CROWDED YEARS

The Reminiscences of
WILLIAM G. McADOO

KENNIKAT PRESS SCHOLARLY REPRINTS
Dr. Ralph Adams Brown, Senior Editor

Series in
AMERICAN HISTORY AND CULTURE
IN THE TWENTIETH CENTURY
Under the General Editorial Supervision of
Dr. Donald R. McCoy
Professor of History, University of Kansas

WILLIAM GIBBS McADOO
At the time he became Secretary of the Treasury

CROWDED YEARS

The Reminiscences of

WILLIAM G. McADOO

With Illustrations

KENNIKAT PRESS
Port Washington, N. Y./London

CROWDED YEARS

Copyright, 1931, by William G. McAdoo
Reissued in 1971 by Kennikat Press by
arrangement with Houghton Mifflin Company
Library of Congress Catalog Card No: 74-137974
ISBN 0-8046-1430-X

Manufactured by Taylor Publishing Company   Dallas, Texas

KENNIKAT SERIES ON AMERICAN HISTORY AND
CULTURE IN THE TWENTIETH CENTURY

PREFACE

I HAD always resolved never to write my memoirs because autobiography is, I think, one of the most difficult of all things to write well, and because, too, I have neither the experience nor the technique of authorship. As time has receded from the notable administration of Woodrow Wilson, it has served to clarify and to mature, to some extent, the perspective upon that great epoch. But even so, a vast amount of misinformation and misinterpretation of events has been published, and I have finally been persuaded, largely by the wish of members of my family and by the importunities of intimate friends, to write my own story as a contribution to the history of that period.

Even when I had reached the conclusion that I ought to undertake the work, my resolution was cooled by the mere sight of the thousands of letters, the huge stacks of records and documents, and the shelves of books that I should, necessarily, have to examine to give the work the stamp of correctness and historical validity.

It was clear that, burdened as I was with an active law practice, I could not do the work without assistance. In this dilemma I thought of my friend W. E. Woodward, a biographer of high reputation, skilled in the handling of historical and literary material. I induced him to spend a week looking over my notes and the piled-up mass of correspondence and documents. I wanted his advice as to the scope and treatment of the narrative and as to how I could compress it into a single volume. I felt that the average reader would not be interested in a voluminous, documented, and dry story, but that he might be interested in the essentials if they could be put in readable form and reduced to the limits of two covers. 'Your career has covered so much ground,' Woodward finally said, 'that you have ten times more history than any man really ought to have; but, of course, we can't help that. The hard part of your job will be to select the essentials that should compose your book. If you want me to, I'll be glad to work with you.'

I have been fortunate in having this brilliant and gifted writer as my collaborator. The book has occupied most of our time for more than a year and a half.

You will observe that this volume has no footnotes. I think their absence calls for an explanation, as it is customary to sprinkle them profusely over the pages of works of this character. I omit them because I am convinced that, in most cases, they are useless appendage. Few people take the trouble to verify references made in footnotes; and, besides, they distract the reader's attention and retard the flow of the narrative. Whenever it has been desirable to indicate chapter and page of a book or a document to which I have referred, the information is embodied in the text.

An autobiography is, of course, a personal story, a self-portrait, and a certain amount of egoism is one of the inevitable qualities of all literary works of this class. I have endeavored to avoid it as much as possible by looking at my career objectively and by treating it as impersonally as I could.

WILLIAM G. MCADOO

CONTENTS

x CONTENTS

ILLUSTRATIONS

CROWDED YEARS

. .

CHAPTER I

THE McADOOS AND THE FLOYDS

I

MY FATHER kept a diary. Year after year he recorded the events of his life in a row of thin brown volumes. There one may read of the ups and downs of his law practice, of his deep devotion to his wife, of the books he bought, and his comments on current events. He was an industrious diary-keeper, painstaking and meticulous, and apparently did not omit very much. Sometimes he would set down the price of a pair of shoes and a record of the fees he had received on the same page with the first draft of a sonnet and the strange Latin names of the flowers that he had come across in his daily walk.

I handle the volumes of his diary with a delicate touch. Their pages are old and tired. They are brittle with too much time, and if I should let them have their way, they would fall apart and disintegrate. Curious to learn of my own coming into the world, I turn to an entry written in pale, home-made Confederate ink at Marietta, Georgia, on October 31, 1863.

Today, about thirty minutes after noon, Mary gave birth to a son weighing nearly eleven pounds, with long black hair. He bawled lustily, showing a fine pair of lungs, is voracious, and seems to have a vigorous constitution. My darling wife went through the terrible ordeal bravely, and appears to be doing well tonight.

Though I was born at Marietta — a town about twenty miles north of Atlanta — my parents had lived for many years in Knoxville, Tennessee. Both of them were well acquainted with Marietta and its people, although they did not consider themselves permanent residents. Before the Civil War it was a summer resort, and my father had met my mother there.

The McAdoos belonged to eastern Tennessee. They had lived among its hazy blue mountains for many years; for so many years, indeed, that the story of their coming and their settlement on the new Tennessee land — as I have heard my elders tell it — is mingled with stout-hearted tales of Indians and camp-fires. These early McAdoos were bearded, vigorous men of Scotch descent, pioneers by instinct, rough and hearty, living close to the soil, and making their own way without seeking help or guidance. They were all Bible-reading Presbyterians who believed in Judgment Day and the efficacy of shotguns.

My father, whose name was William Gibbs McAdoo, the same as mine, was born in 1820, about the time when schooling and book-learning were beginning to get a toe-hold in that pioneer country. He was the first McAdoo who ever went to college, so far as I know. In 1842, he entered the East Tennessee University, at Knoxville, and graduated in 1845. Before going to the University, he had taught school for several years. The citizens of his country must have had a high opinion of him, for he was elected a member of the legislature of Tennessee on the day before his graduation.

Soon afterward — that is, in 1846 — the Mexican War began, and a company of volunteers was enrolled at Knoxville. My father was the chief organizer of the company, which consisted of about a hundred raw-boned, stalwart country youths eager for adventure. In the course of their progress toward Mexico, my father, who began as the company's first lieutenant, eventually became its captain.

The company, with its arms and supplies, embarked on flat-boats at Knoxville and drifted down the Tennessee River as far as Muscle Shoals. There the original flat-boats were abandoned and they proceeded to the bottom of the rapids and built another fleet of boats. That task was a mere nothing; those husky boys were all handy with the axe and the plane. Within a week their new boats were completed. They piled in their belongings, their banjos and their dogs and pet raccoons, and started for New Orleans. It took a long time to float down the Tennessee, Ohio, and Mississippi Rivers to New Orleans.

Eventually they were sent to Vera Cruz in a seasick little

MARY FAITH FLOYD McADOO
At 25

WILLIAM GIBBS McADOO, SR.
At 48

ship that capered and jumped over the waves. For a day or two the farmer boys were too ill to quarrel. Then they got their sea-legs, and — for some reason that is not clear to me — they announced their intention of throwing the captain of the ship overboard. It seems to have taken a good deal of my father's Tennessee oratory to keep them from actually doing it. They were, I fancy, an unruly lot.

They reached Vera Cruz after a while and aided in the capture of the city. Then, with the rest of General Scott's army, they fought their way — disillusioned and very tired — up the steep mountain roads to the City of Mexico. On the way, my father and his company distinguished themselves at the battle of Cerro Gordo.

After the Mexican War was over, my father studied law, was admitted to the bar, and in time was elected to the position of district attorney-general — or prosecuting attorney — for the Knoxville circuit, which included a number of counties in eastern Tennessee.

As attorney-general he gained a reputation for ability and fearlessness which survived long after he had become only a memory in the Tennessee courts. This distinction was probably magnified and colored by time and much re-telling, but from my knowledge of his character I should say that not a great deal of it was fiction. I never knew him to be afraid of anything or anybody.

During the long political agitation that preceded the Civil War, he was on the side that opposed secession; but he thought, nevertheless, that any state had a legal and moral right to secede if it cared to do so. His reading of history had convinced him, to his own satisfaction, that the Union was only a league of states, and that the right of any state to sever itself from the league was implied in the Constitution. This was the conventional Southern opinion at that time. It was held implicitly by millions of intelligent people. My father's opposition to secession was based on grounds of policy. Although he considered secession legally sound, he looked upon it as ill-advised and senseless, and was convinced that it would lead to the South's ruin.

My mother had inherited a considerable number of slaves, but she and my father both thought that slavery was morally wrong and economically wasteful. Like many other intelligent Southerners of that era, my father favored a course of gradual compensated emancipation, extending over twenty-five or thirty years. During this period the freed slaves, he thought, should be prepared for citizenship and its responsibilities by education, as well as by training in industry and self-support. Just before the Civil War, the Southerners who held these views were so numerous that they constituted a respectable political minority, but their ideas contained the fatal defect of compromise. People who stand in the middle of the road are invariably run over in times of great excitement. On one hand the hot-headed secessionists were immune to all argument. They defied the North and the enlightened opinion of the world. They were blind to the obvious fact that slavery had outlived its epoch and its usefulness. On the other hand were the Northern Abolitionists, who wanted immediate uncompensated emancipation, equality, and the right of the negro to vote. They argued that a negro was not only as good as a white man, but even a little better than most Southern white men.

In the squabble over the election of Lincoln, the common-sense of the Southern people curled up and died. One state after another seceded, amid the blare of brass bands and the drone of oratory. With difficulty the secessionists dragged Tennessee out of the Union. It was a close shave. But, although Tennessee thus became one of the Confederate states, the Unionists were in a decisive majority around Knoxville.

As soon as secession ceased to be a theory and became a fact, my father washed the anti-secessionist logic out of his mind and was as patriotically Southern as Jefferson Davis. Every man had to take sides — and my father was a Southerner.

When the Unionists got control at Knoxville, and became the virtual rulers of eastern Tennessee, my father felt that existence there was no longer possible for him. He wound up his affairs, said good-bye to his friends, and started southward with his family, to a region where there were no Unionists except a few who had been put in jail for their own protection.

My mother, who was a Floyd of Georgia, owned an extensive plantation on the Georgia coast, near Darien. I use the word 'extensive' in a geographical, instead of an economic, sense. Although the plantation was many-acred, wide-spreading, and probably of fertile soil, it was lean in profits. The slaves that lived on it consumed about all they produced. My father and his family started from Knoxville with the intention of going to 'Bellevue,' as this plantation was called. He was to leave my mother and the children at the plantation while he went into military service.

On the way they changed their minds. They came to the conclusion that the climate of the lowlands would not do for the young children — I had a brother and two sisters living at the time — and they decided to remain in Marietta among the north Georgia hills. A few miles from the town a house was for sale, and they bought it.

This Marietta house was a large, airy place, with a wide, white-columned verandah in front. It stood on elevated, red-clay land with a vista of green valleys and smoky-hued Kenesaw Mountain in the distance. The house, with its grounds, was called 'Melora' in the high-toned fashion of the old South, where everything in the shape of a mansion had to have a name. That is how I happened to be born in Georgia instead of Tennessee on the last day of October, in the year 1863.

The Confederate authorities made out a commission appointing my father to a place in the army, but before signing it they had the medical men look him over. The doctors discovered that he had a double hernia and a chronic dysentery, which he had incurred in the Mexican War. Crestfallen, he came home with the letter of rejection in his hand. This was early in the war. Later on, when the man-power of the South was on the wane, he renewed his application, was accepted, and fought in the Georgia campaign.

I have no personal memory of living at 'Melora.' When I was about six months old, my family moved to Milledgeville, in the central portion of the state. Milledgeville was then the capital of Georgia.

There was an immense difficulty in getting moved, as I see from my father's diary. This was in 1864; the Southern Confederacy, reeling and staggering, was bled white of men and resources. Affairs were in such hopeless confusion that few people dared to travel, except on military business. The railroads, all of them controlled by the Confederate government, were hardly more than streaks of rust. The weary, scrap-iron locomotives had to stop for breath on every heavy grade.

Nearly every freight car still capable of running on wheels was in the government service. After besieging everyone within reach who had anything to do with the management of the Western and Atlantic Railroad, my father was finally promised a freight car to move his household goods, and was told that it would be left at Marietta on a certain day. Empty promise. The day came and went with the Marietta siding blank and vacant.

One day, while he was wondering what he would do, he saw a gaunt, weather-beaten wreck of a freight car standing on a spur track near the station. It had holes in it large enough for a man to walk through, and part of its roof was gone. He hurried to the railroad station to see the agent, who told him that he could have the car if he would nail boards over the holes. The agent remarked that the car had been abandoned as unsafe. My father and a negro spent the next day repairing this vehicle; then he went home and dismantled the house as quickly as possible, so as to get his belongings into the car before dark.

As they came in sight of the station with the two wagonloads of furniture, they saw a government train standing there. The officer in charge was looking over the battered car and evidently contemplating its seizure.

My father hurried up and explained his desperate plight. The officer was very agreeable. He said he had intended to attach the car to his train, which was taking munitions to the front, but he would always defer to a family in distress. With a polite gesture he turned over the battered car to the McAdoos. There were many bows and courteous remarks on both sides.

In surrendering the car the officer made the depressing remark that the government was seizing all rolling stock for its own use, and that our furniture would not be likely to reach Milledgeville. 'Without red seals on this car,' he said, 'it will probably wind up in Virginia.' A red seal placed on a freight car was a sign that it contained government property and was therefore inviolate.

This was a new dilemma, but the officer soon solved it by taking a lot of red seals out of his pocket and decorating the car with them. My father thanked the officer; the officer bowed and said some gracious words to my mother; my mother and father bowed again; the officer, saying good-bye and good luck, mounted his own creaking and lumbering train, which creaked and lumbered away toward the north.

Not long afterward the passenger train that my father intended the family to take stopped at the station, but he made up his mind not to leave until he had seen his furniture start on its way, so we remained overnight at a neighbor's house. Next morning our car was no longer there; the station agent declared that a freight train had arrived and departed during the night, and that the car had gone on to Milledgeville. My father doubted his word; gloom spreads over the diary. But nothing could be done about it. In those perilous times men and women lived in a sort of quiet desperation.

When the morning train, due at nine-thirty in the forenoon, rattled up to the Marietta station at three in the afternoon, the McAdoo family, including four or five negro household servants — slaves — climbed aboard. Before the train started, the conductor came into the car.

'Do you-all count on takin' them niggers in these kyars?' he asked my father, as he pointed at the shrinking darkies.

'Why, I thought so,' my father replied. 'I've bought tickets for them.'

'Well,' the conductor went on amiably, 'it's a rule that niggers ain't allowed on passenger kyars. I reckon you can't take 'em.'

'Then what am I to do about them?'

'They'll have to go by express,' the conductor announced.

Then followed a long and lazy argument in the Southern style, over this point, while the wheezing locomotive, with its string of ramshackle cars, waited like a tired and wounded animal. In the end the conductor won. The negroes were sent by express, with destination tags strung around their necks. All but one. The conductor was prevailed upon to allow Sukey, a fifteen-year-old girl, to accompany the family.

Sukey was needed as a nurse; she carried me in her arms.

When we arrived at Milledgeville, my father records, there stood our freight car, with its bright red seals, on the side track at the station. Everything was intact.

The negroes did not get there for a week. They were never able to tell where they had been, except that they had stayed for two days in the depot of a place where there were a lot of houses. The Southern Express Company had given them regular meals, they said.

2

We did not live in the town of Milledgeville at first. The house which my father rented was at Midway, a suburb, about two miles from the central square of the town. It was an ordinary frame building, undistinguished in appearance, that had been used as a small hotel before the war. It had many rooms, some of them not needed at first, but after a time our family grew up to the house's large proportions.

There were shady, pleasant woods all around; the sunlight filtered through the leaves and laid a flickering, checkered pattern on the ground. At one side of the house there was an old rose garden. One of my earliest memories is of rain falling on this garden. I stood at the window and watched the huddled roses, beaten by the storm, bend and bow their heads. I felt sorry for them and I fancied that they would like to run away, if they could.

The coziest place in the house was my father's library. It was well-stocked, for he was the kind of man who would save a book from a burning house before he would even think of saving a bed. On chilly winter evenings the library was bright and pleasant, with a crackling pine-wood fire on the hearth. There was a warm leathery smell of imprisoned books, and on the walls the firelight gleamed cheerfully and made amusing shadows.

My father used to tell me of his experiences in Mexico. The flood of years has swept all these reminiscences out of my memory, except his account of the terribly offensive smell of Vera Cruz when the American troops took possession of the city. He said that place smelled worse than anything I could imagine. Naturally, I began at once to do some imagining.

'Did it smell worse than a pole-cat?' I asked. A pole-cat, I may remark, is the Southern equivalent of a skunk. I could not think of anything that smelled worse.

'Yes,' he replied gravely.

'Did it smell worse than a thousand pole-cats?' I demanded.

My father smiled. 'Well,' he said, 'I thought so at the time.'

That did not satisfy me. I wanted more exact data. 'Did it smell worse than a thousand million pole-cats?' was my next question.

'Listen, my son.' My father put his hand gently on my head. 'You have a bad habit of dealing with uncomfortably large figures. Let's say it smelled worse than six or seven pole-cats and let it go at that.'

While I was Secretary of the Treasury during the World War, there were times when I used to think of that conversation. During that period the financial operations of the government grew, as everyone knows, to an incredible magnitude. In the course of a week or ten days I would have to pass out several hundred million dollars to the Allies, and, besides, Congress would appropriate billions for various other purposes. As the head of the Treasury Department I was responsible, to a large degree, for devising means through which this money could be furnished, and the strain was very trying. In the evening I would take great masses of calculations home in a brief-case, put on a pair of pajamas, and lie propped up in bed, a yellow writing-pad on my knees, with sheets of figures scattered around. I would work for hours trying to reduce demand and supply to an equation. The noughts attached to the many millions were so boisterous and prolific that, at times, they would run clear over the edge of the paper. Then, in fancy, I would feel my father's hand on my head and hear him say, 'Listen, my son; you have a bad habit of dealing with uncomfortably large figures.'

When I think of my father there comes into my mind the idea of stature, poise, and courage. He was an unusually tall man. I am six feet one myself, and my father topped me by three inches. Quiet-speaking, gracious in manner, and highly spirited, he possessed a good deal of that stoic dignity that is ascribed to the classical Greeks.

For two or three years after the war he was disfranchised — was not allowed to vote because he had been an officer of rank in the Confederate service. This kept him from practicing law, which was the only way he knew of earning a living.

It was a hard time for us. We had undoubtedly much difficulty in keeping alive and clothed, yet I must say that, as I look back upon those thin years, I remember them without any recollection of unusual privation. The sense of poverty is often the effect of contrast. Everybody in Milledgeville was poor; everybody had fought and lost; everybody had seen better days. The community felt the comradeship and solidarity that come from a common disaster. All had trod, in blood and tears, the road of defeat.

I shall not describe the straitened circumstances of our life as graphically as I might, for such stories bore me, and I have no sympathy with those who lean upon a poverty-bitten youth as a claim to applause and preferment.

Early experiences have much to do with shaping a man's life; of that I am entirely convinced. But it is a false assumption that these moulding experiences can be so largely expressed in terms of poverty or wealth. One's real inspiration is generally far too subtle to be defined in such crude terms. Therefore, as I touch upon the makeshifts and expedients of our life at Milledgeville, I hope my readers will understand that I am not laying the ground for a philosophy of personal evolution, but merely painting a picture.

Within the frame of that picture I must include my mother, bent over her sewing, striving with needle and thread to keep us all from nakedness. She would cut down my father's old clothes to make suits for the boys, and her own dresses were fixed up in some way for the girls. My mother was not an expert tailor, and one may readily imagine that we all looked a little grotesque in our made-over clothes. Yet we did not feel grotesque at all. On the contrary, I felt perfectly grand. My clothes did not fit — but what of it? All the boys with whom I played were in the same fix.

WILLIAM GIBBS McADOO (*right*) AND HIS BROTHER MALCOLM
William was about seven at the time, and his brother a year and a half younger.
Their clothes were made by their mother from their father's cast-off garments.

The 'Bellevue' plantation, according to every reasonable expectation, should have kept us all in comfort, but in that era in the South nothing was reasonable, or turned out the way it should have. It was a nightmare of misgovernment, carpet-baggers, unheard-of taxes, swarms of idle negroes and discouraged white men. The land was filled with low rascals, who had come from the North to make their fortunes. They wallowed over the dead Confederacy like vultures wallowing over a dead lion. The condition of public affairs affected the personal condition of every man in the South. The old economic order had been torn up by the roots too violently, and it was many years before the people could adjust themselves to the new state of things.

The end of the war found 'Bellevue' overrun with weeds. Its buildings had been burned by one of Sherman's raiding parties, or by some band of irregular troops. Its livestock was dispersed; its fences were in decay. My father made strenuous efforts to put the place in working order, but very little could be accomplished on account of the uncertainty of negro labor. The freed slaves had a notion that their new freedom, which had come to them without effort on their part, meant a perpetual license for idleness. They could not understand any kind of freedom that involved work. They had always been made to work; now, if work was still to continue, of what use was this talk of freedom and other devices of the Yankees?

After a year or so of loss and discouragement, my father made no further effort to cultivate 'Bellevue.' He rented portions of it in small patches to white farmers with the idea of getting enough income from the place to pay its taxes and have a little left over. So far as I know the net result was trifling; we got a few barrels of potatoes and rice each year, and occasionally a wagon-load of vegetables. My parents, in their deep necessity, would have sold the land, I am sure, if a purchaser could have been found. A long time afterward, when I was a young lawyer, my father sold a large tract of pine lands — about three thousand acres — for one dollar an acre. A ridiculously low price; the timber on the land was worth many times that amount. It was sold through necessity for whatever it would bring. This tract of land is now owned by Howard E. Coffin, the well-known automobile engineer, and is used by him as a hunting preserve.

As soon as my father's political disabilities were removed by a special grant of amnesty from President Andrew Johnson, he began the practice of law in Milledgeville. It was the poorest place imaginable for anybody who hoped to make a living at the bar. The capital of the state had recently been moved to Atlanta, and nothing of importance was left in Milledgeville but an insane asylum and the state penitentiary. The town had a dejected, grass-grown appearance. In its center stood the abandoned capitol building, a solemn, owl-like structure. Its steps were littered with trash, and many of its windows were broken.

In the dusty streets men pitched horseshoes and talked of the past. Nailed on the doorways were the signs of innumerable lawyers who had done very well while Milledgeville contained the authority and prestige of the state. Now that the capital was gone, they fluttered like dying leaves.

My father's genuine legal ability was wasted. He knew the origin and history of law, and was familiar with the mass of curious subtleties and impressive dicta that constitute the *corpus juris* of our race, but he did not know much about getting ahead in the world. If he had been a practical man, he would have left Milledgeville.

As time passed, our family increased in size. My parents had seven children. Caroline, John Floyd, and Rosalie were older than I; Malcolm Ross, Nona, and Laura were younger. When I was a boy of ten the house was full of children. There was a perpetual running to and fro; the long bare rooms resounded with stir and movement.

3

My mother's maiden name was Mary Faith Floyd. Her grandfather was General John Floyd, who was a figure of distinction in Georgia a hundred years ago. He was an intrepid soldier and a friend of Andrew Jackson, whom he resembled in mind and character. During the War of 1812, General John Floyd was associated with General Jackson in command of the expedition that destroyed the power of the Creek Indians.

General John Floyd had a son named Charles — and Charles Floyd was my grandfather. He might have been created by Sir Walter Scott, as a character in a romantic novel, and sometimes I think he was. There is nobody in either Scott or Dumas that excelled Charles Floyd in a hard-riding, fox-hunting, gallant, dueling career.

Charles Floyd entered West Point at the age of nineteen. He soon got into a series of strange adventures. When he had been at the Academy about a year, a rule was announced to the effect that every cadet had to set down in a register the name of his parent or guardian.

Cadet Floyd refused, and was summoned before the Commandant. 'Have you no parent or guardian?' the Commandant inquired.

'Yes, I have,' said Cadet Floyd, 'but what business is it of yours? I am here to receive instruction — such as you can give me — so why should I write down in a book such personal matters as the names of my parents?'

Then, while the Commandant was staring dumbly at him, he saluted and walked out of the room. He was promptly dismissed from the Academy for insubordination.

Mounting his fine Georgia horse, Charles Floyd proceeded to ride home with leisurely interludes. Somewhere around Baltimore he had an encounter with a stranger. That evening he wrote to his father that he had encountered 'a puppy on a horse in the road.' The man blocked the bridle-path and did not get out of the way when Charles asked him courteously to stand to one side. Thereupon Charles struck him with his riding-whip. He rode on to a near-by inn for the night. Next morning, upon making inquiries, he learned that the man he had struck was not a puppy at all, but a well-known gentleman of the neighborhood. He called for ink and paper and wrote the gentleman a letter in which he said among other things: 'When I struck you with a whip yesterday afternoon I did not know that you have the rank of gentleman, or I would have taken different measures. But your being a gentleman makes your discourtesy even greater than it appeared at first. I anticipate your desire for redress and will therefore await your pleasure. Any friends of yours will find me here. Your humble servitor, Charles Floyd.'

The gentleman sent a friend with a challenge. They met at dawn next day, and at the first fire Floyd shot his opponent in the hip. He was filled with remorse for fear that he had killed him, so he remained in the neighborhood for a couple of weeks, inquiring daily as to his late adversary's condition. The gentleman got well promptly, and Floyd sent him a polite note of good wishes. The two met, clasped hands, drank a bottle of wine together, and the gentleman had Floyd come up to the house and meet his family. He stayed there a few days as a guest, spending his time in festivities and fox-hunting. Then he mounted his horse and rode away, while good-byes were waved from the piazza. He had met a puppy, learned that he was not a puppy, had shot him, had feasted with him, and had made a friend. That was the old South.

Upon the return of this young adventurer to 'Bellevue' plantation, his father, General John Floyd, secured for him a commission as a lieutenant in the United States Marine Corps. Then there followed a long drama of disputes with other officers, the beating of 'puppies,' and duels with gentlemen.

In the meantime he was sending home to Georgia the most delightful letters, written in a copper-plate script. I have many of his letters, and the form and beauty of the writing interests me as much as their contents. Every now and then he would send to his father a book of sketches, done in water colors. He could catch the salient points of character like a Gavarni or a Daumier. The pictures of his fellow officers, or of the people he saw in the streets, reveal, by some gesture of the hand, or the pose of a hat, or the cut of a coat, the inner mood and spirit of the man he portrayed.

When the Marquis de Lafayette made his historic visit to America in 1824, Charles Floyd commanded the guard of honor on his arrival in New York. He wrote some interesting letters about this event. 'The Marquis,' he wrote, 'has strong features, is a tall man, and was dressed in a plain blue coat, yellow nankeen pantaloons and buff vest. His manner is plain and dignified.' In another letter he says, 'If Monsieur lives until the fuss is over, he will be completely soaked with wine and cocktails of every description.'

The Marquis managed to live through it, but I must record that Lieutenant Charles Floyd did not live long with the Marine Corps after the fuss about Lafayette was over. His colonel, who did not like him because he had described the colonel as an 'old woman without the petticoats,' had him assigned for duty in the West Indies. He resigned rather than go to such an unimportant and forlorn post. After his resignation was accepted, he gave his former colonel a beating with a cane in the streets of New York. The colonel cried 'Help' and 'Murder.' The encounter made a sensation in the New York newspapers. One of them said that 'a person named Floyd' had whipped Colonel Gamble with a cane. Upon reading that, the former Lieutenant Floyd wrote the editor an indignant 'Sir' letter. 'Sir: I do not want to take the trouble to hasten your progress toward oblivion, but I will say to you now emphatically that if you refer to me again in your newspaper as a person named Floyd you will reach oblivion much sooner than you expect. I am, Sir, your humble servant. Charles Floyd.'

The newspapers have weapons of their own, and satire is the sharpest blade in their armory. In his next issue the editor said that in the haste of going to press the full name of Mr. Floyd had been omitted. 'He is,' the editor wrote, 'former Lieutenant Charles Rinaldo Floyd of the Marine Corps; now, after a career of great daring and bravery, he has retired and is *Mister* Charles Rinaldo Floyd, of Georgia.' I do not know what my hot-headed grandfather thought of that.

One might think with reason that the fiery spirit of Charles Rinaldo Floyd could lead only to disaster. But it did not; life is full of paradoxes. Charles Floyd either went through a profound spiritual change, or grew out of his youthful impetuosities — I don't know which; but the family chronicles say that in middle life he was a high-minded although spirited man — a careful planter, a generous friend, a kind neighbor. At the age of twenty-nine, he was appointed Brigadier General of the Georgia Militia.

In the middle thirties of the last century some tribes of Indians still remained in Georgia. The Seminoles were particularly troublesome. Large numbers of them lived in the great Okefinokee Swamp — a vast expanse of half-drowned land and forests and creeks in the southern part of the state.

They would make raids from this swamp and, after they had returned to its silent fastnesses, were secure. The government resolved to clear them out, and to transport the entire tribe to the lands beyond the Mississippi. The job of doing this was given to Charles Floyd as the commanding general of the Georgia troops. He surrounded the swamp and pursued the Indians to its depths. When they were all rounded up, after one or two fierce swamp fights, he addressed them and made peace with them. He then moved the Seminoles and the Creeks to the Indian Territory. For this task, ably performed, he was highly complimented by General Winfield Scott.

I never knew Charles Floyd. He died at the age of forty-four while my mother — his daughter — was still a young girl.

By descent I am a McAdoo and a Floyd. Many years of observation of men and women have pretty nearly convinced me that there is not much in heredity, so far as human personality is concerned. But if the conventionally accepted laws of heredity are valid, then I must say that the poise of the McAdoos has beneficially tempered, in my case, the impetuosity of the Floyds. Some deep-lying instinct has kept me outside of the hot and desperate entanglements of the spirit. I have seldom had an impulse to do anything which had no practical justification. The windmills of Don Quixote are far beyond my horizon. I have ideals — have always had them — but I do not nourish ideals which represent the unattainable. Nor do I hold a personal resentment against any man because his opinions differ from my own.

CHAPTER II

MY EARLY DAYS

I

WHEN I first went to school at the age of seven, I could already read and write. My father had taught me at home. I started off feeling much superior to the other boys who were still enmeshed in the toils of the alphabet. This grand beginning was not maintained. I never became a brilliant scholar. I was not the best in the class nor the worst, but my average was good. I was quick and capable at arithmetic, and my spelling was excellent.

At that time there were no public schools, but teachers would get a few pupils of their own. I went to several schools, and picked up a little education, here and there, like a bird picking up crumbs. One of these sketchy, piecemeal schools was taught by my mother's first cousin, a lovely young woman named Julia Floyd. At home we called her 'Cousin Jule.' It was the first school I attended, and I remember it seemed strange to me that in school I had to address my cousin as 'Miss Floyd.'

The teacher whose image stands out most clearly in my recollection was 'Old Man' Carrington, as we called him. I don't suppose he was very old — about forty-five, maybe — but he seemed to me and the other boys almost as old as God. He had old ways; he was solemn and a very strict disciplinarian. He taught the common facts of arithmetic and grammar to his pupils with the air of one who imparts a magic formula. He sat in a web of mysterious knowledge; his mind seemed to hold a nest of secrets, which turned out, after all, to be nothing more mysterious than the information that Columbus discovered America and that the Mississippi is the longest river in the United States.

The professor used to sit in a high chair at one end of the room so he could watch us all the time. Discipline was not only severe; it was rough. The whippings at school had the effect of giving the boys a restless sense of rowdiness. One of

our favorite games after school was to have a 'rock battle.'
For this sport the school divided itself into two groups, approximately equal in numbers. Each side armed itself with
stones, and the game was won by one side driving the other
off the field. It was dangerous, of course. A kindly Providence
kept anyone from losing an eye or being killed.

Another one of our games was baseball, which even that
far back was the great national pastime. The pervading
poverty was so biting and insistent that it reached to the
smallest crevice of our lives. One result of it was that none of
us — I mean the schoolboys — was ever able to buy a real,
honest-to-goodness baseball. As a substitute we made rude,
makeshift baseballs by a method which I shall describe.
First, we got a small round stone and wrapped it with strips
of cloth and such vagrant rubber as we could find — and
precious little rubber was to be found; then we cut out a
leather cover, soaked it so it would stretch and sewed it on
while it was wet. When the leather dried, it shrank and made
a tight fit.

Around that time there was a great deal of talk everywhere
about the fabulous wealth of Commodore Vanderbilt, the
powerful railroad magnate who was at the head of the New
York Central. The idea occurred to me that Commodore
Vanderbilt might lend us a dollar to buy a few baseballs.
I wrote a letter to him, copying it over and over, and improving it, while the other boys stood around and made suggestions as to epistolary style and manner of approach. I
stated the whole case to the Commodore. We did not ask
for a gift, I explained, but merely for a loan; we gave him our
'word of honor as Southern gentlemen' that we would repay
the dollar after a while, as soon as any of us could earn it.
In the South the pledge of one's 'word of honor' was considered the best collateral in the world.

The letter was mailed, and thereafter we haunted the post-
office for weeks. No answer came, and eventually our expectations faded into gray disappointment. Probably the
Commodore never got our letter; some secretary, I fancy,
threw it into a waste-basket.

My failure to borrow a dollar from the millionaire Vanderbilt was a great blow to my faith in human nature. Until

then I imagined that big rich men, with wide vision and generous impulses, spent a lot of time helping poor boys; and what could be more helpful to a poor boy in Milledgeville than a few brand-new baseballs?

Without consulting anyone I resolved to make some money for myself. This was in one of the intermittent periods when there was no school. I got a job at Peter Cline's general dry-goods store.

My duties were to sweep out the store in the morning, wait on customers, and run errands. Saturday was our big day. Then the country people came to town, and the hitching-rail in front of the store had a long line of wagons and buggies, with mules and horses stamping and whinnying. Standing behind the counter, I would get the pungent odor of hay-choked barns and worn leather harness. The store was filled, on these occasions, by sun-tanned cotton farmers and their wives who loitered in the aisles and gossiped. At the coming of dusk, I went about the store lighting the kerosene lamps that stood in brackets on the wall.

In those days country people came early and left early. They lived far away and the roads were bad. One by one our Saturday customers would depart; I could hear the creaking of their wagons long after they had disappeared into the night. About nine o'clock the store would close.

Then I would walk home through the quiet streets, past dark, sleeping houses and gardens that smelled of jasmine and roses. At night when there was no moon the village lived at the bottom of a sea of silence and darkness.

But I did not think of that. As I walked alone through the night my thoughts had wings and soared over the world. I thought of the gleaming cities that I had never seen and could only imagine — of New York, of Chicago, of London. In fancy I saw their streams of people, their great shops filled with fine fabrics and beautiful things, their palatial buildings, their glittering theaters; and I marveled at the uplifting surge of achievement that had created them and kept them in being.

I was thrilled to the heart by curiosity and ambition; and as much by one as by the other. I wanted ardently to know how everything was done; and, then, when I once knew, I wanted to have a hand in the doing.

I was not at all dismayed by the thought that I was only an untaught country boy, or that my entire possessions consisted of the paper dollar that I carried in my pocket as pay for my week's work. I was not dismayed by this reflection because I never had it, and it occurs to me now only in retrospect. No such discouraging discrepancy between ambition and reality entered my mind. Youth does not think of the present, but only of the future. It does not live on memories, but on expectations.

Many times I have seen men of mature talent and experience fumble and hesitate, and turn back just as they were about to scale the high wall of achievement, and the thought has occurred to me that their lackadaisical stumbling was only a mental reverberation of past failures and discouragements. If they could have swept the past out of their minds and looked at their problems with the eyes of unbeaten youth, they would have gone ahead. There is a wise Chinese proverb which says: 'Do not follow on the heels of a sorrow; it may turn back.'

Across the road from our house in Midway there stood a small chapel which housed the Presbyterian congregation. It was built like a box with a V-shaped roof. With its coating of lustrous white paint, it gleamed among the dark and somber pines. Every Sunday I, with my brother John Floyd and my sister Rosalie — and the other children as soon as they were old enough — went across to this chapel to attend Sunday School.

I recall vividly the spick-and-span stiffness of my Sunday suit. I felt very strange and formal in contrast to the easy freedom of week-days. My hair was carefully parted and brushed and my shirt was spotless. Before we left the house, mother always admonished us not to pick up stones or to soil our hands.

We had to learn the Shorter Catechism by heart, as well as innumerable verses of the Psalms and Proverbs. At first I thought Sunday School a dreadful nuisance, but after a while I began to like it, especially when my feats of memorizing brought me some little distinction.

The pastor of the Midway Presbyterian was the Reverend Doctor Lane, a fine man and a courageous, kindly gentleman.

He and my father were great friends. They, and my mother, were interested in botany, and they used to make exploratory excursions in the woods. My mother went along, with drawing-pad and colored pencils, to sketch the flowers that they considered rare or unknown.

When we moved into Milledgeville, my parents, to their great regret, had to dissociate themselves from Doctor Lane's church, as the distance was too great for their attendance. They joined the Presbyterian Church on the State House Square. The pastor of this congregation, the Reverend Doctor Goetchius, had a wide reputation as a powerful preacher. I attended his church regularly for the sake of his sermons. He was a born orator and a clever dialectician. He knew how to make his points with logic as well as with emotion. I was greatly inspired by him.

2

My father used to read the Macon 'Telegraph and Messenger.' He was, I think, the only regular subscriber in Milledgeville. When I was about ten years old, I got an idea that I might establish a subscription route for this paper — in other words, become a newsboy — and was informed that the paper would allow me ten cents a week for each subscriber. I set to work and called, I think, on practically every merchant in the town, but I got only five subscribers, and was never able to get any more. For about a year I delivered the 'Telegraph and Messenger' every day to these five subscribers and made fifty cents a week. Then I had some misunderstanding with the 'Telegraph and Messenger' — I forget what it was — so I switched my entire clientèle of five to the Augusta 'Chronicle and Constitutionalist.' Milledgeville is about halfway between Augusta and Macon.

Every day I read one of my papers from the first to the last page. I was hungry for news, and I devoured everything indiscriminately, including editorials and fashion notes. About that time the presidential campaign of 1876 was stirring the country with its intense bitterness. My newspaper reading taught me so much about Hayes and Tilden, and what they represented, that I believe I understood the vital political issues as well as most of the grown men of the neighborhood.

My father had a fine sense of precision and form. His hobbies and pursuits were all intellectual; I remember clearly his deep interest in literature, and in such amiable sciences as botany, astronomy, and geology. He liked poetry, to read it and to write it, and he had a ready facility in the use of poetic forms, especially in the composition of sonnets.

His poetic and intellectual tastes were shared by my mother. She was dark-eyed and vivacious, and her mind was quick. When I think of her, I get the image of bright music. (I know this metaphor is clumsy, but I cannot help it. I can only tell you what I see, and when I think of my mother, I see bright music.)

Both she and my father liked to write, and a great deal of writing was done. They wrote book reviews, essays, poems, as well as an occasional editorial for the local newspaper. My mother wrote a few novels, now long forgotten, except by antiquarians. I have one of them before me now — a romance called 'Eagle Bend,' which I dimly remember reading years ago. Its theme is chivalry and gentility, as I recall it, and as I turn its time-colored pages I see that gallant cavaliers paid delicate homage to fair damsels. I recollect the event of its production much better than I remember the nature of the book. My mother worked feverishly on it for months, seizing a half-hour now and then in the intervals of her domestic duties. A publisher paid her fifty dollars for it, and I remember her joy when the money came. It seems to me, from looking over the book now, that the mere manual labor of putting the words down on paper would be worth several times fifty dollars. She took the money and bought shoes and clothing for all of us, and a little something for herself. The income from the book was spent the day it was received.

My father insisted that I should read the classics, but I did not care much for them. How could I like Addison or Pope? My intellectual horizon was too limited; I was too young. Dime novels were my literary meat — or poison, if you prefer. A dime novel, I will explain, was a paper-covered story of adventure, which sold for a dime. For some inexplicable reason they were looked upon with loathing by the adult part of the community. Nevertheless, the boys in Milledgeville had a secret circulating library of dime novels which were passed from hand to hand until they were worn out.

I remember telling President Wilson one day of my early liking for this form of literature. Mr. Wilson loved detective stories of the modern type; he read them eagerly, at odd times, in trains or after going to bed. He remarked that these mystery yarns are nothing more nor less than dime novels dressed up in a more acceptable literary form. He thought I would probably like them and gave me two or three, but I could not get much interested in them. I could never recapture the thrill that I used to have when I sat under a secluded pine tree and read a dime novel aloud to a group of listening boys.

In those days, in my juvenile way, I thought of money-making. I do not think so much of it any more. In the final equation of life the enrichment of one's bank account is no good unless it leads to a corresponding enrichment of one's soul and personality — unless it leads to a deeper love of humanity, to a broader vision, to a quickening of the finer impulses. And I must say, judging from my observation of men, that it too seldom leads to any of these elevated states of being. But, however that may be, I thought of money-making when I was a boy, and it occurred to me that a great deal of money could be made by writing dime novels. I asked an older boy who was supposed to know all about everything what he thought of it.

'Oh, dime-novel writers make a pile of money!' he exclaimed. Then he added, 'New York City is just full of rich dime-novel writers.'

'Do you think I could write one?'

'I bet you could,' he said. 'You got a pretty good head.' He went on to say that he had heard that writers got as much as ten dollars apiece for each dime novel. Ten dollars! That seemed to me to be mighty good pay.

I lost no time before starting to work. First, I evolved a title. After much reflection I decided to call my dime novel: 'Ontonawanagan, the Great Red-Handed Slayer of the Northwest; or the Terror of the Plains.' Very secretly, I wrote the first two chapters. It was difficult to carry on such a prodigious literary work without my parents' knowledge, but I managed it. At the end of the second chapter I had the hero and the girl on an island and up a tree with Indians all around, shooting at them, and not a white man within a hundred miles. There the story stuck. While it was resting on this snag, I kept the manuscript hidden under the clothes in my bureau drawer. One day my mother discovered it. She tore it up, burned the fragments, told my father, and in the storm of reproof I gave up the writing, but not the reading, of dime novels.

In the summer of 1877, when I was nearly fourteen years old, news of great import came to the McAdoo family. My father was invited to Knoxville as Adjunct Professor of History and English in the University of Tennessee. This institution was his alma mater, though it had been called the East Tennessee University when he was a student. It had grown in thirty years, and had acquired prestige and dignity as the official state university.

My father was to receive a salary of only fifteen hundred dollars a year. Since I have learned something about the world — about the cost of living and the relation of income to expense — I have never ceased to wonder how our large family was supported on an income of less than thirty dollars a week. When we moved to Knoxville there were nine in the family, my parents and seven children, and not one of the children was old enough to make his own way.

I do not know what my father thought of the financial prospect, but it certainly did not disturb any of his children during the short time that passed between the arrival of the news and our departure. We thought and talked of nothing but Knoxville and our coming trip.

It took us twenty-four hours to go from Milledgeville to Knoxville. Travel was slow in those days, and we had to change trains several times. There were no sleeping-cars, so we sat up all night. When we were not sleeping, we — I mean the children — kept our heads out of the windows, for we did not want to miss an inch of the scenery.

Our faces were literally covered with train smoke and dust. I have an idea that the friends who met us at the Knoxville station went home and told their families that Professor and Mrs. McAdoo had arrived with seven colored children.

3

The difference between Knoxville and Milledgeville was striking. The depressed little Georgia town still felt the social and political shell shock of the Civil War. It stared into the past like a stranded sailor who gazes over a lonely sea and tells the tale of gallant voyages. In its streets men who did not know what to do with themselves whittled sticks.

Knoxville had a brisker tone. There a listening boy might hear the gossip of new careers, the talk of coming destinies. People walked swiftly, as if they knew where they were going and what they wanted to do. The stores shone with bright signs; their windows were full of cheerful things to eat and wear; in the banks there was an impressive counting of money; throngs of joyous students went to and fro about the University; around the hotels there was a confusion of baggage and the chatter of guests; in and out of the public library people passed with books under their arms.

I thought Knoxville a wonderful place, but my enthusiasm for it was cooled, in some degree, by the obtrusive fact that the boys at the Bellhouse Public School, which I attended, looked upon me as an outsider. They had primitive manners, and, according to the custom of primitive people, stranger and enemy were synonymous terms. I wanted to be friendly, while they wanted to fight.

I had to do a good deal of fighting, first and last, for I knew that a boy who would not fight was considered a coward. As fighting appeared to be necessary, I went into it rather thoroughly. I studied the art of boxing as well as I could, and I became so interested that I did not mind taking punishment from a boy of superior prowess if I thought the experience would teach me anything. It did; experience taught me a lot. I learned that it was better not to wait to be challenged. I became a challenger myself and carried a chip on my shoulder, like the ambassador of a military nation at a peace conference. I did not see much sense in all this fighting, but, as it seemed to be an inevitable experience for a new boy, I made the best of it. My inner sense of comradeship led me to prefer friendship to fighting, and eventually I made friends of all the boys.

The Bellhouse School was a good one, and I did very well there. My father felt, at the end of a year, that I knew enough to enter the senior prep class at the University. For a year I attended the preparatory school, and in October, 1879, I became a University freshman.

As I look back upon that faraway time it seems to me that my life suddenly spread out and broadened when I became a college youth. All at once I had a wider range of interests.

I read the newspapers, argued about public questions, took part in the dances, and reflected frequently and seriously on the ways of girls. It was not long before I got into the habit of referring to myself and other college boys as 'University men,' with an accent on the 'men.' I loved the University.

One of the arenas for mental competition at the University was called the Chi Delta Society. It had a regular program which included a debate at each meeting on some public question by four selected disputants. After they had said all they could, the debate was thrown open to any member who cared to participate.

My first cousin, Charles F. Humes, was one of my class-mates and a bosom friend. Together we joined the Chi Delta Society. We attended the meetings and took part in the debates. I was timid at first, but my shyness vanished after I got some practice. I am sure that I made a terrible ass of myself on numerous occasions.

The memory of these obstreperous, dogmatic debates reminds me of something I read recently in a biography of Catherine the Great. During one period of her career the Empress Catherine surrounded herself with learned men in the hope of improving her mind, I suppose, by listening to their discussions. Among those invited for a sojourn at her court was Diderot, the celebrated French philosopher. Upon his arrival in Russia, the French ambassador informed him that a certain Russian savant was bitterly jealous of foreigners. This Russian, the ambassador said, had boasted that he would annihilate Diderot in an argument. Diderot remarked that he could take care of himself. Upon inquiry he learned that the distinguished Russian knew nothing whatever about mathematics. At the first prearranged meeting, Diderot, after making his obeisance to the Empress, turned to the Russian philosopher and asked fiercely, 'Can you explain to me why x square plus y square equals two?' Then he looked at the Empress with a confident air and smiled. To the French ambassador he whispered loudly, 'He'll never answer that.' The poor Russian reflected for a while over this asinine question, became confused, bewildered, and out of his depth. He stammered something that nobody understood, and was philosophically crushed.

I doubt if Diderot could have squelched me and my cousin Humes, for I am sure we would have tackled any question he might have asked, regardless of its profundity. We had the assurance that goes with small knowledge triumphantly asserted.

There were sharp social distinctions between the upper and lower class men at the University, as there is in nearly all higher educational institutions. Most of these distinctions were expressed in petty taboos. The seniors and juniors got the best of everything, while the lower class men were expected to maintain a shy reverence.

The officers of the Chi Delta Society were upper class men, as a matter of course. Humes and I detested this undemocratic system, and we made up our minds to organize a faction of sophomores and freshmen to get control of the society. We did some quiet work, and at the next election of officers we surprised the upper class men by nominating a ticket of our own. Our crowd was in a majority, and we made one of our number, a sophomore, president of the society.

Once a year the society held a public debate in the principal theater in the town. This was a great social event in Knoxville. At these affairs the higher classes were accustomed to shine, and the freshmen and sophomores were traditionally supposed to be mere spectators. Humes and I had ourselves elected to represent one side of the question at the next public debate, to the obvious disgust of the upper class members. We allowed the higher class men to select the other two participants, and they chose a senior and a junior.

It was customary for the four debaters to meet to decide on the question for debate and assign the disputants to one side or the other. Our opponents invited us to a conference for this purpose, but, as we did not consider ourselves on speaking terms with them, we replied with a note in which we said haughtily that they were at liberty to select the subject and give us either side.

They took us at our word, and informed us that the question was, *Resolved, that Mormonism in the United States Should be Abolished*, and also that we were given the negative side. When this happened, in the spring of 1881, a Mormon — or anybody who said anything in favor of Mormonism — was about as popular in the United States (outside of Utah) as an advocate of the German Kaiser would have been in the spring of 1918.

Humes and I were depressed and dumbfounded. We had got exactly what we deserved. We had an idea, for a moment, that if we got up on a public stage and defended Mormonism, we might be run out of town. It may be difficult for you to believe, but it is a fact that we were virtually ostracized for the time being. The nice, respectable people of Knoxville came to the conclusion that there must be something wrong with us, or we would not argue in favor of plural wives, and so on.

To get the facts from the Mormon point of view we decided to write to George Q. Cannon, who was at that time the Mormon delegate in Congress from the territory of Utah. Mr. Cannon rose magnificently to the occasion. He sent us piles of data, and the Book of Mormon. He wrote, to my surprise, that polygamy was not sanctioned by the Book of Mormon and was no part of the Mormon religion. Humes and I studied these documents so thoroughly that on the night of the debate, I felt that I knew almost as much about the Mormons as Brigham Young.

It was customary for the debaters to write out their speeches and memorize them. I was convinced, almost to a certainty, that our opponents would appear with a lot of cold-storage arguments about polygamy, and we resolved to write and memorize only the introduction and the peroration of our speeches, and thus be free to meet with extemporaneous argument the points made by the other side.

The judges were five leading citizens, and the theater was filled to standing room. Exactly as we had calculated, our opponents delivered prepared speeches, and Humes and I took up their points, one by one, and made a perfect hash of them. It was like having a debate with a couple of phonographs. Having delivered their orations, nothing else occurred to them. I proved that polygamy was not sanctioned by the Book of Mormon, and as I waved Mr. Cannon's gift book in their faces I challenged them to point out a single reference to polygamy. Neither of them had ever seen the Book of Mormon before and, of course, they were not able to point out anything. 'Shall all the adherents of a religion be condemned,' I exclaimed, 'just because some of them may be guilty of improper practices? What would happen to Christianity if we applied that rule to Christians?'

Humes and I brought out the Constitution of the United States and recited the First Amendment, wherein it is stated that 'Congress shall pass no law respecting an establishment of religion or prohibiting the free exercise thereof.'

The sympathies of the audience were against us, but before the evening was over, it was obvious that we had made a profound impression. The judges retired for consultation and remained for a short time. When they returned, they announced that Humes and I had won the debate. Their decision, they said, was unanimous in favor of the negative. I was immensely thrilled. We were restored to popularity at once. People whom I did not know at all shook hands with me in the street. The truth of the old adage that nothing succeeds like success was proved again.

Many times in my life the memory of that Mormon debate of long ago has influenced my attitude on public questions. When I hear that a man is a Catholic, or a Protestant, or a Jew, the information carries no more weight with me, in forming an estimate of his character or capacity, than the news that he wears a beard and has a wart on his cheek. I believe in complete liberty of conscience, in absolute religious freedom. A narrow-minded bigot, who hates people because they do not worship God in his particular way, is worse than a knave. You can pick up an out-and-out rascal by the scruff of his neck and throw him into jail, but the only thing you can do about a religious bigot is to avoid him.

4

The problem of having a little money to spend was very pressing. During the whole of one summer I had employment in the printing office of W. J. Ramage, one of the leading job printers of the town. I was a sort of printer's devil, or boy-of-all-work, though my principal duties were to run a Gordon hand press and distribute type. My pay was two dollars and a half a week.

Sometimes on Saturdays I worked on the experimental farm that belonged to the agricultural department of the University. I earned seventy-five cents a day, and it was healthy, perspiring toil. These pickings of a few quarters seem pretty small, but things did not cost as much as they do now. With seventy-five cents in my pocket I could take a girl to a show, or to an ice-cream parlor, or buy myself a new necktie.

I was always on the lookout for earning some money; I had to be. In my father's diary I read the other day: 'As I came home I saw Willie and another boy out in a boat in the river collecting the logs that were floating. They said they intended to sell them.' Reading this entry, I tried to recall the incident, but I have no memory of it. Yet it must have happened.

During the Christmas holidays of 1881, when I was in my junior year, A. R. Humes, clerk of United States Circuit and District Courts at Knoxville, offered me a temporary position, to last through the holidays. The pay was two dollars a day, and it looked big to me. Of course I took it. The work consisted entirely of copying in longhand the final record of Federal cases into large impressive-looking books.

I think Humes must have been greatly relieved by my assistance, as much as I was by the two dollars a day. About the time I had caught up with the work, he came in and made me a new proposition, while I listened and rubbed the writer's cramp out of my fingers. The idea was this: The deputy clerkship in the United States Circuit Court at Chattanooga was vacant, and Humes wanted me to take it. The clerk's office at Chattanooga was under his supervision. Would I go there and take charge? Salary: Eight hundred dollars a year. Duties: Interminable writing in large books; and, besides, I would be expected to sit in the court during its sessions and write the minutes.

At that time I was eighteen years old, and had about a year and a half more to go in the University. What I wanted to do was to get my degree and then take a law course at the University of Virginia, if the money could be procured. As to that, there was considerable doubt. I felt flattered by Humes's offer, was glad he had confidence in me, and the eight hundred dollars a year sounded fine; but I hated to give up my chance at getting any more education.

I talked it over with my father, and in a day or two I told Mr. Humes that I would go. My father thought it might turn out to be an excellent chance to learn law from actual contact with the courts, the lawyers and legal cases.

In May, 1882, I left Knoxville for Chattanooga.

5

I had never been away from home before.

While I was at work at the courthouse in Chattanooga during the day I had no time for homesickness, but as I started toward my boarding-house in the evening dusk, I felt — for the first week or two — a desolate, sinking loneliness, and a longing for my own tribe. In fancy I saw our house in Knoxville. The cheerful gleam of its lighted lamps, my bright mother, and the boys and girls trooping in with their family jokes and their tales of the day's adventures. Then I imagined my father coming home — his footstep in the hall, and his tall form standing in the doorway, a book under his arm.

These images filled me with deep and poignant emotions — love of family, a yearning for familiar objects, a forlorn sense of isolation. Nostalgia is a kind of spiritual seasickness. It is caused by an abrupt transference from the familiar to the strange, just as physical seasickness is caused by the transference of one's body from solid ground to a rolling vessel's deck.

The streets of Chattanooga in 1882 were raw gashes cut across the back of the land, or on the flanks of the hills. When it rained, they turned into bogs of sticky red mud. There was a reddish look about the whole town; when I recall it in memory, it makes me think of a burry red-headed man who had fallen into a roadside ditch and, after scrambling out, went along without taking the time to brush himself off.

The more substantial houses were built of tawny brick, the poorer ones of somber dark-colored wood. In winter the cold wind cut with a shrill insistence around the corners, and the icy rain drove through one's clothing. In summer there were long spells of drought when the red mud caked into disheveled ridges and then fretted itself away into a thin, fine dust which blew about the streets. Most of the houses were large and roomy; inside them there was an air of solid comfort.

The temper of the community might be truthfully described as a sort of hearty, good-natured gusto. The people were energetic, courageous, and unabashed. They had tremendous faith in Chattanooga, and as they went their ways they seemed to say in tone and gesture: Just watch us make things hum.

CHAPTER III
I BEGIN TO PRACTICE LAW

I

WHEN I first went to Chattanooga I lived in a boarding-house of a type that was common everywhere in the early eighties. It was a large, dim, and solemn residence of antecedent splendor, gnawed by time and somewhat musty.

A faint odor of cooking lingered in the house: the whiffy smell of beef stew, of hot biscuit, of ham and eggs. Most of the boarders were large eaters. At mealtime a prodigious clatter came from the dining-room. After a while the young men would come strolling out, picking their teeth, and talking of shows and ball games. Then came the older folks, walking heavily, and talking of relatives and diseases.

Very little of the conversation was in the present tense. Everybody had a past or a future. The middle-aged couples passed the long evening hours relating dull stories of what had happened years ago, of minor triumphs and successes in Tennessee country towns. The young men discoursed on opportunities, and unfolded their rosy dreams. The house was nobody's home, for all expected to move on — back to the extinguished past, if it could be found, or forward to the glittering future.

The landlady was an elderly Southern woman of refinement and breeding. I cannot recall her name, but I do recall her perpetual anxiety about her husband, who had taken up the drinking of whiskey as his life-work. Although he applied himself diligently to this occupation, he was often held back in his career by inability to procure the materials of his trade. Liquor was cheap in those days, but cheap as it was, money was required to buy it. Sometimes he was sober for several days in succession. During these out-of-work periods he would sit around the house, in a state of fidgety and nervous misery. It made me uneasy to look at him; he seemed to be in the toils of a fatal destiny.

He had a fine mind, and his conversation was at times both

interesting and brilliant. He had the enormous egotism of the habitual drunkard. All his talk revolved around himself — his own cares and trials, his ambitions and his enemies. The burden of making both ends meet had to be borne by his wife. It was she who had to carry on, but he paid small attention to her and apparently never gave a thought to her troubles. Liquor had eaten away his will power to such an extent that he had drifted back into a condition of frowzy, adult childhood.

Once I gave him fifty cents to buy some medicine for me at a drugstore. I never got the medicine, and I did not see him again until he had consumed fifty cents' worth of corn whiskey. Though he failed to deliver the medicine, he did bring me a most clever, artistic account of how the money had been stolen from him. I said no more about it; his story seemed to me to be worth half a dollar, at least.

This was my first, close-at-hand experience in observing a confirmed drunkard. Of course, I had often seen drunkards, for heavy drinking was a common vice in that era, but I had never before passed days and weeks under the same roof with one. As I watched his pathetic futilities and listened to his rambling lies, I began to reflect on liquor-drinking as a problem of civilized life.

It is rather curious — so it seems to me now — that I had never considered that aspect of it before. In those days I used to take an occasional drink with the boys, but I never drank enough to get intoxicated. Sometimes late in the afternoon, I would drop into the billiard and pool room of the Read House, the leading hotel, to play a few games of pool. The bar of the hotel was in the pool room. It was a warm and cheerful place. There men met and shook hands and told sprightly stories. Occasionally a drunkard would stagger across the floor and talk nonsense, but we all treated it as a joke. Drinking seemed to be a sort of recreation and nobody thought much of it.

The image of the forlorn, broken man at my boarding-house haunted me. I realized that liquor breeds poverty, that it brings ruin, that it breaks up the moral standards of the race. In my imagination it seemed as if a decaying corpse had walked into my room when this poor derelict appeared.

I felt that I was in the presence of a dead man who appeared to be alive.

A drunkard at one's side will do more toward making one a prohibitionist than listening for a lifetime to temperance sermons.

2

Soon after I settled down in Chattanooga, I made the acquaintance of the Honorable W. H. DeWitt, an able lawyer who was at that time Judge of the Chancery Court, in which all equity cases were tried. As I look back upon my life the light of his personality shines through the years. He had all the qualities that go into the making of a great gentleman: Tolerance, nobility of character, breadth of vision, wisdom, and courage.

Judge DeWitt took a great interest in me. I needed his sympathy and guidance, and he gave them to me freely. I wanted to study law, but I had only a meager notion of how to go about it unaided. When I told him what I wanted to do, he volunteered to give me lessons in the evenings, after I had finished my day's work. My gratitude to him is more than doubled when I reflect that, in doing this, he had to lay aside his own affairs to assist me in acquiring an elementary comprehension of Blackstone and Kent. His mind was rigorously self-disciplined; he had no use for mental sloppiness or half-knowledge. I was eager to keep his good opinion, and the course of study that he laid out kept me very busy.

When I got to Chattanooga, I discovered that the work of the deputy clerk's office was several years behind. There was nothing for me to do except to catch up with it. I began writing at eight o'clock every morning, and I wrote in books of record in longhand until I was sick of writing, and the very sight of pen and ink made me tired. In the evening, after a hasty supper, eaten frequently with a law book beside my plate, I hurried away to Judge DeWitt's house, where I spent many evenings, reciting my lessons and taking notes. I know this sounds like a hard life, but it wasn't, really. I possessed the inestimable buoyancy of youth, good health, and a boundless ambition.

Nor did I work so hard every day. Sometimes I would stop writing early in the afternoon and go to a ball game, regardless of the piled-up documents. I came to know lots of young people. There were parties and dances during the winter months that I attended occasionally.

On warm summer evenings we would organize a picnic crowd, a group of ten or twelve boys and girls, and go to the summit of Lookout Mountain. We would take our supper in baskets and turn some huge rock into a table. Then, as night came on and the Tennessee valleys filled with a dusky haze, we could see the silvery ribbon of the river far below us, and the lights of Chattanooga twinkling in the distance. We liked to go on moonlit nights. I can see now, in memory, the great yellow moon rising in a majestic splendor and enfolding the mountain in a net of ghostly light. On such occasions we would have felt a little creepy if we had allowed the familiar negro superstitions to get the better of us, but we didn't. There was a great deal of laughing and bantering talk, but we never passed beyond the limits of decorum. Young people were not so free and easy with one another as they are now, though we could not have gone very far in the way of license, even if we had been so inclined, for an austere chaperon — the mother or aunt of one of the girls — always sat at the feast like a stolid Buddha. In the shadowy dimness of the moon she generally looked like one, too.

I used to play accompaniments on the banjo. After supper we would sing all the songs we knew. While I strummed my banjo with a circle of moon-washed faces around, we lifted our voices and sang such songs as 'Ca'ay me Back to Ole Virginy' and 'Swanee River' and 'My Old Kentucky Home.'

3

In the spring of 1884 there was much excitement throughout the country over the approaching Presidential campaign. The Republican party had controlled the national government for twenty-four years, since the beginning of the Civil War, and it seemed at last to those who sat in the political watch-towers that the Democrats had a fair chance of winning the election of 1884. Although I was not old enough to vote — I did not reach the age of twenty-one until October 31st of that year — I was tremendously interested in every aspect of the coming political battle.

I was, and am, a Democrat from study and conviction, and not merely because I was brought up in a Democratic community. I have no patience with people whose minds are so flabby that they accept, without questioning, the current ideas of their time or their neighborhood. I have an instinctive reluctance to take opinions at second-hand; I look into things for myself and form my own opinions. Much of my life has been spent in the liquidation of illusions, in the decapitation of useless ideas, in getting down to bed-rock.

Although I did not see how I could manage it, I had set my heart on attending the Democratic Convention, which was to be held in Chicago in July — I mean, of course, in the July of 1884. At that time one of my friends named Frank Sevier was a ticket agent in the Union Station at Chattanooga. I told Frank one day that I wanted to attend the convention, but I could not go, as the railroad fare amounted to more than I could afford. He said immediately: 'I'd like to go, too. I can get railroad passes for both of us.'

'Passes all the way — and back? Free passes, you mean?' I had some difficulty in comprehending the magnitude of his assertion.

'Yes, sir,' Frank Sevier explained, 'free passes. Neither one of us will have to pay a nickel to any railroad, going or coming. Of course, we'll have to pay for eating and sleeping.'

When we got to Chicago and looked up some fellows from Tennessee, I learned that the alternate delegate from the Third Congressional District, in which I lived, would not be at the convention. Someone told me that if I would apply to the Tennessee delegation, then in session at a near-by hotel, I might be elected to the vacancy. I knew that, as an alternate, I would not have a vote, but I would have a seat on the floor of the convention and be close to whatever happened.

I knocked at the door of the room where the Tennessee delegation was in session, and a man opened it about three inches and looked me over. I told him I had something to say to the delegation, and he let me in. A lot of men were sitting in an ocean of cigar smoke; I knew two or three of them. I sat nervously on the edge of a chair and waited for some time, until the chairman asked me what I wanted. I rose, and said, as nearly as I can recall the words:

Mr. Chairman and gentlemen: My name is William G. McAdoo. I live in Chattanooga, and I am a Democrat, eager to do what I can for the party. I understand that the alternate delegate from the Third Congressional District is absent. I know I am not worthy of the great honor I seek at your hands; I know that it is presumptuous for me to seek this honor, but if you will elect me alternate delegate from my district I assure you that I will do my best to be worthy of your confidence.

There was some fumbling of papers to learn if the regularly elected alternate delegate was really absent, then the chairman said: 'Well, why not?' It was moved and seconded that I be made an alternate delegate, and the motion was carried unanimously. The secretary made out a card of credentials in the name of the 'Honorable' W. G. McAdoo. I certainly felt very important.

The convention was, at times, a living roar of voices and brass bands. At other times it was a dreary flat plain of men sitting close together, with somebody on a platform droning out an unintelligible speech.

The situation was interesting. The chief candidates for the nomination — the only candidates, if my memory is correct — were Grover Cleveland, then Governor of New York; Allen G. Thurman, United States Senator from Ohio; and Thomas F. Bayard, United States Senator from Delaware. Before the convention assembled I learned, from listening to the talk of the delegates, that Grover Cleveland was the favorite, and would probably be nominated. He had been Governor of New York for about a year, and had been elected by the unprecedented majority of 190,000 votes over his Republican opponent. The Democratic party, as a whole, had immense confidence in Cleveland, but Tammany Hall was opposed to him. The Tammany outfit had supported him in the gubernatorial campaign under the mistaken impression that he would be a governor of their own kind. They were grievously disappointed when he turned out to be a reformer, a high-minded citizen and a great governor.

So Tammany had come to Chicago full of wrath. On the

eve of the convention the managers of the Cleveland campaign were not sure that the votes of the New York delegates would be cast for the Governor of the State of New York. The unit rule was in force in Democratic conventions then, as it is now. Under the unit rule, when authorized by the state convention, the solid vote of the delegation is cast according to the wishes of a majority of the delegates from that state. It was apparent, of course, that if Tammany had sufficient strength to dominate the New York state delegation, then in that case the New York delegates would have to vote against their own Democratic governor. The convention was saved, however, from witnessing such an absurd spectacle. At a caucus of the New York delegation, Tammany was outvoted by a narrow margin, and the vote of the state went for Cleveland. But not without a bitter fight on the floor of the convention. Tammany tried to have the convention set aside the unit rule, and was voted down after a long wrangle.

Then the convention got down to business. The unit rule controls votes, but it does not control speech. A man whose state delegation, including himself, is committed under the rule to the support of one candidate may, nevertheless, rise and speak against the man for whom he is voting. I remember vividly the appearance of John Kelly, the celebrated leader of Tammany Hall, as he rose to speak against Cleveland. He was a bulky Irishman with a full beard. He spoke slowly, and in solemn tones warned the convention that if Cleveland was nominated he could not carry the State of New York.

Political conventions ride on waves of emotion. Mr. Kelly's speech was swept into oblivion by the rousing pro-Cleveland oration of General Edward S. Bragg, of Wisconsin. He declared that the party, with Cleveland at its head, would carry New York without Tammany, and against Tammany. In speaking of Cleveland, General Bragg said, 'We love him for the enemies he has made.' This sentence became a campaign slogan. During the next four months it was shouted from the house-tops and printed in every conceivable form.

After General Bragg's speech the convention had to suspend business for a while. The Cleveland hosts charged up and down the aisles, bearing their state flags and yelling: 'We love him for the enemies he has made.' The Tammany delegates sat grim and silent. The heat waves rose and shimmered in the air. On the platform perspiring men waited patiently and wiped their bald heads with handkerchiefs. When the Cleveland crowd had shouted itself into a condition of mute hoarseness, and the Wisconsin flag and the other flags had been put back in their proper places, the convention resumed work.

Cleveland was nominated for President on the second ballot, and a few hours later Thomas A. Hendricks, of Indiana, received the nomination for Vice-President.

Frank Sevier and I went to our shabby lodging-house, packed our grips, dug out our railroad passes, bought a bushel of sandwiches for forage on our journey, and started back to Chattanooga feeling like a pair of young statesmen!

4

My twenty-first birthday was on October 31, 1884. A few days later, I cast my first vote for Grover Cleveland. Three months later, in January, 1885, I was admitted to the bar at Chattanooga. During my first year's practice I earned two hundred and eighty dollars. My fees were pretty small. I remember one of twenty dollars, and from that they ran all the way down to thirty cents.

My second year's practice brought me eighteen hundred dollars. Of this amount one thousand dollars was in one lump sum. I was appointed guardian *ad litem* by the court to look after the interest of two little girls, daughters of a man in Chattanooga who had died and left an estate which consisted in part of the majority interest in the stock of the Chattanooga Water Works.

The executor of the estate had petitioned the court for authority to sell this stock for thirty thousand dollars, and I was expected, as guardian *ad litem*, to consent to the sale. I thought the stock was worth more, so I got some responsible men to give me a written promise that they would bid forty thousand if the court would authorize the sale of the stock at auction. The court granted my petition, and at the sale the stock brought more than sixty thousand dollars. The people who had expected to buy the stock for thirty thousand dollars were very much annoyed and I lost their friendship. I was sorry, but I couldn't help it.

The court awarded me a thousand-dollar fee for this job; it should have been five thousand, at least, but I was satisfied, for a thousand dollars looked very big to me.

When I got this fee I put the money in my pocket and walked around the streets of Chattanooga feeling like a cross between Haroun-al-Raschid and Jay Gould. I would stop before the windows of stores and add up the prices of articles displayed there with the cheerful reflection that, if I wanted to, I could go in the store and buy everything in the window.

A well-known jurist at that time was Judge Trewhitt, who presided over the Circuit Court. He was a fine old fellow, with a profound knowledge of law. He was very popular with the profession. Everybody held him in great respect. He did not wear judicial robes and was extremely informal in his courtroom. Frequently he heard cases while leaning back in a swivel chair with his feet on the judicial desk. On these occasions one addressed the soles of his feet. He chewed tobacco continually. Now and then he would lift his head and with unerring aim deluge a convenient cuspidor with tobacco juice.

In my first case before him I committed, in my eagerness, what every seasoned lawyer considers an offense against good practice — I proved my case twice. There is always danger in over-proving one's case, but I felt that I ought to have the thing clinched and nailed down before proceeding with my argument before the jury.

Despite this error I won the case. Later that day I walked up the street with Judge Trewhitt. I felt all puffed up with my success, and I hoped the Judge would compliment me, but he did not say a word. Finally I said, 'Judge, how did I try my case?' He stopped, turned toward me, and said with great emphasis: 'My boy, never prove a case but once.'

This is a saying that I have never forgotten. I remembered it years later, when I was getting together the millions of dollars that were needed to build the Hudson Tunnels. Then I had to 'sell' the idea to men like the elder J. P. Morgan and E. H. Gary. I told them my story as concisely as I could —

and then stopped. Many times I was tempted to start all over again and add something, when I recollected Judge Trewhitt and his advice: 'Never prove a case but once.'

5

While I was studying law I became acquainted with Miss Sarah Houstoun Fleming, a young and very charming Georgia girl who was living at that time with her relatives, the Hazlehursts, in Chattanooga. I fell deeply in love with Miss Fleming, and persuaded her to marry me.

I am not sure that love laughs at locksmiths, but I am quite certain that it laughs at poverty. When I married, on the eighteenth day of November, 1885, I had no material possessions of importance, but we did not let that worry us much. We made our lack of money a sort of running joke, and had a lot of fun over it. One can do such things when one is in the early twenties.

That third week in November, 1885, was a marrying week for the McAdoo family. The day before my own wedding, I went to Knoxville to attend the wedding of my sister Rosalie. Our house was gay with ribbons and flowers. A crowd of young girls in billowy skirts chattered and laughed against the background of our somber furniture. I hardly knew my sister when she came down in her wedding finery. Rosalie married James Saunders O'Neale, a young man from Virginia. After it was all over, most of my family, including the newly married O'Neales, accompanied me to Chattanooga, where I was married the next day. In a cyclone of excitement, with intermittent hailstorms of rice, the four of us started north on our honeymoon trip. In Virginia, Mrs. McAdoo and I left the O'Neales and went on to New York.

That was my first visit to the metropolis. We were there about a week, and I worked like a beaver at sight-seeing. When we got back home in Chattanooga we were tired, happy, and broke.

My responsibilities broadened; I could not live any longer in empty rooms or in the camp-like atmosphere of a young man's boarding-house.

I have observed throughout my experience in life that unforeseen events, both good and evil, often come out of the blue sky and plop down at one's feet without the least warning. It is this quality of Destiny that makes it such an interesting playmate. The episode that I shall relate here shows how well the unforeseen can behave when it really tries.

There was a lot of talk at that time about a projected railroad from Chattanooga, through Rome to Carrollton (in Georgia), where it would connect with the Central of Georgia, and thus furnish a through line from Chattanooga to Savannah. The president of the proposed road, whose name was Williamson, wanted Hamilton County, in which Chattanooga is situated, to vote a bonus of one hundred thousand dollars in bonds in aid of the project. I thought the new road would be a great help to Chattanooga, and I set out to do what I could to make it a reality. I was not employed to do this; I went at it simply as a citizen, but I was very enthusiastic about it, and very pushing.

The bonus was voted and the road was built, but it was not completed in time to get the bonus which expired on a certain date. One day Mr. Williamson came to my small, bare office and, without any preliminaries, said he wanted me to be the attorney for the railroad in Tennessee.

To be appointed the attorney of a railroad company, at so early an age, was considered a decided recognition of one's ability. It was certainly a great help, and the prominence that it created turned out profitably in bringing other clients to me. All the railroads in the region sent me passes over their lines, as a mark of courtesy; and that, too, was helpful. All of a sudden I found myself looked upon as a promising figure at the local bar.

CHAPTER IV
AN ADVENTURE IN ELECTRICITY

I

I DO NOT like ideas that are suspended in the air. There is not much metaphysics in my temperament. My mental pictures are of people and things in action. An idea is usually in the nature of an unborn deed — and when I conceive one that looks practicable and sound, my impulse is to turn it into something that I can see and handle.

This preference for tangible reality has its drawbacks, for tangible realities sometimes possess the characteristics of enraged bulls. Once brought into being, they often have such a ferocious aspect that one can only cling to the tail and pray for help. These thoughts occur to me as I think of my pioneer work in electrifying the Knoxville Street Railroad.

In the decade of the 1880's people talked of electric power in much the same way as they talk of aviation today. It was the great new undeveloped force. For the first time in the world's history men were putting harness on the back of the electric current and setting it to work.

A desire to have something to do with this astonishing development grew in my mind until it was a burning obsession. I looked about for a field of effort and for ways and means. In Knoxville the street cars went like sleepy tortoises; they were pulled by mules. I pictured myself changing all that, but there were difficulties in the way. The Knoxville street-car system was owned by a local company that appeared to be pretty well satisfied with itself. Of course, it might be induced to sell its property; but where could I get the money to buy it?

I have forgotten to say that, in the four years since my marriage, I had saved about twenty-five thousand dollars. Some of this money had been earned through my law practice; most of it had come to me, however, as the profits of real estate deals. Chattanooga had just emerged, in a dazed condition, from the orgy of a fantastic land boom. When this festival of trading was at its height a piece of ground sometimes changed hands two or three times in the same day, and always at higher prices. Much of the buying and selling was done without any attempt to examine titles, or even to look at the property.

Suddenly, the bottom dropped out with a loud bang. Fortunately, I had seen the end approaching, and my twenty-five thousand dollars was safe. I was not only willing, but eager, to put this sum into the purchase of the Knoxville car lines — if they could be bought — though I realized that it would not go very far.

I went to see the principal stockholder of the company. He was one of the wealthiest men in Knoxville, and virtually controlled the whole thing. He knew me simply as a young lawyer without any visible fortune, and I could read astonishment in his eyes when I told him I wanted to buy the street-car system.

He was willing to sell, if I could pay — and, by the way, where did I expect to get the money? I said I would explain all that if we could agree on a price. After considerable bargaining, the price was put at two hundred thousand dollars. It was too high, but I did not know it, and had no means of finding out what the road was really worth. Of this amount he wanted fifty thousand dollars in cash; he would give me time on the balance.

I talked him into giving me an option, and then I set out to raise the money. My plan was simple enough: I hoped to get some financial institution to advance the fifty thousand dollars and act as trustee. Then, with the road in my possession, I intended to reorganize it and issue three hundred and fifty thousand dollars in bonds. When the bonds were sold, and the road paid for, I expected to have one hundred and fifty thousand dollars left which could be used to put in electric power. The discount on the bonds, or commission for selling, I would have to pay out of my own resources. For my work in the reorganization I expected to take the common stock of the company.

My notions about corporation finance were naïve; I was an absolute greenhorn in such matters. At first I had an idea that I could raise the necessary funds in Chattanooga or Knoxville. The bankers in those towns were well disposed toward me and my plan, but they were not prepared to finance permanent investments. I decided to look for the money in the North, so I packed a suitcase and started out. My first stop was at Philadelphia.

I did not know anybody there, and the best thing I could think of was to call on every bank in the city. I walked along Chestnut and Fourth Streets and stopped wherever I saw a banker's sign. I may remark here that I have never had any backwardness about talking to strangers. When I believe in anything, I am not afraid to tell people about it. I believed thoroughly in the future of electric street railroads, particularly in the prospects of the Knoxville lines, and I certainly spread the news of Knoxville's coming glory in the banking district of Philadelphia.

The Philadelphia bankers were either indifferent or bored, and sometimes they did not mind letting me witness their depressing emotions. I remember one frigidly courteous man whose good manners struggled desperately with his desire to get rid of me. His fingers were very white and he wore rings. As he looked out of the window in abstraction, he kept pushing my maps and documents away from him in little delicate nudges until he had unwittingly nudged some of them off his desk. He acted as if he feared they might bite him. As I gathered up my documents to leave, he became very polite, escorted me to the door, shook hands and thanked me for having told him about the proposition.

In another banking house I started to tell my story to one of the chief officials, who was evidently ready to listen, when he interrupted me right at the beginning.

'Knoxville?' he asked. 'You mean Knoxville, Tennessee?'

'Yes, sir,' I replied. 'The Knoxville Street Railroad.'

He folded up the map I had shown him and handed it back. 'I can do nothing for you,' he said. 'Sorry. Not interested.'

'But maybe you'd be interested if you knew the favorable nature of this proposition.'

'No,' he went on. 'No matter how favorable it is, we wouldn't touch it.'

'Why not?'

'Because it is in the South. Our fixed policy is not to make investments south of Mason and Dixon's line.'

Southern enterprises had to contend with that sort of rusty prejudice for thirty years after the Civil War.

At one imposing banking edifice I thought I had struck oil. The president of the institution received me with the cordiality of an old-time friend. He listened to me, when he was not talking himself, as if he wished to burn my words into his memory. He pored over the map of Knoxville and traced various streets and routes with his fingers. The electrical development of the country was an assured fact of the future, he said, and in the growing, progressive city of Knoxville my road ought to be a big money-maker. He read all the papers I handed him — read every word of them and discussed them at length. There was a kind of feverish curiosity in his manner, and I got an impression that he did not mean for me to leave until he had signed my contract.

I stayed there about two hours. His conversation wandered into many byways. He had known some McAdoos in Indiana long ago, and wanted to know if I was related to them. I said I didn't know. That having been settled, he went back to the map and made a few suggestions about straightening out the route of the car lines. He said my plans were eminently constructive. After that we discussed the beauty of Knoxville for a while. He had never been there, but he imagined it was a lovely town. I said it was. He remarked that it must be a place full of Civil War memories. I told him that it had more Civil War memories than it really needed. Then he recollected an incident about some soldiers in Grant's army. It took him about twenty minutes to tell this story; it got more involved as he went on. While he was talking, I resolved to bring him back, at the first pause, to my financial proposition. There wasn't any pause. From Grant's army he went straight, without a break, into the question of politics. Finally I interrupted and asked him when he thought we could get together and close up the Knoxville deal. His eyes opened wide, and he looked at me in an astonished way. For a moment he said nothing — just gazed at me. Then he exclaimed suddenly:

'Oh, that! Why it's entirely out of our line. We couldn't think of going into it.'

'You wouldn't!' I said. 'I thought you were very much interested in it from the way you talked.'

'Of course. I'm interested in everything. But we never undertake that kind of financial operation. Why, we wouldn't touch a thing like that,' he continued hastily. 'Out of our line. Completely.'

That was disappointing. I sat in puzzled silence. While I was thinking it over, I had an idea that, as the proposition seemed to have his personal approval, he might refer me to someone else who would finance the road, even if his bank would not do it. No; he couldn't do that, he said, and his manner was rather cold. He was very sorry; he did not know me; and he didn't like to bother his friends by referring people to them, especially strangers.

I thought for a moment of leaving the map of Knoxville for him to play with at home that evening, but on reflection I came to the conclusion that he didn't deserve it, so I picked up the map and the rest of my playthings and departed.

After several days of such unprofitable experiences, the sum of fifty thousand dollars, which had seemed so small when I first thought of it, now looked like the wealth of Crœsus. The faraway town of Knoxville had dwindled in perspective to an insignificant pin-point. The papers and maps on the bureau in my hotel room seemed dejected and tired. Nearly everybody I talked to stared at me sadly and without enthusiasm.

As I look at these experiences in retrospect, I wonder how I ever got a chance to tell my story at all. I appeared out of the air, as a stranger, without introduction. All I had to show was a map and some pieces of paper covered with figures.

If it had not been for the tacit confession of defeat in going home without the money, I might have started back to Chattanooga. But that would never do; I could not return and tell them that I had been unable to put it over. I know now that it would not have made the least difference to the people in Tennessee, so far as their opinion of me was concerned, for they did not expect me to get the money anyway.

I decided to try New York. There I had the same experience as in Philadelphia, except that there was no prejudice in Wall Street against Southern investments. Everybody I saw in New York — and later, in Boston — was willing to hear what I had to say. Some of the bankers were interested but I was not able to land them. There was always some obstacle that prevented action; the transaction was too small to bother with; electric power in transportation was still an experiment; Knoxville was too far away; money was scarce; public utilities had turned out disastrously on too many occasions. The chief difficulty, or the one that was mentioned more than any other, was the tightness of money. I heard so much about scarce money in Boston and New York and Philadelphia that I became alarmed for the financial stability of the United States. I walked the streets wondering what had happened to all the money. It seemed to have dried up at the source. Scarcely anybody had any, and the small amount of it in existence appeared to be unavailable. As a matter of fact, money is the most fluid of all commodities. It is the easiest thing in the world to get, and at the same time the hardest thing in the world to get, depending on the circumstances.

Something or other came up — I forget what it was — that made me resolve to give Philadelphia another trial. I had not called on all the banking houses there on my first visit. Upon arriving in Philadelphia for the second time, I took an alphabetical list of the banks and checked them off. The Union Trust Company was on the list. I did not remember it. Upon consulting my notes I saw that I had not been to that trust company, and I made it my destination the first thing.

The treasurer of the Union Trust Company was Mahlon S. Stokes. He was a business-like person. Mr. Stokes listened to all I had to say, asked me many questions, and wanted the papers left with him until the next day.

When I appeared again he met me with a smile. 'We're very much interested in your proposition,' he said. 'I want you to tell your story this morning to Mr. Africa.'

Africa. Was it possible that anybody could have a name like that. 'Did you say Mr. Africa?' I asked, in a sort of daze.

'Yes,' Mr. Stokes answered casually. 'Mr. Africa wants to see you.' He led the way down a hall.

'Who is Mr. Africa?' I managed to inquire.

'The president of this trust company,' he replied. 'J.

Simpson Africa.' As he ushered me into the president's office, I half-expected to meet a colored man, but Mr. Africa had no color except white. He was an impressive, cordial man, with a full beard and a strong handclasp.

In a few days an arrangement was concluded. It all went through with amazing ease. The Union Trust Company acted as if it had been waiting for years just to lend me money. The company agreed to advance the fifty thousand dollars to be secured by the bonds of the street railroad company. Not a word was said about money being scarce.

With the signed contract in my pocket I sent joyous telegrams to Knoxville and Chattanooga, treated myself to a grand dinner and went to a show.

I imagined that all my troubles were over. They were, in fact, just beginning.

2

When we got about half the line converted to electric power, our money gave out. The engineers had grossly underestimated the cost. This created a distinctly bad situation, and for some time I did not know what to do or which way to turn. We could not operate half the road with electricity and the other half with mules and hope to make a success of it.

The most unheard-of difficulties came up for solution. Mechanical troubles. Electrical problems. Of course we had mechanics and electricians on the ground, but frequently they seemed unable to make a choice between various technical expedients that lay strictly in their own field. I have noticed on many occasions since those early days that people who are able to do skillful work are often incapable of making decisions. All business requires management. Somebody who can decide and direct and is not afraid to take responsibility is an essential factor in every kind of commercial or technical enterprise.

I knew very little about electricity, and those who wanted my judgment on this and that might just as well have told me their troubles in Greek. There was nothing for it except to learn what it was all about, and that is what I did. In a few months I had a fair working knowledge of electrical engineering. I learned how dynamos are set up, how to rewind armatures, how to calculate electric power and the relation of current to cost of production. I made myself familiar with the mechanism of trolley cars. Of course, my knowledge was superficial. When it was at its full strength I was far from being an electrical engineer, but I could understand intelligently when complicated technical problems were under discussion.

I learned a lot about electricity and the management of street railroads, but my law practice suffered. All the time this was going on I was practicing law in Chattanooga. I had to be in Knoxville, hovering over the street railway, for about half my time. My clients asked me pointedly if I intended to be an electrical engineer or a lawyer.

Chattanooga is one hundred and twelve miles from Knoxville. Sometimes I would take the train and get to Knoxville in the evening, spend most of the night in talking with the street railway people, and then catch the four A. M. train back to Chattanooga. Now and then I would remain in Knoxville for three or four days. To meet this situation I formed a law partnership with J. H. Barr, an excellent lawyer, under the firm name of Barr & McAdoo.

3

In spite of the most desperate efforts the street railroad was not a success. Electrical machinery was so imperfect at that period that it was impracticable to apply it profitably to a small street railway system. I did not know this until I got entangled with the Knoxville road. The cost of replacing a single armature in the old fifteen horse-power double reduction motors was three hundred and fifty dollars — and that sum was more than the gross earnings of the railroad for one day. There were days when we lost seven armatures.

Day and night I thought of ways and means to raise money. One may scoff at money and cultivate a feeling of superiority about it, but let me tell you that if there is anything more distressing than a lack of money when one is in desperate need it has escaped my observation.

There were times when I had the utmost difficulty in raising funds to pay the wages of our motormen and conductors. For months it seemed as if the whole enterprise would simply lie down and die on my hands within the next twenty-four hours. Knoxville at that time was a town of thirty-five thousand people, and the line had all the streetcar traffic there was in the community, but that was not enough to pay for expensive machinery and high-priced mechanics. The company borrowed money on my personal endorsement, and I turned over the earnings of my law practice. My resources were taxed to the last dollar.

At times I had an overwhelming desire to walk away and tell everybody, including the creditors, to go to the devil. However, these spiritual fainting fits were only momentary. I felt that I would be a quitter if I put up the white flag before the last shot had been fired. I resolved to stay right there until the end.

In collaboration with the Thomson-Houston Electric Company, the concern that had supplied our electrical equipment, I got up a plan of reorganization which would have saved the company, in all probability, if it had been carried out. But the bondholders were obdurate and insistent. I cannot blame them. Like everybody else, they wanted the interest on their money when it was due. They refused to go into the reorganization, and in February, 1892, they put the road in the hands of a receiver.

The road passed out of my control, and I passed out into the street without a cent that I could call my own.

I was mortified and embarrassed beyond words. The failure of the road, I thought, reflected adversely on my ability and standing. As a matter of fact, it did nothing of the kind; I merely imagined that it did. On the contrary, the impression of the intelligent public was favorable so far as I was personally concerned. I had brought electric power to Knoxville, and people were pleased with the thought that the road was still there, even though it was owned by Northern capitalists. Its owners could not pick it up and carry it away. I was looked upon as a talented, progressive young man, but I did not realize it at the time; and if I had known it, the knowledge would not have made my defeat any easier to bear.

4

I had lost all the money I had saved, and I owed, besides, a considerable sum. Most of this debt had been incurred through my personal endorsement of the street-car company's notes. Reflecting on the possibilities of my Chattanooga law practice, I came to the conclusion that I would never earn enough money in that or in any other small city to pay off my indebtedness. It seemed urgently necesary for me to get into a larger field, and I decided to go to New York.

The first question was to raise enough money to make the move and support myself and my family in New York until I could build up a law practice. I could not take any chances there with a few hundred dollars in my pocket, as I might have done before I married. We had two children at that time.

My wife owned the house we lived in. It was worth about ten thousand dollars. She and I talked it all over, and we thought the best thing to do would be to mortgage her house and base our New York adventure on the proceeds. I raised five thousand dollars on the house, with considerable difficulty. In June, 1892, we turned toward New York with all the high hopes and buoyant optimism that go with youth.

We arrived there during a memorable hot spell, and I rented a house at Sea Cliff, on the north shore of Long Island, for the summer. The great city, with its teeming crowds, its miles of streets, and its resounding activity, was an unending source of interest and wonder. I was glad to be there. The stir and bustle of the place suited me perfectly. I felt like a born New-Yorker.

I was walking along Wall Street one day, when I saw a sign, 'Office to let.' I went up to the sixth floor of No. 15 Wall Street and met a young Southerner by the name of Eldon Bisbee, who is now the head of one of the largest law firms of New York and counsel for the Chase National Bank. The fact that Bisbee, like myself, was a Southerner, put us on common ground immediately. He said that his firm had more space than it needed and was willing to sublet two rooms. I think Bisbee's firm was having a hard time and that it wanted to reduce its overhead. I took two rooms of his suite.

I had arranged with my partner, Mr. Barr, in Chattanooga, to stay in the firm there and to get the benefit of such business as I might develop for the Southern connection, but at that time I had no law business whatever in the City of New York.

CHAPTER V
NEW YORK

I

THE building-up of a profitable law practice by a young lawyer in any large city where he is unknown is one of the most discouraging things one can imagine. A lawyer can neither advertise nor solicit business. The dignity of his profession, as well as its code of ethics, forbids such direct methods. A law practice, where a lawyer has no large outstanding reputation, comes only from friends and acquaintances. Day after day I sat in my silent office and wondered what I ought to do. The helplessness of my situation was exasperating. It was a predicament like that of standing before a blank wall with no apparent means of going around it and with no ladder to aid one in climbing over it. In such a case one can only hope that something desirable, flying over the wall from God knows where, will land at one's feet.

In October — this was in the year 1892 — I moved my family from Sea Cliff to an apartment house at No. 3 West Eighty-Seventh Street. This was a five-story building without any elevator. I rented a furnished flat on the fifth floor at sixty dollars a month. It was a stiff climb to our apartment, but when we got there the view was beautiful. We could look down on the greater part of Central Park.

The small capital that I had brought from Chattanooga trickled away in a stream of dollars, quarters, and dimes, although I held on to it like a miser. I detest cheap expedients; nevertheless, I became by degrees an expert in using them. Frequently I walked from Eighty-Seventh Street to my office in Wall Street and back again, about five miles each way, not because I needed the exercise, but for the simple reason that I did not possess the ten-cent carfare for the round trip.

Without my wife's inspiration and help I could not have made out at all. She believed in me and met me always with a smile of encouragement. Her wise counsel kept me from making serious mistakes on more than one occasion. Not only that; she learned the art of economy. As a girl she had been reared in the conventional Southern manner, with little thought of money; but, during our hard times in New York, she managed things so well that we got along with the rent paid and no debts; and, through some esoteric feminine magic, she contrived to be well-dressed through all the changing seasons of women's fashions.

2

At that time I knew a young man named Francis R. Pemberton. He was a son of the Confederate General Pemberton who surrendered Vicksburg to General Grant. Pemberton had come to Chattanooga from Philadelphia, about two years before I moved to New York, with the idea of establishing an office in Chattanooga for the sale of securities. He was experienced in the investment banking business and his knowledge of bond values was excellent. He was resourceful and proved to be an effective salesman. However, his Chattanooga venture did not succeed; the community was probably not large enough nor wealthy enough. About the time I was getting ready to migrate to the North, he was also looking forward into the unknown future, and came to me with a proposal that we go into the investment securities business together in New York.

Of course, I intended to practice law, and I did not see clearly how I could take care of my law office and sell bonds at the same time. Pemberton said that he thought the law practice and the investment business might be of help to each other. We discussed the idea from all points of view, and eventually arrived at an agreement which resulted in the partnership of Pemberton & McAdoo: Investment Securities.

As it turned out, the law practice did not, for some years, take up any time worth mentioning, so Pemberton and I went around New York trying to sell bonds. We had no capital, but we arranged with some of the large investment houses to handle securities on commission. The effort to sell bonds was uphill work. We did make sales occasionally, but the commissions were small. We had the greatest difficulty to earn enough at the beginning to keep things going.

The experience, however, was valuable. I could not talk intelligently about corporate securities without knowing a lot about corporations, so I set out in earnest to study financial and corporate structures and corporation law. It was a railroad era; most of the issues that we sold — or tried to sell — were railroad securities. I became a walking encyclopedia of railroad statistics. When I declare that I could give off-hand the capitalization, earnings, and general characteristics of every well-known railroad in the United States, I am not exaggerating in the least. The drawers of my desk were crammed full of railroad maps. I studied them day and night. After a while I had a mental picture of every important railroad system; I could take a map of the United States and mark with a pencil the main line and principal branches of any railroad one might name.

Even more important and interesting was the study of railroad economics; the sources of income, the methods used in making rates, the cost of service, the division of the railroad dollar into its component parts.

One can never tell when knowledge may become useful. Many years later, when I was appointed Director-General of Railroads of the United States, I found that the large and accurate stock of information that I had acquired in those days — and which I had kept up to date ever since — was of enormous value to me.

The investment securities business with Pemberton proved very helpful and, by a sort of miracle, I built up, by gradual accretions, a pretty fair law practice. Some of my clients came through contacts that Pemberton and I had made in our efforts to sell bonds; others were sent to me by Tennessee people.

I was not out of the dark woods, so to speak, for ten years, but long before I could see my road clearly rays of light began to show here and there. By the end of 1894 I had enough faith in the future to feel justified in living in a little better way, and I moved my family to the suburban town of Yonkers, which was then a more countrified place than it is now. We lived in Yonkers about twelve years and in Irvington-on-Hudson about six years. When we moved to Yonkers, we had three children: Harriet Floyd and Francis Huger, born in

Chattanooga; and Nona Hazlehurst, born in New York City. While we lived at Yonkers, we had three additional children: William Gibbs, Jr., Robert Hazlehurst, and Sally Fleming.

In the year 1894, my father died, at Knoxville, in his seventy-fourth year. I went down to Knoxville to his funeral. To say that I was grieved at his death would be an inadequate use of words; my emotion was so much deeper than grief that it is difficult for me to describe how I felt. I was in the habit of imagining him at my side even when we were far apart. I knew his rectitude, his honesty, his high purpose and his courage — and in the dark days he inspired and uplifted me.

All things must pass. I bade my mother good-bye in her silent, darkened house and went back to New York with the feeling that, although I had lost my Pole Star, I would not have to sail an uncharted sea as long as she survived.

3

As I did not have much to do during my first few years in New York, I spent a lot of my time in reading books. My reading extended over a pretty wide area and included some excellent books as well as many poor ones.

I have long since come to the conclusion that the vast majority of books are of no value. Nine out of ten of them are written by those who lack the experience, the capacity, and the ideas which are necessary for the creation of a significant literary work. They write merely because they have read many books themselves and think that writing is the thing to do. Consequently, what they have to say consists of repetitions of old ideas and old facts worked up into new forms and presented without daring or originality.

Yet, when I come to think of it, I realize that these critical opinions are the reflections of my later years. In the last decade of the eighteen hundreds I read everything I could lay my hands on. I 'wanted to find out what men have said and done; and even if their saying and doing touched the zero of banality, it did not make much difference to me.

One end of my intellectual chromatic scale rested on fiction and poetry; at the other end was biology and astronomy.

Though my tastes were characterized by voracity rather than by discrimination, I did acquire a preference for history, biography, and economics. These subjects deal with the structure of civilization, and my chief interest was in the motivation of civilized life.

Our modern civilization, it seems to me, has been profoundly influenced by four major social movements: The Renaissance, the Reformation, the going forth of the English to the ends of the earth, and the French Revolution. Nearly all our prevailing ideas of social structure, as well as our intellectual and æsthetic conceptions, date back to these sources. If I were an historian with the learning and the ability to write world history, I would make this idea the basis of my work. The streams of action that arose in these major movements have come down the years and have spread out over the great level plateau of modern life.

These are social forces; they deal with human rights, with culture, with intellectual forms. Other factors, such as mechanical inventions, also contribute to the shaping of modern history. Certainly the invention of the steam engine was an event of enormous importance. Watt and his tea-kettle were the parents of all modern power devices. Before the discovery of steam as a motive power, mankind did not expect much help from nature. Its immutability was taken for granted. The earth had served, through untold centuries, merely as a food-producer.

The invention of the steam engine, with all its implications, opened up long vistas of industrial progress. Mechanical contrivances acquired a splendid dignity. The minds of men went exploring among cog-wheels and pistons, seeking new combinations that would take the place of hand and muscle.

It was the birth-hour of the industrial age. Machinery required capital; and capital and machinery became the masters of labor. A new set of problems came into the world.

4

The center of gravity in the field of statecraft has shifted, during the last century, from the political to the economic plane.

The patriots who inspired and organized the American Revolution thought only of political rights. In temper and philosophy they were individualists. They rebelled against England because they wanted self-government, and the right of free speech and a free press. They contended that no man should be imprisoned arbitrarily, and that every accused person had a right to be tried by a jury. They held that every man should be allowed to conduct his own affairs in his own way, as long as he obeyed the law; and they argued that law should concern itself with nothing but the cardinal vices.

Before the close of the eighteenth century, these demands were so firmly established that they became political axioms, acknowledged as a sort of Euclidean truth by all intelligent and liberal minds.

The success of the American Revolution was a triumph of individualism, and its propelling spirit surged on into the Constitution of the United States. Though Alexander Hamilton and Thomas Jefferson differed widely in their conceptions of human affairs, they were both individualists. They both thought that the government had done enough for a citizen when it put adequate safeguards around his life, his family, and his property.

This attitude of the government toward the people seemed eminently sound to the four million Americans who saw the birth of the nineteenth century. But even then, while they were contemplating the perfection of their governmental system, a new power was rising silently among them — a dynamic force that operated outside the law and the political scheme. Its terrain was the field of economics. It struck at men where their armor of political rights left them unprotected. Those who liked to give names to intangible realities called it Economic Power.

In the young American republic — saturated, as it was, with a policy of Let Everybody Alone — there existed ready opportunities for the exercise of greed, for the appropriation of natural resources, for the making of money by those who had money-making talents.

But very few people possessed any money-making talents; and the majority of people had other standards of personal worth. They were willing to let money alone if it would let them alone. An ideal arrangement, but not a practical one. Economic Power cannot let people alone even if it should want to, for Economic Power lives and grows on profits; and profits have to come from the mass of workers and producers. Consequently, Economic Power, possessed by comparatively few, grew and fattened in the midst of American affairs like the fabled crocodile in the pool which swallowed every frog that came near him.

The formula of political rights which had been set up by our forefathers and had been cast in enduring bronze as a guide and landmark for future generations was found wholly inadequate as a defense against this new menace.

When the era of mechanical industry began; when the small workshops disappeared and huge factories rose in their places; when railroads displaced the ancient highways; when commerce became nation-wide; when the nation's money fell into the control of a few hands, then Economic Power set out to show what it could do when it really tried. It became the arbiter of destiny, the fixer of fate, the silent invisible government. As its domination extended over men and resources, its unpopularity grew, and the cool, philosophic name of Economic Power gave way to such rough and opprobrious terms as the Money Trust, the Predatory Interests, and Plutocracy.

Something had to be done about it. The writings of the Fathers were thumbed over for guidance and inspiration, but they had not anticipated the rise of Big Business. It became apparent that their placid philosophy of allowing every man a maximum of liberty to conduct his own affairs in his own way was unworkable in the complicated modern world. Experience proved that a maximum of economic liberty meant a maximum of greed; and, moreover, that it led to intolerable confusion and inefficiency.

'The freest government,' said Daniel Webster, 'if it could exist, would not long be acceptable if the tendency of the laws were to create a capital accumulation of property in a few hands. In such a case the popular power must break in upon the rights of property, or else the influence of property must limit and control the exercise of popular power.'

Slowly, and by degrees, the American governmental system

began to evolve from a guarantor of political rights into a supervisor of economic activities. It was an arduous and difficult evolution — a long contest between tradition on one hand and necessity on the other — and the end has not yet been reached. But the process has gone far enough to shock Jefferson, Hamilton, John Adams, and Andrew Jackson into speechless astonishment if they could see what has taken place. The members of Congress used to quote Cicero and Virgil; today they quote the statistics of steel production. We have an Interstate Commerce Commission, to regulate the railroads; a Tariff Commission, to adjust import duties; a Federal Trade Commission, to regulate interstate trade; a Federal Reserve Board, to influence the flow of money and credit; and, besides these, many other devices that have been set up to direct the nation's economic life.

Individualism as a practical working philosophy is coming to an end among the American people. We who are living today are looking upon its dying struggles. The statesmen of the future will have to give most of their attention to measures for the regulation of economic power and the enactment of laws to promote social welfare.

I do not claim to be much of a prophet, but I hazard a prediction that the historians of the next century will look upon this change in the direction of the American mind as the most significant happening of our epoch.

To anyone who comes straight from European to American history, as I did in my reading, the sense of continuity is very striking. The stream of European ideas flowed into this oversea land without a pause or a break. We are transplanted Europeans, not only in the matter of speech and customs, but also in respect to fundamental ideas.

To me this thought has always been depressing. I wish it were not so. Here, in a new world, with all the defects and stupidities of an antique civilization behind us, it does seem to me that we might have struck out on a new and better road. With all the land on the continent at our service we might have built more spacious and more beautiful cities; we might have achieved some effective method of industrial

coöperation; we might have done something to smooth away
the infinite injustices that come from the unequal distribution of wealth; we might have conceived a form of land
tenure and land ownership that would have been more in
conformity with the needs of modern society; we might have
thought of a plan which would eventually raise the great mass
of men to a better grade of thinking and a higher level of
citizenship.

That we did none of these things is one of the tragedies of
history. On the contrary, we came to the new world carrying
our worn-out fallacies and ancient ideas, like travelers who
burden themselves with bundles of threadbare clothes. Upon
arriving here we put on our old garments and have worn
them ever since, except for a few minor changes to fit the
climate.

As I write these words I realize that I am indulging in a
fantastic idealism. The long experience of mankind has proved
that everything that is worth while must come through experiment and error, pain and suffering.

5

In the official family of Grover Cleveland, during his second
administration, there was an Assistant Secretary of the Navy
named William McAdoo. After his term of office was over, he
came to New York to practice law. I had long known of this
namesake of mine by reputation, but I did not meet him until
the spring of 1897, when I went to his office to hand him some
of his letters that had been delivered to me by mistake, on
account of the similarity of our names.

The bewildered post-office could hardly grasp the fact that
there were two William McAdoos, and that both were lawyers.
The postmen scrambled the mail so thoroughly that the opening of letters became a surprise and a delight. Mr. McAdoo and
I got in the habit of sending wrongly delivered letters back and
forth with humorous excuses for having read some of them
inadvertently. In time we became good friends.

Of course we tried desperately to prove ourselves blood relations, and in the effort we twisted the sacred genealogical
tables into all sorts of queer shapes. But we never could es-

tablish any kinship. William McAdoo was Irish by birth. He was brought to the United States when he was a small child, and grew up here. The Jersey City Democrats sent him to Congress, where he served four terms. As Congressman and Assistant Secretary of the Navy he made a fine record.

One day he remarked that as our mail would probably never be disentangled, it might be a good idea for us to occupy the same office, and relieve the postman of needless mental fatigue. That was his way of suggesting a partnership.

'Well, Mac, your plan sounds good,' I said. 'But, in that case, who would open the letters?'

'Why, the first one of us who gets here in the morning would have a preëmption claim on the entire batch,' he answered.

'And the checks?' I continued.

'Oh, we'd divide those up — half and half.'

The law firm of McAdoo & McAdoo came into existence before the end of 1897. It was one of the most agreeable associations that I have ever had in my life. In some respects William McAdoo was as naïve as a schoolboy, and in other ways he was as deep as a well and appeared to possess all the ancient wisdom of the world. He was a whimsical person; his mind ran into delightful similes and comparisons.

Our partnership ceased in about four years, when the work of organizing the Hudson Tunnels companies took up so much of my time that I had to give up almost entirely the practice of law. Later on, William McAdoo became Chief Magistrate of the city of New York — a post that he occupied until his death in 1930. He died a poor man — a convincing evidence of the inflexible integrity of his career.

I looked upon the law as my life-work, and I expected to continue its practice indefinitely. I hoped, or expected, that as my practice grew, I would accumulate a moderate amount of money. Then, with a competence put away securely, I planned to devote less time to the law and more to public affairs. I had a burning desire to acquit myself with distinction and to do something that would prove of genuine benefit to humanity while I lived.

Along this sharply defined life-pattern I made far-reaching

plans, with a mistaken notion that I could see my own future clearly, but I have since learned many times, and in many ways, that the clarity of a conception is no proof of its validity.

My career was entirely different from what I thought it would be when I played with these forecasts thirty years ago.

Intelligent people eventually come to the conclusion that human destiny is incalculable; only fools maintain a permanent faith in fortune-tellers. No man knows what is going to happen tomorrow — and it is just as well that nobody does know, for a foreknowledge of events would pretty thoroughly spoil the quality of adventure in life. And what a dull thing living would be without adventure!

Under the Hudson River, in slime and darkness, lay the ruins of a partly constructed tunnel that was intended to connect New York and New Jersey. It was the grave of a daring idea, the last resting-place of an ambition and an energy that had been crushed by insuperable obstacles. Attempts had been made at intervals for thirty years to drive this bore through the under-river depths, and every attempt had met with failure. Before I came to New York, the project had been definitely abandoned. The fragment of the tunnel was closed and forgotten by everybody except a few bondholders of the last bankrupt construction company. Probably not more than one person in a thousand living in New York in 1900 knew that it was in existence. The tunnel was considered a dead thing, laid away forever in the cemetery of unworkable ideas.

It was dead, indeed, but not dead beyond the power of resurrection. The Fates had marked a day when I was to go under the river-bed and encounter this piece of dripping darkness, and it would rise from its grave and walk by my side. I was destined to give it color and movement and warmth, but it would change the current of my life and lead me into a new career.

6

My law business caused me to make trips frequently to Philadelphia and Baltimore and the South. I had to cross the Hudson River to reach the railroad station, and the only way to get across was to take a ferry-boat.

Of course, this clumsy system, with its complications, led to innumerable delays. The ferries usually ran every ten minutes. If you missed one boat, you had to wait for another. Even when you made a perfect connection, it was slow going. Sometimes, on days when navigation was difficult on account of the thick river fogs, the ferry-boats went very slowly, feeling their way and stopping dead still in the middle of the river now and then, like a blind man halting in the middle of a street.

On such occasions a ferry crossing, if one had the time to spare, was a picturesque experience. Often I have stood on the wet deck of a ferry-boat, drifting uncertainly through a world of gray fog and oily green water, and have felt a thrill of adventure and unreality. Through the fog came a bedlam of mournful sounds — the deep bellowing of ocean liners, the angry screams of tugboats, and the long, eerie cries of the ferry sirens that reminded one of sea gulls. Against the pallid sky, rising above the lower levels of the fog veil, one might see the heavy, broad-shouldered bulk of Manhattan's huge buildings. Sometimes the fog would be a shallow sea, lying low in the river, and then there was a strange effect of the crest of the buildings standing out in sunlight while the blinded river traffic cautiously felt its way. They looked like strong stone houses floating in the air.

It was picturesque, but most people who went back and forth across the river had no time for marine adventures. They were on their way to their daily jobs, or to catch trains, or to keep appointments.

The delays that I experienced in crossing the river on my various trips started me to thinking of possible means of taking people across more expeditiously. I had no particular object at first in applying my mind to the matter of trans-river traffic; I thought about it just to keep myself occupied. But after a while it began to interest me seriously; it was a problem for which I had an instinctive liking.

I had an idea that a tunnel might be driven under the river, and I spoke about it casually to a number of my acquaintances. Most of them listened to me indifferently and remarked that it could not be done. The river was too deep, they said. Others argued that if it were an engineering possibility, it would have been accomplished long ago.

I wrote to the Hydrographic Office at Washington and got some profile maps and some data about the river channel. I learned that the Hudson is sixty-five feet deep at its deepest point between New York City and New Jersey; and that the river bottom rests on a thick layer of silt. The mention of silt started me on an investigation to find out exactly what silt is. I discovered that it is simply mud, highly impregnated with water, but capable of supporting heavy burdens.

One of the strangest things about all this fact-finding and conversation is that I never heard the abandoned tunnel mentioned by anybody or referred to in print — not at that time, while the idea of boring under the river was forming in my mind.

In 1901, I became interested with John Markle, the well-known anthracite coal operator, and his brother Alvin, in organizing the company that owns the Wilkes-Barre & Hazelton Railroad. I was entrusted with the legal work of the organization. My associate was John R. Dos Passos, one of the leading corporation lawyers of New York. One day, while I was talking with Dos Passos, I told him of my plan of building a tunnel under the river.

'A tunnel!' he exclaimed. 'Why, it has been tried. A failure.'

I was astonished. 'Tried when?' I asked. 'Do you mean that actual work was ever done on a Hudson River tunnel, or was it merely an idea?'

'I mean actual physical work,' Dos Passos replied. 'I ought to know; I lost enough money on the thing to make me remember it very well. Why,' he continued, 'there's about half a mile of tunnel out there in the river now, unless the whole contraption has caved in.'

From Dos Passos I gathered an outline of the tunnel's abortive history.

In the early seventies a Western railroad-builder named D. C. Haskin came to New York with a plan for putting a railroad tunnel under the river. He was energetic and confident, with a complete faith in his own ideas. His project was an ambitious one. It included a large underground passenger station at Washington Square. From this point a tunnel large enough for railroad trains was to run, in a southwesterly direction, under the city blocks until it reached the river, and then under the river to New Jersey.

He began work on the Jersey side in November, 1874, midway between the Lackawanna and Erie terminals. Within a month the Lackawanna Railroad succeeded in getting out an injunction which stopped his operations. The Lackawanna objected to the tunnel running under its yards on the Jersey side of the river. This injunction, with its accumulated legal papers and arguments, lingered on in the courts until 1879, when it was dismissed. In December of that year the work was resumed.

In about a year Haskin's money ran out, and he made the most desperate efforts to interest financiers in his project. He did succeed in getting some new money, but not a great deal. The engineering problem, which was a formidable one, had been so magnified in the public mind that most people thought the project a hopeless impossibility.

The Haskin company failed in 1882, and work on the tunnels ceased. The company's failure was hastened by a disastrous accident which happened while Haskin was trying to raise fresh capital. A cave-in occurred, and twenty workmen were drowned in the forward working chamber. Their escape through the door in the air-lock was prevented by silt piling up on both sides of the door in such quantities that it could not be opened.

For six years the uncompleted work remained as Haskin had left it. In 1888, the company was reorganized and a contract for finishing the job was given S. Pearson & Son, of London. This world-famous concern had recently built the Forth Bridge in Scotland.

The Pearsons changed some details of Haskin's plan. Instead of building the tunnel with masonry, they substituted cast-iron rings. These rings were brought into the bore in segments. As they were set up and bolted together, they constituted an iron tube, which grew in length as the work went on.

The English contractors would have completed the work, I think, about the middle of the nineties, but the tunnel company was not able to raise sufficient funds to carry on — so the company failed again. The property was bought at foreclosure

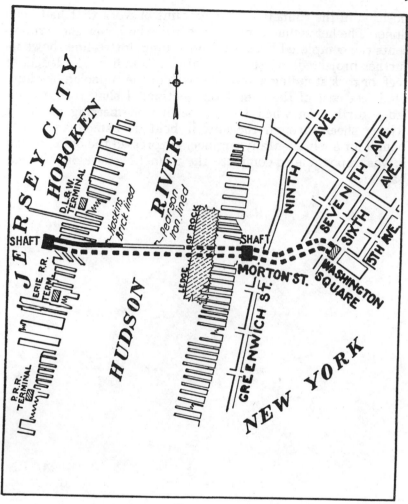

FIGURE I

Black line running out from New Jersey shore shows the section of
tunnel bored by Haskin and the Pearsons — 3800 feet of a single tube.

by a committee of the bondholders, who had no idea what to
do with it.

When the Pearsons stopped, about thirty-eight hundred
feet of the north tunnel had been finished. The width of the
river along the line of the tunnel is about fifty-eight hundred
feet. The rough map which is given here as Figure I shows the

position of the tunnel and the amount of work that had been done. The heavy line running out from the Jersey shore represents the completed bore; the continuing dotted line shows its further projected course. On Figure 1 is indicated a ledge, or reef, or rock standing across the path of the tunnel, a few hundred feet east of the completed section. I shall refer to this ledge further on when I describe our engineering methods. Rising sheer through the silt, it held us baffled and spellbound for a while. Many engineers expressed the opinion that it was impossible to complete the tunnel because of this rock barrier.

CHAPTER VI

BURROWING UNDER THE HUDSON RIVER

I

I TOLD Dos Passos that I had a plan in my mind for building a tunnel under the Hudson River. 'Why not take hold of ours and complete it?' he said. In speaking of the Haskin and Pearson remains as 'ours,' he meant, of course, that it belonged to the bondholders.

Naturally, I felt flattered by his confidence in my ability, and considerably astonished. He knew me to be a lawyer without much experience in engineering or in large enterprises; and I suppose he knew that I had no money. However, I took him at his word, and told him that I would like to get in touch with the bondholders.

The attorney for the bondholders' committee was Frederick B. Jennings, of the law firm of Stetson, Jennings & Russell. I had never met Mr. Jennings, but I knew him by reputation. He was one of the great lawyers of the time. Dos Passos said he would be glad to introduce me to him.

I called on Mr. Jennings one day in October, 1901 and was received with cold politeness. He was a brusque and forceful man, accustomed to brevity and directness. I was a tall, thin young lawyer, without any convincing credentials, and certainly without any experience that would inspire the least confidence in a matter of this kind.

I told him that I had been studying the subject of rapid transit for some time, particularly in respect to the Hudson River, and that I intended to organize a company to construct some tunnels under the river. The thought had occurred to me, I said, that I might utilize the partly completed tunnel under his control, if it was in good condition and could be obtained at a satisfactory price. This was pretty big talk, considering the fact that I had no money and no ideas as to where I could raise any.

Jennings looked at me gravely. I could see that he was

sizing me up, and that he was not enthusiastic over the prospects of selling the property to me.

'Have you any idea how much money would be required to put a tunnel under that river?' he asked, after studying me awhile.

'Oh, yes,' I replied confidently. 'I have a pretty clear notion.'

To that he said 'Huh,' in a colorless tone.

'It would cost several million dollars,' I continued. 'My idea of the necessary capital is only an approximate one, of course.'

I think he wanted me to go away and let him alone, but was too courteous to say so. I asked him if I might be permitted to go into the tunnel and look it over. After some hesitation he said yes, I could see it. Before I left his office, he gave me a note of introduction to Charles M. Jacobs, one of the engineering firm of Jacobs & Davies, who had charge of the abandoned work.

A few days later, Jacobs and I explored the tunnel. Dressed in rubber hip boots, yellow oilskin coats and hats, and carrying oil lanterns in our hands, we descended a vertical shaft to the depth of sixty feet, and stood before the entrance.

As I entered the tunnel, I had a powerful feeling of visiting a place I had known well many years ago. It was a curious impression. I was like a man who walks through a wrecked and dismantled house that he had lived in when he was a boy.

Down the length of the bore a narrow board walk was laid, about three feet above the slime at the bottom. This walk was covered with soft ooze, and was slippery. Moisture trickled along the iron plates that encased the tube. The inside of the tunnel was as dark as midnight. As we walked along the plank, our lanterns cast wavering, fantastic shadows. The gloom lay ahead of us like a long black section of nothing. When we spoke, it sent our voices back to us in metallic, unearthly echoes.

We went clear on to the end, to the steel shield that the Pearsons had used in boring through the silt. The shield was slimy with mud and rusting in spots. It was a hopeless-looking piece of machinery, but Jacobs said that all of its vital parts, such as hydraulic jacks and other appliances, were in good condition.

I was depressed as I came back to fresh air and the gray October afternoon. The whole thing was so inanimate, so ponderous, and so lonely. It was not a ghost, or a skeleton, but a carcass. I felt as if I had seen the body of some long and enormously heavy animal that had lain down and died. Yet, from the moment I saw the tunnel I never doubted that I would get possession of it and complete it. This conviction did not live in my mind as a secret mental boast, nor as a prophecy, nor even as a hope. I can hardly call it a mental idea. It was an intuitive conviction — a presentiment — but it was so overpowering in its simple, colorless intensity that I accepted it instantly as a fact.

Next morning I walked all the way from the Grand Central Station to my Wall Street office while I reflected on ways and means to raise money. The location of the tunnel did not fit well into my scheme; it began casually at nowhere in New Jersey, and it ran in such a direction that it would have to emerge from the river on the New York side at a most unlikely spot for passenger travel. But, in spite of these drawbacks, I saw the advantage of taking over the property if I could get it. In raising capital, it would be much easier to interest investors in a half-completed tunnel than in a mere idea.

After walking to my office in the cool autumn sunshine, I came to the conclusion that I could not proceed intelligently until I had acquired much more engineering data than I possessed at that time. In a day or so I went to see Jacobs and told him all I had in my mind. He was confident that the tunnel could be finished successfully, and, as the art of underwater tunneling had made much progress during the last decade, the work (he said) would cost considerably less than it would have cost Haskin or Pearson.

Jacobs and his partner, J. Vipond Davies, coöperated with me heartily and made up some tentative plans and estimates. We figured that the entire job, as we had planned it, would cost approximately $4,000,000. This sum would complete one tunnel and its approaches. As the tube was eighteen feet in diameter, it would be possible to put two narrow-gauge tracks within it. I knew that one tunnel would be inadequate for the potential amount of traffic, but I decided to accept the situation, as the building of two parallel tubes would require vastly more money. That was something which had to come in the future, and I kept it in the back of my head.

I called on Jennings again, and I think he was surprised to see me. He was much more cordial than he had been on my previous visit, and took a genuine interest in the sketchy plans and figures that I showed him. After this conference I saw Jennings many times and became well acquainted with him. He was a man of the finest type, and pleasant enough when one got to know him. Like many other men of large affairs, he surrounded himself with a chilly atmosphere for the purpose of discouraging bores and time-wasters. When he came down from his iceberg, I found that he had as much good nature and warmth in his make-up as human beings usually possess.

After much negotiation with Jennings, it was agreed that if I could raise the capital for a new company the bondholders would turn over the half-completed bore for $350,000.

I accepted these terms, and soon afterward I incorporated a concern to carry out the project. This corporation was called the New York & Jersey Railroad Company. Its authorized capital was $6,000,000, and I intended to issue at once $5,000,000 of common stock and $5,000,000 of first mortgage, five per cent bonds.

The remaining authorized capital of one million dollars was not to be issued at that time. I planned to hold it back until we were ready to start work on the second tunnel.

I expected to sell, or to have underwritten, $4,500,000 of the first mortgage bonds. Five hundred thousand dollars of the authorized five million were to be issued for the general purposes of the company.

This set-up, considered as a plan of financing, was simple — and it was also thoroughly sound. The weakest spot in it was myself. I had no money, few influential friends, and no experience or record which would justify the financial community in turning over to me such a tremendous undertaking. It was entirely possible that some Wall Street concern, with ample resources, might step in and take the whole thing out of my hands. It was even possible that, after I had raised the necessary capital, the subscribers might decide to give the management of the company to an experienced executive, or engineer of great repute, and dismiss me courteously with a fee for my work in organizing the enterprise.

One of my friends was Walter G. Oakman, the president of the Guaranty Trust Company. I decided to call on him first, and it was a sensible decision. Before becoming a banker, Mr. Oakman had been an engineer and a railroad president, and he understood my problem. He was an exceptionally fine and able man, and his advice and active help were invaluable.

Through Mr. Oakman the Guaranty Trust Company agreed to lend, for a reasonable length of time, the sum of $3,750,000 on $4,500,000 of the bonds, if I could get that amount underwritten by subscribers whose financial responsibility was satisfactory to the trust company. It would undoubtedly take some time to sell the bonds, but, with the issue underwritten, we could lay our hands on the necessary capital at once.

Oakman himself headed the list of underwriters with a subscription of one hundred thousand dollars. Frederick B. Jennings was next on the list, and he put his name down for a hundred thousand. With a letter from Mr. Oakman I called on Anthony N. Brady, who was the controlling figure in the Brooklyn Rapid Transit Company. Mr. Brady read my letter, asked a few questions, and signed for a hundred thousand without any hesitation. I was almost bursting with elation as I left his office. The business of getting wealthy men to write down their names for one hundred thousand dollars apiece seemed very easy. The hard part was to come later. Mr. Oakman, Mr. Jennings, and Mr. Brady all consented to go on the board of directors.

The United States Steel Corporation was conspicuous in the public eye. It had been organized that year (1901), and, as it was the largest corporation in the world at that time, everybody was talking about it. The personalities who directed its affairs were as well known as the President of the United States. Among the men most prominent in the Steel Corporation were E. C. Converse and E. H. Gary. I felt that if I could get these two men into the company it would be a tremendous help. I knew Converse in a friendly way, though I had never had any business dealings with him. He was an informal, hearty person, with a pleasant manner.

One day I went in to see him and told him about my project. He listened to me for a quarter of an hour, asked one or two questions, and reached across his desk for the underwriting agreement, which I held in my hand.

He read the paper slowly and carefully; then he took up his pen. He wrote down his name and paused for a moment before the column of figures. As I sat opposite him, I watched intently every movement of his pen. First he made the figure 2, then a cipher and a second cipher. I thought that he was going to subscribe $20,000 and I felt disappointed. But he put a comma after the second cipher, and followed it with three more noughts. I knew before he handed the paper back to me that he had subscribed $200,000. 'There you are, Mac,' he said. 'How'll that do?'

I looked at it and said 'Fine' — then I added dolefully, 'But I really hoped you'd make it more.'

He laughed, and I laughed. When Converse laughed, one always wanted to laugh with him. 'Liar,' he said humorously, 'you know you didn't expect more than half that amount.' Before I had departed from his office, he agreed to be one of the directors of the company.

I told Converse that I was anxious to get E. H. Gary, whom I did not know, interested in the company, and Converse gave me a letter of introduction. In due course I called on him. He was certainly the antithesis of Converse in manner and bearing. I have never met any other man in public life, or in large financial affairs, whose attitude as a listener was as unresponsive as that of Judge Gary. His clammy unresponsiveness was an efficient squelcher of enthusiastic talk. I was, of course, bubbling over with optimism. I started out on my epic with joy. Before I had talked ten minutes, I found myself discussing the prospects of the Hudson tunnels with the same sad intonation that one uses in talking about the yellow peril, or the boll weevil, or the statistics of the divorce courts. His unenthusiasm was infectious. All at once I realized that he cared nothing whatever for rhetoric, that when he considered anything he did not want his view blocked by verbal flowers. He wanted nothing but the bare bones of the subject, and he would do his own interpretation.

I talked on, and Judge Gary listened imperturbably. When

I paused, trying to think of an accurate expression, he made no effort to help me out, but simply sat there, immersed in a kind of esoteric gloom, and waited until I found my tongue.

When I had told my story, he began to ask questions in a level, monotonous tone. He asked five or six questions of the most penetrating kind, and, at the conclusion, looked more indifferent and gloomy than ever. I felt that I had not convinced him, but I handed him the underwriting agreement, anyway. He glanced at it, signed his name, wrote '$100,000' after it, and handed it back without a word. I was astonished. I thanked him and said: 'Judge, will you go on the board of directors with Oakman, Converse, Jennings, and Brady?' 'All right,' he said, 'put me down as a member of the board.'

Judge Gary and I became warm friends. This fact, and the phrase in which I express it, may seem surprising in the light of our first meeting. He was never a jovial personality, but he was a solid man, of most excellent, sound financial judgment. For eleven years — as long as I was connected officially with the Hudson Tunnel enterprise — Judge Gary never failed to attend the directors' meetings, unless he was out of town. Whenever a perplexing question came before the directors, he would go straight to the inner core of the problem.

With all these big people on my list of underwriters, I thought it would be just too easy to round out the total subscription. It was not so at all. I had to do the hardest kind of work, and to take all sorts of frigid rebuffs. As soon as I spoke of putting a tunnel under the river, most people looked upon me as a crank. Strange, isn't it? I called again and again at offices where I could never manage to see anybody; at other places I was turned away with a shrug of the shoulders. It was a slow, arduous, heart-breaking job, but it was eventually done. I remember the day when I went to Mr. Oakman with the subscription list filled. He looked over the names, said they were satisfactory, and remarked that the young company would soon have $3,750,000 to its credit. Then he said, 'You know, I had an idea that you would never succeed in doing this.'

'Why?' I asked. 'Somebody has to build the tunnel.'

'It's an innovation,' he replied. 'People are scared to death of new things, even if the new things are absolutely necessary.'

At the first meeting of the board of directors I was elected president of the company. My salary was fifteen thousand dollars a year, which was more than I earned at my law practice at that time. I knew that the tunnel would take all my energy and thought, so I retired from the investment securities firm of Pemberton & McAdoo and from the law partnership with my namesake, William McAdoo.

2

I was completely absorbed in the tunnel project during the autumn and winter of 1901. The tunnel lived with me, as an idea and as a picture, every day and all the time. Everything I saw, or heard, or read, trickled back through some intricate and devious route to this controlling idea.

When I first conceived the notion of boring under the Hudson River, my chief motive was to make money for myself; close behind came a secondary desire to perform a public service, to accomplish something that would be of material benefit to people generally.

But as time went on, another motive — a more compelling one — appeared. In some inscrutable way there grew within me a kind of sympathetic relationship between the forlorn, comatose tunnel and myself. It was the same creative urge that sends a painter to his canvas or a sculptor to his modeling clay, the affection of an inventor for the grotesque model of a new machine. I experienced a sense of inner compulsion, a driving desire to do the thing for its own sake. It was also a challenge to do what was supposed to be impossible. In the early summer of 1902, we began work under the river. The construction work was turned over to Charles M. Jacobs and J. Vipond Davies, both able engineers with large experience in sub-aqueous tunneling.

Do you want to know the secret of doing a big job successfully? Well, I'll tell you what it is. Turn all your big problems into little ones. Reduce everything to its simplest form. Do not be overwhelmed by the magnitude of a task, for a big piece of work is, after all, nothing more than a small job seen through a magnifying glass. I felt sure that if we could build ten feet of tunnel, we could build ten thousand feet.

As soon as we began actual work, the sleeping tunnel awoke from oblivion into the glare of publicity as lively as that which surrounds a new operatic star. Everybody was interested. The people of New York looked on and stared as the people of Egypt must have gazed at the building of the Pyramids.

Many of the newspaper descriptions of our methods were loosely worded and full of mistakes, though we told everything we knew, and all we were doing, in the simplest words, to the army of newspaper people that swarmed about us.

One of the commonest of the popular misconceptions concerns the question of how the tunnels are supported. Many people suppose that we had to drive piles under water and lay the tubes on them. Others have some fanciful notion about the tunnels lying placidly in the water on the bed of the river. As a matter of fact they are embedded in silt without piles or other support. The silt, which has lain for thousands of years under the pressure of the river above it, is firm and homogeneous. It sustains easily the weight of the tunnels and the impact of heavy trains in motion. This seems astonishing to people generally — when they first hear of it — but it is a simple physical fact. The silt is quite as firm, and as capable of bearing weight, as the ground on which railway tracks are usually laid.

The Hudson Tunnels were driven under the river by what is known as the shield method. The shield may be described as a sort of mechanical mole. It goes through soft earth in a manner somewhat similar to that of a mole plowing under a lawn.

If you take an ordinary tumbler, place it in a horizontal position with the bottom of the tumbler foremost, and shove it into a bank of earth, you will have a pretty good representation of a boring shield.

The bottom of the tumbler corresponds to the face, or — as the engineers call it — the 'diaphragm' of the shield; the rest of the tumbler is the 'tail of the shield.' Imagine a number of small doors — big enough for a man to pass through — in the face of the shield (or bottom of the tumbler), and picture the whole contrivance being slowly pushed forward by powerful hydraulic jacks.

Now, to carry the tumbler representation further, after you

have forced the tumbler into the earth a little way, you stop and build up within the 'tail' of the tumbler (the shield) a ring of the tunnel, which is composed of cast-iron segments securely bolted together. As the shield goes forward, you erect one ring after another, bolting them tightly together. As a result you will have a permanent tunnel, or a circular tube, composed of massive iron rings. In a general way, and very crudely, that describes the mechanics of tunnel-building by the shield method. I am trying to avoid technical terms.

In boring the 'north' tunnel — which we tackled first, as it was already half-completed when we took hold of the work — the shield was advanced about thirty inches at a time. As the hydraulic jacks were applied, the bottom doors in the face of the shield were opened, and the displaced silt was squeezed through them into the working chamber, or 'heading,' as it was called. This tumbled and sticky mass of material had to be carried to the surface. It was a terrible nuisance and expense. The men in the heading shoveled it into small cars; then it was hauled back to the New Jersey shaft, dumped into scows, and finally dropped into the ocean outside of New York Harbor. That was the only way to dispose of it.

One 'shove' of thirty inches, with the subsequent removal of the displaced silt and the erection of the iron ring, would usually take two or three hours. It was slow and arduous work.

When we began to bore the parallel or 'south' tunnel, we installed hydraulic jacks of enormous power. They put enough mechanical muscle behind the shield to drive it straight through the silt without opening the doors. It was not necessary to move any more silt through the tunnel. We laid away the spades and parted company with the scows. The shield, with the iron-ringed tunnel growing behind it, went into the under-river soil like a walking-stick going into a soft bank of clay. The silt was pushed upward and to one side as our mechanical mole moved ahead. It was a tremendous improvement. With the old process we were never able to advance through silt more than twenty-four feet in a twenty-four-hour working day, but the new process carried the work forward at the rate of seventy-two feet a day. It was the first time in the history of engineering that a tunnel was bored without the labor of excavating and removing the earth that it displaced.

All this work was done under air pressure. In the forward part of the tube, in the heading where the men worked, the pressure was thirty-eight pounds to the square inch. That was enough to equalize the hydrostatic head, as the engineers call it — that is, the pressure of the water — and prevent it from flooding the tunnel, except in case of accident.

The tail of the shield had to be slightly larger in diameter than the iron rings which form the tunnel for the reason that the tunnel was built up inside the tail of the shield. Or, to use a homely illustration, the tail of the shield fitted over the growing end of the tunnel as an office-worker's cuff fits over a sleeve. The danger spot was in the little crevice between the outside of the tunnel rings and the enveloping tail of the shield. The thrust of the air pressure was upward. If the shield moved slowly, or remained stationary for some time, the compressed air would begin to push through this crevice and percolate the silt overhead. Eventually the water of the river would come down on the tunnel, smashing through the crevice at the tail of the shield and flooding the tunnel heading with incredible speed. As long as the shield was kept moving forward, this danger was minimized. That is one of the reasons why we carried on the work twenty-four hours a day.

I have said that the air pressure in the tunnel was thirty-eight pounds to the square inch, but that applies only to the heading. There was no use in keeping such a stiff pressure throughout the completed part of the tunnel. An air-lock was constantly maintained a few hundred feet behind the shield. This air-lock was simply a long steel tube, like a boiler, about five feet in diameter, with doors at each end. It was encased in a concrete bulkhead built across the tunnel. Through the air-locks the men passed from one section of the tunnel to another, and from one stage of air pressure to another. In the heading the pressure was thirty-eight pounds; in the next section, which was also protected by an air-lock, it was eighteen pounds. After that, one came into a long stretch of the completed tube which was at normal air pressure, and which was connected with the main shaft, or entrance.

In case of accident in the heading, the men were expected to make a dash for the air-lock and go through it. Once on the other side, they were safe. They had to run for their lives on several occasions; I shall tell you the story further on.

3

As long as the shield was moving through silt it was relatively a simple process, though one which required unceasing care at all points. When we reached the reef of rock that lies below the bed of the river, a new and unsolved problem stood before us. The reef, a sort of granite backbone which rises up through the silt, is seven hundred feet wide. Its top, at the highest point, is sixteen to twenty feet below the river bottom. Our problem was to bore through the reef, forcing the bottom of the tunnel through the rock and the top of the tunnel through the silt.

This obstacle presented an unprecedented engineering puzzle, and it was considered by many engineers to be an insoluble one. Our engineers had a complete profile of the route, made from borings and surveys, and they knew, of course, that the rock was ahead of us. I remember spending hours in the office of Jacobs and Davies, listening to them and looking over their plans for conquering the buried reef. Surrounded by their huge drawings — circles and triangles superimposed one on the other, intricate diagrams and sheets of cabalistic figuring — they made me think of the necromancers in a sketch by Albrecht Dürer. But these modern necromancers did not rely on charms and omens; their strong points were mathematics and physics.

Engineering is not only a science; it is also an art. Like all the other creative arts, it is vitalized by the use of the imagination. The engineer must be able to put himself imaginatively in the place of material forces in very much the same way that a novelist puts himself in the place of his characters. He should have the imaginative faculty of foreseeing the contingencies of energy and matter, and of devising plans to meet them.

Jacobs and Davies had worked out a solution of the reef problem on paper. It was a simple solution, and that made me think well of it. Simplicity is one of the outstanding characteristics of talent.

The first step in the Jacobs and Davies plan was to push the shield right up to the reef. Then the lower doors of the shield were to be opened and the men were to dig away the silt for six or seven feet in front of the lower half of the shield. While this was being done, the mass of silt overhead, as well as the river above it, would be supported by timber breasting and by compressed air.

When sufficient space had been cleared, a steel apron, or shelf, was to be bolted to the front of the shield, horizontally, on a level with the shield's center line. Figure 2 shows this apron in place. The purpose of the apron was to hold the over-head silt in position and prevent it from coming down on the men as they drilled the rock for blasting. Later, we added another device, also shown in Figure 2. We built a vertical wall, or breasting, in front of the men at work.

The problem was solved, even though the operation was a delicate one and great caution was needed. The explosive charges of blasting powder had to be very light. Above the rock there were only sixteen to twenty feet of silt — and, above that, the ponderous weight of a river more than one mile wide and sixty-five feet deep. A heavy blast would have brought the river down on us.

It took us eleven months to get through this reef. The shield edged along, an inch at a time. It would come to a stop; then there would be more drilling, more feeble blasting, and a few pounds more of broken rock to remove. It was excellent training for the cultivation of patience.

Shortly after we had reached the reef, we had a blow-out which delayed the work for some time. The shield was kept standing still too long. Our thirty-eight pounds of pressure sent a stream of air filtering through the overhead silt, churning it into soup. All of a sudden water began to pour in on the men in the heading. They had the sense not to try to plug the leak, for anything in the way of a stopper would have had to keep back the Hudson River. They ran for the emergency air-lock, and all of them reached it. Before they slammed shut the door of the air-lock, they looked back and saw a string of electric lights still glowing foggily in a mad whirlpool of foaming water. After they had closed the door, they listened. They heard the torrent strike against the steel

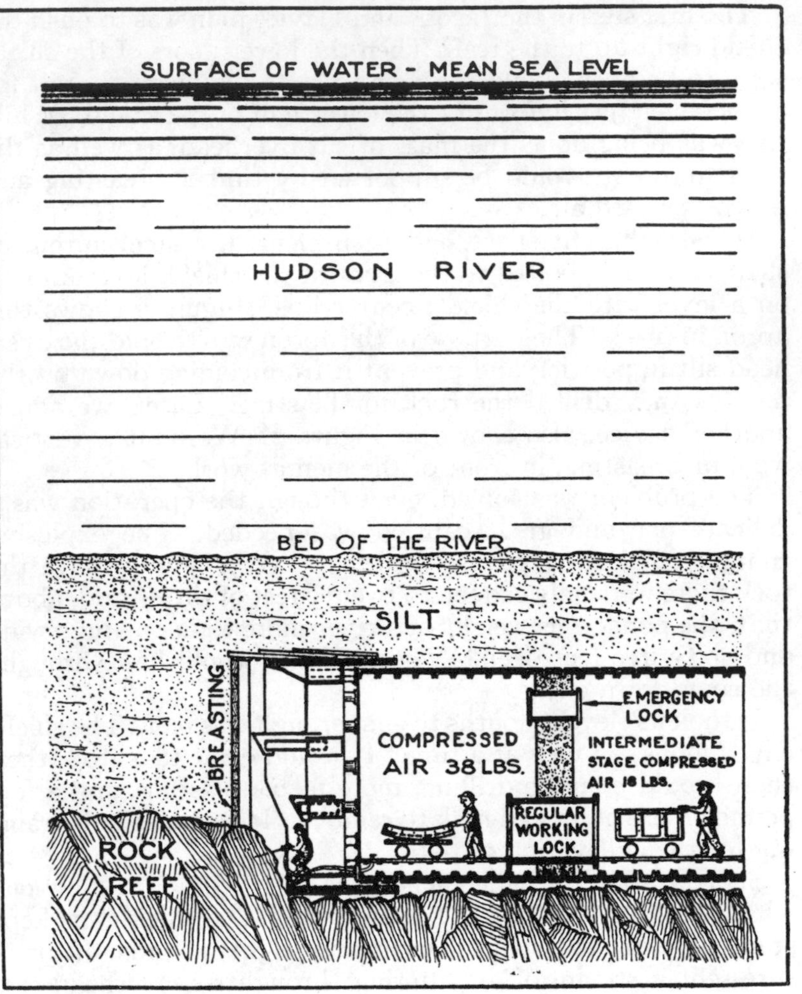

FIGURE 2

Method of attacking the ledge, or reef, of rock under the river bed.

partition like a hundred sledgehammers. Then, streaked with mud from head to heels, they came to the top and told us what had happened.

Repairing a blow-out in an under-water tunnel is not an easy matter. After considering various ways and means, our engineers decided to plaster the hole with clay. Of course, they knew exactly where the break had occurred. Through triangulation they located a spot on the surface of the water that was precisely over the hole in the bottom of the river. With permission from the War Department, which has control of harbors, we dumped several barge-loads of clay into the hole. What we did was to cork up the hole and put a new bottom in the river.

By pumping compressed air into the heading, and opening the valves of the water-lines which connected the various sections of the tunnel, the water was blown from one section to the other until it reached the shaft on the New Jersey side. Thence, it was pumped to the surface. When we got back into the heading, it was a scene of devastation, the muddiest sight I ever saw in my life. We caught a live fish in the heading — the first one ever taken through the bottom of the Hudson River.

More than one blow-out occurred in the course of the work, but we were fortunate enough to lose the life of only one man in these accidents.

4

It was a foregone conclusion, almost from the start, that we would bore two parallel tunnels — although, as I have said, our plans at first included only one tunnel, with two narrow-guage tracks laid in it side by side. Such an arrangement would have proved inadequate to handle the traffic and, in many other ways, was undesirable.

We started to bore the parallel or 'south' tunnel in 1903. Owing to the employment of the high-powered jacks, much faster progress was made than in the first tunnel. Although work began on the south tunnel a year after our start on the first one, the two tunnels were completed at pretty nearly the same time. Progress was hastened by work at both ends of the tubes. As soon as we had got fairly started on the New Jersey side we installed shields on the New York side. Thereafter the working parties advanced toward each other and met under the bed of the river.

Looking at one of these ponderous mechanisms, as it sits in its place underground, and at the adjacent chaotic jumble of pipes and scaffolding and iron and mud, it is difficult to believe that an infallible accuracy in direction could be attained through the use of such unwieldy devices. But engineering is a nest of miracles. The two shields, both enveloped in blind-mole darkness, approached each other slowly, and finally met, face to face under the river with a watchmaker's nicety of contact.

The shields in the north tunnel came together on March 11, 1904. We had telephones in the tunnel headings, and I had arranged with Chief Engineer Jacobs to call me up when an opening had been made. As soon as I heard from Jacobs, I got in touch with Walter G. Oakman and told him the news. He and I and a few others hastened across the river in a ferry-boat and went to the shaft on the New Jersey side. We walked in the tunnel and passed through the air-locks until we came to the shield. The workmen were standing around. The men looked worn and tired; they were covered with mud, of course, from head to foot.

Chief Engineer Jacobs smiled. 'Mr. McAdoo, we've got something to show you,' he said, as he pointed to one of the open doors of the shield.

I knew what he was going to show me, but as I looked through the door my heart leaped. There stood the grim face of the New York shield that had plowed its way under the river to meet us. We crept through the door and the narrow passageway, dripping with water, that connected the shields, and continued on our way. Half an hour later, we reached the New York shaft.

For the first time, in the history of mankind, men had walked on land from New Jersey to New York.

5

From the beginning I had carried a picture of an extensive tunnel system in my mind. I said very little about it, for I have an instinctive antipathy to huge and nebulous programs. In a project of this kind it is better to do one thing at a time and let each new development grow out of an accomplished and successful fact. The thing to do at first was to prove that we could actually put a tunnel under the river, so I kept my

THE FIRST MEN IN HISTORY TO WALK UNDER THE HUDSON FROM
NEW JERSEY TO NEW YORK

Front row, left to right: William Barclay Parsons; G. Tracy Rogers; Walter G.
Oakman; William G. McAdoo; George B. Fry, Superintendent (kneeling); Charles
M. Jacobs, Chief Engineer; John Skelton Williams; P. Fitzgerald, Foreman (squatting). J. Vipond Davies, Deputy Chief Engineer, is just behind Mr. Rogers and
Mr. Oakman.

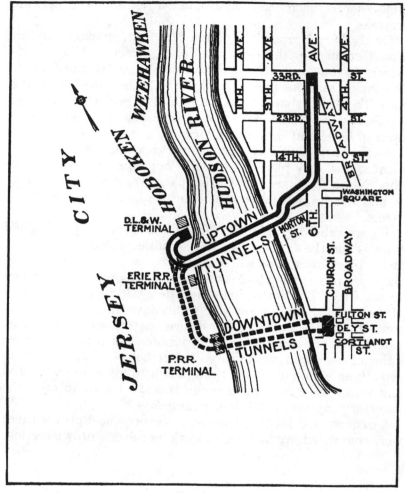

FIGURE 3

This diagram shows the uptown tunnels, as completed (shown in black lines). The dotted lines indicate the route of the downtown tunnels.

plans to myself until our work had progressed to a point where nobody had any further doubts as to its success.

To connect the under-river tubes with the traffic, I proposed to build an extension under the railroad yards on the Jersey side which would run north and south, almost at right angles to the river tunnels. This north-and-south extension would enable us to reach the Lackawanna, Erie, and Pennsylvania stations.

On the New York side, I planned, at first, an extension that would connect with the Christopher Street Station of the Ninth Avenue Elevated Railroad. Later on, I came to the conclusion that our line would have to go beyond Ninth Avenue. To get our share of the traffic, and to perform an efficient public service, we should have to take our passengers to the uptown hotel and shopping district.

At that time Sixth Avenue was the great highway of department stores. My plan was to carry our uptown extension beyond Ninth Avenue — up Christopher Street to Sixth Avenue — and northward under that thoroughfare to Thirty-Third Street.

Figure 3 shows graphically what I had in mind. The original tunnels and the extensions I have just described are drawn in heavy black lines. You will observe also two dotted lines across the river further down, between the Wall Street district and Jersey City. The dotted lines indicate a still further extension of the system. For a while I kept this day-dream of the downtown tunnels submerged in silence, as its accomplishment would involve the building of two more twin tunnels, and require a large amount of money. Nevertheless, I expected to do something about it. After the uptown tubes were completed and trains were running through them, I hoped to raise the necessary capital for the lower tunnels.

Circumstance hastened events. Before the uptown tubes were completed, we had begun work on the downtown section.

CHAPTER VII
THE HUDSON TUNNELS ARE COMPLETED

I

MONTHS before our sandhogs had burrowed their way under the river, the successful boring of the tunnel was conceded by everyone. There were no longer any doubters. The first subway from Brooklyn Bridge to the Bronx was being built, and there had been so much talk and publicity that the whole community appeared to be a little mad on the subject. Nearly every man I met in those days had a new idea for a tunnel.

With all this in the air I thought the time had come for me to do something definite about the downtown tunnels. For a long time I had been carrying the plan in my head. I awoke this sleeping idea, got its eyes open and its face washed, and set it on its feet. I traced a route across the Hudson from the Pennsylvania Station in Jersey City to some point in the neighborhood of Trinity Church, near Broadway, facing Wall Street. Then, going back to the Jersey side, we laid out on the map a subway which would connect the uptown and downtown under-water tunnels, and tie them up with the principal Jersey railroad stations. On the map it looked like a capital letter U, laid flat, with the two horns of the U resting on Manhattan, while the bottom of the letter was on the New Jersey side. I talked over the plan with my friend Mr. Oakman. He was all for it, and agreed with me that if we did not build a downtown tunnel, and begin work on it soon, somebody else among the numerous tunnel enthusiasts in New York might step in and do it ahead of us.

It was evident that, in carrying out the downtown project, the coöperation of the Pennsylvania Railroad was essential. In the first place, the passengers of that great railroad system constituted a large percentage of the across-river traffic; and in the second place, we needed a right of way under their railroad yards and property. I did not know what the attitude of the Pennsylvania would be, but I must say that I was doubtful as to any coöperation, for I could see readily enough that our plans might cut deeply into the railroad's ferry business.

The situation, briefly stated, was this: At that time the Pennsylvania owned the ferry line that ran between its station in Jersey City and the foot of Cortlandt Street, in New York. Passengers of the railroad were taken both ways across the river on their railroad tickets — that is, without charge. In other words, the ferry system was an integral part of the Pennsylvania lines; and, apart from the railroad company's own passengers, the ferries had a large and valuable pay traffic from the street railways and from so-called 'walk-on' passengers from the street. When our tunnels got in operation, we should be able to carry passengers across the river much more frequently, quickly, and comfortably than the ferry-boats could do it; so, if the road made an arrangement with us, the value of the ferries would be greatly reduced. Therefore, anything that we could propose to the Pennsylvania would involve a drastic change in its methods and in the status of its ferries.

However, there was another aspect to the matter. The Pennsylvania was just beginning, in 1903, to build its great terminal in New York uptown at Seventh Avenue and Thirty-Third Street. As soon as this terminal, with its tunnels, was ready for business, it was the intention of the Pennsylvania to send the greater part of its passenger traffic into it. The through trains and expresses would not enter Jersey City at all; they would go straight on through Newark, and under the river, to the new uptown station in New York.

Nevertheless, a large percentage of the Pennsylvania's passengers would have downtown destinations, and in consequence the road could not very well abandon the route through Jersey City without seriously impairing its service. An arrangement of some kind would have to be made for taking these downtown passengers off the through trains at Newark, or at some other convenient point, and sending them to downtown Manhattan. The management of the road had planned, as a matter of fact, to keep the ferries going and to run shuttle trains, back and forth, from Newark to the Jersey City station.

I reflected on this situation and put myself, imaginatively, in the place of the Pennsylvania executives. I tried to look at it from their point of view. This diversion of traffic from the main line through Jersey City was a sort of trailing loose end of their enormous scheme, and I fancied that they considered it a nuisance. Now, suppose I should go to them with a proposal to take it off their hands? The longer I revolved this thought in my mind, the more clearly it appeared to me that here was my logical point of approach.

An essential part of my general plan was the erection of two large office buildings west of Broadway over the underground space which was to be used for our downtown trains. We should have to buy considerable ground for our tunnel station anyway; why not make the investment in land pay for itself? That could be done by putting up two huge office buildings on the property, with our terminal in the basements.

For weeks I studied the terminal problem, and quietly examined every available site. Finally I reached the conclusion that the downtown terminal ought to be on the west side of Church Street, between Cortlandt and Fulton streets. It was the logical location. Oakman and I decided to get options on, or to buy if necessary, sufficient property at that point to provide for our needs. We wanted two entire city blocks, embracing numerous pieces of real estate. Needless to say, this property had a variegated ownership. It was controlled by all sorts of people, some of them business-like, some of them stubborn or suspicious, and some of them unreliable.

Our proceedings were carried on with the utmost secrecy, as a measure of safety. If the least inkling of our intention had reached the public, prices would have gone sky-high. Though we were willing to pay the normal prevailing prices we did not want to be forced into an expenditure of millions of dollars for real estate which might have been bought for much less. The purchasing of this plot of ground would have taxed the skill of a dozen diplomats, but somehow or other our brokers managed it.

That is how the matter stood when I went to Philadelphia, early in 1903, and called on Mr. Cassatt, the president of the Pennsylvania Railroad.

My instinctive feeling for personality told me, before I had been in Cassatt's office five minutes, that any attempt at shrewd bargaining with him would not only be wasted effort, but might be harmful to my proposal. As a rule, great men do not haggle over details. This may surprise some of my readers, but it is so. Big men, I mean men of range and caliber, look at effects and results in the mass rather than in detail. The only way one can meet them on their own plane is by a frank and complete discussion of the subject in all its phases.

I told Cassatt exactly what was in my mind. He looked over my maps and asked some questions. Then he glanced at me and smiled dryly. 'Well, it seems to me,' he said, 'that you're going to destroy our most profitable ferry.'

I said nothing; the fact was obvious. I wondered silently if he hoped to get some monetary recompense for the depreciation in value of the ferry line as the price for coöperating with us. 'You are about to put our ferry out of business,' he continued, 'but the Pennsylvania Railroad believes in providing the best facilities for its patrons, and, as your tunnels will do that, we'll hook up with you.'

This interview had lasted less than an hour. I had expected a long series of conferences, and was agreeably surprised at the quickness of his decision, yet the brevity of the discussion and his readiness to come to terms on such an important question were somewhat disquieting. I did not know with certainty whether Cassatt was merely expressing his own views or speaking formally for his railroad. The directors of the company might not agree with him, and then what? Of course, I wanted to get it all settled definitely, yet I did not want to ask him if he had authority to commit the road to this arrangement without seeing other people.

In my perplexity I thought of our project for a terminal building, and I decided to use that as an indirect means of drawing him out. I told him about our plans for the terminal and the office buildings, and that Mr. Oakman and I had obligated ourselves to raise the money for the ground on which it was to stand. 'If any hitch occurs in this agreement with the Pennsylvania Railroad,' I remarked, 'it will put us in a bad hole.'

'There'll not be any hitch,' he said. 'At any rate, none on our part. You can count confidently on us.'

Then, as if he had read my mind, he went on and said: 'Our board will approve all we've agreed on today. You can go right ahead with your plans, and we will sign the agreement as soon as it is prepared.' I left his office with full confidence in his word, and my confidence was entirely justified. He was the kind of man on whom one could rely absolutely.

We organized a new corporation, called the Hudson & Manhattan Railway Company, to build the downtown tunnels. This was a separate concern, and I was the president of both companies.

The first agreement with the Pennsylvania Railroad was signed on May 16, 1903. Three years later, we made another contract with that railroad under which we pushed an extension of our downtown tunnel westward to the Bergen Hill in Jersey City and made a junction at that point with the Pennsylvania's tracks to Newark. A new station, called Manhattan Transfer, was built by the Pennsylvania at a point just where Newark fades away in the Jersey meadows. Pennsylvania trains stop on one side of this station, and the Hudson Tunnel trains on the other side. Hudson Tunnel trains run straight through between Newark and the Hudson Terminal. They take the place of the contemplated Pennsylvania shuttle service to and from Newark and downtown New York. Passengers are exchanged between the companies across platforms at Manhattan Transfer.

2

The Hudson Tunnel system was like a rapidly growing boy who keeps getting too big for his clothes. We began with a single tube under the river, but before long we had a network of projects on our hands. When the system was finally completed — and that was not until 1910 — it consisted of four under-river tunnels and miles of underground subways; nineteen miles of line in all. Besides, we had constructed office buildings covering two city blocks. At that time they were the largest office buildings in the world.

All this growth required an enormous amount of money. We came to the conclusion that we could no longer depend on the haphazard sale of stock here and there, and decided to put the financial end of the enterprise into the hands of Harvey Fisk & Sons, one of the old established private banking houses of New York. Oakman was a warm friend of Pliny Fisk, the

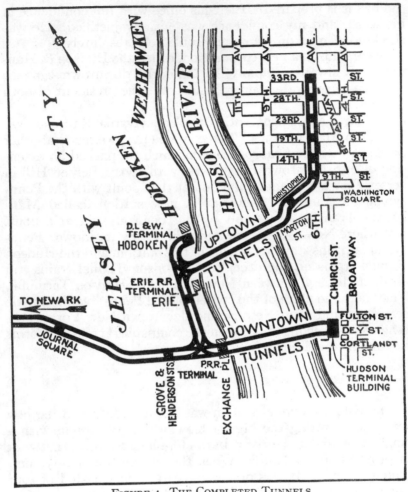

FIGURE 4. THE COMPLETED TUNNELS

senior member of the firm, and it was at Oakman's suggestion that we got the Fisks interested. This connection was made in 1904.

I shall not carry you through all the ramifications of the financial program. It includes a tangled mass of obsolete figures, and you would find it neither interesting nor informative. The whole story is told in outline when I say that it was successful, and that, before the system was completed, about

$72,000,000 had been invested in the enterprise. The Hudson Terminal buildings alone, with the ground on which they stand, cost $13,000,000. Without the aid of Pliny Fisk and his associates, I do not believe we could have ever got that immense sum of money together. Pliny Fisk was an extraordinarily able man; he had courage and vision two indispensable qualities of a great financier.

Subsequently, during the year 1906, we consolidated the two tunnel companies — the New York & Jersey Railroad Company and the Hudson & Manhattan Railway Company — into one corporation, known as the Hudson & Manhattan Railroad Company, and I became the president of this consolidated company. This concern was our permanent establishment; it is today the owner of the Hudson Tubes and the Hudson Terminal buildings.

One day when Pliny Fisk and I were considering ways and means, he remarked that it would be tremendously helpful if we could get J. P. Morgan interested in the tunnels. I agreed with him heartily, and said that, if anybody could get Mr. Morgan, it was Fisk himself. To my surprise he replied that I was the man to see to that. I did not think so, but Fisk kept on urging me, and finally he told me that he had arranged with Mr. Morgan to see me.

I presented myself at the Morgan offices at the indicated hour. It was one of the few times in my life when I approached an interview with inward trepidation. No doubt you have an impression, from reading all I have written so far, that I am not timid about seeing people and talking to them. That impression is correct. But on this occasion so much depended on the result that I had a sinking at the heart. I feared that I would be unable to convince this emperor of finance and would be responsible for a failure.

Mr. Morgan sat in a small, rather bare, room. He was at a desk, signing some papers, when I entered. He told me to take a chair, which I did. I waited, while he went on with his papers. He seemed to me, as I studied his appearance, to be a man of great physical strength. He was broad-shouldered and deep-chested. On his face there was an expression of confidence and power.

He looked up from his papers, pushed them away, and

fastened his eyes on me. 'All right, Mr. McAdoo,' he said pleasantly, 'go ahead.'

I said: 'How much time can you give me, Mr. Morgan?' He asked me how much I wanted, and I said, 'Ten minutes.'

In my memory he stands out as a unique type. I have never met another man who was enough like him to be put in the same class. He had remarkable eyes; they were vividly keen and penetrating. His nose was disfigured by some sort of coloration or eruption. It was large and bulbous. In forming a mental picture of almost any other person with a disfiguration of that kind, the nose would be the outstanding feature in one's recollection. But after you had been in Mr. Morgan's presence for a few minutes, you did not think of it, because his powerful personality reduced this blemish to insignificance. I had been often told that he was gruff and difficult in manner, but I did not find him so.

When the ten minutes were up, I asked if he could spare five minutes more, and he said: 'Yes; go on.' I finished what I had to say, and waited. He seemed to be willing to hear more, but I remembered, from long ago, Judge Trewhitt's advice never to prove my case twice. It is very easy to talk a good proposition to death. After a moment of silence, Mr. Morgan asked a few pertinent questions and said that he would discuss the matter with Mr. Fisk, so I took my leave. Mr. Morgan had not said a word of approval, or of disapproval, while I was with him.

Some days afterward Fisk told me that Mr. Morgan had agreed to take one million dollars of our preferred stock. You can well imagine that we were all greatly set up and elated. We needed the money, but even more than that we needed the financial repute and public confidence that came from association with such a powerful figure in finance.

I thought at the time that I had been the means of bringing Mr. Morgan into the tunnel enterprise, but as I reflect upon the incident now, in the light of my larger experience in life, I doubt if my interview with him had much, or anything, to do with it. Pliny Fisk, I fancy, had already convinced him, and Mr. Morgan probably wanted to see me just to size me up, as I happened to be the originator of the plan and the executive head of the company.

On February 25, 1908, the uptown tunnels were formally opened, and a train service went into operation between Hoboken and the station at Sixth Avenue and Nineteenth Street.

It was a great day for all of us. At that time Charles Evans Hughes was Governor of New York and Franklin Fort was Governor of New Jersey. These two governors, as well as many other distinguished people, were our guests. I had arranged with Theodore Roosevelt, then President of the United States, to press a button at the White House and start the first train on its trip from Nineteenth Street to Hoboken.

President Roosevelt did this gladly, and before the tunnels were formally opened, he wrote me a letter in which he said, in part:

The tunneling of the Hudson River is indeed a notable achievement — one of those achievements of which all Americans are, as they should be, justly proud.... It is a bigger undertaking than any Alpine tunnel that has yet been constructed; and the successful completion represents moving New Jersey bodily three miles nearer to New York in point of time.... It is the kind of business achievement which is in the highest degree creditable to the American people, and for which the American people should feel and publicly acknowledge their hearty gratitude.

We rode under the river in the gleaming new cars, freshly painted, glittering and shiny. The tunnel was a long tubular perspective, with its strings of electric lights receding and vanishing in a golden-yellow blur. In the cool, under-river air there was a faint smell of varnish, of cement, of freshness, of things newly finished. Inside the cars the silk-hatted gentlemen sat in rows, leaning on their canes, and looking a little uneasy as they glanced out of the windows and saw the curving iron walls flash by.

The boundary line between New Jersey and New York is in the center of the Hudson River. When we reached it, the train stopped so that the line was between two cars, in one of which was Governor Hughes and in the other Governor Fort. The two governors shook hands across the imaginary line, signalizing the formal 'marriage,' as it was called, of the two states. A kind of grown-up child's play, of course; but people like such ceremonies. It was all very sedate, and amiable, and pleasant.

The trains in this uptown section had been running for more than a year when the downtown tunnels and the great Hudson Terminal were completed and opened for traffic on July 19, 1909.

The newspapers got in the habit of referring to the system as 'the McAdoo Tunnels'— and anyone who did not know the facts would have thought, after a month's newspaper reading, that I had personally done the whole job. I have as much vanity as the average man, I am sure, but I do not like to be praised for other people's work. About the time the tunnels were completed, I wrote letters to all the New York newspapers and asked them as a favor to suppress the name, 'McAdoo Tunnels.' I called their attention to the fact that many men had contributed to the successful completion of the work — among them our competent and resourceful engineers, the whole army of 'sandhogs,' and a staff of executives and supervisors. It was through my energetic protest that the name 'McAdoo Tunnels' was tabooed in the newspaper offices.

3

One day, some months after we had opened the downtown tunnels, my office boy came in and announced that a Mr. Edison was outside and wanted to see me.

'Edison?' I repeated wonderingly. 'What Edison? What does he want?'

'He didn't say what he wanted,' the boy answered. 'I suppose he wants to sell something. His name is Edison.'

'Did he tell you his business?'

'No, sir, he didn't,' the guardian of the door remarked. 'He's kind of hard to talk to, because he's deaf and has an ear-trumpet.'

Thomas A. Edison! I rose and went out to meet him. My profound admiration for Mr. Edison ran back for many years, but I had never seen him before. When I ushered him into my office, he said diffidently that he was afraid that he might be intruding on me, but his excuse was that he wanted to see and talk to the man who had driven the tunnels under the Hudson River.

I had some difficulty in conversing with him at first, as my voice has a natural low pitch, but pretty soon I got accustomed to his deafness. He appeared to be interested in even the smallest details of our work; in our latest powerful shield for tunneling through silt, in our up-to-date power-house with its turbo-generators, in our multiple unit trains with their all-steel cars and ingenious automatic side-doors. I wanted him to talk, but he preferred to listen.

Mr. Edison is, I suppose, the greatest inventor that ever lived, and history will probably give him that distinction. His career has always seemed fascinating to me. He is a perfect example of a genius, working through the power of inspiration and moved by an inner voice. He was very poor in his youth — a working boy without any advantages whatever and with very little education. His inventive genius expressed itself in his early days and under most discouraging conditions.

A man who knows Edison well told me once about the invention of the quadruplex telegraph. This is a device through which four telegraphic messages are sent over the same wire at the same time, two in each direction.

It was one of Edison's earliest inventions. While he was working at it, he made his living as a telegraph operator in Cincinnati. He preëmpted a little spare room in the offices of the company, and after his day's work was over, he tinkered about in this room with his wires and chemicals. The other telegraph operators, employed in the office, made a practice of grouping themselves in the doorway and asking ironical questions. His ideas appeared to them so preposterous and silly that he was looked upon as the office simpleton. Two messages going one way, and two the other way over the same wire at the same time! All thrown in together, helter-skelter. Who ever heard of such a thing? Why, they would get all jumbled up — just a hash of dots and dashes — and nobody would be able to make head or tail of any of them.

The manager of the office thought Edison was woolly in the head and devoid of horse-sense. Eventually he fired the young dreamer.

The quadruplex telegraph was perfected, however, and is now used by every telegraph company in the world. Although this device is just a mechanism, the imagination behind its invention was of such a high order that it should really be classed as an example of creative art, and stand beside the works of Shakespeare and the paintings of Rembrandt.

A curious thing about Edison is that many of his inventions have been made in absolute defiance of common-sense. He has never been bound by tradition. He belongs to the race of Columbus, Galileo, and Einstein — the race of innovators and scientific free-thinkers.

Common-sense is the attitude of the intellect in felt slippers. They are all right for wearing around the house, but nobody in felt slippers ever discovered a new continent.

I wonder what would happen if a genius like Edison appeared in the field of politics and economics? Imagine a dynamic, clear-thinking, unconventional mind that would approach the vexing problems of social welfare, unemployment, labor and capital, with an uncluttered freedom from traditional modes of thought.

Would a statesman of such high and original talent have a success comparable to Edison's? I should say decidedly not. I am not a prophet, but like everyone else I am entitled to a guess, and my guess is that the mind of the public would be divided as to the correct treatment of such an astonishing genius of statesmanship: some of the people would want to put him in jail at once; others would be satisfied if he were merely subjected to contempt and indifference.

The modern world does not look with approval upon new social and political devices which may lead to fundamental changes in the structure of society, even if such changes would be distinctly for the better. But at the same time the modern world offers every possible reward, in money and fame, to inventors in the field of science, even if their inventions lead to the scrappings of acres and miles of machinery.

The result is that science and mechanical industry are now some two or three centuries ahead of the rest of civilization in the process of evolution. This lopsided condition of affairs has, through the course of years, set up exceedingly dangerous internal strains in the social structure of every civilized country.

Anyone who is interested in this phenomenon may observe

its manifestations best in a time of business depression. On one hand millions of people are out of work and there are bread-lines in the big cities. The farmers cannot pay the interest on their mortgages, factories close, and merchants have few customers for their goods. But, on the other hand, the machinery in the great industrial plants is of the most improved pattern and stands in shining readiness to turn out an immense volume of products, and to give employment to armies of people. The banks are gorged with money; and, although the jobless stand in bread-lines, the land is full of food — and contains, indeed, so much wheat that the government has to buy it and hold it in packed warehouses to keep its price from going down.

There we have a picture of a widening gap that it will take an Edison of statecraft to close.

4

The millions that I was supposed to have made out of the Hudson Tunnel enterprise are mythical millions. A fiction of that sort has the quality of spontaneous combustion — it simply starts into being of its own accord. People generally do not understand how anyone can be at the head of a large corporation and fail to become wealthy.

During the eleven years that I was the president of the tunnel companies I received, in money and stock, what amounted to an average of fifty thousand dollars a year, and this includes my salary for the eleven-year period. Considering the big salaries paid to the heads of corporations, and considering the fact that I conceived the project and carried the responsibility for its success, I think everyone will agree that I was not overpaid.

I am not setting down these facts by way of complaint; they are recorded merely as items of history. I was then, and am now, quite well satisfied. Even if I did not make a great deal of money, I acquired a large and favorable reputation, and I value that more than money.

The ability to make money is a very different thing from what is known as the business sense, though the two are frequently confused and identified, mistakenly, one with the other. Business sense is the capacity to manage a business in an orderly and profitable manner, while money-making is the expression of the acquisitive instinct. Some of the best business executives I know are relatively poor men. They carry on successfully the affairs of important corporations — and make dividends for them — yet they have nothing of their own but their salaries and what they have been able to save.

On the other hand, the art of money-making is inexplicable to one who does not possess it. In it there is mingled an inherent feeling for values, and an intuition that leads one to do the right thing at the right time. I have met many money-makers of great renown, and the ease with which they attract wealth has never ceased to astonish me.

Speaking of money, I shall tell you how one man made a million dollars indirectly from the Hudson Tubes without ever having invested a dollar in them. That man is Arthur Brisbane, the distinguished editor-in-chief of the Hearst newspapers.

I met Brisbane in the early days of our Hudson Tunnel struggles. He was very friendly to our project, and frequently printed editorials and articles about it. His work did much toward popularizing the tunnels. We became good friends. Without saying anything to him about my intentions I resolved to do him a good turn the first time I had a chance.

After all our battles were over and we were at peace with our late foes, we began preparations to extend our lines to Newark. There was to be a station of the line at Summit Avenue — now called Journal Square — in Jersey City. I knew that the opening of this station would create a new business center, and that real estate values would increase tremendously. With this in mind I took Brisbane to Jersey City and explained the situation to him. I advised him to buy all the land around the proposed station that he could get at the low prices then prevailing. I told him that I wanted to buy some myself — and I did intend to, but I never did, for I did not have the money.

Brisbane acted on my advice. Some years afterward he told me that he could sell the property he had acquired at a profit of a million dollars.

5

The test of material progress lies in its relation to human welfare. In the end, when all is said and done, the value of achievement must be measured only in terms of social worth.

You may talk all you please about inventions, and enormous business enterprises, and sky-piercing towers, yet none of these material entities has any intrinsic value of its own. Their worth rests wholly on their use by humanity. No man can make himself independent of other people, and no man-created institution possesses a superiority over ordinary human rights.

All property is created by men and women at work; all material value arises from the juxtaposition of people and things. Machines do not make men; but, on the contrary, men make machines. There is something debasing in the thought of men being the slaves of inanimate things: in the idea that a man is not as good as the machine he operates, or worth as much as the house he lives in, or that he is inferior in value to the street car that takes him to work.

Conceptions of this kind have an enormous potential power for evil in them. They are vicious, but they exist; and many people accept them as unimpeachable truths. These moral fallacies flow, to a large extent, from the modern form of industrial development, in which the machine and the money that it represents are arrayed in tacit antagonism to the worker. And also, to a large extent, they are distorted pictures of the function and status of corporations.

In the eyes of the law a corporation is an artificial person created for a specific purpose; in other words, it is a machine for carrying on a business enterprise. Out of this definition there has grown the idea that a corporation, being impersonal, has no soul; and that men, by combining together in corporate form, thereby manage to rid themselves of their ethical and social responsibilities. I do not believe in this theory; to my way of thinking, it expresses one of the most destructive tendencies of our time.

In an address before the Harvard School of Business Administration, in 1910, I said:

I assert that no corporation is soulless; that, on the contrary, every corporation has a soul; that the soul of a corporation is the soul of its dominant individual — usually the president; that the management of the corporation reflects the prevailing soul almost as infallibly as a looking-glass reflects the object set before it. If that soul be selfish, little, and narrow, the policy of the corporation will be selfish, little, and narrow; if that soul be broad, liberal, and honest, the policy of the corporation will be broad, liberal, and honest. It is inevitable that the rank and file of the corporation, by which I mean its employees, will in time imbibe the spirit of its dominant factor.

I resolved, before the tunnels were opened, that as far as it lay within my power the Hudson & Manhattan Railroad Company would make service to the public its first and most imperative consideration. It was to be a corporation with a soul. This decision was not prompted, in any particular degree, by altruism or generosity; it merely seemed to me that it was the fair and square thing to do. We depended on the patronage of the public for our daily bread; then, why shouldn't we make service to the public our first law of conduct, not merely as a form of words, but in actual daily practice?

For weeks I endeavored to devise something in the nature of a phrase, or sentence, which would express this idea concisely and with a bright upfling of words — something with the same number of words and syllables that would be the antithesis of that famous saying of William H. Vanderbilt, 'The public be damned.' I wanted a phrase which could be used like a trade-mark, and come up in people's minds when the Hudson Tubes were mentioned. If you have never tried to think up a slogan, you cannot imagine how elusive the right words are.

During that period of my life, and for many years thereafter, I used to go to sleep at night with a pad and a pencil on the table by my bed. Frequently I would awake during the night with a thought of something that needed to be done, and I would turn on the light and make a note of it. One night I woke up with Vanderbilt and his 'Public be damned' in my mind. Instantly it was followed by the words, 'The Public be Pleased.' I wrote this sentence down on my writing-pad, then and there — and, as I wrote it, I felt in my bones (as the saying goes) that we had our slogan. Its success was

THE McADOO POLICY.

CARTOON IN THE JERSEY CITY EVENING JOURNAL
July 21, 1909

amazing. Every newspaper in the United States, I fancy, printed it with favorable comment. The company received thousands of encouraging letters about it.

When the downtown tunnels were opened in July, 1909, I made an address in which I said:

We believe in the public be pleased policy as opposed to the public be damned policy; we believe that that railroad is best which serves the public best; that decent treatment of the public evokes decent treatment from the public; that recognition by the corporation of the just rights of the people results in recognition by the people of the just rights of the corporation. A square deal for the people and a square deal for the corporation! The latter is as essential as the former, and they are not incompatible.

While I directed the Hudson & Manhattan, it lived up to its 'Public be Pleased' policy and I think it has continued to do so. Its career proves the effectiveness of a lot of ordinary, good-natured friendliness in the contact of a corporation with the public it serves. During the first year of its operation we carried about forty-nine million passengers, and received less than fifty complaints.

6

When we opened the downtown line in 1909, we employed E. T. Munger, of Chicago, as general superintendent. Munger was a very capable man, with a long experience as an executive of the Chicago elevated railroads.

He suggested that we employ women as ticket-sellers. Since the ticket-sellers on our uptown lines and on all the elevated and subway lines in New York were men, I asked why he wanted to employ women.

He said: 'We use them on the Chicago elevated and have found them, on the whole, more satisfactory than men; they are quick and courteous and the latter squares with your policy in operating our road; and, in addition to that, they are cheaper.'

'Well, if they are just as good or better than men, why should we pay them less?' I asked.

'You want to run the road economically, don't you? If you do, we can save a lot of money by employing women as ticket-sellers,' he replied.

'Of course, we want to run the road as economically as possible, but I am opposed to doing it at the expense of justice,' I replied. 'Let's employ women as ticket-sellers on the downtown lines and give them the same wages as men.'

'All right, sir,' he said, looking a bit sullen, I thought, and dissatisfied about it.

The next day he came in to see me and said that he wanted to apologize; that he had left my office thinking that I was something of a fool to take such a position, but, as he had thought it over, he saw and fully appreciated the wisdom of treating all employees with justice and fairness. He got my idea that with the policy of the 'Public be Pleased' in operating the road, it was necessary to establish a morale and an *esprit de corps* among the employees.

There was a curious result — one of the strange and unexpected things that happen.

For years the women teachers of New York City had tried to get equal pay with men teachers for their work in the public schools. They encountered so much indifference and active opposition that they were not able for several years to get the legislature to vote on the matter. Eventually, however, in the year 1908, they did succeed in putting through a bill which gave them equal pay. They thought they had won their fight, and were naturally elated, but they rejoiced too soon. Charles Evans Hughes, then Governor of New York, and now Chief Justice of the United States Supreme Court, vetoed their bill.

(The women teachers of New York are now paid the same as the men. A Democratic State administration subsequently came in and granted this simple dispensation of justice.)

About the time that Governor Hughes had disapproved the equal-pay bill, the Hudson & Manhattan Railroad Company announced its policy of paying women on the same basis as men. There was no connection between the two events, but unexpectedly I found myself the popular hero of the teachers. Deputations of women called at my office, and I was invited to address a mass meeting in Carnegie Hall. I accepted the invitation, but I did not attend, as I was laid up with an attack of tonsillitis at the time.

Cynical opponents of equal pay for women asserted that I

was playing to the galleries, that I had political ambitions, and that I had placed our women employees on the equal wage scale basis just to discredit Governor Hughes.

Well, all I can say is that none of this has a word of truth in it. I did not want to admit my ignorance at the time — for nobody likes to acknowledge that he does not keep up with current events — but I confess now that, when I decided to put our women employees on the same plane with men in the matter of wages, I did not know anything about the movement among the women teachers. Doubtless I had read of it in the newspapers, but my mind was so full of my own problems that it left no lasting impression.

I mention this story that there was an ulterior motive behind my action as an example of the lies and innuendoes that pester men in public life; or, for that matter, men who have attained any kind of distinction, whether they are in public life or not.

The lie is a potent force in politics, and a clever, well-conceived lie has much more vitality, as a rule, than a dull and stodgy truth.

Professional politicians, whose calculations are disturbed now and then by the political aspirations of public-spirited citizens, are adepts in the invention of slanders, and they have a technique of their own. With the aid of partisan newspapers to supply circulation, a perfect lie-disseminating machine is established. Further on, in the proper place, I shall give some actual specimens of the art of political mendacity, as I have observed it.

The first principle of political lying is to make the lie highly personal, for lies about a party or a class are too cold and abstract to arouse more than a faint public interest.

The second principle of the art is to create and disseminate a vague story, rather than one which hangs on precise data. The more vague and foggy it is the better, as it is likely to live longer than a detailed lie, which can be disputed by facts. Its vagueness is a sort of protective coloration; in the first place, it cannot be pinned on to its originator, for if it comes back to him and is slapped in his face, he will either deny it outright or declare that he was misunderstood. Vagueness leaves a great deal to the imagination, and people are likely to imagine the worst. The great lie-masters have learned by experience that much dependence can be placed on the widely diffused capacity for invention. All you have to do is to launch the lie in general terms, and the public will supply the details, so that the story grows by much retelling.

In Algernon Blackwood's book of memoirs, published under the title of 'Episodes Before Thirty,' he discusses the vitality of lies, and tells of some in his own experience. He is a writer, as you probably know, of novels in which the central point is some diabolic mystery or superstition. In one of his books he described the Black Mass, or the 'Devil's Mass.' In the carrying out of this evil and obscene ceremony, the worshipers of the Devil are supposed to use the holy vessels of a church.

Blackwood says that, after his description of an entirely fictional Black Mass had been published, a story went around England that he had officiated at a Black Mass himself, and that he had stolen the communion vases of Saint Paul's Cathedral for use on that occasion.

After years of telling, this lie — he remarks — is in husky good health and has prospects of rounding out a century of active life. He explains that he never dreamed of taking part in anything as ridiculous as a Black Mass; and that, moreover, the sacred vessels of Saint Paul's are so closely guarded that the most expert thief could not lay hands on them. He goes on to say: 'This capacity for invention and imaginative detail of the most ingenious sort, using the tiniest insignificant item of truth as a starting-point, suggests that even the dullest people must have high artistic faculties tucked away somewhere within them.'

CHAPTER VIII
MEETING WOODROW WILSON

I

I saw Woodrow Wilson for the first time in February, 1909. My son, Francis Huger, then a student at Princeton, was laid up in the University infirmary with an attack of diphtheria, and I was on my way to visit him. The village of Princeton, as you may know, is not on the main railroad line. One waits at the Junction for a dumpy little train which ambles back and forth from the main line to the village.

I was waiting there, on a freezing cold February day — and walking up and down the platform, trying to keep myself warm — when Mr. Wilson got off a train that had arrived from New York. A mutual acquaintance who was at the station introduced me to him and we went on to Princeton together. He walked with me to the door of the infirmary and we had a pleasant chat.

He was gracious and unpretentious in manner. He possessed, to an unusual degree, the indefinable quality of charm. There was an unforgettable clear vividness in his speech. Our conversation on that occasion was nothing more than the casual talk of two strangers who happen to be walking together in the same direction, and yet it was somehow inspiring and stimulating. He had a way of lifting the most commonplace topic, spontaneously and without effort, to a height where it would catch the rays of the sun. But he was not dogmatic, as so many scholarly men are. He carried his knowledge and his ideas easily, like a well-worn coat, and he was without a trace of the intellectual ferocity that frequently goes with superior learning. His casualness was pleasant and disarming. There was not much of the traditional appearance of the college professor about him. Almost anyone, meeting him as a stranger and not knowing his antecedents, would have taken him for a lawyer or a man of large affairs.

In the summer of 1910, the Democrats of New Jersey nominated Woodrow Wilson for governor. When I read the news,

I was delighted. I felt that it was a great thing for the Democratic Party to have men of Mr. Wilson's type among its active leaders. By that time I was well enough acquainted with him to know that he had none of the shifty qualities of a machine-made politician; and that, if the people of New Jersey elected him governor, he would be a public servant of all the people of the state, and not the shop-window of a tight little whispering political ring.

I wanted to help, but I hesitated for fear that I would do more harm than good. I felt sure that, as the head of a large financial enterprise — the Hudson Tunnels — I was considered by many people who did not know me as a tool and office boy of Big Business and Wall Street. This was pure myth, but in American life myths acquire an astounding solidity, and one must deal with them seriously.

As a plain matter of fact, I was never anything more than an outsider in the community of interest that is known as Big Business. I appeared in Wall Street with a constructive idea, and managed to get it turned into a reality. Anybody else might have done the same thing, but it just happened that nobody else did. The conception of me as being hand in glove with great and powerful interests, and playing a deep game in partnership with them, is on a par with the fiction that the Hudson Tunnels had made me a multi-millionaire.

Bigness is admired for its own sake in America. We point with pride to our sprawling, confused, and overcrowded cities, to our unnecessarily high buildings, to the breadth and length of the national domain, to the gigantic floor space of our factories. The American mind absorbs facts more quickly than ideas, and bigness is an imperative fact. We are the only people in the world who consider mere size an admirable quality; it is one of the American traits that always seems puzzling to Europeans.

In the light of this reflection of the public mind, one would say, with reason, that Big Business has, or ought to have, an immense popular predisposition in its favor. But it hasn't. Somehow, it has managed to get itself pretty thoroughly distrusted and disliked by the great majority of the American people. They look upon high finance, and the concentration of authority in the hands of wealthy men and powerful corporations, as a public menace.

Undeniably, Big Business has virtues of its own. It possesses the fine qualities of daring and initiative; and these have at times a high social value, as when they are used to create useful enterprises, to develop natural resources, to promote scientific research, industrial efficiency, and the welfare of employees. Yet, with these points granted, it exercises a dangerous influence in American affairs. It is motivated by a desire for money and power. These objectives cannot be attained, on a nation-wide scale, without some effective control of the country's economic and legislative forces. Big Business attempts to do this — and often succeeds. It displays, in this respect, a purpose that is extraneous and foreign to any acceptable idea of a popular democracy.

Its chief outstanding vice, in my opinion, is its reluctance to accept fair and legitimate profits. It has a passion for unearned money, for watered capital, for fortunes that appear to be created out of the air, but which come nevertheless from the pockets of the people. For that reason the chief item of its political creed is a High Tariff. Its leaders accumulate millions of dollars mysteriously. When one considers the huge surplus funds built up by Big Business corporations and the fabulous salaries paid to some of their leaders, one cannot resist the conclusion that either they have underpaid their workers, or have sold their goods at exorbitant prices, or have managed to secure special privileges. If they are dissatisfied with their reputation, they ought to realize that they are the victims of their own shrewdness.

I know that Big Business is a result of the upward evolution of Small Business. Everything that succeeds has a tendency to get bigger — and any legislative effort to keep a small business from growing is, I think, a fundamental mistake.

The logical remedy for the evils of Big Business — and its brother, High Finance — is not to be found in repressive legislation which attempts to stunt the development of business enterprise. A more efficacious plan, in my judgment, is to let it grow — but, at the same time, surround it with adequate supervision and publicity. This supervision should be intelligent, and not so restrictive as to suppress legitimate initiative; but it should be strong enough to eliminate unearned profits.

Small Business is checked by its own limitations. It is constantly threatened with competition, and is often in danger of extinction. Besides, it is confronted by the sentiment of the locality. A greedy man in a small business cannot be as greedy as he would like to be; the people around him would not stand for it.

But Big Business exists in a different atmosphere. Many huge business concerns are thinly disguised monopolies; or, if not monopolies, they are so completely armed with talent and money that they are able to crush any opposition they may encounter. They are, in effect, public institutions conducted for profit by private interests and without public supervision. Their actions have far-reaching economic results.

Big Business is simply a state of society, a natural product of our form of civilization. Popular imagination is at fault when it pictures the leaders of Big Business as a distinct social class; as an aristocracy of wealth. They lack the repose — and often the dignity — that is characteristic of aristocracies. For the most part, they may be correctly described as talented and energetic men who have managed to accumulate a great deal of money. Though they possess wealth and the authority that goes with it, they still continue to look at life from the standpoint of the money-getter. This trait makes them more menacing to the democratic ideal than any social aristocracy could be. Their wealth, used dynamically, gives them an undue advantage in human affairs. Its effect, improperly used, is to throw democratic institutions out of balance, and to destroy them eventually.

The community of Big Business is conscious of the fact that it exists in a web of antagonisms; moreover, it is conscious of a public sufferance that may some day turn against it. To forestall supervisory legislation that might regulate or curb its activities its leaders are constantly endeavoring to gain control of both major political parties.

To accomplish these ends, Big Business exercises a powerful influence over most of the newspapers and magazines; and this results from its control of the advertising from which the newspapers and magazines receive most of their income. Besides, it has in its service numerous clever publicity agents; and, in fact, the major part of the whole creative world of print. Through these agencies it influences public opinion, and creates prestige and distinction for men in public life who are considered sufficiently pliable to advance its interests.

But, even with all this cleverness at its command, it has not yet been entirely successful in dispelling the popular notion that the head of a big corporation cannot be trusted in politics.

These thoughts were running through my head when I went to see Mr. Wilson in the fall of 1910. I did not want to embarrass him as a candidate for the governorship of New Jersey, so I asked him to tell me frankly whether or not my support, in view of the fact that I was the president of an important corporation, would react to his disadvantage.

He listened to what I had to say, smiled, and said he thought I was too sensitive. He made some highly flattering remarks about my management of the Hudson Tunnels, and said pleasantly that my support would be welcome.

As soon as he was in office, Governor Wilson began a series of reforms that made a profound impression, not only in New Jersey but throughout the country. He was a Democrat of the best traditions; and by that I mean that his political philosophy was a Jeffersonian humanism.

The essential difference between the Democratic and Republican parties is that the vital idea of the Democratic Party is *people*, and the vital idea of the Republican Party is *property*. This difference is immemorial and historic; it expresses a natural division in political thought, and it goes back to the origin of the republic.

Yet, as profound as this distinction is, it is not sharp and clear in its minor shades — and for that reason one often hears people say that there is not really any difference between the Republicans and the Democrats. It is true that, when one looks at them from a distance of six inches or so, they do not seem to differ very much, but when observed from the standpoint of long perspective and policy, the difference between them is pronounced.

The basic policy of the Republican Party is conservative.

It has never exhibited much constructive ability. Although its controlling idea is the rights of property, it does think of people, and it has the welfare of the nation at heart, according to its own interpretation.

On the other hand, the basic policy of the Democratic Party is humanistic and progressive, but it does not hold property in contempt. It stands for property as well as for people, but to its way of thinking people come first. Its philosophy is permeated with human values. To the Democratic intelligence progress and wealth are illusory unless they bring a fair measure of contentment to the whole body of the American nation, including all classes of society.

2

In the spring of 1911, William F. McCombs, who used to come to my house in Irvington for week-ends occasionally, told me on one of his visits that he was working, in a quiet way, to secure the nomination of Mr. Wilson at the National Democratic Convention which was to meet the next year — that is, in 1912. He asked for my coöperation. I told him that I would give it gladly; that I had been thinking of doing something myself in the same direction.

I learned from him, on that week-end in 1911, that he had organized a small publicity bureau in Governor Wilson's interest, with the Governor's approval, and was doing what he could in the way of sending out letters and newspaper articles.

Before I go further with this narrative, I think I had better introduce McCombs, and say something about his strange and erratic personality. I approach the subject with reluctance. If I followed my own inclination, I would gladly allow McCombs' attacks on me to go unanswered, for he is dead, and cannot reply to anything I may say.

But the matter does not concern me alone. McCombs was intimately associated with the Democratic campaign of 1912, and when he died, nine or ten years later, he left as a literary legacy a mass of grotesque and fanciful inventions about this campaign and various people who were active in it. These bitter aspersions, most of them without a shred of fact in them, have appeared in print as a serious contribution to the history of the epoch. Regardless of my own personal preference, I feel that in the interest of truth I ought to discuss McCombs' misstatements, and correct them.

Dr. Freud, or some other modern soul-searcher, says that every man has within him another man, a second personality who hates the outer man and does whatever he can to destroy him. It is an interesting theory; I am sure you will recognize it as nothing more nor less than the ancient idea of demoniac possession, dressed up and put in the language of modern psychology. I cannot say whether or not this theory is sound; I am not sufficiently mystical to accept it at its face value, but when I reflect upon the curious change that took place in William F. McCombs, I realize that the theory of an inner man who is the obverse, or contradiction, of the outer man rests on human experience.

The man who lived inside McCombs — and hated him — began to reveal himself in 1912; and before long he became the dominant, outstanding personality. In the end this inner man ruined McCombs' promising career.

One day in November, 1908, I went to Princeton to see the Princeton-Yale football game. That afternoon, coming back to New York, the train was crowded. I gave my seat to a lady and went to the rear platform. McCombs was standing there. I did not know him; I had never seen him before. I noticed that the man on the platform was slender, well-dressed, and lame; and that he appeared to be about thirty-five years old. We got into conversation, and before we reached New York I had learned that he was William F. McCombs, a Southerner and a Princeton graduate, and that he practiced law in New York City.

McCombs seemed very glad to meet me; he said that he recognized me at once from having seen my picture in the newspapers. Before we parted that afternoon, we made an engagement for luncheon some day during the next week.

I got to know him well. He was a Democrat, was interested in politics, and was a member of Tammany Hall. He told me that he enjoyed the confidence of the Tammany 'boss' — I mean Charles F. Murphy — and that he was also a friend of Thomas F. Ryan, for whom, now and then, he did confidential work of one kind or another.

I liked McCombs because of his agreeable qualities and his engaging personality, but he had disturbing traits, the first faint symptoms of the psychic disorganization that was destined, at a later day, to overwhelm him.

His attitude toward human affairs in general was suspicious and rather cynical. I believe myself that a certain proportion of healthy cynicism is good for the soul. There are so many tricky rascals running loose in the world that the rest of us can hardly afford the luxury of playing the part of naïve children. McCombs went a good deal further. He seemed to think that virtually all successful achievement in the field of politics was a sort of sleight-of-hand trick. In his conversation he laid much emphasis on manipulation and adroitness, and I could perceive clearly that he admired professional politicians and political short-change artists — and, in fact, anyone who thought more of 'trades' and 'deals' than of principle.

But wait. I have described only one side of his personality. He was of two minds. On one hand he had a profound respect for machine politics; and on the other hand his respect for high ideals, for men of lofty character, for those who despise the kind of success that comes only through cunning, was equally profound. His admiration for Woodrow Wilson was genuine and deep; yet at the same time one of his political demigods was Charles F. Murphy, the boss of Tammany Hall.

These clashing contradictions met in McCombs' mind and went along amiably, hand in hand. I wondered at it. The explanation is that his personality was already beginning to split in two, and the two sides of the division were acting independently of each other. This is a phenomenon of the psychology of neuroses. Of course, I did not reach this conclusion at that time. One doesn't understand such things when they appear close at hand and in one's friends. I ascribed his contradictory points of view to nothing more serious than a confused state of mind, and thought it would gradually work itself out.

The qualities that I have described were not mere surface traits, though I thought they were. They were flashes from his inner life — from the man who lived within him. As time went on, this concealed and repressed man burst the outer shell of McCombs' personality and became McCombs himself. The man whom I had known disappeared, vanished, went away. God knows where he went, or what happened to him. The new man — a stranger who had the outer appearance of McCombs and possessed his memories and signed his name — exhibited an egotism of such swollen proportions that it can be described only as a form of megalomania. He was impelled by an insatiable vanity; and by a querulous, nagging, fault-finding suspicion of everything and everybody.

3

McCombs and I used to meet once a week, and sometimes more frequently, at luncheon in a private room in the Railroad Club in the Hudson Terminal Building. There we discussed the progress of the quietly conducted campaign that we were carrying on for Governor Wilson.

To these luncheons came, on my invitation, Walter Hines Page, editor of 'World's Work'; and Oswald Garrison Villard, proprietor and editor of the 'New York Evening Post.' They were both strongly for Wilson, but we soon found that neither of them had any practical ideas about the management of a political movement of this sort. We were very glad of their aid, however, because of the publicity they were able to give.

There was, of course, an urgent need of money. McCombs enlisted the aid of some Princeton men who knew Governor Wilson and approved of his policies. Some of these Wilson men were known to be Republicans, but they were progressive in spirit. During the campaign of 1912 there was considerable shifting of party affiliations.

The largest contributor was Cleveland H. Dodge, a classmate of the Governor's at Princeton. He gave the pre-convention campaign chest $51,300 — or more than one fourth of the entire amount raised from all sources. He was a Godsend.

Mr. Dodge not only gave more than $50,000 of his own money, but he went out among the Princeton friends of Governor Wilson and raised $35,000 more. Through him Thomas D. Jones gave $10,500 and Cyrus H. McCormick $12,500.

Frederic C. Penfield, of Philadelphia, contributed $12,500;

and Samuel Untermyer subscribed $7000; Harvey Thomas, the publisher of a daily newspaper in Atlantic City, sent a check for $6000; and Abram I. Elkus, of New York, gave $12,500. I am not attempting to set down these contributions in chronological order, but am giving them just as they come up in my memory.

McCombs was an excellent money-getter. He went to Chicago, saw Charles R. Crane, and got two checks of $5000 each from him, although Mr. Crane was nationally known at that time as the chief financial backer of Robert M. La Follette's campaign for the Republican nomination for President. Later on, Mr. Crane explained his attitude. 'Wilson and La Follette,' he said, 'were both progressive men. With me, the names Democrat and Republican are obsolete. They were both progressives, both having the same program and method of thought, and I just wanted to have any progressive candidate succeed; I did not care which one it was.'

Altogether, about $193,000 was collected as a pre-convention campaign fund, and it was far from being enough. The allotments to the various state campaigns were so small that they were simply pitiable. McCombs was able to send, for example, only $1000 to Maine, $575 to Connecticut, $1100 to Colorado, $2200 to Iowa. Many states got nothing at all.

I find in my files a copy of a letter that I wrote on April 24, 1912, to Josephus Daniels, of North Carolina, about the situation — particularly in reference to that state — which reveals the straits to which we were reduced at that time. I give the letter in part; it is too long for full reproduction here:

Dear Mr. Daniels:

I am greatly obliged for your kind letter. My observation thus far of the Wilson campaign causes me to feel more concerned because of a lack of organization everywhere than for any single reason. I am sure that if we could have organized everywhere, so that the great popular sentiment for the Governor could have found expression, he would have been irresistible. As it is, the results do not, in my opinion, half measure his real strength....

The chief cry now seems to be money for legitimate expenses. I am going to make a contribution of $500 for North Carolina, although I have already taxed my resources severely in what I have done up here. I asked Colonel W. H. Osborn, of Greensboro, if it would not be possible to raise some money among the Governor's friends in the state. Can you not take this up?

I think that even $1000 for the purpose of maintaining head-
quarters and sending out literature would accomplish much....
I know how much you are doing in this direction, and I hesitate to
suggest that you do more, but we have all got to stand together and
meet the demands as far as it is possible to do.

4

McCombs had a good idea. He persuaded Governor Wilson
to make a trip across the country as far as the Pacific Coast
and to speak in the principal cities. This speaking tour was a
great success. Spontaneously, newspapers in all parts of the
country began to treat Woodrow Wilson as a presidential
possibility. We were glad of that; but so much was said in the
newspapers, there were so many editorials and so many pictures, that we began to fear that the movement would spend
itself in a premature wave of enthusiasm. The political field
is littered with the broken fragments of sky-rockets that went
off too early. Was the Wilson movement destined to be one
of them? We could not say, but we felt doubtful.

The enthusiasm over the Governor's Western trip was encouraging, but about this time (late in the fall of 1911) I found
myself lying awake at night with disquieting reflections about
McCombs.

The quality of his personality that caused so much concern
at that time was his complete lack of organizing ability. There
was an immense amount of activity about the campaign
headquarters, but we appeared to be thrashing around without getting anywhere.

McCombs made trips and conferred with prominent Democrats; contributions were received and money spent on
publicity and speakers; the daily mail kept increasing in
volume; and newspaper clippings poured in on us — yet,
though months went by, still there was no real Wilson organization. There was hardly a state with an active Wilson committee, and very few states in which even one man was
definitely known as a Wilson representative.

The most active of our Democratic opponents was Champ
Clark. He and his lieutenants knew how to organize. There
were Clark headquarters and Clark committees in every state;
at any rate, that was my impression. They had the country

mapped out; wherever they got a foothold, they consolidated their gains. It was perfectly plain that Champ Clark was outstripping us and that his advantage consisted largely in an organization that was skillfully directed and kept well in hand.

I came to the conclusion that the source of our ineffectiveness lay in McCombs' jealousy of everybody who had anything to do with furthering the Governor's interests. Though I was supposed to be his close associate, I was working frequently in the dark. It was like pulling McCombs' eye-teeth to get full information as to what was actually going on. This rendered my coöperation less effective than it could have been. Obviously it was his intention to make the Wilson campaign a one-man show, with McCombs himself as the One Man. That might have been all right if the matter at issue had been the election of a village mayor, but a presidential race is a different thing. No one man can handle satisfactorily all the problems that arise in a national campaign.

CHAPTER IX
THE FATEFUL YEARS

I

IN THE late summer of 1911, I was approached by Henry Green, a talented young man of Jewish descent, who sought my aid in a movement to obtain the abrogation of our treaty with Russia, on account of the Czarist Russian government's treatment of American Jews and Catholics. The Russian-American treaty of 1832 stipulated that: 'They [the citizens of either country] shall be at liberty to sojourn and reside in all parts whatsoever of said territories [Russia and the United States], in order to attend to their affairs, and they shall enjoy, to that effect, the same security and protection as natives of the country wherein they reside....'

For decades the Russian government had persistently ignored this treaty in its passport regulations. American Jews and Catholics were refused permission to enter Russia at all, as a rule. In special cases, when Jews were allowed to go into that country, their passports had the words 'American Jew' — or its equivalent in Russian — stamped across the face of the document. They were frequently subjected to arbitrary arrest; and, in general, the attitude of Russian officials toward them was offensive and contemptuous.

I was already familiar with the terms of our treaty with Russia when Henry Green called on me with a request that I head a committee of protest. The United States government had made protests in the past; all of them without result. Green thought, and I agreed with him, that the only possible way of accomplishing anything effective would be to abrogate, or cancel, the treaty on the ground that Russia had persistently violated its terms, so far as Catholic and Jewish American citizens were concerned.

He said that all previous attempts to have the treaty abrogated had emanated from American Jews, and that, in his opinion, this had not been a wise policy. He wanted to organize a National Citizens' Committee, composed largely of Gentiles, so that the movement could not be regarded as a narrow racial Jewish protest.

I was very much in sympathy with these ideas, and the proposed form of procedure, but I was so busy with my work for Governor Wilson and my duties as president of the Hudson Tunnel system, that I did not see how I could find any time to take on any more responsibility. However, I accepted the chairmanship of the National Citizens' Committee, notwithstanding the new burdens I should have to assume. I gave the committee headquarters in the Hudson Terminal free of rent and we went to work.

We made rapid headway. On December 6, 1911, we held a mass meeting in Carnegie Hall, to which the leading candidates for the presidential nomination were invited. Governor Wilson came and made a marvelous speech. He had prepared a speech to be given in advance to the press, but when he faced the great audience he discarded it, and spoke with extemporaneous freedom and eloquence.

The meeting adopted resolutions demanding the abrogation of the Russian treaty. A committee was appointed, of which I was chairman and of which Jacob H. Schiff and others were members, to present these resolutions to Congress and to President Taft. The committee visited Washington and, as a result of its efforts, Congress adopted resolutions for the denunciation of the Russian treaty and President Taft acted accordingly. Since that time there has been no treaty between Russia and the United States.

On our return from Washington, Mr. Schiff and I sat in adjoining seats in the parlor car. Governor Wilson's speech at Carnegie Hall had made a great impression on him. He had never seen Woodrow Wilson before that occasion, and he questioned me eagerly about him. He told me, as the train was entering the Pennsylvania station, that although he had been a Republican all his life he had decided to do what he could in support of Governor Wilson. Within a few days he sent me a check for $2500 for the campaign fund.

2

McCombs was rather vague about his relations with Governor Wilson. I did not know what kind of understanding existed between them, yet it was important for me to have a clear idea of the situation. The Governor was, of course, the head of the movement, and the reason for its existence. Was McCombs his authorized representative and spokesman?

I asked Governor Wilson for an interview and he invited me to spend a night at his home in Princeton. I arrived in time for dinner and met Mrs. Wilson and their three daughters, Margaret, Jessie, and Eleanor. This was early in the fall of 1911. Shortly after dinner, the Governor took me into his study and there I had my first opportunity to discuss the situation with him alone and quietly.

He told me frankly that he was not an active candidate for the Presidency, but that he would, of course, be gratified to receive the Democratic nomination. He said that the interest McCombs and I and his other friends were taking in the matter was most generous and that he warmly appreciated it; that he was particularly grateful for my interest, not only because he valued my friendship, but because his political enemies were trying to make the business men of the country believe that he was dangerous and hostile to business; that the fact that I was identified with a great business enterprise, the Hudson Tunnels, and was an open supporter, would tend to counteract these false stories.

'Governor,' I said, 'I am very much gratified to have you say that. I shall be glad to devote all the time I can spare to the movement to nominate you, but I beg the privilege of imposing one condition.'

'Certainly,' he agreed. 'What is it?'

'I want you to know,' I replied, 'that my support is absolutely disinterested. If you should be nominated and elected President, I shall not seek or accept any public office, nor shall I ask any favors at your hands. If you believe this, I can enter into the campaign with enthusiasm because I shall know that you will understand always that any advice I may offer will be uninfluenced by personal interest.'

I meant precisely what I said. At that time I had no

thought of getting into public life. I felt that the nation needed a man of Mr. Wilson's courage and ideas, and that if I could contribute toward his election, the event itself would amply compensate me.

The Governor looked at me almost incredulously for a moment, then said: 'This is delightfully refreshing. I have never before had an experience like this. I have already discovered, in my brief public career, that people too frequently are actuated by a selfish purpose in political life. I believe absolutely in your sincerity and I shall be very happy to have your support on your own terms.'

I then spoke to him of McCombs, and of the work we were doing at the New York headquarters. I did not say anything about McCombs' jealousies, or of his incapacity as an organizer, or anything whatever that could be construed in Mc-Combs' disfavor. My chief reason for saying nothing against McCombs was that I thought any statement of the kind would be inappropriate — and, to put it plainly, a stab in the back.

I felt, however, that it was important for me to know the exact status of affairs, so I asked the Governor if McCombs was his authorized campaign manager.

'No,' he said, 'I cannot say that he is. Mr. McCombs has very generously, and of his own motion, set up a publicity bureau in New York for the purpose of distributing my speeches and urging my availability for the nomination. I haven't felt that I should have a campaign manager because I have not yet taken the movement seriously enough to justify an organization. I think McCombs is doing good work and that he can be more effective in his present rôle of a volunteer than if he were designated as a campaign manager.'

He added that if the movement gained sufficient headway, it might evolve into a permanent organization under McCombs' direction. I told the Governor that I agreed with him fully and that I would continue to coöperate with McCombs along the lines he had indicated.

3

Under the surface at campaign headquarters a sort of grim comedy was going on. There were drastic, absurd rules about the most trifling matters, and the employees of the bureau had been frightened almost into a panic by McCombs. His chief obsession at that time was to get every little scrap of publicity and credit for himself — and in this effort he managed to alienate many Democrats of national influence.

One day the head of the publicity department committed an offense of enormous gravity. He signed his own name to some letters. McCombs had made a rule that no letter was to leave the place until he himself had read it and signed it. On some days the dictated letters ran into the hundreds. Frequently he got days and days behind in his reading and signing.

The head publicity man at that time was Frank Parker Stockbridge, a journalist of excellent repute who had been recommended by Walter H. Page. Stockbridge had been in charge of the publicity from the beginning. It became his duty to arrange the details of the Governor's speaking tour in the West. In the course of this work he wrote a number of letters to party leaders and newspaper men and signed them himself.

McCombs considered this an insult and brooded over it. He decided to get rid of Stockbridge.

The manner in which he approached the problem was characteristic. One day he remarked to me casually that Stockbridge was not making good; did not know how to write political articles.

I did not know Stockbridge well, but I had heard him spoken of most favorably, and I told McCombs that I was surprised. McCombs said sadly that he, too, was surprised and grieved; that he wanted to keep Stockbridge, but it was impossible on account of his inefficiency. 'Perhaps,' he said, 'you might suggest a good man to take his place.' After some reflection I recommended Byron R. Newton, whom I knew to be a capable man, and as fine and clean a fellow as I have ever met. He had been connected with various New York newspapers for years as a reporter and political writer. McCombs

saw Newton within the next day or two and employed him.
He told me that he was impressed by Newton and felt sure
he would do splendidly.

Newton had been at work about a month when he came to
me in a state of excitement. He told me, to my astonishment,
that McCombs detested me beyond all mortal beings. Mc-
Combs, he said, had read in some newspaper a paragraph in
which my work in Governor Wilson's interest was commented
on favorably.

'When he saw your name in the paper,' Newton said,
'he had an expression on his face like that of an infuriated
animal. He locked the door, seized his cane and beat it into
splinters over his desk. In the mean time, he cursed and
shrieked with rage, and called McAdoo every hideous name
in the vocabulary.'

You may imagine how I felt at this sudden, explosive
revelation. At one o'clock that same day McCombs was to
be my guest at luncheon. I met him at the Railroad Club,
and he was as agreeable as ever. I did not say anything to
him about what I had heard from Newton.

I did not know exactly what to do about this state of affairs, and in the end I decided to do nothing in the hope that
time, which is the great solvent of most human problems,
would eventually lead to a solution. A public row between
McCombs and myself would have given the campaign a terrible blow. Even a private disagreement, with one of us
resigning in a cloud of mystery, would have been harmful.

I do not know when the Governor began to suspect that
something about McCombs was functioning badly. The
Governor had keen perceptions; he understood men and their
motives, but he had a way of keeping his knowledge to himself. He never discussed McCombs with me until after the
Baltimore convention; but judging from various bits of evidence, too numerous and too trivial to relate here, I got a
notion that, in the spring of 1912, the Governor had pretty
well taken McCombs' measure.

His position was delicate and trying. McCombs was a self-
appointed campaign manager who had taken hold on his own
initiative. Whatever organization there was had grown up
around him. He had alienated many strong Democrats and

had failed to develop anything like a national organization; but he had given his time and money and had accomplished much during the period when the Governor needed friends. In these circumstances, could Governor Wilson tell McCombs that he was not doing his job well, and that somebody else had better take hold? I think not. Such a procedure would have been looked upon as — and would have been, in truth — an exhibition of ingratitude. I felt that way about it, and I am sure the Governor had the same point of view.

One day in the fall of 1911 — according to my memory it was in October — McCombs asked me to call with him on a wealthy man from Texas, Colonel Edward M. House. I had never heard of Colonel House before. McCombs and I went to see him at the Hotel Gotham. On the way I asked McCombs who Colonel House was, and all about him. I was informed that he was an influential man in Texas politics, or — as McCombs put it in his characteristic manner — 'He has the entire state of Texas in his vest pocket.' I also learned that the Colonel was reputed to be a man of wealth, dignity, and honor; and that he had never run for a political office and had never held one. We went to see him for the purpose of getting him interested in Governor Wilson's behalf.

I was favorably impressed by House. There was an air of quiet good breeding about him. He was a small man, apparently somewhat fragile and delicate, with fine blue eyes. When we arrived he was surrounded by books. I judged, from the look of them, that they were all new publications, and that he had been amusing himself by cutting their pages and looking them over.

Although he talked freely on this occasion, he was non-committal about Governor Wilson, and I left with the notion that his preference was for someone else.

Colonel House was turned into a Wilson man by Woodrow Wilson himself. He invited the Governor to run up to the Gotham and have a chat. The Governor went there (alone) on November 24, 1911. Colonel House says, in his 'Intimate Papers':

The first hour we spent together proved to each of us that there was a sound basis for a fast friendship. We found ourselves in such complete sympathy, in so many ways, that we soon learned to know what each was thinking without either having expressed himself.

From that time on, Colonel House was one of the Governor's warm supporters. The Texas delegation, with its forty votes, was an unshakable fortress of Wilson strength at the Baltimore Convention. Colonel House had something to do with that, I think, but Texas was strongly for Wilson from the beginning. Thomas B. Love was one of the most influential Wilson men in that state — and there were others; Cato Sells and Thomas H. Ball, to mention two among many.

4

In January, 1912, I went to Albuquerque, New Mexico, where my eldest daughter, Harriet Floyd, was to be married to Charles Taber Martin. The wedding occurred in Albuquerque because Mr. Martin had been threatened with tuberculosis and it was considered imprudent for him to come to New York in the winter. The young couple went to Prescott, Arizona, to live.

On this trip, I met Democratic leaders in New Mexico and Arizona and tried to enlist them in Governor Wilson's support, but they were already committed to Clark. Returning, I stopped at El Paso, Texas, to see what I could do for Governor Wilson there, but I found that Clark had captured the leading Democrats.

I then proceeded to Jackson, Mississippi, where I addressed, by invitation, a joint session of the legislature. I knew, before I entered Mississippi, that our cause in that state was hopeless. Senator Vardaman seemed to have a virtual control of the Democratic Party, and he was for Underwood. However, I learned while I was in Mississippi that many Democrats in that state were Wilson men, and I hoped to create sentiment for Wilson as the second choice of the Mississippi delegation.

In February of 1912, I had the great misfortune to lose my first wife. She died at Irvington, shortly after my return from our daughter's wedding in New Mexico. She had not been sufficiently well to accompany me on the long journey to the West.

I have never known a more noble and devoted character, and her death was a great blow to all of us — to me and our six children. Through the long years of our struggle she had stood at my side with unfaltering faith and encouragement.

Her death meant the breaking-up of our country home at Irvington. My three boys were in college or preparatory school, and my country house was too large and too expensive to maintain for myself and the two children who were at home. My daughter Nona was then a young girl in her teens and Sally, my youngest daughter, was a small child. I moved to an apartment at 405 Park Avenue, in New York City. It was like beginning life over again — but a beginning that was full of long memories.

The test of the work that had been done for Governor Wilson was now approaching as the state conventions and primaries began to be held. As time went on, the Democrats of Texas, Pennsylvania, Wisconsin, Minnesota, and Oregon instructed all, or most, of their delegates to vote for him, but the total amounted to only 164 in a convention of more than a thousand delegates.

Besides the states I have mentioned we had delegates from Kansas, Maine, New Jersey, North Carolina, and South Carolina. But while some of these delegations were uninstructed — which left the delegates the right to vote as they pleased — others were instructed for Clark or Underwood. The total of the Wilson delegates, even if we added up everything we could think of, and gave ourselves the benefit of all doubtful situations, amounted to less than one third of the convention.

Clark was running like a prairie fire.

He carried Illinois April 9, New York April 11, Nebraska April 19, Massachusetts April 30, Washington May 7, Wyoming May 13, New Hampshire May 14, Nevada May 14, California May 14, Iowa May 16, District of Columbia May 16. Missouri went for him, of course. He was Missouri's most distinguished son.

These blows, coming one after another, fell upon us like high-explosive shells on a dug-out. Within five weeks Clark had gained 324 delegates — all with hard-and-fast instructions to vote for him — and, over and beyond these certainties, there were probably one hundred and fifty additional Clark votes in delegations that were not instructed. As we gloomily looked over these figures, it did seem that the Clark crowd, in the convention, might flatten us out on the very first rush.

Despite the prevailing gloom and depression, I did not have any doubt of a Wilson victory. There was no particular reason for my confidence; that is, nothing that I can define precisely, but I felt it powerfully just the same. In attempting to analyze my conviction in the face of negative facts, I came around eventually to the thought that Woodrow Wilson was in contact with the heart of the people, that deep down in the American nation there was a dynamic impulse toward him that no manner of political manipulation could turn aside.

Champ Clark had been in politics practically all his life, and he had an enormous following. He was an old-line politician, with liberal tendencies. He knew everybody, and the ins and outs of things. For years he had been in Congress, and in 1912 was the Speaker of the House. He was a formidable opponent.

The other two candidates for the nomination were Oscar Underwood, of Alabama, and Judson Harmon, of Ohio. Both of these gentlemen were conservatives; so conservative, indeed, that they were classed, in a general way, as representatives of the vested interests. I say this without casting any imputation on their honesty and good intentions.

The chief financial backer of both Underwood and Harmon was Thomas F. Ryan. An official investigation disclosed the fact that Ryan had given more than half of the entire amount raised in Harmon's behalf, and about two thirds of the amount raised for Underwood.

We had great hopes of a Wilson victory in Georgia and Virginia. The Governor was born in Virginia, had spent a part of his boyhood in Georgia, had practiced law in Atlanta, and had married a Georgia girl. On the ground of sentiment, if nothing else, he had special claims upon these two states.

The Underwood forces in Georgia were highly organized and were making a vigorous fight for their candidate in the state primary. With the hope of carrying the state, we ar-

ranged a speech-making tour for the Governor. It was decided that I should accompany him. There were large and
enthusiastic meetings in Atlanta and Savannah, and the
Governor made many short speeches on the way between
those two cities from the platform of the train. After the
Savannah meeting I left him and went over the state. I
made a lot of speeches, and I have hardly ever seen popular
enthusiasm so fervid and so loud. The Democrats of Georgia
seemed to be unanimously for Wilson, but the impressions
that one gets on a speech-making tour are very deceptive.
Despite all the loud hurrahs for Wilson, the state primary
was carried by Underwood.

On the day after the Georgia primary I wired to Governor
Wilson: 'Too bad about Georgia, but don't be discouraged.
We shall win yet.'

5

In the midst of our various defeats there came a backfire
from New Jersey. Mr. Wilson had made himself a national
celebrity as a governor who stood for good government,
honesty, and decency, but his performances were displeasing
to the Democratic machine of New Jersey, which was at
that time in the hands of ex-Senator James Smith, Jr.

Smith and his friends had determined to prevent the election of a Wilson delegation to the Baltimore Convention, and
they devised a clever scheme to put the Governor in a hole.
If they could convince the voters of the state that he was a
wild and irresponsible radical, without any respect for the
just rights of property, it would be a severe blow, and might
prevent a Wilson delegation from being selected.

The state legislature, under the manipulation of Smith,
aided by the Republicans, was induced to pass a bill abolishing
the railroad grade crossings in New Jersey. For years the
abolition of these grade crossings had been agitated, and the
Democratic Party had specifically urged a grade crossings
measure in its platform. The bill which the legislature passed
was so cunningly contrived, however, that it was grossly unfair
to the railroads. In some respects it was confiscatory, and in
other respects impossible of performance. If the Governor
should approve the bill, his action would confirm all the

stories and charges that had been circulated about his radical-
ism and destructive attitude toward private rights and property. On the other hand, if he vetoed the bill, it would be a
terrific disappointment to the people of the state and identify
him with Big Business and corporate interests. It would in-
cline the people to believe that he had a more tender regard
for property rights than for human life.

The New Jersey machine got the bill put through the legislature by a large majority, not long before the date set for the
New Jersey primary. I studied the provisions of the bill, as
they were published in the newspapers, and I was perfectly
confident that the only real purpose of the measure was political.

The railroads in New Jersey were greatly concerned as to
what action the Governor would take. My activities for Governor Wilson had become well known by this time and my
influence with him was supposed to be much greater than it
really was. About this time the general counsel of one of the
largest railroads in the state called to see me. He said that he
was speaking for the leading railroads; that the grade crossing
bill, if approved by Governor Wilson, would be disastrous to
them; that on its merits the bill ought to be vetoed, and that
the railroads would like to employ me as counsel to argue the
case before Governor Wilson.

I discussed the legislation at some length with him without telling him that I had already been looking into it, because I wanted to get a full expression of his views.

'What compensation do you think the railroads would be
willing to pay if they win this case?' I inquired after a while.

He didn't know, but he thought the fee ought to be a
large one — say, one hundred thousand dollars.

I told him that it would be impossible for me to accept
a retainer in the case. 'It wouldn't be fair to me or to Governor
Wilson for me to do so,' I said, 'and I don't think it would
be fair to the railroad companies. In the first place, you don't
need a lawyer. What you evidently want is my supposed
political influence with the Governor. I haven't any. But
if I had, I could not, and would not, capitalize it.'

Then I went on to say: 'There is no man on earth who will
give you a fairer hearing and no man on earth who will be

more courageous in deciding the matter on its merits, regardless of personal or political consequences, than Governor Wilson. My advice to you is to ask the Governor to give you a hearing, then present the matter to him, fairly and squarely, and I am sure that you will get justice.'

He thanked me and said that he would take that course. After he had gone, I called the Governor on the telephone and told him that I had been going over the bill and that I thought it was an unfair and confiscatory measure and that I hoped that he would, upon full investigation, reach the same conclusion.

He realized that if he vetoed the bill, it would be a great disappointment to the people, who were anxious to get rid of the menace to human life caused by the great number of railroad grade crossings. On the other hand, he said that he could not approve of anything which was confiscatory, unjust, or unreasonable.

Governor Wilson also said that he did not believe the measure had been passed by the legislature in good faith; that he thought a political purpose was back of it; that if he was convinced that the bill should be vetoed, he would not hesitate to do it; that if the legislature was acting in good faith, it could demonstrate it quickly and conclusively by passing the bill over his veto, as that could be done in New Jersey by a majority, instead of a two-thirds vote. He assured me that he would consider the matter on its merits and act accordingly.

Within a reasonable time and before the New Jersey primary on April 28, the Governor vetoed the grade crossing bill with a message which was unanswerable. The legislature did not pass it over his veto, which showed conclusively that it was merely a political trap.

The effect of his action, and particularly the tone and reasoning of his veto message, made a highly favorable impression on the rank and file of New Jersey Democrats. At the primary Mr. Smith and the machine politicians were decisively defeated. Governor Wilson got twenty-four members of the delegation, while his opponents managed to elect only four.

6

After all the state primaries and conventions had been held, McCombs and I made a careful check of the first-choice strength of Woodrow Wilson. There would be 1088 delegates in all, and, as the two-thirds rule prevails in Democratic national conventions, 726 votes were necessary for a nomination. Our check-up showed that we had about 350 votes, or thirteen less than one third of the convention. This was very disappointing. We had hoped to go into the balloting with at least one third of the convention back of us.

I felt confident, however, that our vote would grow as the balloting went on and minor candidates began to drop out. Throughout the pre-convention campaign we had made a great effort to build up a large second-choice sentiment for Wilson. In this we had been successful beyond expectation, but it was not possible to tell in advance just how strong this second-choice strength would be, measured by actual votes.

Both McCombs and I came to the conclusion that nothing should be left undone to obtain the support of William Jennings Bryan. His following was large, and he was certain to be one of the outstanding figures at Baltimore. We thought that he was for Wilson, but we were not sure of it, as he had not committed himself, in a definite way, to any candidate. There were rumors that he wanted to capture the nomination for himself. I decided to see Mr. Bryan personally and have a talk with him. Within an hour I was on my way to Chicago, where the Republican National Convention had assembled. Mr. Bryan was there, as a newspaper correspondent.

I found him at the Congress Hotel, at eight-thirty in the morning. He sat in a room facing Lake Michigan, in his shirt-sleeves, with a palm-leaf fan in his hand. The day was very hot. There was a crowd in the room. Bryan was always surrounded by people. They came and went about his rooms with the nonchalant freedom of people going in and out of a railroad station.

He had never seen me before. When I had introduced myself, he looked around at his assembly of callers, and said: 'I think we had better go out in the hall.' We went out where a window in the hall overlooked the lake, and stood there talking.

I tried to impress Bryan with the fact that Wilson was the only progressive in the race and that he was thoroughly and dependably so. I stated what I believed to be a fact; namely, that it would not be long after the balloting began before the machines and bosses would line up behind Clark as the only way to beat Wilson.

Bryan was very cordial in his response to my talk, and I saw clearly that he was favorably disposed toward Wilson. He agreed with me that the nomination of a reactionary or conservative would defeat the Democratic Party. It seemed likely that the Republican Convention, then in session, would renominate President Taft, and that Roosevelt would run independently as a progressive. Bryan thought that if that occurred, Roosevelt would defeat any conservative Democrat.

'I am very much impressed by Governor Wilson,' he told me. 'I am convinced that he is thoroughly progressive and that he is courageous and dependable. But my state, Nebraska, has instructed its delegation for Clark. I, as a member of the delegation, am bound by my instructions. I must honorably carry them out.'

'Yes,' I remarked, 'I understand that. I'm in the same fix. I'll be in the New York delegation, but under the unit rule I shall have to vote as Tammany Hall tells me; and I'm sure they will not tell me to vote for Wilson.'

We both laughed. It seemed absurd that I, who was so completely identified with the Wilson campaign, would have to vote for somebody else.

'Who's Tammany's choice; do you know?' Bryan asked, looking up quickly.

'Harmon,' I said. 'At any rate, I think that Boss Murphy is going to start off by casting our ninety votes under the unit rule for Harmon. But this is a blind; the delegation will be switched to Clark as soon as the boss thinks it will secure Clark's nomination.'

'Humph!' he exclaimed. 'That may be the plan. Now, as I said before, I am obliged to vote for Clark; but after I have complied with my instructions, in good faith, I shall feel free to take such course in the convention as my conscience shall dictate. Moreover, if, during the course of the convention, anything should develop to convince me that Clark cannot or ought not to be nominated, I shall support Governor Wilson.'

'Colonel,' I said, 'I don't see how you can take any other position. I am sure that Governor Wilson's friends will be entirely satisfied with the course you have indicated.'

From Chicago I went straight to Baltimore, where the Democratic Convention was to meet in a few days. On the way I read the newspapers. Many of them contained well-written obituaries of the Wilson movement. Clark seemed to have the best of it.

CHAPTER X
THE BALTIMORE CONVENTION

I

FOR a week the city of Baltimore laid aside its serene urbanity and gave itself without stint to the joys and alarms of politics. It sang and roared like a country town on circus day. Rivers of men flowed through the streets. Most of them wore badges or buttons with inscriptions which proclaimed their political allegiance in terms that were sharp and curt. Overhead the June breeze stirred the folds of gaudy battle-flags and wrinkled the vast, solemn pictures of the rival leaders. Underfoot the ground was speckled with the fragments of speeches and diatribes; one walked on a printed litter of argument. In the hot and jangled air there was a faint, pervading note of hysteria.

The convention was to meet and organize on Tuesday, June 25. I arrived in Baltimore on the preceding Saturday. McCombs had arranged for Wilson headquarters at the Hotel Emerson. From these rooms we had a private telephone line to Governor Wilson's summer home at Sea Girt on the coast of New Jersey.

When I reached the Hotel Emerson, I found McCombs already there. He seemed to be on the ragged edge of a nervous breakdown. His condition was pathetic, and I felt sorry for him. With a hand that shook like that of a man in a fit of ague, he passed over to me a telegram and said, in a trembling voice, 'Bryan has thrown a bombshell into the situation.'

I read Bryan's telegram carefully, pausing at each word, so as not to miss its full import; but, before I reproduce it here, I had better give the reason for its existence.

Under the rules of the Democratic party organization, the National Committee (or a sub-committee of that body) proposes the name of a prominent Democrat as temporary chairman of each national convention. The temporary chairman holds his office only a few hours, but the position is an important one for the reason that the temporary chairman makes

the 'keynote' speech in which he outlines the policy of the
party and its attitude on current political questions. He is
supposed to confer with the leaders of the party in formulat-
ing what he intends to say, but he has much latitude, and
the speech inevitably carries the tone and temper of his own
views.

The sub-committee for the nomination of a temporary chairman was not unanimous in its choice, but eight of its sixteen
members voted for Alton B. Parker, while the votes of the
remaining eight were scattered. Parker was, therefore, proposed as the selection of the committee for temporary chairman. Judge Parker was usually called a conservative Democrat, which I must say is a definition tinged with charity,
for all his ideas and motives were thoroughly and definitely
reactionary.

The news that Parker was the choice of the committee came
out just before I left Chicago. Bryan told me at the time that,
in his opinion, this was the first move of the reactionary
element to capture the convention, and I felt quite sure that
he was right.

Bryan's telegram, addressed to the four candidates for the
presidential nomination — to Wilson, Clark, Harmon, and
Underwood — was an adroit maneuver to defeat this effort;
or, if it could not be defeated, to put the sentiment of the
progressive element of the party before the country in unmistakable terms.

Here is the text of the telegram:

In the interest of harmony I suggest to the sub-committee of the
Democratic National Committee the advisability of recommending
as temporary chairman some Progressive acceptable to the leading
Progressive candidates for the presidential nomination. I took it
for granted that no committee interested in Democratic success
would desire to offend the members of a convention overwhelmingly Progressive by naming a reactionary to sound the keynote of
the campaign. Eight members of the sub-committee, however, have,
over the protest of the remaining eight, agreed not only upon a reactionary, but upon the one Democrat who, among those not candidates for the presidential nomination, is in the eyes of the public
most conspicuously identified with the reactionary element of the
party. I shall be pleased to join you and your friends in opposing
his selection by the full committee or by the convention. Please
answer here. (Signed) W. J. Bryan.

While I read, McCombs stared at me in breathless excitement. 'Well, that sounds pretty plain,' I remarked. 'What's wrong with it?'

'Everything's wrong with it,' McCombs replied gloomily. 'Let me read you a telegram which I have sent on to the Governor as a suggestion for his answer to Bryan.'

I listened as he read the draft of a message to Bryan which he expected Governor Wilson to sign and forward. It was rather long and somewhat involved in phraseology, but the gist of it was a feeble evasion of the issue. It wound up by saying: 'My friends in Baltimore are on the people's side in everything that affects the organization of the Convention. They are certain not to forget their standards, as they have already shown. It is not necessary that I should remind them of these standards from New Jersey and I have neither the right nor the desire to direct the organization of a convention of which I am not even a member.'

This proposed reply to Bryan's outspoken announcement conveyed nothing more to me than a mealy-mouthed, half-hearted surrender at the first appearance of the enemy. My earnest hope at that instant was that the Governor had not sent it on to Bryan — and I did not think he had, for I knew how thoroughly he hated indecision.

'That won't do at all!' I exclaimed. 'Governor Wilson can't afford to beat about the bush. I think he should unhesitatingly tell Bryan that he agrees with him.'

McCombs fidgeted with the paper in his hands, folding and refolding it. 'If the Governor,' he said, 'takes that course, he'll destroy all his chances.'

In trying to get this idea out of his mind, I told him of my conversation with Bryan in Chicago and of my confidence that Bryan would throw his powerful support to Wilson at the proper time in the convention unless he became convinced that Wilson was trying to play to the reactionaries and the bosses.

McCombs disagreed with me emphatically. 'He'll never get New York,' he remarked gloomily, 'and without it he can't be nominated.'

'You're chasing shadows. He'll not get New York, anyway,' I said. 'We are bound by the unit rule, and that means that Murphy will never let New York vote for Wilson. We've got to nominate Wilson without the help of Murphy.'

McCombs' persistent error throughout the convention was in believing that we had to play politics with the bosses in order to nominate Woodrow Wilson. He did not seem to understand that Wilson himself would have repudiated any such conciliatory tactics.

He sat dejectedly on a bed while I went into the next room to call up Governor Wilson at Sea Girt.

'Governor,' I said over the telephone, 'McCombs has just read to me the reply which he has suggested that you send to Bryan. I am absolutely opposed to the McCombs suggestion. While I was in Chicago I saw Bryan; had a long talk with him. He didn't say in explicit terms that he was on our side, but I am confident that we can count on his influence and support at the proper time in the convention if you do nothing to impair his confidence in you as the leader of the progressive element in the party. I know how he feels about Tammany and the bosses because he told me himself. I earnestly urge you to stand with Bryan in the position he has taken as to the election of a progressive chairman of the convention.'

'I agree with you,' he said. 'Let me read to you the telegram I have just sent to Mr. Bryan.'

The Governor read this message over the telephone:

W. J. Bryan, Chicago: You are quite right. Before hearing of your message I clearly stated my position. The Baltimore Convention is to be a convention of progressives, of men who are progressive in principle and by conviction. It must, if it is not to be put in a wrong light before the country, express its convictions in its organization and in its choice of the men who are to speak for it. You are to be a member of the convention and are entirely within your rights in doing everything within your power to bring that result about. No one will doubt where my sympathies lie and you will, I am sure, find my friends in the convention acting upon clear conviction and always in the interest of the people's cause. I am happy in the confidence that they need no suggestion from me. (Signed) Woodrow Wilson

'That's fine,' I said. 'Have you sent a copy to McCombs?'

'I have just done so,' the Governor replied.

When I returned to the room, I found McCombs lying on the bed, sobbing hysterically, with the Governor's telegram in his hand. Weeping men puzzle me, for I never know what to do with them. I was sorry for McCombs; I felt a wave of pity for his lack of stamina. Suppose it all came to the worst possible end; suppose Governor Wilson was completely beaten on the first ballot. Such a turn of events would be a terrible blow, but men ought to be able to stand heavy disasters. Why weep?

'McCombs,' I said soothingly, 'what's the matter?'

He raised his head and turned toward me a face which revealed his painful emotions. 'All my work has gone for nothing,' he declared. 'The Governor needs all the friends and all the votes he can get — and now he's backing Bryan in a quarrel with the most powerful men in the party.' He rose and walked heavily to the window, where he leaned against the wall and gazed into the street. 'The Governor can't afford to have a row,' he added.

I said: 'The Governor can't afford to have anything but a row. The bigger the row the better for us. Our candidate can be nominated only by progressive votes. The votes will be there; he'll be nominated.'

McCombs would not be comforted, however. After a long silence he said: 'I'm sick and I am going to my apartment to rest.' He had taken an apartment in the Latrobe, a small hotel, where he could retire and get away from the crowd. I had breakfast there with him the next morning, which was Sunday. He looked better then, and said he felt better. He had come to the conclusion, after a night's sleep, that all was not lost.

Wilson was the only one of the candidates who realized the tremendous significance of Bryan's telegram. Clark replied grumpily that the Clark candidate for temporary chairman was Senator Ollie James, of Kentucky, who was one of Bryan's close friends. He said nothing in his reply about the issue between the progressives and reactionaries, but he did say that the 'supreme consideration should be to prevent any discord in the convention.'

The key to history is often found in small events. My own conviction is that Champ Clark lost his chance of becoming President of the United States when he failed to repudiate the reactionaries in his reply to Bryan. He left Wilson as the only candidate in the field who was ready to take a bold and courageous stand.

The truth is that the convention was a battleground between two conflicting ideals of government. Clark did not appreciate this fact with vigor and clarity. It was an error, on his part, of the first magnitude.

2

The confidence of the Clark people ran obstreperously all over the place, like the Mississippi in a spring flood. They had come to Baltimore with the idea of sweeping the convention right off its feet, of carrying everything by storm. I saw clearly that our imminent peril lay in the first few ballots, and that our most favorable line of strategy would be simply to hold tight regardless of what happened. Every successive ballot, with Clark still lacking the necessary two thirds, would be in our favor.

I did not see how Clark could possibly line up two thirds of the 1088 votes if every Wilson man stood firm. To be nominated he had to get 726 votes. Now, I knew for a certainty that the Wilson strength would amount to 300 votes at least, and Harmon and Underwood could hardly run under 100 apiece. Besides, there would be at the beginning some scattered votes, complimentary ballots for favorite sons.

It seemed to me, and to all of us at the Wilson headquarters, that neither Harmon nor Underwood had a chance; their following would begin to disintegrate as the contest went on. Wilson was the *second choice* of a great many delegates, and in the elimination of the minor candidates we expected to get more new votes than Clark.

Weeks before the convention met, Stuart G. Gibboney, a New York lawyer and a Virginian, who was devoted to the Wilson cause, had applied himself to the task of getting a complete list of the delegates: a list in which every man's predilections, and preferences and temperament, so far as we could learn, were recorded. These facts had been dug out by Wilson men in each state. The information, which we had tabulated and indexed, was invaluable. As I write this chapter, eighteen years later, I have that bulky list before me. Here is a specimen: I omit the name:

—— Mayor for sixteen years. For Underwood first, and Wilson as second choice. Very vain. Treat him like a big man, and you can handle him. Has three children. Wonderful children. Likes to talk about them.

Here is another, some pages further on:

—— Strong Wilson man. Elected as such. Uninstructed. Employed as a local manager of —— Insurance Company. Believes in currency reform. Bryan is his second choice.

We decided to keep in touch with every delegate, and we got together a lot of unalloyed, enthusiastic Wilson men for that purpose. Each of these men was given a list of, say, five delegates, with all the facts we had been able to gather, and his duty was to fraternize with the delegates on his list and use every possible opening — without being offensively insistent — to bring anti-Wilson men to our point of view.

The slogan of the Clark forces was the tag end of a song about hound dogs, and so on — and it ran in these words:

> I don't care if he is a houn',
> You gotta quit kicking my dawg aroun'.

This strenuous objection to the kicking of hound dogs was shouted, screamed, whispered, and cat-called until the air quivered with its echoes. It was silly and meaningless, of course, but if you think it was ineffective, you would change your mind if you ever watched a political convention. The Clark men seemed to be comforted by saying it over and over, as the old lady in the story was by the word 'Mesopotamia.' They shouted it in chorus; they shouted it to strangers who shouted it back. We had nothing in the way of a battle-cry that was the equal of the 'houn' dawg' in noise.

The day before the convention assembled, one of our Wilson men, attached to headquarters, said to me: 'I'm going to get a hound dog, take him out on the street, and kick him around — just to see what happens.'

'Do you want to be lynched?' I inquired with a good deal of solicitude. I hated to lose an active worker.

'No, I don't want to be lynched,' he said, 'but what do you suppose they'd do if I started to kick one around?'

My advice was not to do it, and he didn't. The whole place was in such a turmoil over the sanctity of hound dogs that I would have let one bite me without the least resistance, for fear of reprisals.

In reading over what I have just written, I see that I have unintentionally made the Clark campaign sound foolish and trivial. I do not mean that, and I hasten to correct the impression. What I have tried to do is to depict the scene on the surface. The ideas and driving power behind the Clark effort were neither foolish nor trivial.

Champ Clark was an honest man and a distinguished citizen, and he had already had a great career. He was a powerful and skillful adversary; I had much respect for him, not only as a political opponent, but also as a man. Yet, notwithstanding his long experience in public affairs and his personal rectitude, I cannot believe that he would have made a good President. He was not, according to my opinion, a good judge of men. In that respect he was like Bryan. Neither of them could conceive of anything being wrong with any of their friends — an excellent trait, if one's friends are not evilly disposed, and have nothing wrong with them. In depth of intellect and clarity of ideas he did not measure up at all to the stature of Woodrow Wilson.

Besides their slogan, the Clark people had a map — and their map was an excellent piece of propaganda for their cause. It was a map of the United States, colored to show the political preferences within the Democratic Party. The states that had voted in the primaries, or in their conventions, for Clark were shaded red on the map, and the Wilson states were shaded green. The four states that had gone for Underwood — Mississippi, Alabama, Georgia, and Florida — were white with red bars across them. At first glance the entire map looked as red as a boiled lobster. The green patches — signifying Wilson — included the states of Oregon, Texas, Minnesota, Wisconsin, and Pennsylvania. The map made Wilson out as a rather feeble candidate. It was an effective piece of paper; the Clark crowd had bunches of maps in their pockets and gave them away to everybody. People like to be on the winning side. The map seemed to prove that Clark would win easily.

I think that he was defeated for the nomination, in large measure, by his intense desire to be nominated. He was willing to accept the support of anybody, no matter whom. Many a good man has been damned by his friends.

Before the convention assembled, a meeting of the New York delegation was held, and Charles F. Murphy was elected chairman. He said to the delegates that the meeting was not a caucus, but merely a conference for the exchange of views; and while the unit rule had been imposed on the delegates, he thought, nevertheless, that it would be helpful if every delegate would say, frankly and without reservation, who was the best man for the convention to nominate.

The roll being called, Senator James A. O'Gorman, one of the delegates at large, led off for Wilson. The fact was developed that eighteen of the ninety delegates favored Wilson. The Tammany men, of course, all voted for Harmon under Murphy's instructions.

The unit rule is one of the most stupid devices ever conceived by the human intellect. Its operation leads inevitably to rank injustices — and to grotesque situations which would inspire gales of laughter in a comic opera. For instance, I was known to every well-informed man in the convention as a Wilson lieutenant, but under the unit rule which bound the New York delegation I had to vote with Tammany. Murphy voted me for Harmon on the first nine ballots, and then he switched me and the rest of New York's delegates to Clark. In the mean time I was active all over the floor trying to get Wilson votes.

William Jennings Bryan was the most powerful personality in the convention, and his activities were entirely devoted to furthering the interests of Woodrow Wilson. Yet he had to vote for Clark, as the Nebraska delegation, to which he belonged, was so instructed. Can you beat that for absurdity?

Under the unit rule it is possible for a candidate who has a majority of the delegates on his side to be defeated. To illustrate that point, let us take a few states and work out a calculation. Any number of states, picked at random, will do for this purpose; but, suppose we take three: New York (90 votes); Texas (40 votes); Illinois (58 votes). Now, let us assume that A and B are candidates for the nomination, and that the preferences of the delegates from these states are as stated here:

	A	B
New York......................................	40	50
Texas...	30	10
Illinois.......................................	28	30
Total...............................	98	90

A's total is 98; and B's is 90. But under the unit rule B would carry the New York delegation, with its 90 votes, and the Illinois delegation, with its 58 votes. In short, the votes actually cast for B under the unit rule would amount to 148. On the other hand, A, although he is the preference of 98 delegates, would carry only the Texas delegation, and therefore he would have 40 votes, and no more.

In the Baltimore Convention, Wilson's strength was much greater all along than the balloting indicated. Hundreds of Wilson men were sewed up, as it were, in delegations that voted under the unit rule for other candidates. A delegation sent to the convention with instructions to vote as a unit for a candidate was bound to vote for that candidate until he appeared to be out of the running, or until they were released by the candidate himself.

The two-thirds rule, which requires any candidate to get two thirds of all the votes in the convention before he can be nominated, is equally mischievous and asinine. It usually results in the elimination of all the powerful candidates who might lead the party to victory and the selection, as a compromise, of some colorless personality who receives the nomination because nothing can be said against him, or for him.

Our difficulties in handling the problems of the convention were immensely increased by the fact that McCombs was in a desperate state of nerves and indecision. We could not get him, as our official leader, to decide anything — yet, at the same time, his extreme resentment at interference kept the rest of us from giving him as much assistance as we might have given him otherwise.

Nevertheless, McCombs — in one way or another — did some excellent work during convention week. He was close to the big political chiefs, such as Roger Sullivan, of Illinois, and Thomas Taggart, of Indiana, and I think he had a great deal to do in bringing them around finally to the Wilson side.

He was in his element when he was in contact with a high-geared, intricate political machine.

Eventually A. Mitchell Palmer, then a congressman from Pennsylvania, was agreed upon as spokesman of the Wilson forces on the floor of the convention. Palmer was an able man, clever and resourceful, and devoted heart and soul to the Wilson cause.

3

When the convention assembled, the first fight that we had on our hands was over the selection of Alton B. Parker as temporary chairman. Bryan headed the opposition to Parker, and nominated John W. Kern, of Indiana, for the place. Kern declined to make the contest in a speech in which he praised everybody impartially, and which was obviously conceived with the idea of smoothing things over. But things wouldn't be smoothed. Bryan himself finally ran for temporary chairman, and was defeated by Parker, who received 579 votes, against 508 for Bryan. It was really a victory for the progressives, although Bryan was beaten by a narrow margin.

On this vote the Clark forces stood by Parker, and the vote measured their strength with accuracy. I knew it at the time, and I felt confident then and there that they would never be able to nominate Clark. Besides, it was a serious strategic error on their part, for it definitely aligned the Clark sentiment on the side of the reactionaries.

Parker's 'keynote' speech was a mere blur of words, a dull-gray affair. He attempted to give it a progressive tone, in keeping with the temper of the convention, but his progressiveness was so palpably artificial that the speech was received without enthusiasm.

Senator Ollie James was elected permanent chairman — unanimously, I think. He was fair and impartial and made an excellent presiding officer.

In this convention, contrary to general practice, the platform was brought in by the platform committee at the tail-end of the proceedings on the last day, after the candidates had been selected. It was adopted by the convention unanimously, and without debate. This circumstance reveals, perhaps more clearly than anything else, that the attention of the delegates was centered on personalities rather than on issues. The Democratic Party that year wanted a *man* rather than a *set of arguments*.

All political conventions are emotional; it is the essence of their being; and politics is, very clearly and in certain aspects, an emotional adventure. Two or three political ideas, thrown like bombs into the convention, burst with explosive violence. Their emotional fragments touched every man in the assembly and swept the entire convention off its feet.

The first one was the opposition to Judge Parker as temporary chairman. It consolidated the Wilson forces, brought them into cohesion, and revealed their strength.

The second one was launched at the evening session of the third day — that is, on Thursday, the 27th. Until then the convention had been in the throes of organization.

The session had just begun, and the New York delegation was in conference in an anteroom of the convention hall when one of the delegates rushed in and excitedly announced that Mr. Bryan had introduced a resolution which was an insult to New York and that there was great turmoil on the floor. The New York delegates hurried in and took their seats. Bryan held the platform and was endeavoring to speak, but was being continually interrupted by various delegates who opposed his resolution:

Resolved, That in this crisis in our party's career and in our country's history this convention sends greetings to the people of the United States, and assures them that the party of Jefferson and of Jackson is still the champion of popular government and equality before the law. As proof of our fidelity to the people, we hereby declare ourselves opposed to the nomination of any candidate for president who is the representative of or under obligation to J. Pierpont Morgan, Thomas F. Ryan, August Belmont, or any other member of the privilege-hunting and favor-seeking class.

That sounded all right, though a trifle personal, especially in view of the fact that Mr. Ryan was sitting in the convention as a delegate from Virginia, and Mr. Belmont was, at that moment, sitting near me as a delegate from New York.

The Bryan resolution had a second paragraph, which was expressed in these words:

Be it further resolved, That we demand the withdrawal from this convention of any delegate or delegates constituting or representing the above-named interests.

You have heard of Bedlam, I am sure, but not many people have seen Bedlam in full career. I am one of those who have seen it, and you would have seen it, too, if you had been a spectator of the Baltimore Convention for an hour or so after Bryan had introduced the resolution which I have given here.

It was an indescribable, turbulent chaos — a cacophony of howls, groans, and yells, punctuated by futile attempts to obtain some kind of order. Some of the delegates ran like madmen through the surging crowd on the floor, and as they ran they shouted, 'Lynch Bryan!' 'Throw him out!' 'He's a disgrace!' and other phrases of similar import. A delegate from Virginia leaped on the platform and shook his fist in Bryan's face. This Virginian became so hysterical that his friends had to lead him out into the open air.

In the end Bryan's friends shouted down the opposition. They were more numerous. One of them, the Honorable Cone Johnson, of Texas, had a voice of immense capacity and carrying power. It sounded over and above the roar like a steamship siren. He mounted a chair and said, in his loudest tone, 'All I know and all I want to know is that Bryan is on one side, and Wall Street is on the other.' He made this observation over and over again. The floor was stunned into silence. The voice of Cone Johnson made a mere yell sound like a whisper.

Bryan's resolution is an example of his extraordinary cleverness in political strategy. It contained two paragraphs, as you have seen. Certainly, the convention could not vote down the first paragraph and still pretend to be on the side of progressive liberalism. One can readily understand why many delegates did not want to vote on it at all — but, since it had been introduced, it could not be voted down without implying that the Democratic Party had committed political suicide.

The second paragraph, which demanded the withdrawal of certain regularly elected delegates, was wholly indefensible. The convention had no power to expel delegates, or to set up standards of admission. Bryan knew that very well; he put in the second paragraph, I am sure, for no other purpose than to be able to withdraw it later. He understood the psychological value of making an exorbitant and indefensible claim to screen another and more desirable objective — and in withdrawing later from the indefensible attitude as a concession.

There was a bitter debate as soon as the convention calmed down sufficiently for speakers to be heard. Bryan sat on the platform, imperturbably fanning himself, his inevitable glass of water on a table by his side. He had introduced his resolution on his own initiative, and without notifying any of the leaders of the Wilson forces.

After various speakers had wrangled over the question, Bryan got up and, with apparent reluctance, withdrew the second paragraph of the resolution. By withdrawing that paragraph he created the effect of having toned it down, although it remained essentially as it was before. As the roll of states was called, the voting showed that the resolution would be carried overwhelmingly.

I sat directly behind Charles F. Murphy. Though we disagreed in our political views, Murphy and I got along well enough personally. He was pleasant and agreeable, even if his good humor did cover a good many mental reservations. He knew that I was a tenderfoot in politics, and for the purpose of teasing me, I suppose, he would sometimes ask my opinion, with great solemnity. When the voting on the Bryan resolution began, Murphy turned around to me and said: 'How do you think we ought to vote on this?' I replied, 'There's only one way we can afford to vote, and that is for the resolution.' Of course, my view of the matter had no effect on Murphy, who did his own thinking. When New York was called, he cast the ninety votes of our delegation in favor of Bryan's resolution. It was carried by a vote of four to one.

4

On the first ballot, taken on Thursday (June 27) Clark polled 440½; Wilson, 324; Harmon, 148; and Underwood, 117½. This was the only ballot cast that day.

The next day Clark started out with 446½ votes, against

Wilson's 340. Harmon and Underwood had both dwindled slightly.

The Wilson managers knew that Murphy intended to switch from Harmon to Clark, but we had no idea when the switch would occur. Murphy was, of course, in constant touch with the Clark leaders on the floor — Senator W. J. Stone and others — and we were sure that the switch to Clark would be dramatic, and at an opportune time, with the idea of stampeding the convention. It would come, when it came, with a boom and a roar, and a big bass drum, and the unfurling of flags. If we could find out just when it would take place, the knowledge would be useful.

The broad back of Tammany's Czar was right in front of me. I might have touched him on the shoulder and asked him point-blank when he expected to vote me — and the rest of New York's ninety delegates — for Clark, but I didn't, for I knew that all I would get would be a soothing dose of verbal camouflage.

But I had a friend among the Tammany delegates, a man for whom I had once done a favor. He was close to the inside group, Murphy and others, that ran everything. I do not give his name because the arm of vengeance is long, and Tammany might make him quite uncomfortable.

I called him out to an anteroom and told him that I would like to know when New York was to be switched to Clark. 'I don't know anything now,' he said, 'but I'll listen, and find out, if I can.'

Just before the roll call on the ninth ballot was concluded, my Tammany friend beckoned for me to come out into the lobby.

'They're going to switch on the next ballot,' he whispered. 'After the voting begins, Murphy is going through the form of taking a poll of the New York delegates. We'll all be for Clark — except you and a few others — and Murphy will then cast our ninety votes for the great houn' dawg statesman.'

'Do the Clark people know it?'

'Know it? Sure! I mean their leaders know all about it, and, believe me, there'll be a demonstration that'll shake the roof. Clark's daughter's here; they're all set to bring her out.'

I went rushing around the convention to give this news to every leader of a Wilson delegation that I could reach. We decided to treat the Clark demonstration as a matter of course, and to appear undisturbed. If we held tight, we were safe enough. With New York added to his list, Clark would have a majority, but not two thirds, though the Clark cheerleaders would no doubt try to make us believe that it was all over but the shouting.

It all went according to schedule.

When New York's vote was announced for Clark, his followers went wild with joy. The noise was deafening. They seized the banner of the New York delegation and marched around the hall with it. Clark's daughter, a young and attractive girl, appeared suddenly in front of the speaker's platform with an American flag. She was picked up and carried on the shoulders of her father's admirers. The Wilson men sat silent.

After a while the smoke and fury subsided, and the votes were counted. The Wilson crowd had stood like a stone wall. The stampede of our forces had fizzled out, for upon taking stock of the situation, we found that we were only two votes short. On the tenth ballot Clark had 556 votes, and Wilson 350½ — or two less than on the previous ballot.

Clark had touched high-water mark.

We were fortunate in having a considerable number of skillful and active Wilson men who acted as floor-leaders. They were of inestimable help in holding the Wilson forces together during the Clark cyclone. Such men as Willard Saulsbury, of Delaware; Charles F. Johnson, of Maine; A. S. Burleson and Thomas B. Love, of Texas; A. C. Weiss, of Minnesota; John Gary Evans, of South Carolina; Senator Gore and W. H. ('Alfalfa Bill') Murray, of Oklahoma; P. H. O'Brien, of Michigan; Joseph E. Davies, of Wisconsin; and Robert Ewing, of Louisiana; and there were others who did great work, but whose names I do not recall at the moment.

5

Saturday, June 29, was a critical day. The convention was to reconvene at 1 P.M. Before it met, I went to see Mc-Combs. I had slept about four hours, and it was then around ten o'clock. I found McCombs in a hysterical condition; he had simply gone to pieces.

'The jig's up,' he declared as soon as he saw me. 'Clark will be nominated. All my work has been for nothing.'

I was amazed.

'Do you mean that you are giving up the fight?' I asked.

'Why, Governor Wilson himself has given up,' McCombs replied.

'What do you mean?' I exclaimed.

'I talked to the Governor on the telephone fully about the situation,' he said, 'and told him he could not be nominated and that I thought he ought to release his friends, and the Governor has authorized me to release them. I told the Governor that I would have to have a telegram from him authorizing me to do so, as his friends in the convention might not accept my statement.'

I understood McCombs to say that he had such a telegram from the Governor, but I cannot recall whether or not he showed it to me. In my haste to denounce McCombs for what I considered his betrayal of the Governor, I didn't think much about the telegram. We had some hot words.

'You have betrayed the Governor,' I said. 'You have sold him out.'

McCombs denied the accusation.

My remark was merely a sudden and hot-tempered reaction to his statement that he had advised the Governor to quit the race. On reflection, I am confident that he did not attempt to betray the Governor or to sell him out. His trouble was a bad case of fright; the Clark outburst of enthusiasm had scared him into a nervous spasm. Besides, he had an unconquerable itch to be on the bandwagon, which Clark seemed at that moment to be driving.

I went to the telephone and got Governor Wilson at Sea Girt.

'I am dumbfounded,' I said to the Governor, 'by what

McCombs has just told me about releasing your delegates. You must not think of accepting his advice. You are gaining all the time. Clark can never get two thirds of the convention. I am sure that your nomination will be the inevitable outcome if you stay in the race. Please call McCombs immediately on the telephone and tell him not to release your friends.'

The Governor was evidently astonished by my statement. He said that McCombs had told him positively that Clark's nomination was inevitable and, therefore, he had felt that it was unfair to bind his friends any longer. He said that he had instructed McCombs not to release his delegates, however, without conferring with me and getting my approval. He authorized me to countermand his instructions to McCombs.

I went back to McCombs and told him what the Governor had said; whereupon he called the Governor on the telephone and received full confirmation of my statement.

How strange are the ways of destiny! If McCombs had released the Wilson delegates that morning, the history of the next ten years would have presented a different picture to the world.

There is hardly a vestige of truth in McCombs' story of this incident, as it appears in his book. He says the Governor called him on the telephone and said he wanted to quit the race. He goes on to say: 'I was thoroughly enraged. I felt that if loyal Wilson men were willing to fight to the last ditch for the Governor, he at least might maintain his nerve and stand with them.'

He says a little further on: 'I tucked the Governor's instructions into my pocket. They remained there until the convention nominated him.' Perfect rot! J. P. Tumulty, the Governor's secretary, was at Sea Girt when McCombs called on the telephone to tell the Governor that the situation was hopeless. His testimony confirms everything I have related in these pages. He says, in his book, 'Woodrow Wilson As I Knew Him,' that McCombs 'would make it appear that Governor Wilson had got in a panic and tried to withdraw from the race; whereas, the panic was all in the troubled breast of McCombs, a physically frail, morally timid, person, constitutionally unfit for the task of conducting such a fight as was being waged in Baltimore.'

The Wilson family, at Sea Girt, sat down to breakfast in a gloomy frame of mind that morning, all except the Governor, who bore his apparent defeat with good humor. His daughter Eleanor — now Mrs. McAdoo — says there was a touch of gayety in his manner, as if he felt relieved that the struggle was over. While they were at breakfast, the postman came, and in the mail the Governor found a large, impressive catalogue of a concern which sells coffins. 'This coffin company is certainly prompt in its service,' he remarked to the family. 'They've got their catalogue here by the first mail.' He passed the illustrated booklet around and asked the family to help him select a defeated candidate's coffin.

6

When the convention reassembled on Saturday, a tense feeling of excitement pervaded the entire body. Everyone seemed to be expecting something unusual to happen. I thought I knew what it would be because of my conversation with Bryan in Chicago. I knew that when Murphy threw the New York delegation to Clark, it was likely to convince Bryan that the reactionary forces were behind Clark and that he would feel that he was no longer bound by the instructions of the Democrats of his state; that he was free to do what his conscience told him he ought to do in behalf of the progressive cause.

The secretary began to call the roll for the fourteenth ballot. When Nebraska was reached, Mr. Bryan rose and asked permission to explain his vote. In the course of his speech he said:

When we were instructed for Mr. Clark, the Democratic voters who instructed us did so with the distinct understanding that Mr. Clark stood for progressive Democracy. [Applause.] Mr. Clark's representatives appealed for support on no other ground. They contended that Mr. Clark was more progressive than Mr. Wilson, and indignantly denied that there was any coöperation between Mr. Clark and the reactionary element of the party.

He went on to say that neither himself, nor the Nebraska delegates for whom he spoke, would vote for any candidate whose nomination depended on the vote of the New York delegation, 'ninety wax figures,' controlled by Mr. Murphy. 'Speaking for myself,' he said, 'and for any of the delegation who may decide to join me, I shall withhold my vote from Mr. Clark as long as New York's vote is recorded for him.'

Clark began the day with 554½ votes, against 356 for Wilson. At the time of adjournment, after the twenty-sixth ballot, Clark had gone down to 463½ votes, and Wilson had gone up to 407½.

Sunday was an anxious time. We feared that the long recess would give the bosses a chance to make new deals or to attempt new alignments, to Wilson's disadvantage. As a matter of fact, they did attempt that very thing.

A. Mitchell Palmer, as leader of the Wilson forces on the floor of the convention, had conducted himself so admirably and with such ability that he had made a highly favorable impression upon everybody. The bosses conceived the idea of tempting Palmer to enter the race. It was understood that they had proposed to switch the Clark support to him. With this accomplished, the bosses figured that they could demoralize the Wilson following and divert enough of it and of Underwood's strength to assure Palmer's nomination.

It was not, by any means, an illogical or chimerical scheme. It had at least one fatal defect, and that was that Palmer wouldn't consider it. He stood loyally and steadfastly by Wilson. He would not betray his trust. I never talked personally to Palmer about this incident, but I am sure that I state it with substantial accuracy.

On the twenty-seventh ballot — this was on Monday — I had the vote of the New York delegation challenged. This means that the secretary of the convention calls the roll of the delegation, each member by name, in open convention, and each member rises as his name is called and states what candidate he favors. I knew that it could not change the casting of our ninety votes for Clark, under the unit rule, but the strategical effect would be good, as it would reveal to the convention that a certain number of Wilson men were tied up in the Tammany vote for Clark.

You will remember that Murphy had the delegation polled prior to the first session of the convention, and there were eighteen Wilson men in it, but that took place in a private room. Senator O'Gorman, who was strongly for Wilson, told me that there would certainly be less than eighteen delegates willing to announce their preference for Wilson before the whole convention, as some of these men feared Murphy's displeasure; he also advised me to have an up-state man make the challenge. I asked Walter H. Edson, a Wilson man from upper New York, to challenge the vote — and the result showed nine men out of ninety who were willing to announce themselves for Wilson, despite the black looks of Mr. Murphy. The nine were: James A. O'Gorman, Abram I. Elkus, William G. McAdoo, Lawrence Godkin, John B. Stanchfield, Thomas F. Conway, Thomas W. Meachem, Benedict Brooks, and Walter H. Edson. Samuel Untermyer, who was not present, was voted by Murphy for Clark, although he was a well-known Wilson man and a large contributor to the Wilson campaign fund.

The effect of the challenge was excellent. It showed the convention that the New York delegation still had some independence — not much, but a little — left in it.

It was at this psychological moment that the Indiana delegation, under the leadership of Tom Taggart, cast twenty-nine of its thirty votes for Wilson. Up to that time, it had voted consistently, ballot after ballot, for Thomas R. Marshall, Governor of Indiana, and that state's favorite son. This accession of strength to Wilson produced a magnificent effect upon the crowded galleries. Enthusiasm for him burst out anew and his supporters made the most of it on the floor of the convention.

Tom Taggart had done a grand thing for Wilson. It was the first break to him of the delegates from any of the large states. It disheartened the Clark forces and, from that time on, Clark's strength disintegrated with every ballot. The forty-second ballot was the last one on Monday — and it gave Wilson 494 votes to 430 for Clark. I think every man in the convention felt that Wilson would be nominated next day — and he was.

On Tuesday, July 2, Roger Sullivan switched the fifty-eight votes of Illinois from Clark to Wilson. That ballot — the forty-third — gave Wilson 602 votes, and it was the beginning of the end.

Sullivan, though a typical politician, was a man of his word, and he had what is unusual in the average political boss — a lot of idealism in his composition. I always regarded Taggart and Sullivan as far superior in character to Murphy. Aside from that, both Taggart and Sullivan lived in important mid-western states. They had a better comprehension of the spirit and needs of the country than Murphy, as well as a larger outlook upon public affairs. They each took a pride, I think, in contributing their large influence to the nomination of a man for the Presidency who would worthily sustain the high traditions of the presidential office.

The enthusiasm for Clark that had poured in a rushing torrent through the convention no further back than the previous Friday had subsided without leaving an echo. As I listened to the thunderous cheers for Wilson, and witnessed the swift breaking-up of the Clark forces, I marveled at the mutability of public opinion.

Every delegation on the roll hastened to scramble aboard the Wilson bandwagon. On the last ballot I had the honor of casting my vote for the Governor for the first time. Murphy had decided that, since Wilson was nominated anyhow, he might as well make it unanimous.

The noise and the shouting died. The delegates sat in tired silence, a sea of white faces, rumpled clothes and limp collars.

But there was work still to be done. A platform was in the making — in the hands of a committee — and a Vice-President had to be nominated.

The convention adjourned around four o'clock, to meet again at nine that evening.

7

The harsh electric light glared once again upon the thousand men on the floor. The galleries were almost deserted. Interest had dropped from fever heat and was hovering around zero.

A hoarse reading clerk gabbled swiftly through the planks of the platform. It was adopted without discussion.

During the recess I had got in touch with Governor Wilson and told him that the convention would nominate anyone he

desired for the Vice-Presidency. He said he did not care to
offer a suggestion; that he would prefer to have the convention exercise complete freedom of action about the vice-
presidential nomination. I told the Governor that his friends
in the convention would want an indication of his preference
and that if he failed to point the way for them there was no
telling what might happen. He then asked me to suggest the
best available man. I suggested Thomas R. Marshall, of
Indiana, whom I did not know personally, but only by reputation. The reason I suggested Marshall was because he was
the governor of a mid-western state; because his reputation
was that of a liberal, and because he seemed to be generally
well regarded. I thought that his nomination would balance
the ticket well, so far as political considerations went. Governor Wilson authorized me to say that Marshall would be acceptable to him.

I conveyed this information immediately to Taggart.
He was immensely pleased. A listless convention, yawning
and looking at time-tables, voted Marshall in for second
place. Then we went home.

CHAPTER XI

WOODROW WILSON IS ELECTED

I

THE convention had left me so exhausted from loss of sleep that I passed most of the day of July 3 at my hotel in Baltimore, in bed. Then I set out for Bayhead, New Jersey, a small summer resort on the shore where my family had been accustomed for many years to spend the summer. Bayhead is about eight miles south of Sea Girt, the summer home of Governor Wilson. Upon arriving at home, I decided to take a rest over the week-end and not to call on the Governor for a few days, as I knew that he would be continually surrounded by people, and as busy as a dozen men.

On Sunday, July 7, McCombs came to see me at Bayhead, and said that he had just come from Sea Girt. We had a pleasant conversation, as veterans of the hard-fought battle of Baltimore. After a while he disclosed the reason for his visit. He wanted me to speak to the Governor in his behalf. In the Democratic Party the presidential candidate always has the privilege of naming the chairman of the National Committee, and McCombs was desperately anxious for the place. Would I help him?

To refresh my memory of this meeting I wrote Stuart Gibboney, who accompanied McCombs from Sea Girt, and he replied under date of September 9, 1930:

I remember the occasion clearly. It was the Sunday following the adjournment of the Baltimore Convention. I met McCombs at Sea Girt and he asked me if I would drive down with him to see you at Bayhead. He told me that there was an effort being made to sidetrack him and prevent his selection as Chairman and that he was anxious to secure your support and influence with Governor Wilson, and he asked me to help him with you. We drove to Bayhead in his car and he solicited your aid and support.

I was disconcerted, for a moment, by McCombs' appeal for my help. It was in bad taste, to say the least, considering our disagreement over his proposal to withdraw the Governor's name at the convention. I do not often have much difficulty in making up my mind, for I hate to be in a state of indecision; but, in this case, I was decidedly perplexed.

There was no doubt as to McCombs' unfitness for the arduous duties of conducting a nation-wide campaign. He had revealed his lack of executive capacity, his small jealousies, and his unlimited egotism so clearly that I had a perfect mental picture of his limitations. Besides, he was ill; what he really needed was a long rest in some quiet place.

But one thing was certain; if the Governor dropped McCombs, it would undoubtedly cause misunderstanding and discord at the very beginning of the campaign. To most of the people of the country, McCombs was merely a name, and they knew nothing of his failings. To them he appeared, on account of the publicity which he had put out for himself, as the whole pith and core of the Wilson campaign management. I had no idea what the Governor proposed to do, but it seemed to me, after reflection, that the only course open to him was to make McCombs chairman of the National Committee. We would simply have to put up with him, and hope for the best.

Having reached this conclusion, I told McCombs that I would see the Governor and recommend his appointment. He said he thought me very generous and declared his undying friendship.

2

Governor Wilson was seated on the porch of his house, facing the Atlantic and its infinite blue vista of sky and water. But he was not alone. A swarm of people — politicians, Democrats, disguised Republicans, well-wishers, fortune-hunters, and newspaper reporters — was around him. A long string of motorists drove by in the road, and as each car passed, a pointing hand and peering eyes turned toward the house. The Governor had the uncomfortable look of a modest man who has been sentenced to sit in a show window.

As soon as he saw me, he excused himself to his callers and led me to a room inside the house, where, after a few exchanges about the Baltimore Convention, the Governor brought up the question of the national chairmanship.

in close communion with the party leaders. Contact and influence do the rest.

3

When I went into the management of the campaign, I thought I knew something about people, but I acquired considerably more data on the subject of the human race during that crowded summer of 1912. I learned, among other things, that it is impossible to defeat an ignorant man by argument. If a man does not know anything to start with, you cannot argue with him; you can only tell him, and let it go at that. I discovered also that vanity is a stronger impelling force than reason; also, that no matter how big a liar a man may be, he wants and expects everybody else to tell the truth.

During the course of the campaign I became acquainted with leading Democrats throughout the country, and I must say that on the whole these leaders made a favorable impression on me. Naturally, they were partisans and their views were limited frequently to purely party advantage; but they were earnest, able, vigorous men, who believed in Democracy and in Woodrow Wilson, and they coöperated with me loyally in the conduct of the campaign.

Among the problems that rose to plague us was the so-called Catholic question. In 1912, the A.P.A. (American Protective Association) was still in existence and active in every direction. This association was anti-Catholic, and its leaders endeavored to drag the religious issue into every political campaign. The late General Nelson A. Miles was, as I recall it, president of the organization. He and two other members of the association constituted a committee which called on me during the campaign with a demand that President Wilson express himself on the so-called Catholic question. I told the committee that Governor Wilson and I deplored religious issues of any kind; that we believed in freedom of religious worship and could not see where a religious issue entered into this campaign or had any part in American political life. The committee left, breathing dire threats against the ticket, but, so far as I am aware, nothing ever came of it. The injection of this question, however, caused me some concern because I did not know how far-reaching it might be. Martin J. Wade, of Iowa, a Catholic, was attached to our headquarters. Judge Wade was one of the leading Democrats of the Middle West, and a citizen of high character. He told me that the course I had taken with the A.P.A. committee was absolutely right and said that, if I would leave the general direction of the matter in his hands, he would look after it. I gladly delegated it to him; meanwhile, calling into headquarters, at Judge Wade's suggestion, James K. Maguire, ex-Mayor of Syracuse, New York, an able politician and himself a Catholic.

These two gentlemen looked into all questions or inquiries of a religious nature that came up during the campaign, and I must say they handled them with great tact, discrimination, and judgment.

The Catholic issue, so-called, is nothing new in American politics. I cannot recall any time in my life when it has not appeared in some form in American presidential campaigns. These anti-religious movements have been sporadic and ephemeral throughout our history. They have never amounted to anything in the long run, although they have at times exercised a great influence upon the decision of the electorate. One has only to go back to 1826, when a man named Morgan was supposed to have been murdered in the State of New York by a 'secret society' known as the Free Masons, the Masons being the present Masonic order in the United States. The Masonic lodge of which he was a member was charged with the crime. Excitement was intense, and suppression of Free Masonry in the United States became such a political issue that a national anti-Masonic political party was organized.

This party existed for something like ten years and was a factor in presidential and state campaigns. Clay sought its support in 1832 when he ran against Jackson, only to suffer defeat. President Jackson was a Mason, whereas Thurlow Weed and William H. Seward were members of the anti-Masonic party. It was believed at the time that Catholic influences were strongly behind the anti-Masonic movement.

The persecution and ostracism of Masons during this period of the existence of the anti-Masonic party were as notorious as they are amazing to the student of American history. The movement failed eventually and we hear no more about suppressing the Masonic order.

The anti-Masonic party had been dead only a few years when the so-called Know-Nothing party appeared upon the scene. The Know-Nothings were anti-Catholic and anti-foreign. This party also became temporarily an influence in our political life. But, like the anti-Masonic party, it disappeared after a relatively brief period and has remained unhonored and unsung.

Too many people take these ephemeral movements seriously. Being based upon no principle of political action or sound economic policy, but appealing only to the prejudices of men, they have no solid ground for existence and disappear inevitably in the course of time.

4

Shortly after I had taken charge of the national campaign as vice-chairman, I began to be mentioned, here and there, as the probable nominee of the Democratic Party for Governor of New York. I did not pay much attention to it, at first, as it seemed to be merely idle gossip or the speculations of political reporters of the newspapers. But, before long, I realized that it had some substantial basis.

The Tammany chiefs saw clearly that Wilson would be elected, and, as they were anxious to put themselves on some sort of solid footing with him, they sent word that Tammany would gladly support any man as nominee for governor that was acceptable to him. I do not know how this information was conveyed to Governor Wilson; but, at any rate, he told me about it and said that he would be happy to see me Governor of New York.

It was a Democratic year and there was hardly a doubt that the gubernatorial candidate of the party would be elected. The governorship of New York State is an important position, and to be governor is a great honor for any man. But I had no desire for any political office; and, besides, how could I make the race for governor with so much of the responsibility for the national campaign on my hands?

The talk of nominating me persisted, however, so I finally gave out a public statement on September 11, in which I said that, while I appreciated the interest of my friends, 'Under no circumstances could I entertain the nomination.'

Continuing, I said:

Without my seeking there has been thrown upon me grave responsibilities in connection with the national campaign. Every energy and power that I have must be devoted to it.

To be even suggested for office puts me in an equivocal position and reacts to the disadvantage of the national campaign, particularly in this state, because the inference will be inevitably drawn by some people that I am using the powers of the National Committee to advance my personal interests. This would be an intolerable situation for me, and I could not permit it.

It is an honor far beyond my deserts to be mentioned for such a great office, and I feel deeply grateful to those of my friends who think me worthy of it, but I must ask that my name be dismissed from further consideration.

I hope that is clear. I mean it to be final.

I have devoted some space to this episode, which is of small importance considered by itself, in order to clear up a mistaken impression concerning my attitude toward Tammany Hall. Mendacious people, both inside and outside of the Tammany organization, have said from time to time that I disliked Murphy and Tammany because they refused to give me the nomination for Governor in 1912. There is not a word of truth in that story. I could have had the nomination. Tammany did not refuse to give it to me. I declined to take it.

5

I have never believed that political platforms have an important part in determining the preferences of the public for one party or another. They are nothing more than abstract and rather vague generalizations of current political ideas. The average voter pays little or no attention to political platforms, and has little desire to learn anything about them; but he has usually a pretty clear idea of what his party stands for in general — of its tone and purpose. If one could get enough data to make a statistical tabulation, I think it might be shown that the independent voter is the deciding voice in all closely contested national campaigns; and that the independent voter is attracted more by a single leading issue or an outstanding personality than he is by a party. We won in 1912 because the personality of Woodrow Wilson had captured the country.

Governor Wilson didn't believe in 'barn-storming,' and it was with considerable difficulty that I induced him to make some speeches at important points throughout the country. His speaking engagements were always made by me for the reason that the chairman of the committee quite naturally should determine where the candidate can speak with the greatest advantage, since important questions of political strategy are involved.

This brings to mind an interesting incident. George M. Palmer was chairman of the New York State Democratic Committee. One day he called me on the telephone and asked me to persuade Governor Wilson to speak at the Syracuse State Fair. I told him that I thought Governor Wilson's energies ought to be used where they would be of greater benefit than in New York, because, with the split in the Republican ranks, the state was safe anyway. He admitted this, but said that if the Governor would speak at Syracuse we could capture two or three up-state congressional districts which would otherwise be doubtful.

I took the matter up with the Governor. He did not want to speak at Syracuse, but, when I told him about the chance to elect several Democrats from the upper districts of New York, he said he would be willing to go, though he feared that he might be embarrassed by the presence of Charles F. Murphy, the boss of Tammany Hall. Someone had informed the Governor that Murphy would be at Syracuse.

He was emphatic in saying that he did not want to be brought into contact with Tammany in this way; and that he did not want any sort of identification with it or what it stood for. I asked the Governor if I could make an engagement for him provided I got assurances that he would not have to meet Murphy, and he replied that I could.

He would not have been at all squeamish about meeting Murphy, as one man meets another, I am sure, but in the circumstances their meeting would be twisted around by our

Republican opponents to the detriment of our campaign. Speakers in both divisions of the Republican Party — Roosevelt, particularly — were going up and down the land making loud assertions that the election of Wilson meant the election of Tammany. Cartoonists for Republican newspapers were busy with pictures which showed Woodrow Wilson standing in the foreground, or sitting at a desk, or doing one thing or another, with Murphy's rotund but ghostly shadow hovering over him.

Without telling Palmer of my talk with the Governor, I asked him if he did not think we would be stupid to give Roosevelt an additional club to pummel us with by having Governor Wilson appear at Syracuse with Murphy and the Tammany chieftains. Palmer agreed with me, and said that if the Governor would accept the invitation he would be spared any embarrassment of that kind. Having this assurance from him, I agreed that the Governor would visit the fair on the appointed day.

I decided to run up to Syracuse with Governor Wilson. We left New York on the midnight train — September 11 — and arrived in Syracuse around noon of the next day.

When we got to the clubhouse in the fair grounds, Palmer led the way into a public dining-room, and headed for a large round table. No sooner had I got inside the room than I saw Murphy seated at this table with a number of gentlemen, among whom I recognized Governor Dix and Norman E. Mack. I was astonished at seeing Murphy there, and my astonishment was not diminished when Governor Wilson was placed in the seat next to Murphy. I sat on the Governor's left.

The Governor did not recognize Murphy until he had sat down beside him. It was a tense and disagreeable moment. Governor Wilson returned Murphy's greeting with a stiff nod and sat for a moment without saying a word; then he arose abruptly and left the table. I followed him, as a matter of course. As soon as we got outside, I said: 'Governor, I am amazed by what has happened; it is a complete violation of the promise that was made to me and I hope you don't think that I am in any way responsible.' He said that he knew it was not my fault, but he expressed himself vigorously about

ity, that he ordered me brusquely to vacate his office. This assertion is so far from the truth that it is comical. Instead of ordering me from his office, McCombs was, on the contrary, suave and courteous, although he was evidently laboring under suppressed excitement. I welcomed him back, turned everything over to him, gave him as full information as possible about the state of the campaign, and resumed my desk in the vice-chairman's office.

The election was already won because the effective work of the campaign was finished when McCombs returned. All that we had to do was to hold our ground. McCombs, however, began to call in various machine politicians and affected to believe that the campaign was in dire extremity and that only he could save it.

The smouldering discord was soon fanned into a full flame, however, and for the last two weeks of the campaign we all lived over a volcano. It is a good thing that the election took place early in November. If the campaign had lasted a month longer, I fear that Democratic headquarters would have exploded with a bang.

I felt a deep resentment against McCombs for a while, but as time passed it disappeared, and now, as I look back in retrospect on our disagreements, my feeling for him is one of pity. I am sorry that I have been obliged to say so much about him that is not favorable.

7

Cranks appear in all exciting political contests. The campaign of 1912 stirred up a lot of them. At headquarters I received scores of menacing letters and threats against Governor Wilson. Inexperienced as I was, I did not know that most crank letters are harmless. I was afraid that some irresponsible person might attempt to kill the Governor and I wanted to provide him with a bodyguard, but he objected.

While this was going on a crank in Milwaukee shot Roosevelt. The Colonel's escape from death was miraculous. The incident created a tremendous sensation. I decided to get a bodyguard for the Governor, whether he liked it or not.

But where could I find one who was unobtrusive, who had

good judgment, who was quick as lightning and a dead shot? In my perplexity I called Colonel House on the telephone and explained the situation. He recommended Bill McDonald, ex-captain of the Texas Rangers, as the ideal man for the job. I asked House to wire for Captain Bill, and the Captain came. He had started immediately after he got House's wire. There had been no time to pack anything, so all he brought with him was a spare shirt and two blue-barreled revolvers. I liked the Captain. He was lean and eagle-eyed. The hard pavements of New York bothered him. After he had been there about a week, he went to House and complained: 'Ed,' the Captain said, 'I get awful tired walking on these rocks.'

One day, when the Governor and Captain Bill were taking a walk, they came to a store window in which there was a news photograph of Mr. Wilson and the Captain entering a taxicab. They looked at the picture a moment and went on. Mr. Wilson told me that for the rest of their stroll Captain Bill appeared to be dispirited and out of sorts.

'What's the matter, Captain?' the Governor asked eventually.

'It's that picture in the store window,' said Captain Bill, gloomily. 'That photograph.'

'Why, what about it? Didn't you think it a good one?'

'It's not that,' the Captain replied. 'What worries me is that I didn't see that man when he took it.'

'I didn't either; but that makes no difference.'

'Yes, but it is my business to see things,' said the faithful Texan, 'and I missed him completely.'

Shortly after his inauguration, President Wilson made him United States Marshal for the northern district of Texas — a job that suited him perfectly.

When election day came around in November, Wilson was elected overwhelmingly. In the electoral college he carried forty states, with four hundred and thirty-five electoral votes; Roosevelt came next with six states and eighty-eight electoral votes, while Taft carried only two states — Vermont and Utah — with eight electoral votes.

In the election of Woodrow Wilson, the American people broke away from the narrow and cramping tradition that the high office of President is the peculiar perquisite of politicians and soldiers. No man of his type had ever before been at the head of the nation. He was a scholar, but not a recluse. He had the vision and knowledge of a sound-minded man who has read much and thought profoundly; yet, at the same time, he possessed the energy and practical sense of a man accustomed to large affairs.

After the election, I resumed my duties as president of the Hudson & Manhattan Railroad.

CHAPTER XII
THE FIRST WILSON CABINET

I

I HAD just finished lathering my face and was putting a fresh blade in a safety razor on the morning of February 1, 1913, when my servant came to the bathroom door and said that someone speaking for Mr. Wilson was on the telephone. It turned out to be the Secret Service man who had been sent from Washington to act as the President-elect's bodyguard. He informed me that Mr. Wilson was at the University Club, and asked if I would run over right away, as he would like to see me.

When I got there I was told that the Governor wanted me to go up to his room. It was the first time I had met him since election day, except for a brief moment at the annual dinner of the Southern Society in December.

He said that he was making up his Cabinet and that he would be very glad if I would accept a place in it as Secretary of the Treasury. He had a delightful way of putting things; he created the impression that by accepting this great honor I would be doing him a favor.

Colonel House had already told me that I was being considered for the Treasury, but I had not taken it seriously. Early in the campaign I had let the Governor know that, if he were elected, I did not expect or desire a political office, or favors of any kind. I meant it, and he knew that I meant it. So, when Mr. Wilson offered me a place in his Cabinet, I was surprised, though I felt that he would not have made the offer without having a good reason.

Moreover, I seriously doubted my own fitness for the place. It seemed to me that the Treasury Department, with its complicated technical problems, should be managed by a man of long experience in banking and finance. Also there was another reason — a personal one — for my hesitation. I was not wealthy, and I knew that the twelve-thousand-dollar a year salary of a Cabinet officer would not go far in meeting the necessary expenses of such an elevated and spacious position.

But I was flattered by his offer. I appreciated his confidence in me, and I made that moment the opportunity for saying so. 'But you know, Governor,' I said, 'that I am neither a banker nor a financier.'

'I don't want a banker or a financier,' he exclaimed. 'The Treasury is not a bank. Its activities are varied and extensive. What I need is a man of all-round ability who has had wide business experience. I know you have the necessary qualifications.'

He paused a moment while I sat reflecting on what I had better do. 'We must enact a new tariff bill and a new currency or banking measure to fulfill our platform pledges,' he went on to say. 'The Treasury will have to play an important part in this legislation. It would relieve my mind to have you in charge of that department.'

I referred to our conversation at Princeton in 1911, when I had told him that I did not care for a public office and I said, 'I hope you do not feel under obligation to offer me anything.'

'No; it's not a matter of obligation,' the Governor replied. 'I remember our conversation distinctly, but the responsibilities of the Presidency are great and I cannot perform them alone. If I can't have the assistance of those in whom I have confidence, what am I to do?'

'Of course, Governor,' I said, 'if you feel that way about it, I shall be glad to accept. There is nothing on earth that I wouldn't do for you and for the success of your administration.'

2

As I was leaving the club he remarked that there were difficulties in selecting a Cabinet, in getting the right men for the right places. He did not say anything else about the Cabinet, except that Mr. Bryan was to be the Secretary of State. I went away with the impression that he had not, up to that time, decided on any members of the new Cabinet except Bryan and myself. The Governor asked me to keep my talk with him strictly confidential except to the extent that I might be obliged to use it in closing up my business affairs and relieving myself of the presidency of the Hudson & Manhattan Company.

I have always believed that no one should seek a Cabinet position. It is entirely different from an elective office where our system necessarily compels one to seek election at the hands of the people. A place in the Cabinet implies a very intimate and confidential relation to the President, and it has always seemed to me extremely indelicate for anyone to try to push himself into such a position.

However, in politics there is, as a rule, little delicacy of feeling where selfish ambition and desire for place are concerned. Governor Wilson was besieged by friends of candidates for places in his Cabinet. He wanted to give careful consideration to all the suggestions, but obviously he could not make inquiries himself about individuals without great embarrassment. Someone had to do this for him. Who more competent and discreet than the faithful House? Clearly he was the friend to whom he could turn and to whom he did turn.

House had therefore an important part in making the Cabinet. I do not mean to say that he actually selected any one of the department heads — for Governor Wilson would not have turned over the prerogative of the President to another person — but I do mean that Colonel House, moving outside the periphery of official life, was better situated than the Governor to look into the merits and capacities of those who were being considered. His function was to see and hear and to give the President-elect the benefit of his judgment. During the four months between the election and the inauguration, I saw a good deal of him. We became good friends.

House's coöperation and unselfish interest were invaluable to the President and the administration, not only during this formative period of Democratic control, but also later on, when we were confronted by the perplexing problems of the World War. He possessed an extraordinary political clairvoyance, a subtle feeling for the inwardness of events and the drifts of public opinion.

Soon after the election he told me that he was investigating a number of men, at Governor Wilson's request, for places in the Cabinet, and that he wanted to get the benefit of my judgment. Now and then he would invite me to his apartment to meet somebody or other. It was a matter of impressions — the kind of snapshot that one man gets of another in an hour's talk.

There was no doubt, from the beginning, that William Jennings Bryan was to be the Secretary of State. His distinguished position in the party and his great service to Mr. Wilson at Baltimore and during the campaign entitled him to recognition. But over and beyond all that, there was a manifest political advantage in having him in the Cabinet. A very large element of the Democratic Party stood squarely behind Bryan. His coöperation with the Administration meant the smoothing-out of many diverse views about the currency and the tariff.

As for the rest of the Cabinet there were many possible choices; so many, indeed, that Mr. Wilson did not decide on the last one of his official family until his inauguration day was close at hand.

Albert S. Burleson, of Texas, was made Postmaster-General on the recommendation of Colonel House. He had been long in public life, as a representative in Congress, and he knew the mechanism of governmental administration thoroughly. Although he had not been for Wilson in the Texas Democratic Convention — which sent a solid Wilson delegation to Baltimore — Burleson was allowed to go as an alternate delegate at large. His delegate stayed home, and Burleson went in his place. He had a seat in the Texas delegation at Baltimore, and he had been loyal to Wilson throughout those trying days.

Men in politics often possess a histrionic sense. There is, in fact, a lot of unconscious play-acting, not only in politics, but among people in every sphere of life. Shakespeare was right when he wrote: 'All the world's a stage, and all the men and women merely players.' Burleson acted the part of a homely, uncouth politician, which he was not. In reality he was a gentleman of education and ability. But he had a slovenly way of dressing. His clothes were frequently rumpled and rusty. I think he intended to create the effect that he was no better than the humblest citizen of the republic. The effort was successful.

One day House told me that he was thinking of recommending David F. Houston, of Missouri, for Secretary of Agriculture. It happened that I had never heard of Houston, although he had a wide reputation in university circles as an economist. At that time he was the Chancellor of Washington University, of St. Louis. House had known him a long time; had become acquainted with him in Texas, where Houston served for some years as President of the State University. I was invited to meet him at House's apartment, which was just then one of the most important spots on the political map of the United States.

My first impression of Houston was disappointing. He was cold and uncommunicative, and his personality was not engaging. Despite his taciturnity, I felt that he was a man of intellectual force and solid information. I did not consider him a progressive, in the political sense. He seemed to me to be a conservative of a rather conventional pattern. I thought that he would be out of place and somewhat at odds with the liberal Democrats of the incoming administration.

When my opinion was asked, I said merely that I did not think Houston would bring any political support to the President; also, that as far as I could learn he was not in contact with the farmers throughout the country and, therefore, did not enjoy their confidence; and it seemed to me that, for this particular place, it would be better for the President to select some man of distinction in the agricultural world. As I saw that House was thoroughly convinced of Houston's fitness for the post of Secretary of Agriculture, I said no more. The Colonel's judgment, I felt, was worth more than mine, as he knew Houston better than I did.

Franklin K. Lane, who was placed at the head of the Department of the Interior, was another man suggested by Colonel House. He was from California. President Roosevelt had appointed him a member of the Interstate Commerce Commission and he had made a fine record. He was a Democrat, though many leading Democrats considered his political orthodoxy a little doubtful. Mr. Wilson did not know Lane personally, and, for some reason or other, they did not meet until the day before the inauguration, when Lane went up and introduced himself.

Lane was plump, well fed and well groomed. He had a jolly look and he was charming socially. He loved to go out to dinners; I thought that he impaired his strength and usefulness by too much social life.

House told me that the Governor had decided on Newton D. Baker, then Mayor of Cleveland, as Secretary of the Interior before the post was offered to Lane. At the Governor's request, House invited Baker to come to New York and talk it over. He declined the appointment on the ground that he was needed in Cleveland as the mayor of a reform administration.

3

It is a pity that Mr. Wilson's ardent desire to give Louis D. Brandeis a place in his Cabinet was buried under an avalanche of invective and depreciation.

Brandeis is a humanitarian; an idealist, but not a dreamer, for no man living has a firmer grasp of business or of economic actualities. He has an unusual capacity for looking at civilization objectively, as if he were not a part of it, and reducing its activities and results to the common denominator of human welfare.

The Governor had Brandeis on the slate as Secretary of Commerce. When the news came out he was deluged with protests. A crowd of politicians invaded Princeton for the purpose of denouncing Brandeis as a radical, an irresponsible meddler with the sacred traditions, a misty-minded scarecrow who would surely frighten away the hoped-for Democratic prosperity if he had anything to do with the Department of Commerce.

Mr. Wilson took no stock in these aspersions; he did not believe them for a moment, and he kept Brandeis' name on the Cabinet list. But the anti-Brandeis movement spread from New England over the rest of the country. It was plainly an organized campaign to keep this forward-looking progressive out of the Cabinet. Five days before his inauguration the Governor concluded that, in the interest of harmony, he had better put another man in the Commerce post and hold Brandeis in reserve for something else. Such a tremendous hullabaloo had been raised in business circles that the appointment of Brandeis as Secretary of Commerce might have had, in fact, a harmful psychological effect.

With Brandeis out of consideration, and the inauguration at hand, it looked as if we might go to Washington minus a Secretary of Commerce. While House and I were talking over the situation, the name of William C. Redfield, of Brooklyn, came up as a possible choice. He appeared to me to possess some strong elements of availability. Redfield was an executive in a large manufacturing concern, and was considered by all who knew him as a business man of experience and capacity. He had served as a member of Congress, where he had a reputation as a tariff specialist. He not only knew a great deal about that complicated subject, but he had a faculty of presenting very dry and dreary tariff information in digestible form. I was favorably impressed by him. Governor Wilson agreed with House and myself as to Redfield's qualifications, and he was appointed.

Redfield wore side-whiskers, ruddy in hue and sedate in pattern. He seemed the very image of cautious mercantilism, safe investments, and industrial peace. Radicals and side-whiskers do not go together. Redfield looked somewhat as George F. Baker, the great financier, must have looked in his younger days. Those who had fallen into fury at the thought of Brandeis had no more to say.

Colonel House had me up to his apartment one day to meet James C. McReynolds, whom he was considering for Attorney-General. Mr. Wilson's first choice for that post was A. Mitchell Palmer, but there was so much opposition to Palmer's appointment that the Governor ceased to think of it, and wrote down Palmer's name for Secretary of War. When Palmer was consulted, he said that as he was a Quaker and therefore a pacifist he could not consistently be at the head of a department devoted to war.

House considered McReynolds a progressive; in fact, he believed him to be somewhat radical. House's opinion — as he explained it to me — was based largely on the fact that McReynolds, as an Assistant Attorney-General in the Taft

Administration, had carried on the government's prosecution against the tobacco monopoly. On the other hand, he was entirely without prominence in the Democratic Party; he was not widely known; and he had not achieved any outstanding distinction as a lawyer.

Shortly after McReynolds became Attorney-General the President discovered that he did not get along smoothly in harness with others. He appeared to lack the coöperative spirit, and he became unpopular with the leading members of the Senate and the House. This was unfortunate, and it distressed the President.

McReynolds served only a year and five months in the Cabinet. In August, 1914, President Wilson elevated him to the Supreme Court as an associate justice. He was succeeded as Attorney-General by Thomas W. Gregory, of Texas, who was at the time of his appointment an Assistant Attorney-General under McReynolds. In that position he had made a first-class record.

Gregory was a modest man, without even the touch of vanity that most people ordinarily possess. One day, just before the President named him as Attorney-General, I met him and, in course of conversation, I told him that the President was considering him, and that he would probably be put in McReynolds' place.

He looked surprised. 'I don't consider myself suitable,' he said diffidently.

'Why not?' I asked.

'Well,' he replied, 'it's a big job. Anyway' — he paused a moment — 'I'm all right where I am.'

I assured him that he had all the qualities, the knowledge and the experience to make an excellent Cabinet officer.

'But there's another thing,' Gregory said diffidently. 'You know I am a little deaf. Sometimes I have to ask people to repeat their remarks. That might be embarrassing at Cabinet meetings.'

He was only slightly deaf, in fact. His lack of egotism was, I thought, extraordinary. He made an excellent Attorney-General and was a valued member of the Cabinet.

In the evenings, when he was in the company of congenial people, he liked to tell amusing stories. He knew hundreds

PRESIDENT WILSON AND HIS CABINET, 1913

Left to right: The President; McAdoo, Treasury; McReynolds, Attorney-General; Daniels, Navy; Bryan, State; Houston, Agriculture; Wilson, Labor; Garrison, War; Redfield, Commerce; Burleson, Postmaster-General; Lane, Interior

of them, and he used to tell them with an unusual sense of mimicry.

For the head of the Navy Department the Governor selected Josephus Daniels, of North Carolina. This was done, I think, on the suggestion of William Jennings Bryan. Daniels was well known as a loyal Wilson man who had done splendid work during the campaign as publicity director of the National Committee.

Daniels was ridiculed throughout his entire term without justification. Colonel House says that when Walter H. Page heard of Daniels' appointment, he (Page) remarked that it was just too bad, or words to that effect. 'You do not seem to think that Daniels is Cabinet timber,' House remarked. Page replied: 'He is hardly a splinter.'

It was easy for Page to say that, but the result showed that he did not know what he was talking about. The navy went through the World War under Daniels' direction; it has never been, at any period of its history, more efficient, yet its excellent record did not silence Daniels' critics. The President used to say that the vilification of Daniels emanated wholly, he thought, from disappointed contractors who found the stream of easy money dried up when Daniels was put in charge of the department.

The appointment of William B. Wilson as Secretary of Labor appeared to please almost everybody; at any rate, I do not recall any diatribes against him. Wilson's life had been one of hard realities. He had begun, as a mere boy, in the Pennsylvania coal mines, and had risen by degrees to a high position in the councils of organized labor. He was a level-headed, able, and trustworthy man, and had made a creditable record as a member of Congress.

The post of Secretary of War was still open on the first of March, after A. Mitchell Palmer, conscientious Quaker, had declined it. The President-elect asked his secretary, Joseph P. Tumulty, to suggest somebody. Tumulty says, in 'Woodrow Wilson As I Knew Him' (p. 138):

I informed the President that I would suggest the name of someone within a few hours. I then went to the library in my home in New Jersey and in looking over the Lawyer's Diary I ran across the name of Lindley Garrison, who at the time was vice-chancellor of the State of New Jersey. Mr. Garrison was a resident of my home town and although I had only met him casually and had tried a few cases before him, he had made a deep impression upon me as a high type of equity judge.

Mr. Tumulty goes on to say that he telephoned Garrison's name to Governor Wilson, who already knew him by reputation. Thereupon Chancellor Garrison was summoned, and to his surprise, a place in the Cabinet descended upon him like manna from heaven. He walked in as Lindley M. Garrison, a little-known but worthy citizen, and he walked out as Secretary of War Garrison, with the bugles blowing and the flags waving, and the guns throbbing.

Some of these selections were not fortunate, and a year later the President was sorry that he had made them. The judging of men is difficult at its best. When it happens to be entangled in a web of extraneous political considerations, it becomes frequently a matter of luck.

4

The day after I saw Governor Wilson and accepted his offer of the Treasury portfolio, I received a telegram from Knoxville saying that my mother, then in her eighty-first year, was critically ill. When I arrived at Knoxville, she was in a coma; I am not sure she recognized me. As I took her pallid white hand and leaned over with my face close to hers and said, 'Don't you know me, mother?' I thought I felt a slight pressure of her fingers.

There was nothing to do but sit quietly by and see her die. I cannot write of this event. When I think of her warm and noble heart, my eyes are misty. It was all long ago, yet I remember her so clearly that she seems to be here with me now.

5

Any notary public is empowered to administer the oath of office to a member of the Cabinet, and the ceremony is about as impressive as the swearing in of an income tax return. Some of the men in the new Cabinet who came from states which were represented in the membership of the Supreme

Court conceived the idea that they would like to have the justice from their state administer the oath instead of a notary public. I decided to invite Charles Evans Hughes, then an associate justice, to officiate at my assumption of office. Mr. Hughes graciously consented, and I was sworn in by him.

The Secretary's room in the Treasury Building is large and dignified. It is on the second floor, a corner room overlooking the White House grounds and Potomac Park. I have not been in it for some years, but when I was its occupant the rigid austerity of its walls was softened by long blue velvet curtains at the tall windows, and by handsomely framed portraits of former Secretaries of the Treasury. On the floor was an Oriental rug. The furniture of the office — the wide desk, the dark leather-covered chairs — looked as if it had come from the president's room of any large and wealthy bank.

The room was full of people — my invited friends, the higher officials of the Treasury, the heads of bureaus and divisions, and Mr. Justice Hughes. The brief ceremony over, they departed, shaking hands and murmuring polite phrases about good luck.

When I found myself alone in the big, quiet room a feeling of desolation came over me, and, as I stood looking out of the window across the spacious Park lawns, these lines flowed into my memory:

> I feel like one who treads alone
> Some banquet hall deserted,
> Whose lights are fled, whose garlands dead,
> And all but he departed.

There was no sensible reason why I should have been depressed at that moment, but how can one govern one's formless and unbidden moods? I was like a sea captain who finds himself standing on the deck of a ship that he has never seen before. I did not know the mechanism of my ship; I did not know my officers — even by sight — and I had no acquaintance with any of the crew. Within me there was a gray emptiness and a nebulous fear that, after all, I might always continue to be remote from the intricate machinery of the department. The thought of passing my official existence as a figurehead distressed me. It would naturally be distressing to any one of my temperament. I resolved that, no matter what happened, my hand would be on the steering-wheel — that is, as soon as I could find out where the steering-wheel was.

I was beginning the busiest and most strenuous period of my life. I hardly realized that fact; nor did I realize that I was starting out on a career where every casual gesture is given an exaggerated importance and intensity. However, I soon learned that I could not buy a railroad ticket or talk to a man in the street without an esoteric meaning being attached to my action.

That same day I appointed as my private secretary Byron R. Newton, of New York, whom I have already mentioned in a previous chapter; and as confidential clerk William J. Martin, who had been on my staff while I was president of the Hudson & Manhattan Company.

One of the first things to be done was to sign the Secretary's mail. There was a huge pile of letters on my desk and now and then a clerk would bring in more. I hesitated to sign my name to letters that I knew nothing about. The correspondence of the department is so huge that many letters have to be prepared for the Secretary's signature by the various heads of bureaus and divisions.

While I was turning over these documents gingerly and wondering what to do, John Kieley was introduced. He had a peculiar and interesting job. It was his business to keep himself informed about everything that was going on in the department, and he had come in to explain my mail to me. He knew perfectly what every one of the letters was about. When I asked him questions about this and that, with my pen poised in hand over an unsigned letter, he would give me not only the reason for writing that particular letter, but also the history of the subject with which it had to do. He was a wonderfully efficient man. Toward the end of my term, I made him my private secretary. He is still in the Treasury as one of Mr. Mellon's assistants.

The burning question of patronage was the first and the most pressing matter with which I had to deal. For sixteen years the Democrats had been out of office, and it was natural that thousands of them in all parts of the country should expect recognition. Prior to President Wilson's administration, each President in person had handled the patronage question. I do not know how they ever managed to do it and give proper attention to their exacting duties.

There was nothing that President Wilson disliked so much as picking men for office. Immediately after he was inaugurated, we discussed this subject and I suggested that he relieve himself of the burden by placing on his various Cabinet officers the responsibility for making recommendations in their respective departments. I urged this as good organization from a business point of view, because the heads of departments ought to know better than anybody else who is best qualified to fill positions in their departments, and I also commended it as the proper and wise way to take from the President the burden of investigation and selection so that his energies could be released for the more important work. He was delighted with the suggestion and adopted it immediately.

Under this plan the Cabinet officers would make the recommendations, but since all presidential nominations must be confirmed by the Senate, it was necessary to consult the Democratic senators of the states from or in which the appointments were to be made.

Perhaps I ought to explain how a single senator can prevent the confirmation of a person nominated by the President. Patronage is, and always has been, regarded by the senators and the members of Congress as of great value to them in building up party organizations in their states and districts. They are jealous, therefore, of their right to be consulted and of their power to reject nominations. Every senator wants to control the situation in his own state and by common consent they all act together for mutual protection. It is a sort of club in which an immutable rule prevails. That rule is that when a senator says that a nomination made by the President is 'personally obnoxious' to him (and he doesn't have to give any reasons unless he wants to), the nomination will be rejected.

This custom, or tradition of the Senate — for it has become a traditional usage — is fundamentally bad. President Lowell, of Harvard, says that the great outstanding vice of American politics is log-rolling. Whenever I think of the log-rolling that I saw at first hand while I was in office, I am convinced that President Lowell is right. Senatorial courtesy, so-called, often leads to unfortunate results — to the rejection of efficient men and the appointment of the less worthy. But I do not see how the system can be changed with advantage. It would not do to give the President the unrestricted power of appointment, for it might be used arbitrarily or corruptly. Senatorial ratification of the President's selections is, in spite of its defects, better than the only possible alternative. The outstanding vice of the system is that a single senator, standing alone, is able to block an appointment, if the appointment is to be made in his state, or if the appointee is a citizen of his state. The system of senatorial approval would be bettered greatly, I think, if it were done by a majority vote, or a two-thirds vote.

The members of the House of Representatives were not willing that the senators alone should have a voice in the selection of these numerous federal officials, and a good many years ago — I don't know how long, but it certainly is established custom now — the members of the House and Senate came to an agreement with each other under which all post-masters are conceded to be 'congressional patronage,' by which it is meant that Congressmen shall make the recommendations. All other officers of the government are conceded to be 'senatorial patronage,' the recommendations to be made by senators.

Under this arrangement I found that the presidential appointments in the Treasury came under the head of senatorial patronage. This brought me into close contact with all the Democratic senators, and it was by no means an easy job to smooth out the innumerable difficulties which were always coming up; for instance, where there were two Democratic senators from a state, it sometimes happened that they were unfriendly to each other and could not agree upon the candidate. How could I discriminate between them in my recommendations to the President? The only thing to do in such cases was to try to find somebody upon whom they could agree. In states where there were no Democratic senators, it was customary to consult the Democratic national committeeman.

President Wilson began his administration by establishing

a rule that the members of the Cabinet should get opinions on appointees from Republican as well as from Democratic senators. This was an unheard-of procedure, and it revealed — as hardly anything else could so effectively — the generosity of the President's mind. After trying it out for about two years he abandoned the practice. It wouldn't work. We found that the Republican senators sometimes recommended the most incapable man on the list. Why? I don't know. Your guess is as good as mine.

6

The country as a whole looked upon the new Cabinet as a collection of mediocrities. This widespread opinion was created and nourished by the Republican press, which included then, as it does now, most of the wealthy and powerful newspapers in the United States. Not only the success of the Republican Party, but even its continued existence, depends on the fiction that it possesses the 'best minds.' On the numerous occasions when the emptiness of this shallow myth has been disclosed by the incapacity and wide-open corruption of Republican leaders, the newspapers of that party have been depended upon to elbow the ripening scandal gently into oblivion.

If the Republican Party has all the really good brains, then it follows as a matter of course that any Democratic Cabinet, if not actually deficient mentally, consists of adolescents and small peanut politicians.

As a matter of fact, the administration of Woodrow Wilson was responsible for more genuine constructive legislation in its eight years of existence than all the Republican administrations of the past fifty years. This is a fact that belongs to history; no Republican newspaper or Republican spokesman seriously tries to deny it. They simply say nothing about it, hoping that in time the voters will forget the great achievements of the Democratic Party under Wilson as well as the disgraceful incompetency of the Republicans under Harding. That is what they hope and expect; and, judging from my knowledge of the natural forgetfulness of mankind, I have an idea that their expectations will be realized.

The weak point of the Wilson Cabinet, it seemed to me, was not in the essential qualities of ability, knowledge, and initiative, but in the matter of political prestige. Most of its members were unknown to the country, and were without political experience or following. From the beginning I saw clearly that the Cabinet would be unable to give the President the effective support which he needed to meet the strenuous opposition that was certain to confront the Administration.

Bryan was the only one of the entire list who had a large and compact following. Burleson was a man of considerable influence among his former colleagues in the House of Representatives, where he had been an important figure, but he was not well known nationally.

William B. Wilson, the Secretary of Labor, was highly regarded by the laboring classes, and was strongly supported by the leading union labor organizations. Franklin K. Lane had some following, but not much, on the Pacific Coast. The rest of the Cabinet, including myself, possessed a very limited political influence. Mine amounted only to what I had acquired in my association with the presidential campaign.

CHAPTER XIII

THE ADMINISTRATION GETS TO WORK

I

THERE was an informal meeting of the Cabinet the next day after the inauguration. We assembled in the Cabinet room of the Executive Offices, adjoining the White House, and were there about ten minutes before the President arrived. The time was spent in getting acquainted with each other. I knew three of my fellow members — Bryan, Daniels, and Burleson — fairly well; and, of course, I knew Redfield, who had served at the National Democratic Headquarters during the campaign. McReynolds, Lane, and Houston were almost complete strangers to me; I had met them casually only once or twice, and as for William B. Wilson and Garrison — I had never seen them until the day before.

The President came in, shook hands all around, and took his seat at the head of the table. He said that he looked forward with genuine pleasure to his association with us in the great opportunity that was offered for service to the country; and that he hoped each member of the Cabinet would feel that he could, at all times, express himself with absolute frankness on any questions that might arise. He said he thought it ought to be understood that all discussions in the Cabinet should be confidential, and that if anything was to be made public about proceedings of Cabinet meetings that he, himself, should be the spokesman.

No minutes are kept of discussions in the Cabinet. The talk is informal, and of course many immature ideas come out, such as plans and proposals which would be withdrawn after riper consideration. President Wilson talked before the Cabinet without reserve, relying on the implicit pledge of confidence which was supposed to bind all of us to secrecy. It went on all right for a few months; then we began to see references in various newspapers to what had been said at Cabinet meetings.

In December, 1913, some measures — I do not recall what

they were — which had been the subject of discussion in the Cabinet were commented on in the newspapers in such a way that there could be no doubt of a leakage of information. Secretary Houston, at one of the Cabinet meetings, brought up the matters which the newspapers had been discussing with apparent authenticity. In his 'Eight Years with Wilson's Cabinet,' Houston refers to this incident, and goes on to say that he knew 'one or two members of the Cabinet' had been talking too freely about 'matters of a non-departmental nature in respect to which he (the President) had to assume the immediate responsibility.' I have always thought it rather unjust on Houston's part to say that one or two members were guilty of indiscretion without naming the men, as his comment reflected on us all.

Upon hearing Houston's remark, the President took advantage of the opportunity to repeat, quite pointedly, what he had said at the first Cabinet meeting about the confidential nature of our discussions. He said that he wanted to advise with the Cabinet freely and fully, but that he could not do so unless the rule of confidence was kept inviolate.

Everyone agreed that the President was right. Mr. Bryan then said that he had never given anything to the press about the Cabinet discussions. I followed with the same assurance, and each member of the Cabinet said the same thing until Lane was reached. He admitted that he had given out some information, and he went on to say that he would not have done it if he had thought that what he had told the newspaper reporters was a matter of importance. He said he was sorry, and that it would not happen again. The rest of the Cabinet, following Lane, denied having said anything.

2

At the first opportunity I had a long talk with the President about the questions of the tariff and the currency. In respect to the tariff, the Democratic Party was bound by its platform to effect a downward revision, but in dealing with it as a practical problem, the leaders of the party realized that the American high tariff system had existed so long that it had become an accepted part of our industrial life.

The Democratic Administration was like a man who finds himself in possession of a house that has been built wrong. He contemplates its badly shaped rooms, its dark halls, its insufficient plumbing, and its poor lighting, and wonders what to do. Manifestly, it would be unwise to tear the building down because he doesn't like it. If he is a sensible man, he sends for an architect and a plumber and sets them to work with the idea of improving the house.

The platform of the Democratic Party embodied that thought in a paragraph:

> We recognize that our system of tariff taxation is intimately connected with the business of the country, and we favor the ultimate attainment of the principles we advocate by legislation that will not injure or destroy legitimate industry.

The architects of the new tariff measure were Oscar W. Underwood, Chairman of the Ways and Means Committee of the House, where all revenue measures must originate, and Senator F. M. Simmons, Chairman of the Finance Committee of the Senate. These two committees have charge of tariff legislation. The President desired me to coöperate with these gentlemen in every way, and I did. The Treasury, as I suppose everyone knows, controls the official machinery for the collection of customs duties, and the department had a vast store of information as well as a staff of assistants who might have qualified as tariff experts.

A protective tariff was a part of Alexander Hamilton's financial system. It was intended, primarily, to protect infantile American manufacturing industries against foreign competition by putting a duty, or frontier tax, on imported commodities.

In other words, our tariff policy at the beginning was designed to support young and weak industries at the public expense. Now, that may be a good thing to do if the industry is a desirable one and of such a character that it is adapted to the American genius; but the theory falls to pieces if the protected industry never gets beyond the protective stage. I have no doubt that good oranges might be produced in Wisconsin, if grown in hothouses, at a cost of several dollars apiece. But would it be worth while for the people of Wisconsin, or of the United States, to encourage the orange-growing industry under such conditions?

The tariff raises the entire level of prices of the protected commodities, which means that the general public has to pay more for the necessaries of life than a similar community of consumers in a low-tariff country has to pay for the same articles. A high tariff increases the cost of living and builds up fortunes, running into the millions, for its beneficiaries — for the manufacturers who are protected by it. It is a general tax on the entire population for the benefit of private industry.

One of the effects of the tariff is not only an increased price for the imported article, on which a tariff is collected, but also an increased price for similar domestic articles. When a duty is put on watches, for example, what is really meant is that a license is given to every manufacturer in the United States to levy a tax on Americans who purchase watches. This is counterbalanced, to some extent, by the competition of American watchmakers with one another. But if they should happen to have a price-fixing understanding among themselves — and in numerous industries such secret agreements exist — then, in that case, they can put their prices to a point just below the tariff level and absolutely monopolize the domestic market on their own terms.

It is a common misconception that the protective tariff system is responsible for high wages. Even if it were true, it would apply only to the wages of workers in protected industries. Millions of clerks and other wage-earners get no direct benefit in the way of higher wages. Like the great body of consumers, they face a higher cost of living without a corresponding increase in income.

Edward P. Costigan, of Colorado — now a senator from that state — has a national reputation as a tariff expert. He was a member of the Tariff Commission, by appointment of President Wilson, and served continuously for ten years, through the administrations of Harding and Coolidge. In resigning from his post on March 14, 1928, as a protest against the high tariff, he wrote a remarkable letter in which he exposed many fallacies of the protective policy. Speaking of the effect of the tariff on wages he said, in part:

American wages, though relatively higher than foreign, are not in the main the consequence of protective tariffs, but rather of the remarkable skill with which human and other power has been applied to the enormously rich natural resources of the United States.

Even when wages are raised under a high tariff, the fact is deceptive; money wages may increase and real wages remain unaffected. Wages go up, but the price-level of all commodities goes up, too. What good is done by raising a man's wages from, let us say, thirty to forty dollars a week when the cost of living goes up in the same proportion?

The high tariff system is one of the chief causes — but not the only one — of the strikingly unequal distribution of wealth in the United States. Its direct benefits go to a very small minority of the American people; its indirect benefits reach, in one way or another, a wider circle; then we find that an enormous section of the population receives no benefits from it at all — or, if any, they are too microscopic to be discerned.

Consider the cotton farmer, for example. A high tariff does not increase the price of cotton as much as one cent a pound, but it makes the cotton farmer pay higher prices for his shoes and plows and pots and pans and his clothes and the glass in his windows — and, in fact, for virtually everything he and his family use in the way of manufactured articles. The same set of facts, and the same results, exist in the case of the wheat farmer and almost every other kind of farmer. Study the tariff awhile, and you will understand clearly why the farmer has to mortgage his farm. He is milked dry.

In the face of these fundamental objections, it may still be claimed that the protective tariff system has encouraged the investment of capital in untried fields, and has advanced the diversification of our industries. This would have come about anyway, in all probability. Our great wealth of resources and the technical genius of our people were certain, with or without tariffs, to have given us industrial independence within a reasonable period.

Even if we admit the desirability of protecting infant industries, the question is, how far should it go? A child needs protection, but ought one to coddle an infant after it has grown a beard, and is six feet tall, and has the muscles of a prize-fighter?

3

It is increasingly evident that more liberal trade throughout the world is indispensable to general prosperity. The dangers of international hostility culminating in war, growing out of international high tariffs, can hardly be exaggerated.

At the present time (I am writing early in 1931) more than forty nations have raised retaliatory and countervailing tariff walls against us because of the enactment of the Tariff Act of 1930. Clearly the natural flow of commerce is greatly impeded in consequence. The closing, or restriction, of our foreign markets keeps the surplus commodities of farms and factories within our gates and plays havoc with our domestic prices. No wonder that we are suffering from an unparalleled depression.

The situation is plain enough for anyone to see; yet a drastic reduction in tariff schedules, if put into effect all at once, would dislocate the entire structure of American commercial enterprise.

The only practicable method of getting the tariff down to a reasonable, justifiable economic level would be to spread the reduction over a considerable term of years; but the policy behind such a plan would have to be consistently maintained. That cannot be accomplished without the continued political success of a national party devoted to tariff reform. American political opinion is, however, so mercurial that it is almost impossible to realize continuity and consistency in such a policy.

Nevertheless, we should strive constantly to mitigate the evils of the high tariff on the one hand, and to distribute its benefits as equitably as possible on the other.

In doing this, it would help greatly if an immutable rule could be established that, in all tariff legislation, duties will be granted solely on the ground of demonstrated economic justification. Why would it not be wise for the Congress to establish by law a requirement that every industry, acting direct or through an association or attorney or representative, shall, within thirty days before any session of the Congress from which it intends to seek tariff increases or benefits, file with the Ways and Means Committee of the

House and with the Tariff Commission a formal application therefor, containing:

1. A complete schedule of the rates applied for and a full statement of the grounds upon which the applicant justifies the request.
2. An estimate of the amount of increased earnings, gross and net, which the industry expects to receive if the higher tariff duties are granted.
3. A statement of the proportion of such increased net earnings which the industry intends to pass along to its employees, in addition to the wage scale in effect when the proposed legislation is enacted, as labor's just share thereof.

The data in items 1 and 2 should be checked by the Tariff Commission, perhaps aided by an alert and able people's counsel, intent on resisting, except on a showing of national advantage, the use of the government's taxing powers for private benefit; and the Commission's findings should be presented to and considered by the committees of Congress before any law is enacted. The filing of the petition and the findings of the Tariff Commission should be given to the public through the newspapers.

It should be provided in the law that a certain percentage of the increased profits resulting to the manufacturer shall be paid to its wage-earners and employees, in addition to the wage scale prevailing on the date when the law is approved by the President.

It may be asked how labor's share is to be determined. The law might provide that this shall be decided by a joint committee of the owners of the industry and its wage-earners, and in case of disagreement, that arbitration shall be resorted to.

The law should also provide that no applications for increased tariff duties shall be considered unless filed in accordance with the rules prescribed in the statute.

Under this procedure the country would be notified in advance of each session of the Congress of the names of those seeking tariff benefits, the schedules of the proposed rates, and the grounds upon which increased tariff duties are sought. The impartial investigation and report of the Tariff Commission would be of great value to the members of Congress in the discussion of the question.

There is not the least doubt that, under the prevailing

method of enacting tariff measures, increased duties are frequently granted to favored industries as a reward for contributions made by them, either directly or indirectly, to the successful political party. Tariff schedules are usually so intricate that only experts can understand them, and this situation leads to all sorts of trickiness and concealment. You may be sure that the technical details are so framed that the beneficiary is enabled to take out of the pockets of the American people many times more than his contribution to the campaign chest.

The practice of permitting favor-seeking industries to write their own schedules is a scandal of the first magnitude. The proposed procedure should put an end to it.

4

General Winfield Scott Hancock—bluff, unsubtle soldier—was a candidate for President fifty years ago. Somebody who was listening to one of his speeches heckled him about the tariff, and the General, tangled in a bog of unfamiliar verbiage, asserted that 'the tariff is a local issue.'

Local issue! His statement appeared in the newspapers and was received with a lot of good-humored laughter; and with more than a lot of ill-humored scorn. The General's campaign was ridiculed into oblivion. Long afterward his idea of the tariff as a local issue was held against him as a comic example of an addle-headed soldier's state of mind. He may have died, for all I know, in the belief that he had committed a ridiculous blunder.

Well, the tariff *is* a local issue. If there is anything more local than the tariff I have never encountered it. Nine tenths of the arguments that were so vehemently brought out when the Underwood-Simmons Tariff Bill was being discussed were not only local in outlook, but also incredibly narrow and selfish. Everybody wanted something for himself, for his local industry, and hardly any of the manufacturers or their paid agents who appeared before the committee seemed to think of the nation at large.

Consumers are never represented at these hearings. The testimony comes almost altogether from those who have axes to grind, and extravagantly inaccurate statements are made, and go unchallenged, as to the relative costs of production in this country and abroad. During those months of controversy and conflicting evidence, I learned that the great majority of men conceive the state simply as a projection of their own personal interests.

The cheese manufacturers declared that the country was going to the dogs because it was proposed to lower the duty on cheese; and the cotton-mill owners threw up their hands in horror on account of the attempt to reduce the tariff on cotton cloth. They claimed that without a duty they could not compete with the English factories. Their argument was not easy to understand; our factories — many of them, at least — stand among the cotton fields, while the English mills are obliged to ship their raw cotton from America to England, and send back the finished product.

The woolen mills made a tremendous fight. If we should make a material reduction in their schedule, their managers declared that they would be sunk. We could not turn around without stepping on somebody's toes. Herbert Spencer's definition of a tragedy was 'a generalization slain by a fact.' If Mr. Spencer had been a spectator of the tariff battle in 1913, he would have thought that he was witnessing a massacre. Dead generalizations lay all over the field.

There was the sugar situation, for instance. Sugar is produced at a lower cost in Cuba, in Porto Rico, and in the Philippines than in the United States. Why not admit sugar into the United States duty free? As it happens to be a universal household necessity, the complete relinquishment of the sugar duty would be of direct benefit to every American family.

The sugar planters of Louisiana wept on our shoulders. They declared, and supported their assertions by figures, that Louisiana would fade away and expire if the duty was dropped. The difference between affluence and poverty lay in the one or two cents a pound that the existing tariff imposed on foreign sugar. The beet-sugar industry joined in the protest. But, as the inquiry went on, we learned that a substantial part of the Far Western beet-sugar growers and refiners did not need any protection; they were able to compete with anybody. If the Administration protected the sugar industry at all, it would be just so much clear profit for them.

5

The tariff bill was finally brought in and passed on October 3, 1913. It embodied, on the whole, a lower and more rational tariff. Wool was admitted free, and sugar also — but the duty was to be taken off sugar gradually over a two-and-a-half-year period, in order to give the sugar people an opportunity to adjust themselves to the new conditions. The lowering of the sugar tariff went only partially into effect. The World War came on, and Congress voted to retain the duty as a revenue measure.

Sugar prices at present are ruinously low, in part because the tariff against imported Cuban sugar operates, in the way of a huge tariff subsidy, to stimulate the production of sugar in America's island possessions — in Porto Rico, Hawaii, and most notably in the Philippine Islands — in which cheap labor, as in Cuba, produces the sugar crop.

The fact that sugar produced in our island possessions is admitted to the United States duty free while Cuban sugar must pay a duty of two cents a pound draws a flood of Oriental sugar into the American market to depress prices and make the lot of United States sugar producers definitely worse. Or, to say it more concisely, the present sugar tariff has defeated its own purpose.

The Underwood-Simmons Bill was, on the whole, an unusually sound and reasonable tariff measure. It was intelligently framed by men of ability and integrity, wholly free of selfish interest. It is a pity that the World War prevented a test, under normal conditions, of the economic ideas embodied in the new tariff. I have always felt that such a test would have demonstrated the wisdom of that measure and that it would have exerted a permanent influence for good upon all future tariff legislation, to say nothing of the benefits that would have resulted to all the people from a more rational tariff level than that which exists at the present time.

The Sixteenth Amendment to the Constitution, which authorized a federal tax on incomes, was ratified early in 1913. A provision for an income tax was added as an amendment to the Underwood-Simmons Tariff Bill and went into effect with the new tariff. Income taxes were expected to take up the deficiency in the revenue which would result from smaller customs receipts.

The drop in customs receipts was considerably less than we had anticipated. During the year ended June 30, 1913, the Treasury received $318,000,000 from customs duties. Our statisticians and tariff experts figured that, under the lower tariff, receipts would fall to $270,000,000. They didn't. The Treasury income from the customs for the year ended June 30, 1914, was $292,000,000; and the government collected $71,000,-000 of income taxes.

The growth in income tax receipts is one of the marvels of government finance. For the year ended June 30, 1929, there was paid into the Treasury a total of $2,331,000,000 as income taxes — of which $1,095,541,000 came from individual incomes and $1,235,733,000 from corporations.

During the same year the receipts from customs (net) amounted to $583,686,000.

The receipts from the income tax — including individual and corporation taxes — now amount to fifty-eight per cent of the total revenue of the federal government.

6

Any man who faces a problem in life, or an event, has within himself an attitude — often unrevealed — that is peculiarly his own. Outwardly he may take on the color of his surroundings, he may melt into the current purpose of his time, but in his deeper self he retains his own way of thinking and his own inclinations. These inner impelling motives make people different from one another. Two men may do the same thing in precisely the same way, yet their objectives may not be at all alike.

The Secretary of the Treasury is obliged to follow a prescribed formula. I did. I carried out the formula, but at the same time I endeavored to soften the cold, hard opulence of the Treasury. I wanted to give it a touch of human warmth, to make it a people's Treasury instead of a bankers' Treasury.

As the keeper of the nation's money, the Treasury is surrounded by many safeguards. Not even the President, or the

Secretary of the Treasury, can draw out a cent of Treasury funds without the authority of an act of Congress and a lot of bookkeeping and paper-stamping. This is, of course, as it should be, but at times I was exasperated by the inflexibility of the appropriations made by Congress and the circumlocution encountered in meeting the most obvious emergency.

I shall give an example of what I mean. In March, 1913, so soon after my induction into office that I still lost my way when I walked in the corridors of the Treasury Building, a great storm swept over the Ohio valley. The city of Dayton suffered greatly from the ensuing flood. There were rivers of muddy water in the streets, and thousands of people were marooned in their homes. The Dayton local authorities, or some other representative body of citizens, appealed to me, as head of the Treasury Department, to send lifeboats from the Great Lakes to Dayton to aid in the work of rescue. Most of my readers know, I presume, that the Life Saving Service — now the Coast Guard Service — is one of the bureaus of the Treasury.

I sent for the superintendent of the Life Saving Service, and told him that I wanted every available lifeboat on the Great Lakes forwarded at once to Dayton.

He gave me a look of dismay. 'We can't do it,' he said. 'Why not?'

'Because I have no appropriation for this purpose from Congress,' he answered. 'We might get an authorization from Congress if it were in session,' he went on to say, 'but it won't be in session for some weeks yet.'

'Well, I want the boats sent anyway. It's an emergency that admits of no delay.'

'I can't do it, Mr. Secretary,' said the superintendent. 'Under the law, it would be an offense for which I could be sent to jail.'

The bureaucratic mind is an interesting phenomenon, but I did not stop at that time to reflect upon its peculiarities. I resolved to cut that piece of red-tape.

'All right,' I said. 'You send the boats to Dayton and I'll serve the jail sentence. I'll be responsible.'

The boats started from the Great Lakes forthwith. They did excellent life-saving work at Dayton, and I think the citizens of that community, and the whole country, were immensely pleased with our promptness.

Formality and red-tapism and a strict letter-of-the-law spirit are all right at times; at other times they are a nuisance and do nobody any good.

7

You may picture me, during those early weeks in office, as a learner as well as a director of affairs. I studied the technique of the Treasury, I got acquainted with hundreds of employees, I set out to learn what was being done and how it was being done.

One of my first official acts was to appoint John Skelton Williams, of Richmond, Virginia, Assistant Secretary of the Treasury, in charge of the fiscal bureaus.

Mr. Williams was a member of the old and well-known banking house of John L. Williams & Sons. I needed a man in the Treasury who understood business as well as finance. Williams was admirably equipped for the service. The compensation of an assistant secretary of the Treasury was the small salary of five thousand dollars a year.

He accepted the office, at my earnest solicitation, notwithstanding the serious sacrifices involved. They were serious, in earnest, for Mr. Williams had suffered heavy losses in the failure of the Seaboard Air Line system ten years before. When I offered him the place in the Treasury, he was endeavoring to build up his private fortune again, but he gave up his own enterprises cheerfully and became one of my invaluable assistants.

As another assistant secretary I chose Charles S. Hamlin, of Massachusetts. He had served as an Assistant Secretary of the Treasury under Mr. Carlisle during the second Cleveland Administration. Hamlin was a man of high character and a lawyer of ability.

About the middle of April, I learned, to my astonishment, that a private employee of the National City Bank of New York and of the Riggs National Bank of Washington had a desk in the office of the Comptroller of the Currency. This clerk was kept in the Treasury, in the pay of the two banks I have named, for the purpose of reporting on the business and transactions of the department.

It was irregular and improper, of course. The fact that such a situation had been allowed to exist at all was an indication of the attitude of preceding administrations toward certain privileged banks, and to large financial interests in general. I promptly excluded this privately paid employee from the department and said, in a public statement, that the practice could not be permitted because it gave the favored banks an undue advantage in the way of advance information over all other banks in the country; that all must obtain information from the department in the regular way.

For many years — since 1896 — the national banks had not been required to pay interest on government deposits. I decided that they would have to pay at the rate of two per cent per annum. Practically all of them paid their ordinary depositors interest on daily balances — as much as three or four per cent — so it was difficult for me to understand why they should not pay interest to the government also. There was some argument over my ruling. The objections must have been flimsy and incomprehensible, for as I turn my memory back to that time, I confess that I cannot recall what they were.

At any rate, the interest ruling was put into effect on June 1, 1913. Only seven banks declined to accept government funds on these terms — three banks in New York City and four elsewhere. The National City Bank of New York was one of the three. The president of that institution, Frank A. Vanderlip, said he considered it 'unsound banking.' At various times during the past eighteen years I have thought of his remark, and have wondered what he meant, exactly. I am still wondering. If a national bank can afford to pay John Smith and Thomas Brown two per cent, or more, without wrecking the institution, what is 'unsound' about paying the government interest at the same rate on deposits of public money?

Our statisticians figured that if the banks had been required to pay two per cent on Treasury money for the sixteen years prior to 1913, the net revenues of the government would have been increased during this period by more than thirty million dollars.

CHAPTER XIV
THE NEED FOR CURRENCY REFORM

I

THE problem of maintaining a sound and stable monetary system is entangled in the most perplexing uncertainties, yet the essential elements of money are quite simple.

The government does not create values in issuing money. It is merely an agency through which actual existing values are turned into currency. Nevertheless, this truth — which is almost axiomatic in its soundness — is not clearly perceived by many people. Surging political movements have grown out of the erroneous notion that the government, by printing a piece of paper and calling it a dollar, can actually make it worth a dollar. The Greenback Party, in the 1870's and 80's, was founded on this error.

It is quite true that Congress has the power to call any worthless thing money by passing a law to that effect, but the law would not make it money in actuality. Neither the principles of economics nor the laws of nature can be changed by legislative process. You may call your dog a cat, if it pleases you to do so, but he would continue to be a dog, just the same.

Sound paper currency represents stored wealth. If it does not represent wealth in storage and subject to demand, then it is a fictitious and defective currency.

The stored wealth behind paper money may consist of gold or silver — or of bonds and securities, or commercial paper, or staple commodities; but in any event it is something of recognized value. To vitalize actual wealth and make it liquid and serviceable, by turning it into money (when money is required), is the fundamental idea behind all sound systems of national finance.

Credit and money are economic twins, and each of them is, in a sense, a function of the other.

Business concerns, as a rule, do not finance altogether their current operations. They resort to their credit at the bank. If they carried enough cash to finance themselves, it would

mean a large and unwieldy increase in their working capital;
and, in fact, such a policy would be economically unsound, for
at times they would be encumbered by a great deal of idle
money. Instead, they establish a 'line of credit' at a bank, and
the volume of loans ebbs and flows with the seasonal changes
in trade. Credit, to the average business enterprise, is therefore as important as cash in hand — and is, in the ordinary
course of events, equivalent to cash in hand.

A wholesale merchant, for example, sells his goods to re-
tailers on three or four months' time, but he has to pay his
running expenses in cash, in actual money, from week to week.
When he needs money to settle his bills, or to pay his clerical
help and salesmen, he takes his customers' paper — that is,
their promissory notes — to his bank and borrows money.
The bank is protected in these credit operations by the wholesale merchant's own note, or promise to pay at a stipulated
date, as well as by his customers' notes. The bank loan to the
wholesaler is liquidated when his customers pay their bills.
His customers may, in turn, borrow from their neighborhood
banks on their own assets. These transactions are going on all
the time, all over the country. In their totality they build up a
credit structure which rises, step by step, by the side of industrial and agricultural production.

2

Business runs in cycles. Sometimes trade is poor, sometimes
normal, and sometimes it goes ahead with a tremendous rush.
In good times manufacturers increase their output, merchants
enlarge their stores, crops sell at high prices, wages rise, people
everywhere buy in unprecedented volume, a tide of speculation sets in. More money is needed than ever before. Bank
credit becomes strained because so many concerns want
credit all at once.

Under a stiff and inflexible banking system, such as we had
in the United States before the Federal Reserve Banks were
created, money panics were inevitable. A manufacturer, let
us say, who has had the most profitable season in his history,
goes around to his bank for a loan and is met by a courteous
refusal.

'But here is my customers' paper,' the manufacturer says; 'all the best people in our line. I put up their paper as security.'

'Yes,' the banker replies, 'the paper is good, and your own credit is excellent, but we haven't got the money to lend.'

'Why not?'

'Because we have loaned our funds right up to the limit. Business is so good that everybody is making record sales, and everybody is discounting bills. This bank can only lend its available resources; we haven't an unlimited supply of money.'

'Then if business generally was bad,' the bewildered manufacturer is likely to say, 'I suppose you could make me a loan?'

'Certainly,' the banker replies. 'If business was dull, this bank would be full of money, and we wouldn't know what to do with it. You could easily get a loan in that case.'

The manufacturer goes back to his office, oppressed by gloomy reflections. He comes to the conclusion that he will have to curtail production. He draws in his salesmen, and shuts down a part of his factory. There we have the beginning of a money panic.

One of the principal reasons for the creation of the Federal Reserve Banks was to provide a remedy for this recurrent disease.

The root of the trouble lay in certain defects in the national banking system.

The system was established in 1863, during the Civil War, and the national banks played an important part in solving the difficult financial problems of that period. The war bonds of the Lincoln Administration did not sell very well; there was much difficulty in raising money. Salmon P. Chase, Secretary of the Treasury, recommended a national currency system based upon government bonds. In carrying out this idea, national banks came into existence.

A national bank with United States bonds in its possession could turn them over to the Treasury as security, and the Treasury would hand the Bank an equivalent amount of banknotes with the bank's name engraved on them. By means of this arrangement the bank still owned the bonds, and received the interest on them, and it also had the use of the money.

bankers, and the Treasury itself, through politics and manipulation, acted in sympathy with them.

This was revealed clearly in the 'Money Trust' investigation conducted by the Pujo Committee of the House of Representatives in 1912. Samuel Untermyer, who was the counsel
for the Committee, proved conclusively by a swarm of unwilling witnesses that a money trust existed. He showed that
the funds of banks all over the country were diverted from
their normal uses, and that control was centered in five or six
financial institutions.

The testimony of the leading bankers and financiers who
appeared before the Pujo Committee is extraordinarily interesting. Not one of them — so far as I can discover by reading
the testimony — had any conception of the true relation of
banking to the social structure. These guardians of other
people's money revealed, in themselves, the mind and spirit of
small tradesmen. The verbatim report of their testimony presents a picture of reticence and poor memory for which it
would be difficult to find an equal. Some of the witnesses
seemed to be half-witted — but this assumption of naïveté
was merely the spontaneous device of ingenious gentlemen to
conceal information that belonged to the public.

Ignorance of everything that the interrogator (Mr. Untermyer) wanted to know was the chief characteristic of most of
the witnesses. Nevertheless, through this chaos of defective
memory, imperfect understanding, and general lack of knowledge, one may discern the shadowy outlines of secret agreements, the manipulation of depositors' money in masses for
the benefit of a few insiders, the formation of quiet syndicates
with huge profits quietly collected, the outlawing of banks
that did not fit into the schemes of high finance, and the curious interweaving and interlocking of corporations — one sliding in and out of another, like the parts of a Chinese puzzle.

As long as American business was on a small scale, and
provincial in character, the national banking system func-
tioned satisfactorily. But business grew at a tremendous rate
in the 1890's and the onward rush was carried over into the
new century. Great industrial organizations appeared on the
scene. The need for commercial credit increased enormously.
The antiquated banking system received a terrific jolt in

1907. That year there was a disastrous money panic. Business and production were going along normally, and an exuberant bull campaign in stocks was registering a new high mark day by day. All of a sudden the banks threw up their hands and declared that they had no more money to lend. The funds of most of the big city banks were tied up largely in loans on Stock Exchange collateral. The country banks were out of money. They had loaned part of their funds in New York; as for the rest, it was in 'frozen' assets — that is, invested in commercial loans at home, backed by perfectly sound collateral. These good business loans would mature some three or four months in the future. In the mean time there was nothing to do but wait, and let business go to the devil. Every banker was anxious to get as much cash as he could, for fear that his depositors would come down on him in an avalanche and demand their money.

The system had no expansive power — no way of meeting an emergency. The United States Treasury came to the aid of the banks. Thirty-one millions of dollars were deposited in the large city banks in forty-eight hours, but even that amount was not enough to save the situation. The money panic lasted for months.

From its enactment in 1863 until the Democratic Administration of 1913, there had been no change of vital importance in the National Banking Act, though in minor details it had been frequently amended. It was suffering from hardening of the arteries and general senility.

One of the first imperative duties of the Administration was to devise a better currency plan. It was a formidable problem, made more vexing and arduous by the opposition of banks and moneyed interests generally.

I learned, during the year of 1913, that, although the banking business as a whole may be competent enough to take care of deposits and make loans, it has very little social or economic vision. Bankers fought the Federal Reserve legislation — and every provision of the Federal Reserve Act — with the tireless energy of men fighting a forest fire. They said it was populistic, socialistic, half-baked, destructive, infantile, badly conceived, and unworkable. I could put down many more adjectives of the same character if I had the space and did not mind boring my readers. Many of the national banks threatened to leave the system and take out charters as state banks if the Federal Reserve Act became a law.

Of course, the Republican Party was like adamant against it. Further on I shall quote some characteristic Republican opinion, as well as a few excerpts from the speech of Elihu Root — then a senator from New York — in opposition to it. We — I mean the Democrats — put the Federal Reserve Act through Congress in spite of them, as we had a workable majority in both houses. Now they are all for it — Republicans, bankers, and everybody — so much for it, indeed, that the claim is not infrequently made now that the Republican Party, inspired by its great bankers and men of vision, originated the Federal Reserve System!

3

In the spring of 1908, Congress — alarmed to its marrow by the money panic of the previous year — took up the currency question. For months it wandered in dim regions, through the Abyssinias and Cathays of economic philosophy. Few members of either house knew anything worth mentioning about the subject. Eventually the suave Senator Aldrich, apostle of high finance, led the way to a Promised Land of his own. A feeble emergency measure, known as the Aldrich-Vreeland Act, came into being.

Under the Aldrich-Vreeland Act of 1908 the national banks in any district were empowered to form what was known as National Currency Associations. Through its local association a member bank could apply, in time of stress, to the United States Treasury for emergency currency, which was to be issued against pledges of bankers' collateral, such as sound commercial paper, or securities other than government bonds.

I shall not go into full details as to the operation of this supposed remedy for tight money. It was a mass of encumbrances and defects. Not the least of these drawbacks was the requirement as to interest. The Treasury was to lend the emergency currency to the banks, and interest was to be charged at the rate of five per cent per annum for the first month; six per cent the second month; seven per cent the third month — and so on, upward, until a rate of ten per cent per annum was reached! If the currency was not returned for six months, the borrowing bank had to pay ten per cent for its money. It is clear that any bank in need of funds would exhaust every other possible device before applying for currency on these terms.

The original act also provided that no bank should receive emergency currency unless it had outstanding banknotes secured by the deposit of United States bonds to an amount not less than forty per cent of its capital. This provision excluded hundreds of national banks; among them were some of the largest financial institutions in the country.

The Aldrich-Vreeland Act was born half dead, and it remained for five years in a state of suspended animation. I have mentioned it here, not merely because it belongs to history but because you will find it further on cutting across my own narrative. No currency was ever issued under its provisions until I became Secretary of the Treasury. When we were confronted by the extreme emergency of a world plunging into war, I brought this clumsy act out of the legislative garret and succeeded in getting Congress to amend it radically so that it would work. We did not use it long, as it was succeeded by the Federal Reserve, but while it was in use it served fairly well, in spite of its obvious disadvantages, for the crisis was acute in August, 1914, and anything that promised relief, on any terms, was welcome.

Concurrent with the passage of the Aldrich-Vreeland Act in 1908, Congress authorized the creation of a National Monetary Commission, composed of members of Congress, with Senator Nelson W. Aldrich at its head. The Commission was instructed to study European currency systems, to take evidence, both American and European, and finally to recommend a plan for improving our currency situation.

The National Monetary Commission was certainly an imposing affair. It went to work with the stately deliberation of a slow-moving natural force. The Commission sat for four years, visited Europe, employed a host of experts listened to enough evidence to fill thirty-eight volumes — and, in 1912, during the Taft Administration, made a report and a recommendation.

The Commission proposed a plan for a new banking and currency system. The plan made no headway, and the bill embodying it never came to a vote, but its provisions are interesting, historically, as a background for consideration of the Federal Reserve System.

The keystone of the National Monetary Commission's scheme was a central bank. The capital of this proposed bank, which was to be called the National Reserve Association was to be three hundred million dollars, and all of it was to be subscribed by the national banks that desired to enter the system, or association. Banks were not obliged to become members. They could stay out if they wanted to, but any bank that entered the system had to purchase stock in the National Reserve Association to the extent of twenty per cent of the capital and surplus of the subscribing bank.

Now, let us assume the National Reserve Association organized and ready to function. The next step would be to organize the United States into fifteen districts. In each district there was to be a branch of the association, or central bank. This branch was not intended to be an independent concern; it would have no capital stock of its own; it would be a part of the central association, operating under certain restrictions.

With the country cut up geographically into districts, there was to be another, and smaller, division. The member banks in each community were to form local associations — not less than ten banks in each association. In this arrangement there is a vague analogy to the political divisions of the United States. Perhaps some such idea was in the mind of the Commission. The local associations correspond to counties, the fifteen districts to states, and the National Reserve Association to the federal government.

The central bank was to be a bankers' bank. It was to accept deposits only from the United States government and the banks which had become members and stockholders of the system.

The national banks in the system were to cease issuing their own banknotes. That function was to be taken over by the National Reserve Association, which was to purchase two per cent bonds (on which notes were issued) from the member banks, and thereafter the banknotes were to be notes of the National Reserve Association. Against these notes, and as a cover for them, the Reserve Association was to keep a reserve of fifty per cent in gold.

The National Reserve Association was also empowered — according to the plan — to issue its notes against ordinary banking collateral. It was not intended that the notes should be obligations of the United States government. They were to be obligations of the central bank.

The members had the privilege of borrowing from the Reserve Association — through its branches — on commercial paper, bonds, or other valid security. But there was a curious restriction as to the time limit of these loans. A member bank might borrow funds for twenty-eight days only on its own name, supported by such tangible assets as the promissory notes of its customers; but if money was needed for more than twenty-eight days, then the local association to which the borrowing bank belonged had to guarantee the loan, or it could not be made.

These conditions were simply absurd. Money for twenty-eight days is not, in the ordinary course of things, of much use to a bank doing a general banking business with merchants and manufacturers. The twenty-eight-day idea probably came from the Commission's study of the operations of the Bank of France. That great central institution does an enormous volume of business with small tradesmen. They discount the monthly bills of the customers at the bank's branches. Long established in France, this method of financing is little known in the United States.

To obtain a loan for a longer period than twenty-eight days, a member bank under the Aldrich plan would have to persuade the members of the local association — and among them its own competitors — that the loan was really needed, and get them to guarantee it. Not only that; the borrowing bank, to get a loan, would have to reveal the business of its customers to other banks in the community, and that is something no bank cares to do.

The National Reserve Association was to be governed by forty-six directors, all of them (except four *ex-officio* members) to be elected by the member banks. The *ex-officio* members included the Secretary of the Treasury, the Secretary of Agriculture, the Comptroller of the Currency, and the Secretary of Commerce.

The plan, as a whole, was hopelessly bad. It provided for a central bank, whereas centralization was the very thing from which we were trying to escape. It was to be governed entirely by bankers. (The four votes of the *ex-officio* representatives of the government would have been of no avail in a board of forty-six.) There was hardly a trace of public control provided for in the scheme. Moreover, the proposed arrangement for lending money to member banks was such that a bank out of favor with the prevailing financial hierarchy of its community could have been effectively ostracized by its local association, even though its solvency was unquestioned.

The hand of Senator Aldrich appeared in every section of the plan, and he was a standpatter and conservative of the most whole-hearted kind. His proposal, veiled in a fog of false altruism, was essentially a scheme for a powerful, centralized and ruthless engine of high finance.

The Democratic Administration disregarded it. We had to; it was in direct conflict with the fundamental ideas of the Democratic Party.

CHAPTER XV
THE BEGINNINGS OF THE FEDERAL RESERVE

I

I DO NOT know how many people claim the credit for having originated the Federal Reserve Act. There must be at least a dozen. Some of them have published books to sustain their contentions; and others have gone into print voluminously to justify or condemn various features of the plan.

As a matter of history, and not as a matter of mere surmise or belief, I have no hesitation in asserting that the Federal Reserve Act is a composite creation. I was there during its entire period of gestation, and, as the whole thing revolved around the Treasury, I knew what was going on.

Shortly after the inauguration, in March, 1913, I had a long talk with President Wilson on the subject of currency reform. I wanted to get an outline of his views, and also to clarify my own. I found that we were in agreement on all the important phases of the problem. This was gratifying to me, for I saw that, in coöperating with the President, I should not have to work at cross-purposes with my own opinions. That day we discussed, rather sketchily, the Aldrich plan — that is, the banking scheme of the National Monetary Commission — to which the President was strongly opposed. The keystone of the Aldrich plan was a central bank, and the President expressed himself definitely in favor of a system of regional banks.

The President asked me to get in touch with Carter Glass, who became (some weeks later) chairman of the Banking and Currency Committee of the House, and Senator Robert L. Owen, who became the head of the corresponding committee of the Senate. He remarked that Glass had already done considerable work on a currency reform bill and that he would like me to coöperate with him. A draft of this bill had been taken by Glass, in the latter part of the previous December, to Princeton, where it had been shown to Governor Wilson. Later on, I think it was in January, Glass went to Princeton again with a revised copy of the bill. The President suggested that I look over this Glass bill as a preliminary to a general discussion of the subject.

Before I left the White House that day, I asked the President if he did not think, in view of the highly controversial nature of the problem, that it would be wise for me to give consideration to all plans for currency or financial legislation, regardless of their origin or character, which might be presented by responsible people. The President agreed with me thoroughly, as I knew he would. It was his invariable custom to look at all sides of every important question.

I saw Glass soon after my conference with the President and got a copy of his proposed currency bill. I had never met him before, but I knew that he had been for years an advocate of currency reform. From the moment I saw him I was attracted by his personality. He is a red-haired fighter, the kind of man who stands by his opinions and defends them with spirit and pugnacity. I do not care for soft, doughy people, and I must say that there is nothing soft or doughy about Carter Glass. Yet his manners are so courteous that anyone who meets him casually is likely to consider him an urbane easy-goer moving along the line of least resistance.

The copy of the currency bill which Glass handed me — and which I still have, with his annotations and interlineations — was not, I think, his first draft. It had been revised since he had shown it to the President-elect in January. He called it a 'scratch-pad draft,' and remarked that it was not to be taken as final. I shall give a brief description of the Glass plan — as it was then — for the purpose of tracing the evolution of the Federal Reserve Act.

The drafting of a measure of such far-reaching importance is a highly complicated matter. I knew this very well, and I was not surprised, therefore, to find upon close reading that Glass's plan was immature. It was really an outline rather than a perfected document. In its fundamentals it was essentially sound, but some of its features were unsatisfactory.

He had adopted the regional bank idea as the basis of his proposed bill. There was to be no central bank, but a national board of supervision and control. All this was in accord with Democratic policy. There were to be twenty regional banks, known as National Reserve Banks. Each of the twenty regional reserve banks was to be an independent organism, operating in a geographical district of its own.

The system was to be governed by a Federal Reserve Board consisting of forty-three members. Twenty members were to be elected by the directors of the member banks, one for each regional district, and these twenty members were to be practical, working bankers or bank directors. Twenty additional members were to be elected by the stockholders of the member banks — again one for each regional district. The three remaining members of the Federal Reserve Board were to be, *ex-officio*, the Secretary of the Treasury, the Secretary of Agriculture, and the Comptroller of the Currency. The Federal Reserve Board, as one may see at a glance, was to be, therefore, a bankers' board and practically outside of government control.

This was undoubtedly a weak point in his early scheme. If it had been carried out, we should have had a network of huge, privately owned banks with extraordinary powers, managed by a committee of bankers. The three votes of the government officials on the Federal Reserve Board could not have had any appreciable effect upon the conduct of these twenty financial institutions.

The stock ownership of the Reserve Banks — to go on with Glass' plan — was to be held by the member banks. Each bank in the system was required to subscribe to an amount of stock equal to twenty per cent of its own capital. National banks had to join the reserve association or lose their charters. These features were retained in the matured bill, though in the bill as it became a law the compulsory stock subscription of the member banks was reduced from twenty per cent of their capital to six per cent of their capital and surplus.

The plan provided for the issue of National Reserve Association notes. The existing national banknotes were, apparently, to be retired gradually and the National Reserve Association notes were to take their place. The Federal Reserve Board was authorized to issue the notes of the Reserve Association upon application by any National Reserve Bank, but there was a curious restriction: no National Reserve Bank was entitled to receive, in the aggregate, more than twice the amount of its capital stock in National Reserve notes. In this provision there was a lack of flexibility which, in case of a money panic, might have led to serious trouble.

In the Federal Reserve System, as it was finally created, the note issues are based primarily on commercial paper or other liquid assets, whereas in the original Glass plan the amount of the notes bore a hard-and-fast relation to the capitalization of the National Reserve Banks.

While Glass was getting up his preliminary draft, Senator Robert L. Owen was at work independently on a plan of his own. Owen had a thorough knowledge of the banking business; he was, at that time, and had been for years, the president of a bank in Oklahoma. His interest in the subject was intense; he had made several trips to Europe to study European banking systems and his knowledge in this field was large and well-grounded.

There was considerable difference of opinion between Owen and Glass as to certain important features of the proposed measure. Owen thought that the system ought to be wholly under government control. He objected to the board of forty-three members, forty of them representing the banks. In his book, 'The Federal Reserve Act,' he says:

In effect this control of the system I regarded as practically the same as the Aldrich bill, which would have put the management of the system in the hands of persons chosen to represent the banks, and I insisted that the control of the system was a governing function to be exercised alone by the government of the United States.

On first consideration of this question, it seemed to me that, as the member banks would own the system, they were entitled to some representation on the governing body. The Board might be divided about equally, I thought, between the representatives of the people, appointed by the President, and representatives of the member banks. Later on, as I turned the matter over in my mind, I saw clearly that the Federal Reserve Banks were destined to be such an integral part of public finance that it would be a fundamental error to treat them, in any sense, as private business institutions.

The Federal Reserve System, as it finally came into being, and as it functions today, is really a public utility in the service of the nation.

I do not believe in government *ownership* of any industry or commercial concern that can be carried on efficiently and honestly, and with due regard to the public interest, by individual enterprise. But I do believe in government *regulation* of commercial activities that impinge in a powerful manner on the social economy of the nation.

Money and banking are terms which cover energies that affect every person in the United States. I came to the conclusion that it would never do for the Administration to attempt any reform of banking and credit that would, in the end, turn over the new system to a board of self-interested individuals. It was imperative that we should erect a final authority above and outside the banking business, just as the Interstate Commerce Commission is above and outside the railroad business.

I am trying in these few paragraphs to outline the evolution of my own thought on the subject. We were feeling our way, and as the banking and currency measure grew into shape, we all had different ideas at different times.

2

The differences between Glass and Owen as to the composition of the Federal Reserve Board continued, and eventually the matter was laid before the President for decision. I accompanied Owen and Glass to the White House one evening and we discussed the question with the President for a long time.

The judgment of the President was that the government should appoint every member of the Board. Sometime before this conference the idea of having the Board consist of thirty or forty members had been abandoned. On that evening we discussed a Board of seven members, of which at least two (or maybe three) would be *ex-officio*. The supervision of the system, the President said, was essentially a governmental function, and no individual representing private interests ought to have a place in it.

Though the President's decision was accepted reluctantly by Glass, he became later on completely in accord with it, and heartily approved the plan for a board of seven members —

two of them *ex-officio* (the Secretary of the Treasury and the Comptroller of the Currency), the other five appointed by the President.

When the bill was before Congress, a committee of bankers appeared in Washington with a list of criticisms that would fill pages of this book. Among the manifold defects of the bill, they declared, was the section which dealt with the make-up of the Federal Reserve Board. They had an interview with the President. Their contention was that, as the banks would own the Federal Reserve System, on account of their ownership of all the stock of the Federal Reserve Banks, the supervising board ought to be selected in whole or in part by them.

After a while the President said: 'The railroads are owned by the railroad companies, are they not?' Yes, of course they are. 'Which of you gentlemen,' he continued, 'thinks the railroads should select the members of the Interstate Commerce Commission?'

The silence that followed was of a thick consistency. Nothing more was said on that subject.

As a consolation to the crestfallen bankers, President Wilson suggested that a Federal Advisory Council be created to coöperate with the Federal Reserve Board. His idea was incorporated in the Federal Reserve Bill, and the Council was formed simultaneously with the organization of the Federal Reserve Banks. Its members, one from each federal district, are elected by the banks. The Advisory Council has no actual power or authority, but it recommends and criticizes. It has proved to be, I think, a helpful adjunct to the Board.

Although I have pointed out some of the defects and immaturities in the early drafts of Glass's bill, I have done this merely for the sake of historical perspective, and without any intention of minimizing his important part in the creation of the Federal Reserve System. On the contrary, I think his work was admirable and revealed conspicuous ability in the field of financial legislation. The bill, even in its early stages, was essentially sound in purpose and objective.

We had to fight at every step, and as I look back on that ardent summer of 1913, I wonder how the Federal Reserve Act ever struggled into existence. There was a general belief on the part of bankers that governmental control of the Federal Reserve System would be ruinous. George M. Reynolds, one of the leading bankers of Chicago, declared that the Act would 'put the whole fabric of credits into politics,' unless the bankers were allowed to run the system themselves. Paul M. Warburg, of Kühn, Loeb & Co., objected to the bill because it would bring about 'direct government management.'

Ex-Senator Nelson W. Aldrich, whose National Monetary Commission plan had been gently cast into oblivion, said that the Federal Reserve Board would have unheard-of power and that it 'might be able to control elections and insure the success of a political party.' Mr. Aldrich was perfectly willing, however, to have a Federal Reserve Board composed entirely of bankers. In that case the future did not seem to him so threatening. A board of bankers would not attempt to control elections or insure the success of a political party. Of course not; their minds would be on higher things.

With a few exceptions the Republicans in Congress made no creative suggestions. On the whole they preferred to play the rôle of obstructionists. Their vitriolic comments on the floor of the national legislature and in the press consisted chiefly of mere verbal spitballs thrown in a prevailing mood of political sabotage.

As for my part, I made up my mind not to let myself fall into a partisan attitude, and I believe I may truthfully say the same of Owen and Glass. My door was always open to anyone who had anything to say; and frequently, while the bill was in legislative progress, I went to New York and made my headquarters at the Sub-Treasury. I invited Wall Street to call and talk it over. Many of the most important people in the financial district came, and I patiently discussed the essential features of the Federal Reserve Bill with them.

Late in the summer it was obvious to those even faintly endowed with the spirit of prophecy that the bill would be passed. The financial world then took off its coat and proceeded to buckle down to a real consideration of what we proposed to do. Until then we had had to deal, for the most part, with mere biased and unintelligent aspersions and criticisms.

These interviews with bankers led me to an interesting conclusion. I perceived gradually, through all the haze and smoke of controversy, that the banking world was not really as much opposed to the bill as it pretended to be. At the core of its critical objection was a profound opposition to the Democratic Administration. Almost all the leading financiers and bankers — and representatives, generally, of Wall Street interests — were Republicans. Like those ancient shriveled sages, mentioned in the Bible, who knew that no good could come out of Nazareth, they were convinced that something or other must be wrong with anything conceived by the Democratic Party. They thought, without a shadow of excuse for thinking so, that the Administration had set out consciously to cripple the banking business.

The New York 'Times,' on June 30, 1913, depicted this state of mind concisely in an article on its financial page. It said, in part:

The spirit and policy back of the bill, bankers said, were regarded as linked with suspicion of the business and banking interests of the country on the part of the framers, namely, the Administration, and so long as such conditions existed, they felt that it would be impossible to obtain coöperation between the government and the banks....

I realized that two things were essential: First: that the leading financial interests must be shown the merits of the bill by calm and patient exposition. It was our duty — and to a great extent my duty, as far as the bankers were concerned — to prove that the bill before Congress was in the direction of sound money and sound credit. Second: that it would be very helpful if the Administration could start a nation-wide backfire of public sentiment in favor of the bill; and by that I mean a wave of favorable opinion from business men, the newspapers, and the general public. We knew very well that we could put the measure through Congress regardless of the opposition, but we wanted to put it through with such a torrent of public approval that the leading national banks would be ashamed to stay outside the Federal Reserve System when it came into being.

A great deal of my own work during the next several months was devoted to the accomplishment of these two objectives.

Every banker, without exception, that I saw in my trips to

New York was against the regional bank system. They were all strongly in favor of one enormous central bank, and to support their arguments they pointed to the Bank of England, the Bank of France, and the German Reichsbank. These comparisons were unsound for the reason that the conditions are different here. England, France, and Germany are relatively small and compact countries. Not one of them is as large in area as the State of Texas. The population of each of these European nations is homogeneous; and their economic interests run naturally into centralization. New York is the largest and wealthiest city in the United States, but it is not the financial capital of this country in the sense that Paris is the financial capital of France. As for England — anyone who has been there knows that the whole of England is a suburb of London.

3

I have not said anything about the bill which Senator Owen, as chairman of the Senate Banking and Currency Committee, had prepared. The Owen and Glass bills ran along the same general lines, though I do not mean to imply that they were practically identical. As a matter of fact they differed from one another considerably in details. I do not consider it worth while to discuss these differences; it is sufficient to say, I think, that the bill which was introduced in both houses of Congress on June 26, 1913, was the draft that had been agreed upon by the President, Glass, Owen, and myself at a White House conference. This was not the original 'scratch-pad' draft that I have described in the foregoing pages, but an outgrowth or development of Glass's first outline. When brought into Congress and handed to the press, it was in a more complete and well-rounded form; and before its final passage by both houses, it was amended many times.

I shall not give a complete digest of the Federal Reserve Act in these pages. Such detailed treatment belongs more properly to technical works on finance; but I take this opportunity to point out some of the outstanding features of the Act and the system of banking that grew from it.

As finally constituted, the Federal Reserve System is composed of twelve regional Federal Reserve Banks, geographically distributed in sharply defined and numbered Federal Reserve districts, from Boston to San Francisco; and from Minneapolis to Dallas. The member banks belonging to the system, including national banks, state banks, and trust companies, number between eight and nine thousand. There is no central, or master, bank.

The entire system is under the supervision of the Federal Reserve Board at Washington. It consists of seven members. Two of them are *ex-officio* — the Secretary of the Treasury (who is the chairman of the Board) and the Comptroller of the Currency. The other five members are appointed by the President and confirmed by the Senate. Of the five members appointed by the President, at least two shall be 'persons experienced in banking or finance.'

All the stock of the Federal Reserve Banks is owned by the member banks. The government is not a stockholder, neither can any individual hold stock. A member bank, upon entering the system, is obliged to purchase stock in the Reserve Bank of its district to an amount equal to six per cent of the member bank's capital and surplus.

Each Federal Reserve Bank is governed by a board of nine directors. Three of these directors are bankers, chosen by the member banks of the district; three, also chosen by the member banks, are not bankers; they must be business men or agriculturists; and three are appointed by the Federal Reserve Board. The latter three are called government directors. None of the government directors may be an employee, a director, or a stockholder of a bank. One of them is designated, at the time of his appointment, as chairman of the Board and Federal Reserve agent of the Federal Reserve Bank in his district; in other words, he represents the government through the Federal Reserve Board and carries out its authority.

Under the law the member banks are required to deposit a certain proportion of their cash reserves in the Federal Reserve Banks, and the national government, at the discretion of the Secretary of the Treasury, may deposit public funds in them. No interest is allowed on deposits. The Federal Reserve Banks do not accept deposits from, or lend money to, individuals or business concerns. They are strictly bankers' banks.

The dividends on stock in the Federal Reserve Banks are limited to six per cent and this is exempt from taxation. All earnings above six per cent go into a surplus fund, until the surplus amounts to one hundred per cent of the subscribed capital of each Federal Reserve Bank. After a one hundred per cent surplus has been built up, all earnings above six per cent a year go to the federal government as a franchise tax — except ten per cent of such net earnings (above the dividend), are turned into the surplus. Including the year 1929, the Federal Reserve Banks have paid to the United States government, since their organization in 1914, a total amount of $147,109,574 as its share of their net earnings.

The automatic mobilization of reserves is one of the important and beneficial features of the system. Before the Federal Reserve Act came into being, the banking reserves were either scattered in thousands of banks — every village banker holding tightly to his own — or had drifted to New York, where they were used in financing stock speculation. The country as a whole was like a town of wooden houses, where the only water for fighting fire was in barrels in back yards, except for one gigantic reservoir many miles away — too far away to be effective.

This wooden-built town, to continue the comparison, now has twelve large and efficient reservoirs located at strategic points in the community itself. There is no longer any need for the ineffective water barrels in the back yards; the reservoirs are so near, and they are always full.

In outlining the set-up of the system, I have passed over the battle-field of controversy, but I shall go back to it a little further on, and discuss in a general way the adventures of the Federal Reserve Act in its passage through Congress.

4

The backbone of the Federal Reserve, and the principal reason for its existence, is the power of the Federal Reserve Board to issue banknotes — or Federal Reserve money — against commercial collateral. It is a device of great simplicity.

This is the way it works.

John Brown & Co., of Toledo, let us say, are customers of a national bank in that city. They have a line of credit at the bank, and to secure their loans they give the firm's promissory notes, to which are attached the notes, or accepted bills, of their own customers. Under the law this commercial paper must represent actual transactions in the selling and buying of merchandise or the producing of crops or the raising of livestock — and not dealing in stocks or bonds.

The national bank in Toledo has many concerns like John Brown & Co. among its customers. Their business is good; they are all extending credit to retail merchants or farmers or cattle men; they all want loans at the banks. Under the old system the bank would reach a point along the line of these operations when it would have no more money to lend, even to finance the soundest business transaction. The bank would run into a state of 'tight money,' like a sailing ship on a pleasant voyage running into a dead calm.

Under the Federal Reserve System there is relief for this condition of affairs.

The Toledo bank applies to the Federal Reserve Bank of Cleveland for a loan, or what is technically known as a rediscount of the commercial or agricultural or livestock paper in its hands. This is eligible paper under the provisions of the Federal Reserve Act — that is, eligible for rediscount by a Federal Reserve Bank.

The paper sent by the Toledo bank to the Federal Reserve Bank may include the notes and securities of various concerns, but, to simplify the illustration, I shall assume that, in this case, the Toledo bank applies only for a rediscount of John Brown & Co.'s notes.

The first thing that the Federal Reserve Bank does is to turn to its files of credit data and look up John Brown & Co. Loans are made, not on the endorsement of the member bank alone; the accompanying security must also be sound.

Now, assuming that the application is satisfactory, the Reserve Bank may loan the Toledo bank any amount, in its discretion, which does not exceed the face value of the collateral. The essence of this transaction is that the Toledo bank turns over John Brown & Co.'s notes, with its own endorsement, to the Federal Reserve Bank of Cleveland and receives Federal Reserve banknotes in return.

Now, where does the money come from?

It comes, in the shape of Federal Reserve notes, from the United States government, and is issued under the authority of the Federal Reserve Board. The representative of the Board at the Federal Reserve Bank of Cleveland is known, as I have said above, as a Federal Reserve agent. He has the engraved notes in his possession — engraved and ready to issue, but not yet issued — and is responsible for them. Upon proper application, accompanied by adequate collateral, he issues the money to the Cleveland Reserve Bank. When these notes are put in circulation, the Reserve Bank must hold, in its vaults, or in the United States Treasury, a gold reserve of not less than forty per cent of their face value.

The money is sent to the Toledo bank, and is used as current funds; or the Cleveland Reserve Bank may give the Toledo bank a credit on its books for the amount, against which it may draw at will. With this new money in hand, the Toledo bank is able to make new loans. The transaction has transformed sound commercial credit into Federal Reserve money. The Toledo bank pays for the use of the money. This payment, or interest, is determined by the Federal Reserve Bank, subject to review or revision by the Federal Reserve Board.

When John Brown & Co. pay off their loan, the Toledo bank returns the Federal Reserve notes, or their equivalent, — to the Federal Reserve Bank of Cleveland; in this way the transaction liquidates itself.

Section 16 of the Act provides that Federal Reserve notes 'shall be obligations of the United States.' I have quoted the exact phrasing of the law, but from a practical standpoint the obligation of the government is really a guarantee instead of a direct obligation. It is a fact that the notes, in any quantity, may be exchanged for gold on presentation at the Treasury, or for 'gold or lawful money' on presentation at any Federal Reserve Bank; and it is also a fact that, in case of a collapse of the Federal Reserve System, the United States government would be responsible for the redemption of the whole note issue; yet, nevertheless, in daily practice, the operation of redemption and exchange is carried on, not with Treasury gold, but with gold owned by the Federal Reserve Banks.

Every Federal Reserve Bank is required by law to keep a reserve in gold in its vaults equal to forty per cent of its outstanding notes; also another and entirely separate gold reserve equal to thirty-five per cent of its total deposits.

There was a terrific fight over the provision of the bill which made Federal Reserve notes an obligation of the government. The original draft of the Glass bill provided that the Federal Reserve notes were to be obligations of the Reserve Banks and not of the government and Glass made it clear that he stood flat-footed on this feature of his bill. Senator Owen, on the other hand, was in favor of government issues.

The chief reason for making the notes a government obligation was not to strengthen their safety, for they would be sound enough without the guarantee; but by putting the government behind the notes the issue of money naturally fell under government control. It seemed unwise in the extreme to charter a system of twelve powerful banks and give them authority to issue their notes at will without close supervision, not only of note issues, but also of the credit structure from which the bank currency would emanate.

The Bryan Democrats in Congress, and Bryan himself, were unanimously in favor of making the notes obligations of the government, while Glass and his supporters stood on the other side. The situation was growing critical, as a continuous solidarity of the Democrats was necessary if the bill was to go through Congress successfully.

The President told me that he thought the situation might be clarified if I would have a quiet talk with Bryan about the bill and explain all its features to him. I said that I should be glad to confer with him, but that the President himself could no doubt accomplish more. The President wanted me to see him first and reduce the points of difference to a minimum; then the three of us would get together, if necessary, and reach an understanding.

A day or two after my talk with the President I asked Bryan to meet me at the University Club, in Washington, for luncheon. On that occasion I explained to him the major features of the Federal Reserve Bill.

Bryan listened to my discourse, necessarily a long one, and when I had finished, he said that he objected to the Federal Reserve Banks having the power to issue their own notes. 'The government alone should issue money,' he remarked. I agreed with him and said so. As he went on, I saw that he did not appear to understand the basis of the note issues. The fact that Federal Reserve money was to be issued against commercial paper did not seem to make much impression on him. He said he thought the notes ought to be issued by the government without any security behind them; the responsibility of the government ought to be enough.

'I agree with you,' I said, 'that the notes should be issued by the government, but they should be based on such unquestioned security that no liability can ever attach to the government.'

Bryan thought over this awhile. 'But how are you going to secure them? Anyway,' he said, 'I don't see that security is necessary. The government can issue the money and the Reserve Banks can borrow it from the government when and as they need it.'

It did not seem to me either wise or tactful to go into the basic theory of money, so I approached the subject from the flank. 'If the government issues the bank notes, it will be liable for their payment,' I said. 'Why shouldn't it require the banks to turn over good commercial paper as security? You see, the fundamental theory of this bill is to promote commerce through a credit system that can expand and contract automatically with the varying needs of trade.'

'But that is asset currency,' Bryan remarked, 'and you know I've always been opposed to asset currency.' For the benefit of those who do not understand this term, I may say that 'asset currency' means currency issued against tangible commercial values, instead of being issued against gold or silver.

'I don't quite understand why you are opposed to asset currency,' I argued. 'Why should there be any objection to the government making itself secure? Why shouldn't the banks put up security and protect the government's liability?'

He remained silent a moment, thinking it out. 'Yes, I see,' he said, after a time. 'That's all right. What about interest

on the money that the government advances to the Federal
Reserve Banks?'

'I presume you speak of interest in the nature of a circulation tax,' I replied. 'We have, as you know, a circulation tax
on national banknotes. It is an inflexible tax, imposed by
statute. I think it is a mistake to impose a statutory tax, because there are times when expansion of circulation ought to
be encouraged and there are times when contraction will be
demanded.

'Therefore, no fixed interest rate or circulation tax should
be arbitrarily placed on Federal Reserve notes. What we
ought to do is to give the Federal Reserve Board the power to
impose, from time to time, such rates of interest as in its judgment may be wise, or to charge no interest or circulation tax
at all. This will make the arrangement flexible and responsive
to the needs of the country. Suppose we put a provision to
that effect in the bill?'

'I think you are right,' he agreed. 'If the provisions we
have discussed are inserted, the bill would satisfy me and I
could give it my hearty support.'

I told him that I would make every effort to have these
ideas incorporated, and when I saw the President I reported
the result of the conference. He said he would act in the matter. The features that I discussed with Bryan were put in the
bill soon afterward.

The Republican members of the House Committee on
Banking and Currency presented a minority report against
the bill in which governmental guarantee of the notes was
made one of the chief points of criticism. The Merchants'
Association of New York also argued that this feature was a
fatal defect. The Association sent a resolution in that tenor
to Congress. The New York 'Times' characterized the entire
bill as a piece of 'Bryan banking,' and said 'the radical vice
[of the bill] lies in making the circulating notes an obligation of
the government instead of the banks.'

This rather adolescent view of the matter was not the exclusive possession of editorial writers and theoretical economists; it was presented vigorously by a considerable number
of men experienced in financial affairs. As I listened to their
arguments and read their letters, I wondered at times if I were

a fool myself, or whether these dissenters simply did not know what they were talking about.

Paul M. Warburg, who certainly ranked high as a financier, presented a long memorandum in opposition to many features of the bill, and particularly in opposition to the idea of making the notes an obligation of the government. Mr. Warburg said that:

No government of repute assumes the function of a direct issue of elastic notes (that is, against commercial paper). The state may issue its own obligations to pay its own fiscal debts, but it is not the function of the state to buy commercial paper and issue its demand obligations for it, so that if Mr. Jones wants to do a large business in sugar, tea, cotton, or in manufacturing, the government would have to increase its debts in order to pay for the same.

Mr. Warburg's argument was so remote from all actuality, and rested on ideas so foreign to anything in my own mind, that I could only stare at it in astonishment. Under the Federal Reserve Act the government does not 'buy commercial paper.' It does not buy anything. It issues money in the form of banknotes against adequate security, highly fortified by the endorsements of banks and business concerns. It may not be the function of the state to go into the promissory note business, but it is certainly the function of any decently conducted government to provide sufficient currency to carry on legitimate commerce. And what could be a better measure of the amount of currency than the legitimate requirements of business itself?

As for the fear that the government's credit would be injured, consider for a moment the formidable mass of stored wealth and financial value behind the Federal Reserve notes. Inability of the system to redeem them is inconceivable unless one goes so far down in the scale of pessimism as to imagine a complete collapse of the entire financial and commercial fabric of the American nation; and in that case I do not suppose a little thing like an unredeemed banknote would make much difference one way or another. However, this sadly pessimistic view was advanced with such vigor that the Administration had to devote valuable time to exposing its fallacy.

These fears were mere phantoms of the thinnest of thin air. No Federal Reserve Bank has ever defaulted, nor has the government ever been called upon to redeem a dollar of Reserve banknotes with Treasury money. And as for the credit of the government, the guarantee of the Federal Reserve notes has not affected it in the least. In the period of five years, from the passage of the Federal Reserve Act to the close of the World War, the government sold to the American people more than thirty billion dollars in bonds and short-time obligations. This was far more, in amount, than the total bond issues of the federal government from the founding of the nation up to 1914; yet all of these enormous Liberty Loan issues were floated at low rates of interest; so low, indeed, that the banking community protested, and declared that the interest rates were not high enough.

CHAPTER XVI
THE BATTLE-GROUND OF CONTROVERSY

I

WHEN the Wilson Administration was about three months old, a presentiment of coming disaster began to pervade business circles in all parts of the country. It was accompanied by a propaganda of pessimism which apparently had its source nowhere and in nothing. In some places it was said that the Democratic 'tinkering with the tariff' had brought both men and money to a deplorable state of uncertainty. In other places, it was not the tariff, but Democratic 'tinkering with money and banking' that caused the feeling of gloom. These were not the only reasons; there were others — all intangible and shadowy, but nevertheless potent. A statement does not have to be true to be powerful. Some of the most effective assertions in the history of the world have been shown to be pure lies.

Many men of understanding, including friends of mine in whom I had great confidence, told me in discussing the situation that the great financial interests were contributing to these apprehensions for the purpose of defeating the proposed currency and banking legislation, and also to force sweeping changes in the vital features of the tariff bill. They whispered to me that a 'Wilson panic' was in the making. I do not know whether this was so or not; one can never have a certain knowledge about such matters; they are always vaguely defined, even in the inner circles of finance. The powerful moneyed interests do not disseminate commands, or threats, for such directness is unnecessary. They distribute impressions and forecasts, and their policy comes to life through a series of hints.

Naturally, this was very disquieting. At that moment the most Herculean efforts were being made to block currency legislation. Could the blocking be done more effectively than by creating a 'Wilson panic'? One thing I have learned from experience and observation is that the great drama of human affairs is made up largely of stage-setting. Very few events and very few people are what they seem to be. A deft manipulation of mass psychology is often behind historic happenings and popular movements of all kinds.

I decided that, if the drama of a 'Wilson panic' was to be played, I did not intend to be left out of the cast. Uninvited actors in stage plays are seldom welcome; but I made up my mind to be in the scene, welcome or unwelcome. Thereafter I waited and studied the daily reports of money conditions. They became more and more alarming. Money was tight, and getting tighter. It was beginning to strangle the body of commercial enterprise. I felt that the curtain was rising and that it was time for me to do something.

On June 11, 1913, I issued a public statement that there was absolutely no necessity for any legitimate business, with sound resources, to be restricted in the way of banking credit. There was at that time, I went on to say, in the United States Treasury five hundred million dollars of new banknote currency, which the Treasury was prepared to issue to all banks applying for it under the Aldrich-Vreeland Act of 1908.

This statement from the Treasury was printed in every daily newspaper in the United States. The people were told something they did not know, namely, that, if the banks needed additional currency to carry on the business of the country, there was a huge amount in the Treasury to which they could resort upon compliance with the law. It put the banks on the defensive. It was difficult for them to explain to the ordinary borrower why they could not make good loans when they could get currency from the Treasury if their supply was short. Of course, I knew the imperfections of the Aldrich-Vreeland Act and how onerous the conditions were for the issuance of this currency. But that was for the banks to explain.

As an evidence of the spurious character of all the talk about tight money and disaster at that time, I may say that not one bank in the United States applied for any of the emergency currency.

The episode had a country-wide reverberation. It contributed materially to the building-up of popular confidence in the ability of the Administration and its freedom from Wall

Street control. A Western newspaper expressed this feeling precisely. 'When Secretary McAdoo walks in Wall Street,' it said, 'he carries his hat on his head instead of in his hand.'

The New York 'World,' on June 15, printed a long article by S. S. Fontaine, its financial editor, which said, in part:

Since the ultimatum of the Secretary of the Treasury was sent out from Washington on June 11th the entire aspect of the financial situation in this country has changed. On that day conditions in Wall Street were approaching chaos. The prices of investment securities had reached levels lower in many instances than were touched in the great financial upheaval of 1907.... There was indeed very grave danger, and none knew it better than the great financial groups that sat idly by and watched the peril grow....
... They [the people] were told that the tariff readjustment was bound to breed anxiety and unrest throughout the whole business community, and that everybody must prepare for a hard winter.... It is true enough that there was no need for this money — not after the Secretary had spoken. The mere knowledge that it was there, ready and waiting, was all that the reassured business world wanted.

Theodore H. Price said, in 'Commerce and Finance,' on June 18:

Probably nothing for which the Administration is responsible since the fourth of March has done as much to reassure the business community as the psychological aptitude of the Treasury announcement....
Mr. McAdoo doubtless understood as well as anyone else that there would be no call for the emergency currency, but a capacity for leadership requires, preëminently, courage and a knowledge of psychology, and of these two attributes the President and his Secretary of the Treasury have undoubtedly shown themselves possessed.

I have recorded this incident at some length, not because of its historical importance, which is slight, but because of its psychological effect on myself. It proved to me, in the most practical way, something that I already knew theoretically; and that is that the United States Treasury is a more powerful financial authority — when its power is really exerted — than any group of financiers, or, for that matter, of all financial groups combined.

It is for this reason that every effort is made by Wall Street to induce each successive President to appoint, as Secretary of the Treasury, some person who either belongs to them, as a blood brother in high finance, or who is at any rate sufficiently pliable to let the controlling money powers do his thinking for him.

2

Wall Street is the last refuge in America of the romantic spirit. It exists in a world of adventure. In an age devoted to steel skyscrapers and gasoline engines, Wall Street still dreams of a pot of gold at the foot of every rainbow. Within its gates Imagination and Arithmetic remain on friendly terms, and sit down together to plan events which resemble masquerades.

Unfortunately, Wall Street as a financial community does not understand the United States. The reason for the misunderstanding is that the ideals of Wall Street are very different from the ideals of the great mass of the American people. This is really the cause of its unpopularity; and it is so unpopular, indeed, that many a political career has been made on nothing more substantial than a fluent facility in abusing Wall Street and all its works. A politician devoid of ideas, or who has something to conceal, can always divert attention from his own shortcomings by dragging in the Wall Street specter — a device which is rendered more effective by the popular conception of the Wall Street spirit as undemocratic and ominous.

I have no patience with such an attitude of flat, undiscriminating hostility, or with the cheap demagoguery that habitually lays all the ills of the American nation at the door of the New York Stock Exchange.

The fact is that Wall Street plays an important part — an indispensable part, even — in the financial mechanism of the United States. It provides the means, and the machinery, for the flotation of large-scale enterprises, for the purchase and sale of securities in a broad and free market, and for the conversion of liquid capital into forms of productive wealth. These are all legitimate functions of collective finance. It is a pity that, for its own good, and the good of the nation, it does not restrict its activities to these lines in which it is so competent.

But, because of motivating forces which arise within itself,

Wall Street and High Finance cannot remain content with the ordinary profits that come from investments and the ebb and flow of funds. Such a state of being would clash irreconcilably with the spirit of romantic adventure. The Wall Street mind is obsessed with the idea of getting something for nothing, with the allurements of over-capitalization, with the image of vast financial deals which bring fortune to those who neither toil nor spin, but who flourish through the sustaining force of cleverness.

Not only that; it dreams of empire, and is constantly attempting to develop a plutocratic control of the government. Its finger is in every pie. It endeavors to create economic situations which will influence elections, and often succeeds. It buys men in political life; not outright, but by giving them subtle monetary advantages. It bores within each of the great political parties, and its secret representatives sit in their councils. It finances campaigns and expects adequate recompense. It employs smooth-tongued lobbyists who speak in sugary words, and in whispers; their writing often appears mysteriously in the text of legislative acts.

The Wall Street idea of a perfect government is one in which all authority is in the hands of the most able men — meaning, of course, those who have made the most money, and who have, therefore, 'the largest stake in the country.' In the circles of High Finance ability and the capacity for money-making are synonymous terms.

As a result of this outlook on life, Wall Street, as a community, is strikingly deficient in social vision. It has an instinctive opposition to all genuinely progressive ideas. I do not say, nor do I believe, that everyone in Wall Street is a conservative or a reactionary; I have in mind the temper and tone of the community of High Finance taken as a whole. Wall Street does not believe in old-age pensions, in unemployment insurance, in profit-sharing with workers, in the regulation of Big Business in the interest of society, or in any form — even the mildest form — of economic democracy. It considers labor unions a national menace, to be fought at every step. But, at the same time, the Wall Street mind looks upon bankers' and manufacturers' associations as salutary and beneficent.

When I speak of Wall Street I do not speak of individuals. I speak of the 'system' and what it signifies to the popular mind. There are many men of character and ideals in Wall Street and it would not be fair to reflect on them even by implication. But the system, its motivations and operations, is another thing.

Like most human institutions, and most people, there are two sides to Wall Street's character. While it is spinning its webs of plutocratic and political intrigue with one hand, its other is employed in work of real utility. I recognize the usefulness of Wall Street, and that is why, in these comments, I treat its shortcomings with a gentle hand.

3

One day, while the Federal Reserve Bill was still in its preliminary stages, and was being attacked on all sides by powerful banking interests, somebody in the Treasury (I do not remember who it was) brought me a sketchy draft of an entirely different plan. It was proposed — in this outline, or draft — to establish a bureau of discount in the Treasury Department, to be called the National Reserve. This Treasury bureau was to be, in effect, a central bank owned wholly by the government and financed largely by the Treasury. The essence of the idea was that the government itself was to become the rediscount agency for the entire reserve system, including seven or eight thousand banks.

It was proposed, further, that this National Reserve should be managed by a board of seven governors, all appointed by the President except two members *ex officio*; namely, the Secretary of the Treasury and the Secretary of Agriculture.

At that time the attacks of the opposition were directed mainly against the regional bank feature of the Glass-Owen Bill. I have said already that every prominent banker with whom I talked urged the establishment of a privately owned central bank; all of them were vehemently opposed to the provision in the bill for twelve or fifteen independent regional institutions.

I read over the skeleton outline of a National Reserve with headquarters in the Treasury, and the thought of using it as a strategical device occurred to me. If they want a central bank, I reflected, we'll give them one — or make them think so, at any rate, but it will be a government bank. I felt convinced that when the large banking interests saw a plan sponsored by me for turning the Treasury itself into a rediscount bank for commercial paper they would be genuinely alarmed. I hoped that their concern would temper their opposition to the regional bank system. In their view the regional banks would certainly be the lesser of two evils.

I explained to the President the strategy I had in mind. I thought it best not to let anyone else know either the motivation or what was in the background of this maneuver. Of course, neither I nor President Wilson had any idea of transforming the Treasury into a bank, but I felt sure that this reserve plan, coming from me, would start something — and it did.

I discussed the plan with some of the leading bankers, confident that they would condemn it. They did, with the exception of a few who said unenthusiastically that it had some merit and might work. It did not require keen perception on my part to see that these few were merely trying to be polite to the Secretary of the Treasury.

I am sorry now that I did not disclose what was in my mind to Carter Glass. If I had known that my adventure in strategy was going to disturb him so desperately, I should have taken him into my confidence. I was not well acquainted with him, at that time, and I feared that if I told him about it he might think that I expected him to share my responsibility for the scheme; so I thought it best to go it alone.

Glass says, in 'An Adventure in Constructive Finance' (page 100):

Mr. McAdoo 'phoned for me to come to the Treasury on an important matter, and there handed me the outline of a proposed bill to create a bureau bank in the Treasury with all the elements of a central bank. The scheme involved a tremendous issue of treasury notes to supersede the outstanding greenbacks and gold certificates and seemed to contemplate a seizure of the gold in trust behind the certificates. I had not gotten far in my examination of the proposal before I looked up from the paper and asked the Secretary if he was serious about it. With characteristic point and punch he exclaimed, 'Hell, yes!'

In novels one reads of people who deliver solemn utterances with a twinkle in their eyes — meaning that they are not saying all they think — but I doubt if twinkling is so effective in practice. When I said 'Hell, yes!' there was a twinkle in my eye, but Carter Glass was not looking for twinkles that day. He continues in these words:

Needless to say I left the Treasury Building astounded. It seemed an end of currency reform for the time — a nullification of fourteen months of hard work and inconceivable nervous strain.

While he was in my office I told him that George M. Reynolds, who was president of the Continental and Commercial National Bank of Chicago, had expressed himself favorably about the National Reserve plan when I discussed it with him. Glass says that he went out immediately 'to make the wires hot.' Reynolds replied to the hot wire from Glass with a statement that he was opposed to the scheme and did not think much of it when I had explained it to him, but that he thought it wise to handle me 'with as great consideration and courtesy as possible.' There was no reason why he should not have told me that he was against the idea; I asked for his candid opinion. I see clearly now that Reynolds was insincere and that he was trying to play Glass off against me.

Shortly afterward, in a letter to Glass, Reynolds said:

I am rather inclined to believe it [the Treasury plan] may, in the end, prove to be more or less of a blessing in disguise in helping to concentrate favorable opinion on your bill. Possibly the fear of the adoption of some such scheme as has been proposed... may cause many who have been more or less rigid in their views of this question to be a little more yielding.

That was precisely the effect that I wanted to bring about.

The President and I had a conference on the matter a few days later. I expressed satisfaction with the effect that the suggestion of the Treasury plan had already produced on the bankers, as shown not only by the Reynolds letter, but from my own contacts and discussions. The President agreed with me, but was concerned by Glass's anxiety. I told him I thought the object had already been achieved and that we could abandon any further discussion of the Treasury plan. I said that I would notify Glass at once to this effect.

Glass did not know anything about my understanding with the President. He says that the President turned down the scheme and that

McAdoo met the situation like a prince. Not for an instant did he exhibit a sign of resentment or even of disappointment... From that moment he never wavered. Every hour he could spare from more exigent duties he gave to the currency problem... Without his fine spirit and absolute dependability, the task of the Committee would have been infinitely harder, if not well-nigh impossible. But, Heaven help us, what a narrow escape that was from wrecking currency reform and precipitating another government bank upheaval!

I had played the part of a scarecrow rather effectively, it seems. But I made up my mind never to do it again. It is a thankless job.

4

Annually, during the harvest season, or from about the first of September to the first of December, a large amount of credit is needed in the agricultural sections of the country to move the crops. If there happens to be a shortage of money, interest rates go up and the prices of farm products go down.

As the fall of 1913 approached, the talk of tight money and coming distress, which had been so ominous during the early summer, was again heard. The agricultural states were greatly disturbed over the probability of a money panic. I did not take any stock in the prevailing pessimism, as I was confident that we had the remedy in the United States Treasury. The spreading gloom seemed to me to have a purely political origin.

It had been the practice of my predecessors in the Treasury to assist crop-moving operations, if they assisted them at all, by depositing government money in the big city banks — principally in the banks of New York City. It was a clumsy, roundabout way of approaching the problem. Why deposit Treasury funds in New York and Chicago when the idea is to help the farmers in Kansas and Mississippi?

Anyway, that was the practice. The big city banks, receiving the money on deposit without interest from the Treasury, would lend it to the country banks, usually at high rates, and in turn the country banks would extend credit to the farmers and local merchants at higher rates.

In the spring or early summer of each year, bankers in the agricultural sections of the country always sought to make a reservation with their New York correspondents of sufficient credits to meet their seasonal needs. To make sure that they would get what they wanted, it was customary to ask for more than they really needed, with the idea that they would be allotted approximately what they actually required. This created an artificial demand far in excess of actual needs.

On June 30, 1913, there was approximately $165,000,000 in the general fund of the Treasury. According to the best estimates this amount was much more than would be needed to move the crops. I determined to deposit the necessary money, not in New York, but in the leading cities in the agricultural states.

During the early days of August I called into conference at the Treasury Department bankers from the South, Middle West, and Western states, for the purpose of determining how much money would be needed in their respective sections for crop-moving purposes. Their combined estimates called for $46,500,000, and accordingly I prepared to deposit funds to that amount in the banks of the agricultural regions.

It was necessary, of course, for the banks to give security for these deposits. Usually United States and state and municipal bonds were accepted for this purpose. If I had required the usual security, the deposits would have been of little or no help because many banks would have been compelled to buy bonds with the money the Treasury proposed to deposit with them. I decided, therefore, to accept the kind of securities which the banks were most able to furnish, namely, high-class commercial paper, in addition to government, state, and municipal bonds.

There was some doubt about my power to accept commercial paper as security; but, backed by competent legal advice, I went ahead. By taking such paper the Treasury was, in effect, rediscounting for the national banks, thereby giving an object lesson in the benefits which the new banking legislation would provide.

Although I gave the banks credit at the Treasury for the

full amount of crop-moving funds they asked for — namely, $46,500,000 — they withdrew only $37,386,000. The operation was highly successful. The full amount was repaid to the Treasury in April, 1914. In my opinion, this stimulated interest in the new banking legislation and brought to its support influences of importance throughout the country which could not have been enlisted except by a practical demonstration of this sort.

As time went by, we observed that the public generally — I mean the ordinary, average citizen — was in favor of the Federal Reserve Bill. The bankers in the larger money centers were almost to a man bitterly opposed to it, and many business men shared their views. Sentiment among the smaller banks was divided — those against the bill being largely in the majority.

At the national convention of the American Bankers' Association, held in Boston, October, 1913, only two delegates attempted to speak in favor of the legislation; each was howled down until the chairman managed to make himself heard, and begged the convention to give them the courtesy of attention.

Dr. Joseph French Johnson, professor of political economy at New York University, said at a dinner of the Academy of Political Science, that the bill, if passed, would bring on a dangerous credit expansion and that it would cause 'a collapse of the banking system.' He added that 'blacksmiths could not be expected to produce a Swiss watch.' The blacksmiths were, in this case, I suppose, the Democrats, and the Federal Reserve Bill was the Swiss watch. So I infer, and I fancy that another meaning, to the effect that Professor Johnson himself was an excellent watchmaker, lurked in the background.

And from Chicago came reports of a speech of Senator Lawrence Y. Sherman, Republican member of the Senate from Illinois. In addressing the Illinois Bankers' Association he said: 'I would support a law to wind a watch with a crowbar as cheerfully as I will support any such bill.'

But James B. Forgan, banking magnate of Chicago, was more direct in his expression of opinion. He said nothing about crowbars and blacksmiths and Swiss watches. He declared that the bill was 'unworkable, impractical, and fundamentally bad.' It would bring about, he said, 'the most damnable contraction of currency ever seen in any country.'

Forgan's idea that the currency would be damnably contracted was not shared by all the opponents of the Glass-Owen Bill. Many bankers and economists proved, to their own satisfaction by figures and diagrams, that the Federal Reserve System would produce an extraordinary inflation. These vast and irreconcilable differences of opinion between the various groups of our adversaries had the effect of lessening my respect for so-called banking experts. I found that they could take the same set of facts and reach two diametrically opposite conclusions.

For example, Forgan estimated that the currency would be *contracted* to the extent of $1,800,000,000, while Senator Elihu Root, using the same data, predicted an *inflation* of at least $1,800,000,000.

President Arthur T. Hadley, of Yale, who had a high reputation as an economist, believed that the bill, if passed, would lead to inflation on an unparalleled scale, with a consequent depreciation. He was so deeply moved that he wrote a personal letter to President Wilson on July 1, 1913, for the purpose of pointing out to the President that the Act would 'involve the country in grave financial danger.' Practically all of our gold would leave for Europe, he thought. He was greatly mistaken. There is now in the United States about forty-five per cent of all the gold in the world.

Frank A. Vanderlip, president of the National City Bank of New York, declared that the notes of the Federal Reserve Banks would be 'fiat money,' and James J. Hill, the famous railroad builder and financier, said the plan was 'socialistic.' James R. Mann, Republican leader of the House, condemned the bill as all wrong, badly conceived, and impossible as a practical measure. However, he added bitterly, it did not matter; the national banks would not go into the system, anyway. Most of them would become state banks and the Federal Reserve would just lie down and die for lack of support. Saying this, he washed his hands of the whole affair.

Ex-Senator Aldrich now appeared on the scene again, bearing in his arms the lifeless body of his own National Monetary

Commission plan. Like Antony fulminating over a slain Cæsar in the Roman Forum, Senator Aldrich spoke before the Academy of Political Science. The Glass-Owen Bill, he asserted, was 'revolutionary, socialistic, and unconstitutional.' It was not practical; it was dangerous; it would be to America what the plague of locusts was to Egypt.

Among the opponents of the bill was Charles G. Dawes, then a Chicago banker, who has since been vice-president of the United States and is now our Ambassador to England. Dawes predicted a sad future for the country if the bill got through Congress. It would prove 'calamitous to the nation,' he said, 'and would cripple the present national banking system and pave the way for panic.'

I did not know Dawes personally at that time, but I met him two or three years later. We have been good friends ever since. He has a wide reputation as a picturesque personality, but there is much more than mere picturesqueness about him. He is an honest man — honest in his convictions and frank in his speech — and he has ability and courage. The Republicans, in my opinion, made a great mistake in not putting him in the White House instead of Hoover. He was wrong about the Glass-Owen Bill, and he does not hesitate to say so himself. For years he has been a strong believer in the value of the Federal Reserve System to the banking and business interests of the country.

On September 18, 1913, after eight days of debate, the Administration currency bill passed the House of Representatives by a vote of 285 yeas to 85 nays, and was sent to the Senate.

5

The Glass-Owen Bill was beset by perils in its passage through the Senate; time and time again it was on the verge of shipwreck. The opposition was led, strange as it may seem, by a Democratic senator, a circumstance which greatly encouraged the Republicans, in and out of the Senate.

Gilbert M. Hitchcock, of Nebraska, one of the ablest members of the Banking and Currency Committee, objected to so many features of the plan that he gradually edged himself out of the Democratic and into the Republican side of the committee; or, it would be more accurate to say that the Republicans sided with him. He proposed numerous changes in the bill, yet his opposition was not directed primarily against the underlying idea; he simply wanted to reshape the entire plan.

This unexpected defection was distressing. It was the duty of the Banking and Currency Committee to consider and report the bill. In organizing the committee the Democrats had unwisely failed to give themselves a safe majority of its members, as they could and should have done. There were seven Democrats to five Republicans. The withdrawal of one Democrat, therefore, divided the committee into two equal sides. This created an extremely awkward situation. The Democrats of the committee lost their slender working majority and were at a decided disadvantage, not only in reporting the bill promptly to the Senate, but in dealing with the measure itself.

Every man has a right to his own opinions, and certainly Senator Hitchcock was within his rights in contending for his views, but he did not seem to realize that the only possibility of securing satisfactory banking legislation was through united party action. Hitchcock was unwilling, apparently, to make any concessions and so he found himself in the anomalous position of siding with the bitterest adversaries of his own party.

Senator James A. Reed, of Missouri — another Democratic member of the Banking and Currency Committee — soon joined Hitchcock in antagonism to the measure. With the Reed desertion the opposition within the committee was in the majority — seven against five.

I do not think there was any special reason for Reed's secession, at that time, except the fundamentally antagonistic and controversial quality in his character. He did not seem to understand clearly the essential nature of the currency problem, but that did not keep him from talking about it or from taking sides.

In Reed's opinion, the Glass-Owen Bill was a menace — a device of the Philistines, etc. — besides being defective in almost every particular, so he was against it for a time. He looked over the bill, struck it with his hand, and thundered: 'What is the use of the massing of reserves, as proposed in this bill?' Then he paused for a reply. It was embarrassing. When this Jovian bolt was hurled, the bill had been before Congress for months. One of its major objects was the mobilization of reserves so that they might become an effective aid to business, instead of being scattered in every county in the United States. All this had been explained so many times and in so many forms that everyone was distinctly reluctant to go back to the beginning in order to tell Senator Reed what it was all about.

We felt much greater concern when we learned one day that Senator O'Gorman, of New York, also a member of the Banking and Currency Committee, felt cold toward the bill and was disinclined to support it. I knew O'Gorman to be a man of substance and ability; I feared that if he should become a determined opponent of the measure, favorable action at that session of the Congress might be endangered. In those days we maneuvered on the slenderest of margins. O'Gorman's defection threw the committee wholly out of balance, with five Republicans and three Democrats against the bill and only the four remaining Democrats for it — Owen, Shafroth, Pomerene, and Hollis.

In view of this alarming situation I thought that the Democrats in the Senate ought to hold a conference (the euphemistic term used in the Senate to mean a caucus) and make the Glass-Owen Bill a party measure.

All along I had hoped that this would not be necessary because I felt that the legislation should not be dealt with as a partisan matter. There was no other way, however, in which the Democrats in the committee could be brought into line, if at all.

The first conference of the Democratic senators adjourned without action to allow the Democratic members of the Banking and Currency Committee a few more days in which to reach an agreement. On December 1, 1913, a final conference was held. Hitchcock was not present, but Reed and O'Gorman were there. The bill, as reported by Owen, was overwhelmingly adopted as an Administration measure. Reed and O'Gorman resisted no longer, although Hitchcock continued to vote with the Republican members of the committee and brought before the Senate an opposition bill of his own. This was defeated by the narrow margin of two votes.

One of the rather curious episodes of this period was the reappearance on the congressional scene of Frank A. Vanderlip, president of the National City Bank of New York. In the early summer — in June or July — Vanderlip had denounced the entire Federal Reserve plan as it appeared in the Glass-Owen Bill. It meant political control of the banking business, he declared. Not only that; as a banking mechanism it was unsafe; its note issues would be nothing more than fiat money; it dissipated the nation's bank reserves instead of concentrating them. That was what Vanderlip said in July. In October he appeared, however, in Washington with a carefully prepared plan of his own which contained many of the features of the Glass-Owen Bill that he had criticized so sharply.

In laying his plan before the Senate Committee on Banking and Currency, October 23, Vanderlip said that his ideas had been shaped, to a considerable extent, by conversations with various members of the committee. Among others he mentioned Senator Bristow, of Kansas. Bristow was a confirmed obstructionist with the mentality of a third-rate lawyer. He made a specialty of turning the most insignificant difference of opinion into a long, mouthy debate. Bristow, it appears, was one of Vanderlip's advisers in the realm of governmental finance; and he also mentioned Senator O'Gorman, Senator Reed, and Senator Hitchcock.

Vanderlip's plan was based on a hundred-million-dollar central bank with twelve branches. The bank was to be controlled by the government; all its seven directors were to be appointed by the President. The stock in the central bank was to be owned, in its entirety, by the government — or by the government and the general public. The bank was to rediscount commercial paper and issue notes. Behind the notes there was to be a reserve of fifty per cent, in gold.

This Vanderlip plan resembled, in many respects, the so-called Treasury plan which I have already described and to which all the leading bankers violently objected. It was decidedly amusing to read the favorable comments of some of these same bankers on the Vanderlip plan, which contained provisions to which they had expressed themselves as unalterably opposed, but which, dressed up in a National City Bank costume, took on an alluring mien.

When I read the Vanderlip plan, heard how it came into being, and learned who its sponsors were, I felt absolutely confident that the Glass-Owen Bill was safe. The Vanderlip scheme was the last expiring effort of our adversaries. It revealed a confusion of strategical purposes, a condition of disorganization behind their lines. It was their forlorn hope; their attempt to save the central bank idea by throwing everything else overboard; or, if that could not be done, to defeat the Glass-Owen Bill by creating a division among the Democrats.

The Vanderlip plan was a nine-days' wonder. It received such glowing endorsements from leading bankers and newspapers that anyone who was not familiar with its stage-setting would have thought that it was going to displace the Glass-Owen Bill immediately.

But it was all smoke and no fire. The endorsements were shallow and enameled over with pretense; the newspaper enthusiasm was artificial. The Vanderlip plan died in its early infancy and there were few, if any, mourners at its obsequies.

6

The bill, as reported to the Senate by Owen, contained a provision for insuring the deposits of member banks. The insurance fund was to be administered under the supervision of the Treasury. Into this fund there was to be paid a certain percentage of the net earnings of the Reserve Banks 'for the benefit of depositors in all failed member banks.'

There was no such provision in the House bill. When the Conference Committee of the two houses met to reconcile the differences in the two bills, the Senate provision was rejected.

It was a mistake, I thought, to eliminate the deposit insurance feature. While the Senate provision was immature and inadequate, it might have been reshaped in conference with the House committee; and, at any rate, it was a definite step toward the protection of bank depositors from the calamitous losses which they always suffer from bank failures.

The frequency of such failures is a severe indictment of our banking system. So long as each of the forty-eight states charters and supervises a banking system of its own, we shall continue to have scattered throughout the country many weak units, inefficiently supervised. In periods of business depression and public apprehension they fall like houses of cards.

One of the greatest reforms, as well as one of the greatest blessings, that could be achieved in the banking world, is an organization that will save the depositor from loss, no matter what happens to the bank.

You may ask how a deposit insurance plan can be worked out. It would be practicable, I should say, to impose a small premium upon the amount of deposits or resources of the member banks, to be paid into an insurance and liquidating fund, to be administered by the Comptroller of the Currency or by the Federal Reserve Board. When the fund has reached a prescribed amount, premiums would cease until it became impaired, in which event premiums would be resumed automatically until the integrity of the insurance and liquidating fund has been restored.

It may be argued that the unusual number of bank failures these past few years condemns the insurance of deposits idea. I do not agree with this view. If the banks involved had been members of the Federal Reserve System, they would have been more efficiently supervised and, undoubtedly, the percentage of failures would have been greatly reduced. Moreover, where depositors know that their funds are safe, as they would feel that they were under an insurance of deposits provision, many failures due to bank runs would undoubtedly be averted.

I am well aware of the stereotyped objection that deposit insurance would encourage unsafe banking; that the banks, especially the smaller ones, would be likely to take undue risks on the theory that, in any event, the depositors would be paid in full. This objection would be sound and unanswerable if the deposit insurance law was not accompanied by the strictest regulations for bank inspection and supervision.

No bank should be allowed to enter the Federal Reserve System and take the benefit of deposit insurance unless it could pass successfully the most rigid tests for financial stability and character of its personnel. When a man applies for life insurance, he is examined from head to foot, and if he is found to have incipient Bright's disease or tuberculosis, or even a bad family history, the risk is declined. Something like this should be done in the case of banks. It would not be long before banks that could not obtain insurance would have to reorganize or go out of business, as they would find it impossible to keep their depositors.

On December 13, 1913, Senator Elihu Root, the greatest Republican statesman of the time, rose in the Senate to speak on the Glass-Owen Bill. He was the heaviest gun in the artillery of our adversaries. To make his utterances more effective, his energy and logic had been kept in reserve, and during the months of skirmishing he had had but little to say. He spoke for three hours, without notes, with the impressive dignity of a Webster replying to a Hayne.

His manner was impressive, but his speech was unworthy of his fine intellect. Senator Root has a remarkably lucid and forceful mind, yet he uttered on that day a mass of erroneous premises, *non sequiturs*, and illogical conclusions. I do not believe that his speech represented his best thought. In all probability it was induced by a spirit of partisan loyalty.

He said that the Federal Reserve Act would lead to an extraordinary inflation, and that 'If this bill passes as it stands, America stands to lose all we saved when Grant vetoed the Inflation Bill, all we saved when Grover Cleveland abolished the Silver Purchase, all we saved when we elected McKinley, all the Republicans, all the Gold Democrats saved when they helped in the repudiation of the vital principle which has been put into this bill.'

The Federal Reserve currency would be, in his opinion, merely greenbacks or fiat money, for the redemption of which the faith of the nation would be pledged. 'This bill proposes,' he declared, 'to put in pawn the credit of the United States; and when your time of need comes it is the United States that is discredited by the inflation of its demand obligations which it cannot pay.'

This was more than seventeen years ago. None of Senator Root's emphatic predictions has been realized.

On the Democratic side the bill was ably defended by Owen, John Sharp Williams, Pomerene, and Reed.

In its final form the Federal Reserve measure passed the House December 22, 1913, by a vote of 298 to 60. Two Democratic representatives voted against it, and 35 Republicans for it.

On the next day — December 23 — it passed the Senate by a vote of 43 to 25. The twenty-five negative votes were all Republican. Senator Hitchcock, who had opposed the bill consistently all along, took the Democratic side on the final vote. Among the forty-three senators who voted for it were three Republicans — Jones, of Washington; Norris, of Nebraska; and Weeks, of Massachusetts; also one Progressive, Poindexter, of Washington.

That same day, at about six o'clock in the evening, the bill was signed by the President, with three gold pens. One was given to Glass, one to Owen, and one to me. The President departed immediately for a Christmas holiday at Pass Christian, in Mississippi.

I wrote the President a note of congratulation and he replied graciously from Pass Christian, on December 27, with a letter that gave me more credit than I deserved. The letter reads, in part:

All here join in sending the warmest holiday greetings to you and yours.... In looking back upon these months of struggle, I realise how absolutely indispensable and invaluable the part was which you, yourself, played.

I think that Owen and Glass would agree with me that without your constant guidance and mediation the task would have been well-nigh impossible, and I am sure they would join with me in the warm and deep admiration and gratitude which I feel for the part which you, yourself, played. I am sure they would also feel as I do an immense satisfaction that the organization of the new system is to be so largely in your hands.

I did not feel as much satisfaction as the President did in the thought that the organization of the new system would be largely in my hands. Every important city in the United States would certainly consider itself entitled to a Federal Reserve Bank, and I saw that there would be many disappointments. The Act provided for a minimum of eight banks and a maximum of twelve. The locations of the banks and the boundaries of the Federal Reserve districts were to be decided by an Organization Committee — under the terms of the Act — consisting of the Secretary of the Treasury, the Secretary of Agriculture, and the Comptroller of the Currency.

7

The President had just nominated, upon my earnest recommendation, John Skelton Williams as Comptroller of the Currency. I regarded him as admirably fitted for this place and for service on the Federal Reserve Board. He had provoked, however, the hostility of the bankers of the country because of his firm and inflexible performance of duty, resulting in part from his close coöperation with me in the vigorous steps the Treasury Department had taken throughout the fight for the enactment of the Federal Reserve measure.

I am inclined to think that, if I had been nominated as Secretary of the Treasury at that time, my confirmation would have been strongly opposed by the same interests. In any event, Williams' nomination was held up in the Senate so that Houston, Secretary of Agriculture, and myself were the only members of the Organization Committee who could function. Fortunately, the Act provided that two members of the Organization Committee constituted a quorum.

Houston and I decided that the most practicable method of getting the facts on which we were to decide about the location of the Federal Reserve Banks and the division of the United States into districts would be to hold hearings in various parts of the country. The trip around the country was made in a private car, equipped as an office, with a sufficient force of secretaries and stenographers. The first hearing took place in New York City on January 4, 1914. From there we went to Boston, and then to the West.

Before we started, Houston said that he did not see how we could ever cover the ground in a reasonable time, since everybody would want to make long speeches about the merits of the cities they represented, and he was at a loss to know how we could limit them. I told him I had a plan which I thought would be effective; that it had resulted from my own experience. My plan was to treat everybody as a witness — orators, as well as experts — and to require them to sit while presenting their cases.

The sitting posture is an effective squelcher of oratory. In all my experience I have known but one man who could deliver an oration while seated, and that was Richard W. Knott, at that time editor of the Louisville (Kentucky) 'Post.' He appeared before the committee and, with genuine Kentucky eloquence, made a splendid speech from the witness chair.

We saw early in our investigation that twelve Reserve Banks would serve the banking needs of the country better than eight; and, of the twelve, one would have to be in New York, as a matter of course — and another in Chicago, and another in St. Louis. There would have to be one on the Pacific Coast, either in San Francisco, Los Angeles, Seattle, or Portland.

Before I started on the trip, I was quite definite in my mind that a Reserve Bank should be located in New Orleans and another in Baltimore, but when all of the testimony and arguments had been put before the committee, the problem had so resolved itself that Richmond, instead of Baltimore, and Atlanta, instead of New Orleans, were indicated as the Reserve cities for their respective districts.

I was also surprised to find it necessary to establish a Reserve Bank in Kansas City as well as in St. Louis, in the same state, but the testimony clearly justified the Kansas City decision. All this goes to prove the value of knowledge and the necessity of hearing all sides of a case. No question of any kind that involves intricate and doubtful points can be properly decided offhand.

Naturally, a considerable number of cities that had deserving claims, like Pittsburgh, Cincinnati, Baltimore, New Orleans, Denver, Omaha, and Louisville, were disappointed. But it could not be helped; we were obliged to base our findings on the facts as established by the testimony and we consoled ourselves with the reflection that the disappointed cities could be effectively served by branch banks.

Under the provisions of the Act, any national bank that failed within sixty days to apply for membership in the Federal Reserve System was to lose its standing as a Reserve agent. At the end of twelve months, all national banks still outside the system were to be deprived of their charters.

In the fall of 1913, while the bill was in Congress, the National Surety Company of New York sent a questionnaire to all the national banks in the country for the purpose of ascertaining their attitude toward the Federal Reserve plan. The number of national banks that replied was 2395, and 1272 were opposed to the bill. Six hundred and forty were so thorough in their opposition that they declared their intention of becoming state banks if the measure was enacted.

How vain were these resolves and prophecies! Within ten days after the passage of the bill, a score of the largest national banks in the country had notified the Treasury that they intended to enter the Federal Reserve System. On February 3, 1914, while Houston and I were in California, considering the conflicting claims of the various cities of the Coast, I received this wire from John Skelton Williams:

Six thousand one hundred and three national banks, whose combined capital aggregates approximately ninety per cent of the total national banking capital of the country have passed formal resolutions accepting provisions of the currency law.

When I returned to Washington about the first of March the number of member banks had increased to 7571. Only eighteen national banks in the entire country were still outside the system.

Bank secession was dead and the Federal Reserve System was assured!

CHAPTER XVII
WASHINGTON LIFE

I

WASHINGTON society is so formal, so carefully arranged, that it appears to have behind it the studied premeditation of a play on the stage. One suspects rehearsals in private. Everybody in official life has a definite place in the social scale. It is not a simple arrangement, and not many people understand the scheme in all its convolutions.

Before I took office and got enmeshed in the toils of Washington life, I had an idea that I would divest myself of official rank and ask to be treated like any other private citizen. But I soon found that it was impossible. Custom and tradition in Washington are so immutable that one in high official station cannot be the master of his social destiny.

In the end, no matter what you think, you have to paw over lists of names and titles and wonder vaguely whether an Assistant Secretary of State does, or does not, take precedence over an impressive-looking gentleman from a foreign embassy. If you do not place your guests according to the precise gradations of rank at a dinner table, or at a reception, you are likely to cause a 'diplomatic incident'; or, at any rate, a lot of heart-burning and jealousy. Official etiquette is composed of an infinite number of small things fitted neatly together to form an imposing ritual.

The members of the diplomatic corps are sensitive about these matters, of course; it is necessarily a part of their job. But the diplomats are not the only ones. The idea of relative rank and precedence pervades the atmosphere; I have heard clerks and doorkeepers arguing over it.

It is all further complicated by the division of Washington society into classes. The so-called 'aristocratic' Washington consists, generally speaking, of wealthy people who live there permanently. Then there is what is known as 'political' society, and which includes the members of Congress and the officers of the government. The place is full of important nonentities — people whom one meets at dinner and who live in memory only as a white shirt front and a black coat.

The attitude of 'aristocratic' Washington toward 'political' society, except for those in the higher ranks of the government, is said to be one of cool disdain. I doubt it. I never saw anybody treated with disdain, and the 'aristocrats' look for invitations to dinners and official receptions as eagerly as the newest congressman; that is, if the invitation comes from a high official source. But I may be mistaken. I am not a social observer, nor an authority on etiquette, so there may have been a lot of disdain flying around that I never saw. How can a man with the United States Treasury on his hands worry over the social status of anybody?

A senator or congressman, according to an inflexible tradition, has the right to call on any member of the Cabinet at any time and be received ahead of all other callers. This rule plays havoc with the order of the day. Every morning my private secretary would make out a schedule of my appointments and lay it on my desk. The time was divided into small fractions of an hour. Five or ten minutes, or even less, were allowed usually for each caller. Frequently this carefully worked out daily calendar went completely to pieces before noon. A senator would drop in around eleven, let us say, and push by everybody else. He would stay half an hour; and sometimes members of the House and Senate came in a procession all day. Meanwhile, my reception-room would be full of indignant gentlemen who had prearranged appointments. Many of them who did not understand the situation must have thought that I was very careless with other people's time.

In Washington, politics meets one with the ingratiating air of an eager hostess. Everybody talks politics every day and at all hours. It is the one universal topic, like the climate in southern California. A great many people play at the political game. I found, often enough, that some enchanting woman sitting next to me at dinner was a lobbyist in disguise and had designs on the Treasury.

The subtle, suggestive work of lobbyists is going on all the time at Washington, and they manage to influence legislation to an astonishing degree. They are so numerous that they are sometimes spoken of humorously as 'the third house of Congress.' It is impossible to eliminate them, or to devise any law that will curb their activities effectively without doing a grave injustice to citizens who have a legitimate right to bring their views to the attention of Congress.

2

Men in Cabinet positions are usually wealthy, more or less, but the Wilson Cabinet was an exception. There was not a man in it who had much money except Burleson, who was reputed to be well-to-do. Some of them, indeed, had no income beyond a Cabinet member's salary of twelve thousand dollars a year.

As for me, personally, the problem of living within my means was insuperable. I tried to live on my government salary, but I was never able to do it, and when I resigned, after almost six years of service, I was much poorer than I had been on March 4, 1913.

When I first went to Washington, I made up my mind not to pay more than one fourth of my salary, or three thousand dollars, for the annual rent of a house. It was difficult to find a suitable residence at that figure, but eventually I leased a four-story house at 1709 Massachusetts Avenue, next door to the palatial home of Senator Henry A. Dupont, of Delaware. It was not a comfortable house; it was too narrow — about twenty feet wide — and its rooms were too small. However, it was within ten minutes' walk of the Treasury Department.

At that time only two members of my family were with me — my daughter Nona, then under twenty, and my daughter Sally, nine years old. Francis Huger, my eldest son, was just finishing his course in the Columbia Law School, in New York. The two other boys — William Gibbs, Jr., and Robert H. — were at St. Paul's School, in New Hampshire. My eldest daughter Harriet was married and lived in Prescott, Arizona.

As I was a widower, my daughter Nona was the head of my household and its social arrangements. It was a rather formidable undertaking for such a young girl; however, she met the situation splendidly, despite her inexperience. At that time it was customary for the wives of the members of the

Senate and the House to make formal calls on the wives of the Cabinet officers or the heads of their households. These were duty calls; they merely left their cards, as a rule. But the calls had to be returned. Nona was kept on the go for some time. It was really absurd. Imagine five hundred or more women going around leaving cards with the stolid industry of mail-carriers.

One day I discovered that my daughter's status was the subject of some criticism on the part of one or more of the ladies of the Cabinet. As the social head of my household she had the same rank, naturally, that my wife would have had if she had been alive. That meant that she had precedence of all the Cabinet ladies, with the exception of Mrs. Bryan, the wife of the Secretary of State.

Shortly before the first official reception at the White House, Mrs. Wilson asked if she might discuss with me, frankly, a purely personal matter. Of course I said yes. She then told me that she and the President would be delighted to accord my daughter the rank to which she was entitled and that I must feel that they would welcome her in that capacity. However, she said that she ought to tell me that some of the ladies of the Cabinet, whose names she did not mention and concerning whom I did not inquire, had raised the question with her; that as my daughter was so young she should not, they thought, outrank most of the ladies in the Cabinet.

Mrs. Wilson said that she had no sympathy with this attitude, but she wanted me to know about it, so that I might decide, myself, what should be done. I thought it a very narrow view for anyone in the Cabinet to take, but I kept my opinion to myself. I assured Mrs. Wilson that there need be no embarrassment, because I had already discussed the matter with my daughter, and she had told me emphatically that she did not want to assume any such position; that it would force her to take on duties which would restrict her opportunity to associate with younger people. I was proud of my daughter for having such a level head. I could see that Mrs. Wilson was surprised, as well as relieved at this prompt settlement of the incipient controversy; she remarked that Nona was a very sensible girl. The incident passed and the serenity of the ladies of the Cabinet was undisturbed.

3

The habit of taking a worm's-eye view of the universe, commonly known as the inferiority complex, is not prevalent in Congress. The average senator or representative is ready to talk instantly and with complete assurance on any topic connected with the government or politics.

He may be right or wrong in his facts and assumptions — and is just as likely to be one as the other — but he is seldom, or never, bashful. The keynote of his character is triumphant self-confidence. When he rises to speak in Congress, he is not talking merely to a large room full of men in Washington; he is talking to the folks back home. He has in his mind's eye the dull acreage of the 'Congressional Record' with his speech shining and glowing on its surface. He is thinking, too, of the newspapers in his district, and of the discussions in the local drug-stores. Consequently, he cultivates an attitude, and almost never grows out of it during his career. These persistent attitudes frequently develop into idiosyncrasies. Newspaper correspondents have told me that they can tell what a man is going to say when he rises to speak — provided that they know beforehand the subject of his remarks — and provided also that he has been in Congress long enough for them to become acquainted with his 'line.'

This manner of striking poses and playing to a distant gallery is the reason, perhaps, for the assertion of high-brow commentators and magazine writers that Congress has no real ability, that it is composed entirely of blatant mediocrities.

That is not so; it is a false conclusion. I have never known a Congress that did not contain many able men; and by that I mean men of genuine understanding and accurate knowledge. They are in the minority, but they have an influence out of all proportion to their numbers.

The outstanding defect of Congress year in and year out is not lack of ability or lack of knowledge, but lack of statesmanship. The average congressman goes to Washington almost bent double with a weight of pre-election promises on his back. He has got to do something to redeem them; he must look out for the folks. And the pressure is often so great that he is willing to surrender his point of view on almost anything, as long as he does not give up the basic principles of his party, if he can get through an appropriation for a magnificent post-office building in Riddletown. He has much more vision than he appears to have, but he suppresses it except in time of a national crisis. Then, all of a sudden, he is likely to astonish the country with a display of unexpected altruism, sagacity and foresight.

The device of the party 'conference' obviates, to a certain extent, the vicious results of the political situation. Under this system the leaders in each house shape the policies of their respective parties. They do the thinking on large affairs, with the consent of their colleagues. The conference meets, argues and winds up by adopting, eventually, the views of the leaders. Then the rank and file of congressmen go their way, and when an important question comes up they can be depended upon to vote according to the decision of the conference.

The result of all this is that about forty or fifty men, divided about equally, I should say, between the Democrats and the Republicans, direct the work of Congress.

Politics should be the science of humanity. Its subject-matter is, or ought to be, human welfare. When we compare it with other sciences we find that it creeps along far behind them. The motive of all science is a search for truth, but in political affairs very few people try to find the truth. Politics lumbers through the world like a half-witted giant, yelling slogans and campaign songs.

Professional politicians never want to be pinned down to anything definite; they exist in a cloud of generalities. They fill their political platforms with long-winded talk about human liberty and freedom, and various varieties of verbal fog. We must begin to let them know that a political platform is not worth the paper it is written on unless it touches the vital, everyday problems of men and women.

Among other things of primary import, it is the business of political science to consider the deeply rooted defect of our civilization which makes a part of our people extravagantly rich, and another part of them desperately poor; and which causes cycles of economic depression with their evil accompaniment of widespread unemployment and distress. We must find out the exact causes of poverty, not as politicians but as scientists of humanity, and then we must set about devising remedies.

We must try to discover why there are so many unhappy people in a country that is so rich in material wealth.

These are fundamental problems. They go deeper than the income tax, or the tariff, or the building of battleships. The politics of the future will have to deal with them, not in a spirit of partisanship, but with the fair-minded attitude of the scientist.

4

In the course of time my acquaintance in Washington became extensive. I knew personally, of course, all the prominent figures of both parties. There were many interesting men on each side of Congress. John Sharp Williams, of Mississippi, for instance. At that time he was a leading Democratic senator. He was a scholar, and a brilliant one. He was probably the best-read man in either house. And there was F. M. Simmons, of North Carolina, whose mind was a ready reference library on everything connected with the tariff and public finance; and Robert L. Owen, of Oklahoma, vigorous, industrious, and progressive; and Martin, of Virginia, a country gentleman with the fine manners of an *ante-bellum* aristocrat; and John W. Kern, of Indiana, at that time the Democratic floor leader of the Senate.

Ollie James of Kentucky was certainly the most impressive-looking member of the Senate. He was a giant in stature; a good-natured, jolly giant with a nimble and fluent mind. James was, I think, the most effective rough-and-ready debater that I have ever heard.

Joseph T. Robinson, of Arkansas — now the Democratic floor leader in the Senate — had just become, in 1913, a member of that body.

And there were William J. Stone, of Missouri, able tactician and effective debater; Thomas P. Gore, blind senator from Oklahoma — of marvelous memory and a formidable antagonist on the floor; Claude A. Swanson, of Virginia, active, capable, and effective in reconciling party differences; Henry F. Hollis, of New Hampshire, energetic, able, and, although a new member, quickly taking high rank among his colleagues; William E. Chilton, of West Virginia, solid and dependable supporter of the Administration; Morris Sheppard, of Texas, author of the Eighteenth Amendment to the Constitution; Thomas J. Walsh, of Montana, also a new member, but, through industry and ability, quickly gaining the commanding position in the Senate which he still occupies; and James Hamilton Lewis, of Illinois, picturesque and courteous.

Claude Kitchin, of North Carolina, was one of the ablest men in the House of Representatives. He succeeded Oscar Underwood as chairman of the Ways and Means Committee when the latter went to the Senate. Kitchin was a man of distinguished appearance and pleasant personality. He was one of the best-equipped debaters who has appeared in the last generation on the floor of the House. I was not always in accord with Kitchin's economic views, and we used to have some pretty hot discussions over revenue bills, but these controversies never weakened our friendship. Although he held hard to his opinions, he had a fair mind and was willing to be convinced when the argument went against him.

Another member of the Ways and Means Committee, Cordell Hull, of Tennessee, was one of the best-informed men on the vexatious subject of the tariff in either house. Hull has recently gone to the Senate. For some time he was chairman of the National Democratic Committee.

In 1913, Underwood, of Alabama, was the Democratic floor leader in the House, as well as chairman of the vitally important Ways and Means Committee. Underwood was a genuine, well-grounded tariff expert. It was largely through his efforts that the Administration tariff bill passed the House.

One of the men in the House for whom I had, and still have, much admiration and friendship was John N. Garner, of Texas; and another was Carter Glass, whom I have mentioned extensively in previous chapters of this narrative. Garner is now the Democratic floor leader of the House and Glass is in the Senate.

Another able Democrat in the House was Joshua W.

Alexander, of Missouri, chairman of the Committee on Merchant Marine and Fisheries, a strong supporter of the Administration's shipping bill and effective in that notable fight. He was subsequently appointed Secretary of Commerce by President Wilson.

I must mention, also, Victor Murdock, of Kansas — militant, progressive, and able citizen — inevitably drawn to the support of President Wilson by the force of principle and conviction.

Among the Republicans I had a great liking for La Follette. We got along together splendidly and agreed on most subjects. He was, in my judgment, one of the greatest men in the history of the Republican Party.

I also knew Senator William E. Borah pleasantly and favorably. He was then, and has been ever since, one of the outstanding personalities in the Senate. And there was George Sutherland, the able Senator from Utah, now an Associate Justice of the Supreme Court of the United States; and Albert B. Cummins, of Iowa; and Henry Cabot Lodge, of Massachusetts.

Lodge and I met with the coolness of men who come from different ends of the earth and bring to their meeting two opposing sets of ideas. After a while we became friendly, although we were never intimate. Lodge was a member of the Senate Finance Committee, and in all the legislation that the Treasury needed during the war I was able to secure his support.

He was a cultured man, but his mind was almost wholly without vista and singularly inflexible. His ideas were colored by prejudgments and prejudices. He had already made up his mind about everything, and his conclusions formed a museum of wax figures which were not to be touched. Lodge never liked the South and was annoyed at seeing so many Southern men in office. But despite these various inhibitions he could be agreeable and, in fact, thoroughly charming.

I often wondered, as I heard him talk, why a man as gifted as Lodge undoubtedly was had not played a greater part on the national stage. The reason is, I believe, to be found in his intense partisanship. He could not see any good whatever in the opposition. That is unfortunate for anyone in any sphere of life; for a public man it is tragic. All the truth, all the goodness, and all the greatness are never on one side. You may not like the other fellow, but do not forget that God made him, too.

One of the picturesque characters in the Washington of that period was Thomas R. Marshall, Vice-President during the Wilson Administration. I call him 'picturesque,' even though the term is hackneyed, because that appears to be the only single word which fits him. He was picturesque but not flamboyant. He was small in physique, provincial in manner, and he had a wide streak of dry humor. I can imagine him sitting with a swarm of cronies in a country grocery-store telling stories, and the scene would have fitted him perfectly.

He was fond of puns. When President Wilson started for Paris in 1918, Marshall sent him a book inscribed, 'From your your only *Vice*, Thomas R. Marshall.' In the midst of the alarms of the World War, Marshall declared, 'What this country needs is a good five-cent cigar.' This saying caught the public fancy. It has lingered in the air long after Marshall has gone to another world. Men are often remembered by such things.

He was not a liberal, as many people thought when he was Governor of Indiana. He struck me as a decided conservative. I think he was an over-judicial man. As the presiding officer of the Senate, he sometimes disappointed his party because, on some crucial points, his rulings favored the opposition, when they should have favored, and could very properly have favored, his own party. He was so anxious to appear impartial that he sometimes leaned back the other way.

He was a great job-hunter for his friends. When he came to see me at the Treasury, he wound up his conversation almost invariably with an effort to put somebody on the payroll, and I have an idea that his feelings were often hurt because he did not get what he thought he was entitled to as Vice-President of the United States. I was always anxious to oblige him, but the difficulty was that the two senators from Indiana had the right, under a long-established rule, to make the recommendations for their state for appointments in the Treasury Department. I did the best I could for him, but he was never satisfied. I do not think Marshall ever knew to what extent I was instrumental in having him nominated as Vice-President at the Baltimore Convention.

As Speaker of the House, as well as on his own account, Champ Clark was a personage of high importance in Washington. I frequently saw him, and, while I admired him as an able man and a sound Democrat, I used to wonder how he ever became a popular figure before the public. He had a cold manner and a listless handshake; besides, he seemed morose and to bear deep-seated grudges. He said as few words as possible, and what he had to say appeared to be tacked on to a tacit background of discontent. But I had a genuine liking for the Speaker and was always glad to render every possible service to him. My opinion is that he never got over the disappointment of his defeat for the presidential nomination by Woodrow Wilson.

He did not bear any grudge against President Wilson, nor against me, to the best of my knowledge and belief. The devil in his cosmos was William Jennings Bryan. I have recently read his autobiography, 'My Quarter Century of American Politics,' and in it he says in downright phrases that he would have been President if it had not been for the perfidy and double-dealing of Bryan. I do not agree with him. After Tammany switched the ninety votes of New York from Harmon to Clark in the Baltimore Convention, Bryan, who had supported Clark up to that time, came out openly and frankly against him. Moreover, I am convinced that, if Clark had been the Democratic nominee in 1912, Roosevelt and his Progressives would have won. It was a year of liberalism and reform.

George Creel has a funny story about Champ Clark, though in telling it he always prefaces the anecdote by saying that it did not seem funny to Clark himself. It appears, according to Creel, that Clark was on a political speaking tour and got in the habit of making the same speech at every stopping-place. He was accompanied by several newspaper men, and of course, they memorized the speech from having heard it so frequently repeated.

At one stop Clark was late; had taken the wrong train. While the audience was waiting one of the correspondents on the platform suggested to the chairman that he would like to make a speech himself, and the good-natured chairman thereupon stepped forward and presented the young man to the audience.

This reporter, beaming on the people, gave Clark's speech — every word of it — and received great applause. While he was bowing in appreciation he saw, out of the corner of his eye, Champ Clark coming from the railroad station. He wasted no time in getting away, and when Clark had been introduced briefly and had started on his oration the young man was seen disappearing across a field. The chairman timidly twitched the coat-tails of the Missouri statesman and whispered, 'That speech has just been made.'

'What do you mean?' Clark demanded.

'Why, that boy,' the chairman said, pointing at a speck in the distance, 'has just said the same thing, word for word, on this platform.'

Clark's brow was as black as thunder. His sense of humor was all gone. 'I'll kill him,' he rumbled, 'if I ever see him again, and I mean it, too.'

Among my good friends in Washington was Cary T. Grayson, then a surgeon in the United States Navy and personal physician to the President. He was subsequently made an Admiral, and is now retired. Grayson and I used to go horseback riding in Rock Creek Park and Potomac Park whenever I could spare the time. He was a great enthusiast over the benefits of exercise on a horse, and is responsible for the aphorism: 'The outside of a horse is good for the inside of a man.'

Besides being a competent physician, Grayson was one of the most agreeable of companions. He was just the man to look after the physical welfare of the President — quiet, unobtrusive, tactful, discreet, and an excellent story-teller. He was trusted by the President and won his lasting friendship and affection.

Grayson was then unmarried, and he and I used to go, occasionally, to dances. The fox trot was just coming into fashion; also the tango. I learned the fox trot quickly, but I never danced the tango, although some newspapers seemed to delight in referring to me as a 'tango artist.'

My taking part in dances caused considerable astonishment in Washington, and in turn the astonishment astonished me, for I could see no reason why I shouldn't dance if I wanted to. But it seems that it was considered somewhat undignified for a Secretary of the Treasury to dance. There was a tradition about it. My predecessors wore frock coats, high hats, and walked with stately deliberation, like a man carrying a bucket of water on his head.

5

I have said that I went riding in the parks and along the country roads with Grayson. But he was not always my companion. Occasionally Miss Eleanor Wilson, the youngest of the President's three daughters, went horseback riding with me. We rode and played tennis and danced together, and talked about almost everything. I got into the pleasant habit of calling on her in the evening. At that time the Federal Reserve Bill was in Congress, and it was on my mind, of course. One day, while I was with Miss Eleanor, I fell into a sort of monologue, or disquisition, on the Federal Reserve plan, but I cut myself off short in the middle of my talk, as I feared that I was boring her. To my surprise she continued the topic, and revealed an unusual understanding of the subject.

After that I began to discuss all sorts of political questions with her. She took an enthusiastic interest in them and in the many problems which faced the Administration. This might have seemed remarkable to me if I had not known of the President's way of talking freely about every subject in the family circle. He would never talk of the day's work at the dinner table, as many men do; but after dinner, or at any other period of leisure when he was surrounded by his family, he would frequently discuss in the most interesting and charming way political issues and the current problems of government; the personalities of important men and women; and sometimes his mind would range over the field of literature and history; economics and sociology. It was a liberal education and a privilege to hear him on these occasions. He did it not only because he wanted Mrs. Wilson's reaction to the im-

ELEANOR WILSON McADOO
Photograph taken at the White House in 1914, shortly before her marriage

mediate problems in which he was concerned, but also because he wanted his three daughters to understand and learn as much as possible about the vital questions of the time.

He expressed himself with the utmost freedom, trusting to his daughters' discretion, which they never failed to observe. The knowledge of Administration measures that Miss Eleanor possessed came from these discussions as well as from her own interest in public affairs.

She was neither argumentative nor angular, but entirely womanly — a charming girl, without affectation or pedantry. It was not long before I discovered that my interest in her was more than platonic. Being twice her age, I resolved that I could never tell her about it; it didn't seem quite fair to her, in the first place, and again, I was not vain enough to believe that she could ever consider me in any other light than that of a friend. Moreover, I felt at a great disadvantage with the young and gallant officers of the Army and Navy, the accomplished diplomats, and other eligibles who swarmed around her on all occasions. I laid my affection for her away in the attic of the soul where one stores lovely but hopeless emotions.

While I was pondering over all this, Miss Eleanor's sister Jessie was married at the White House on November 18, 1913, to Francis B. Sayre, an able and interesting young man who is now a professor in the Harvard Law School.

It was a brilliant and impressive occasion. After the wedding there was an informal dance. Miss Eleanor and I danced together frequently. At such times, with the rosy unfolding of waltz music in the air, stern resolves against self-revelation are likely to dissolve in a mist. I made up my mind to propose to her.

I did not know when I would make my confession; I awaited a favorable moment. It is rather curious about proposals. I do not believe one in a hundred of them are made in conventional form. In the prim novels of the eighteenth century, we read of men proposing in long and precise letters that sound like literary essays. In the Victorian age the man was supposed to fall on his knees on the carpet while the lady sat on a sofa. I wonder how many men have actually fallen on their knees before the ladies of their choice?

It was hard to find time in the midst of my pressing duties

and Miss Eleanor's numerous engagements to see as much of her as I should have liked, but now and then we used to steal off at dusk, between tea-time and dinner, and take a walk. One of our favorite places was the Ellipse, that lovely park that lies immediately south of the White House and along the Potomac. We would climb the diminutive hill where the great Washington Monument soars into the sky and watch the dull red winter sunsets. We both liked to be there; it seemed so remote, so far away from all problems and exigencies.

One evening she remarked that she was leaving in a few days to spend Christmas at Pass Christian, on the Gulf coast. That was in December of 1913. I knew that I should not see her again for several weeks; it seemed a long time. So there, sitting on a park bench in the evening twilight, I made my confession.

Now I had to face an important question. My marriage into the President's family, I realized, might cause considerable embarrassment, officially and politically. I could conceive that differences might arise between myself and other members of the Cabinet, and between myself and the leaders of the party. If I should stay in the Cabinet, these differences, or at least some of them, might cause an awkward situation for the President if he should be called upon to decide them. If he should uphold me, no matter how clearly I might be in the right, there were plenty of people who would be small enough to say that the decision was induced by family relationship.

The only thing to do was to tell him what was in my mind. I gave him the substance of my reflections — then I said:

'Mr. President, I think, in the circumstances, that I ought to resign after my marriage, and I should like you to feel that my resignation is at your disposal, to take effect at your convenience.'

'I don't agree with you,' he replied. 'I appreciate warmly your generous and considerate attitude, but I hope you will dismiss all thought of such a thing. You were appointed Secretary of the Treasury solely on your merit. No one imagined, at that time, that the present situation would arise.'

He paused a moment, and looked at me humorously. 'But I must admit,' he continued, 'that, if you had married into my family before I became President, I could not have offered you a position in the Cabinet, no matter how outstanding your record and qualifications might have been. You are now organizing the Federal Reserve Banks and engaged in other matters of vital public interest. Your resignation would be a serious blow. I cannot conceive of any embarrassment that could result from your remaining in the Cabinet.'

I was gratified by his expressions of confidence and told him that I was glad to yield to his judgment.

The rumor that I might resign got abroad and it pleased me greatly to have a Republican paper — the Kansas City 'Journal' — say: 'It is gratifying to learn that the marriage of Eleanor Wilson and Secretary of the Treasury McAdoo will not result in the latter's resignation.' I am not vain enough to quote the remainder of this article or the commendatory things the press, without regard to partisanship, so generously said about me in this connection.

The newspapers of March 14, 1914, carried the following:

The President and Mrs. Wilson announce the engagement of their youngest daughter, Eleanor Randolph, to Honorable William Gibbs McAdoo.

On the day of the wedding, my fellow members of the Cabinet invited me to a luncheon, which was strictly within the Cabinet circle. It was a jolly and informal occasion. After luncheon, Secretary of State Bryan took charge of the meeting and called on each member of the Cabinet. They responded with brief speeches; felicitations and so on. Finally Mr. Bryan laughingly told me to stand up and 'give an account of myself.'

Well, what could a prospective bridegroom say when commanded to tell his life-story? It sounded ominous, that question. I thought for a moment of making a speech, one hour long, on the subject of the grand old currency, and watching the members of the Cabinet squirm and yawn. But that would have been too much of a joke, so I compromised with my inclinations by telling this story:

An illiterate mountaineer, who lived in his lonely cabin high up in the Great Smoky Range in eastern Tennessee, had for years courted unsuccessfully the girl with whom he was desperately in love. Sitting one moonlight night by the fireside in his cabin, a knock called him to his door. There he found the rural mail carrier, who handed him a letter. By the light of the fire he saw the handwriting of the girl he loved. He opened the letter with trembling hands and was filled with joy to find that it contained the answer he had so long prayed for. He stepped out of the cabin into the bright moonlight, and with hands uplifted to Heaven said: 'Oh, Lawd, I ain't got nuthin' agin' nobody, no mo'.'

The wedding ceremony took place in the Blue Room of the White House the evening of May 7, 1914. The attendance was limited to our families and relatives and to the members of the Cabinet and their families. About a hundred people were present.

My little daughter Sally acted as flower-girl, and my friend Cary T. Grayson was best man. The maids-of-honor were Mrs. Francis B. Sayre and Miss Margaret Wilson. The Reverend Sylvester W. Beach of the Presbyterian Church and pastor of the President's Church at Princeton, performed the ceremony.

My wife and I decided to avoid newspaper publicity as much as we could and to slip away to some quiet place for our honeymoon. We had planned to make a short trip to Europe, but the situation in Mexico became so alarming by the time the wedding occurred that I felt I ought not to go far away from Washington.

The President and Mrs. Wilson had rented 'Harlakenden' at Cornish, in New Hampshire, as a summer home. They offered it to us for a couple of weeks' stay and we decided to go there. Our destination was kept a carefully guarded secret. After the wedding, followed by a supper and a reception, the problem was to get away from the newspaper men. This was made more difficult by the fact that I was on friendly terms with the Washington correspondents and I had a natural impulse to give them all the information they wanted. But

I restrained this good-natured urge and was as silent as the Sphinx. They said, humorously, that it did not make much difference, as they would easily find out where we were going. I saw that they planned to follow us to the station. During the evening of the wedding, the parking area before the White House was full of newspaper automobiles, chugging away, their engines running.

I engaged a private car and had it placed on a side-track at College Park, a Washington suburb. The railroad officials were enjoined to secrecy. Then I had three White House cars parked at the south entrance, instead of the main entrance facing Pennsylvania Avenue.

Mrs. McAdoo and I took one car; the other two were taken by Mr. and Mrs. Sayre, Miss Margaret Wilson, and some of the guests. These cars, with curtains drawn, left the White House grounds through the southwest gate and immediately separated, going in different directions. The maneuver was completely successful. The watchful reporters were at the north gates on Pennsylvania Avenue and did not learn that we had left the White House until some time afterward.

When the regular train from Washington to New York reached College Park, our private car was hooked on and we were off for New Hampshire. I had also arranged for my motor to meet me at a side-track at West Deerfield, Massachusetts, where we arrived the next morning about eight o'clock. We reached 'Harlakenden' the evening of May 9.

Our whereabouts was a mystery for only a day or two. One morning a pleasant-voiced newspaper man stood bowing at the door, and I learned that he was not the only one who was camped at the hotel in the village.

CHAPTER XVIII

OPENING OF THE FEDERAL RESERVE BANKS

I

DURING March, 1914, my office looked like a cross between the map-room of a geographical society and the statistical division of the United States Census Bureau. Houston, Williams, and I spent hours defining the exact limits of each Federal Reserve district and fixing the location of the Federal Reserve Banks.

The next thing on the program was the appointment of five members of the Federal Reserve Board. The personnel of the Board was a matter of immense importance. The entire scheme was novel and untried. We were dealing with experimental formulas, with principles that had existed only in theory, and which were to be put to the most practical of tests. For the Board we needed men who were not only able, but who possessed the gift of working with other men without friction.

The President's first choice for Governor of the Board was Richard Olney, a distinguished Massachusetts Democrat who had been Secretary of State under Cleveland. Olney was a man of the highest character; and besides, he had the wisdom that grows from a combination of common-sense and experience. To my regret he felt that he was too far along in years to undertake a large new responsibility.

'You can hardly be sorrier than I am,' Mr. Olney wrote, 'that I am able to do so little in aid of an administration whose first year of achievement makes it one of the most notable the country has ever known.'

The President asked me to suggest someone, and I proposed the name of Charles S. Hamlin, of Massachusetts, who was serving at that time as an Assistant Secretary of the Treasury. Hamlin was a sound and cautious man, and a capable one. On my recommendation President Wilson designated him as Governor of the Board for the first year. This was a wise selection.

Perhaps I should explain here that the Board has both a Chairman and a Governor. The Chairman is the Secretary of the Treasury, while the Governor is the actual executive officer. The five appointed members give their whole time to the work of the Board, and are in effect the managers of the system.

At the suggestion of Franklin K. Lane, the President made Adolph C. Miller, who was one of Lane's assistants in the Interior Department, a member of the Board. Both Lane and Miller were Californians. Miller's fitness was based on his qualifications as an economist. He had been a professor of finance in the University of Chicago for ten years, and was afterward in the faculty of the University of California.

Another member was W. P. G. Harding, of Alabama. When the President appointed him, at the suggestion of Colonel House, Harding was president of the First National Bank of Birmingham. He was a thoroughly trained banker. After the Board got under way, and I began to know all these men well, I came to the conclusion that Harding was the ablest man on the Board, so far as the practice and technique of domestic banking was concerned.

One of President Wilson's lifelong friends was Thomas D. Jones, of Chicago. They had known each other since their college days, and Jones was a trustee of Princeton University. The President named him as a member of the Federal Reserve Board, and the result was a bitter contest in the Senate over his confirmation. Jones was a director of the International Harvester Company and of the New Jersey Zinc Company — the so-called Zinc Trust.

The Harvester Company was, at that time, hated like poison throughout all the agricultural states. Besides being in popular disfavor, it had been charged by the government with violations of the Sherman Anti-Trust law.

In the Senate it was shown by the spokesmen of the Administration that Mr. Jones possessed only an insignificant amount of Harvester Company stock, and that he had taken no part in the formation of the concern. He became a director seven years after the corporation was organized. He was not a member of the finance committee, which was the dominating power in the corporation, nor had he ever been one of its executive officers. The attack, therefore, was against his affiliations rather than against him personally.

The President refused to withdraw the nomination and the situation became strained and ominous. I am sure, however, that Jones would have been confirmed eventually, but, after the wrangle had gone on for some weeks, he removed himself from the contest by writing a letter to the President in which he said that he would prefer not to be considered any longer, as he did not want to embarrass the Administration.

That was the first of President Wilson's collisions with the Senate, and it was by no means the last one.

The President asked Jones if he could recommend a suitable man for the place, and Jones suggested Frederick A. Delano, of Chicago. Delano was a well-known railroad executive and, at the time of his appointment, was president of the Monon Road. His nomination was readily confirmed.

There was a vast amount of controversy over the appointment of Paul M. Warburg. As soon as his nomination reached the Senate objections arose. Warburg was identified with Wall Street; he was a member of the banking firm of Kühn, Loeb & Company, and was a director in a number of railroads and other large corporations. Personally, I favored his appointment. It seemed just and right that a member with the Wall Street point of view should be on the Board, if it was to be well-rounded and representative of all classes of American finance.

He had been an American citizen for only three years; and this, too, was the subject of criticism. Many senators and a large section of the public maintained that an official position of such importance to the country's welfare should not be given to any man who, only a few years before, had been a foreigner. I may explain, to make the incident clear, that Warburg was born in Germany, and that his family had been international bankers of renown for several generations. He had lived for years in the United States before he became a citizen. His English, both spoken and written, was perfect; he was, in short, a man of education and understanding. He was a 'scientific' banker; that is, he knew banking — especially that part of it which relates to international transactions — with the precision of a scientist.

The controversy about his appointment was further complicated by the fact that Warburg refused to appear before the Senate committee to which the nomination had been referred. He was the only nominee who was requested to appear before the committee, and that was the basis of his objection. He declared that he would not mind being questioned if all the other nominees for places on the Board were also summoned.

Finally, in July, after the nomination had dragged along for weeks, he consented to appear before the committee, on the advice of his friends, I suppose. He was subjected to some questioning — nothing especially harsh — and the committee made a favorable report. The Senate confirmed both Warburg and Delano on August 8, 1914.

The appointment of Warburg to the Federal Reserve Board is a striking instance of the broad-mindedness of the Wilson Administration. He was appointed in spite of his criticisms of the Federal Reserve Act because it was thought that his technical knowledge of international finance would be useful. It was useful; in some respects it was invaluable.

2

There seems to be an impression among Warburg's friends, and perhaps elsewhere, that he contributed largely to the shaping of the Federal Reserve Act; some of them — Professor E. R. A. Seligman among others — go so far as to declare that he practically wrote the bill, or inspired it. In his preface to 'Essays on Banking Reform,' Seligman says: 'In its fundamental features, the Federal Reserve Act is the work of Mr. Warburg more than of any other man in the country.'

On March 27, 1915, the New York 'World' in a leading editorial asserted that Warburg 'had more to do with the actual drafting of the Federal Reserve Law than any other man, either in Congress or out of Congress.' This assertion is so completely erroneous that it must have emanated from ignorance rather than from mendacity. I must say, in justice to Warburg, that he has never, so far as I know, made such a claim in his own behalf.

As a matter of pure history, I may record the fact that Warburg was opposed to the Glass-Owen Bill, although he approved its underlying intent and objective. He thought that we were going about it the wrong way, and he said so in many letters and conferences, also in magazine and newspaper articles.

A draft of the Glass Bill was shown to Warburg by Colonel House in June, 1913, while they were both on a steamer going to Europe. That was the first time Warburg had seen the bill. He remained in Europe all, or most, of the summer while the bill was being discussed in Congress. From Switzerland he wrote a number of letters criticizing the plan, as set forth in the Glass-Owen Bill, and he emphasized his objections in a couple of pamphlets, which he prepared while in Europe. These were printed and widely circulated. On his return in the late summer or fall of 1913, he was very active in connection with the bill: criticizing, suggesting amendments, and proposing alternatives. At that time the measure had been before Congress for months, and it was then essentially in the form in which it finally became a law. His suggestions and comments had no appreciable influence in shaping any of its vital features.

While the New York 'World' thought Warburg had more to do than any other man with the actual drafting of the Federal Reserve Act, its neighbor the New York 'Times' pinned its medal on the breast of ex-Senator Nelson W. Aldrich. On November 19, 1914, the 'Times' printed an editorial on the creation of the Federal Reserve which was a marvel of weighty and profound misinformation. The 'Times' declared that 'Nelson W. Aldrich will in financial history be known as the Father of the Federal Reserve banking system.'

In view of the fact that Aldrich was bitterly opposed to the Glass-Owen Bill, and that his own plan for establishing a reserve banking system differed materially in almost every important feature from the one that was adopted, the 'Times' editorial might be considered nothing more than an amusing specimen of ignorance if, in reading it, one did not have the melancholy reflection that the historians of the future would probably look upon it as an authoritative statement. The 'Times' said:

In any distribution of praise, in any acknowledgment of the country's debt to the builders of the country's Federal Reserve banking system, the name of Nelson W. Aldrich, lately Senator from Rhode Island, must and will stand first upon the list of those to whom credit is due.... By whatever name we call it, that bill [the Aldrich bill] was the source and origin, it contained the spirit and substance, of the present Federal Reserve banking act.

The editorial goes on to say that 'due credit and reward' should be accorded to Glass and Owen, and then editorial applause is given to the bankers of the country. As the bankers, with a few exceptions, fought the bill with the desperate resolution that people usually display in fighting the bubonic plague, it is difficult to see where the applause comes in, but the 'Times' says that credit should not be withheld from 'any of the laborers in the field'; and 'certainly not from the bankers of the country, to whose priceless services and advice, given often in circumstances of extreme discouragement, the country owes the final shaping of the measure and the exclusion from it of unnumbered crudities and much false doctrine.'

The 'Times' does not mention President Wilson in this editorial. Somehow it overlooked the news that the President was a potent factor in shaping the Act and in putting it through Congress. Without his constant coöperation and powerful influence, the Federal Reserve System never would have come into existence.

I have not set out with the intention of showing up the New York 'Times' in a sorry light, and I am conscious of the fact that misleading editorials, like the one from which I have just quoted, are not customary, but rare and exceptional in its columns.

Later on, the 'Times' became a warm supporter of the Wilson Administration. The President appreciated its friendly attitude. To Louis Wiley, general manager of the 'Times,' he wrote on February 26, 1919: 'Even when I do not agree with the "Times," I am often very much instructed by what it says, and its support of the League of Nations has given me the greatest gratification.' And on October 6, 1920, he wrote — again to Louis Wiley: 'May I not say how much I admire the splendid course the "Times" is pursuing editorially? Please convey my warmest regards to the editorial staff.'

3

The month of August, 1914, was a fateful one for President Wilson.

In that month Europe became a battle-field, and half the man-power of the civilized world rushed to an orgy of slaughter and destruction.

From the instant it began, all sensible men realized that the World War was moving with an enormous centrifugal force. Its fragments were flying in all directions. The President and his advisers had to think of the war with urgent and instant concentration. Thereafter, the current of emotions generated by the European struggle seeped into American thought and action, inevitably and continuously. We were like a family that lives next door to a house in which everyone has a contagious disease.

The burden of unpredictable, and often insoluble, problems fell heavily on the President.

And, in the midst of these worries and distractions, came the great tragedy of his life, the loss of his wife, who died at the White House late in the afternoon of August 6. She had been in poor health for months; during July she was desperately ill.

Before she lapsed into final unconsciousness, she said to Grayson: 'Doctor, if I go away, promise me that you will take good care of my husband.' These were her last words; her thoughts in her dying moments were of the man with whom she had lived so long and so happily.

Mrs. Wilson was one of the most unselfish people I have ever known. She was devoted to the people she loved, to her husband and daughters, to high and noble ideals, to the helpless and the poor. The World War, if she had lived to witness its progress, would have caused her unutterable pain.

For the President her death was a genuine disaster. She supplied a calm excellence of judgment which had contributed uniformly to his happiness and success in life. I do not mean by this to imply that the President himself was lacking in calmness and judgment. There was, however, a strong quality of impulsiveness in his nature, though I am sure that those who did not know him well never thought so.

He was also inclined, because, I think, of an innate and un-

ELLEN AXSON WILSON
The President's first wife

suspected shyness, to withhold himself too much from contact with people whom it was important for him to know and
whose coöperation was highly desirable in the conduct of public business. The pressure of great affairs absorbed his mind
so thoroughly that he often disregarded personal contacts and
became impatient of their necessity. Mrs. Wilson, with an
extraordinary understanding that might be truthfully characterized as a prescience, or intuition, was keenly alive to
these subtle influences in political life.

She possessed a quiet dignity which radiated a degree of
happiness and contentment in the Wilson household that was
exceptional. It was surprising to me, too, that, with her slight
experience in public life, she had such a clear judgment of
actions and motives.

Her knowledge of human nature was remarkable. The
President had an enduring confidence in her estimates of men
and their ideas. She proved to be one of the soundest and most
influential of his advisers. Perhaps it would not be too much
to say that she was *the soundest and most influential* of them
all. Yet she did not abuse her power; nor did she thrust herself into situations and try to run affairs. The well-rounded
development of the President's personality was undoubtedly
due, in large measure, to the influence of this rare and beautiful spirit.

I was as deeply grieved by her death as if she had been my
own mother. We were great friends and grew to love each
other devotedly after I became a member of the family.

4

A distressing lack of harmony soon revealed itself among
the members of the Federal Reserve Board. An anti-Treasury
faction developed even while the Board was in its formative
stages. The members of this group — Miller, Delano, and
Warburg — were in opposition, as a rule, to myself, Williams,
and Hamlin. Harding did not side with either group, but remained a neutral, and held the balance of power. They seemed
to think that I had set out deliberately to make the Board a
subsidiary of the Treasury Department, and they acted and
voted frequently on that assumption. Nothing could have

been further from the truth. I had troubles enough of my own without taking on the management of the Federal Reserve System.

The first dissension arose over quarters in the Treasury Department. The Federal Reserve Act, in Section 66, says: 'The Secretary of the Treasury may assign offices in the department of the Treasury for the use of the Federal Reserve Board.' That is a simple statement. I accepted it in good faith and made room for the Board in the Treasury Building. To do it was something of a nuisance; I had to move a number of grumbling gentlemen out of their offices into less agreeable quarters.

The Federal Reserve Board came in, and then the fact developed that the Warburg group was opposed to this arrangement. They thought that by occupying quarters in the Treasury Department they would become an adjunct of the Treasury — a mere cog in a vast machine.

The long argument that followed this move and its resultant discontent worried me a great deal. I did not care anything about the discussion; what bothered me was that the argument had come up at all.

I said as little on the subject as I could, hoping it would die out in the course of time. It did; the Federal Reserve Board still has offices in the Treasury Building; it is not at all subservient to the Treasury Department — and never was.

Then came the unexpected question of social precedence, and it agitated some members of the Board for weeks. The newspapers were partly responsible. Some of them had referred to the Federal Reserve Board as 'the Supreme Court of finance.' The fact is that there is no resemblance, in reality, between the Supreme Court and the Federal Reserve Board. The functions of the Board are mainly executive, though it has some traces of judicial power. Nevertheless, the anti-Treasury group took the designation seriously.

Being the Supreme Court of finance, the Board, they thought, was entitled to a pretty high place in the social scale.

Well, how high?

They didn't know, but they were intent upon having proper recognition. They were not to be pale and distant stars, lost in a Milky Way of obscure officialdom; they must swim in the luminous ether close to the sun!

The battle of the Marne was being fought and all the world was looking on. But Marne or no Marne, what about official and social rank? I didn't know; I had not the least idea. So far as I was concerned, I was perfectly willing that the Board should come ahead of the Supreme Court.

That's all very well, but who settles such questions?

I had learned that somewhere in the State Department there was an official whose duties embraced the intricate formula of social precedence. The dispute found its way to the State Department, and I believe the verdict was that the Board, as an independent commission, should take rank with the other independent boards or commissions, whose relative place is determined by the date of their creation.

The Smithsonian Institution was the first independent commission created; therefore, it had the top rank among the commissions. The Pan-American Union came next. Then, in order, the Interstate Commerce Commission, the Civil Service Commission, and the Federal Reserve Board. Naturally, the Federal Reserve Board, being an independent commission (the Warburg group were especially insistent upon its being so considered), had to take the rank which would be accorded to it as the last independent commission (the fifth) created up to that time.

This did not satisfy the social aspirants on the Board. I was urged to put the question up to the President. I hated to do it, for the President detested all such matters. However, I decided to speak to him. If the thing was not settled definitely, I did not know how long it would continue to agitate the Board.

I shall never forget the day I brought up the subject at the White House. The President sat at his desk, glancing restlessly now and then at some papers that lay on it. As he gathered the import of my statement, I could see the shadow of a frown pass over his face. He turned over one of the papers before him with an irritable gesture.

'I can do nothing about it,' he remarked, when I had finished my story. 'I am not a social arbiter.'

'I know that, Mr. President,' I said, 'but they want you to decide.'

'Decide what?'

'Decide their rank in the scale of social precedence,' I answered.

He reflected a moment, then looked up with a broad smile. 'Well,' he said, 'they might come right after the fire department.'

I never told the members of the Board what the President had said. It would have caused needless pain.

5

The Federal Reserve Act was signed by the President on December 23, 1913. Ten months later, the system was still in embryo. The banks had been organized, the districts defined, the officials selected, and practically every national bank in the country, as well as many state banks, had joined the system.

But the machine, though apparently complete in all its essential features, did not start. Time went on, and the only thing wrong with the Federal Reserve System, so far as I could see, was that it did not exist. Arguments against opening the banks appeared here and there; and besides, there were unaccountable and intangible obstacles which can hardly be defined.

I had a feeling that, if the system did not get into active operation soon, it might never come to life at all; that it might fall into the limbo of things devised but never used. There already existed a body of opinion to the effect that the Federal Reserve System should not be made a permanent financial institution, in daily operation; that it ought to be considered an emergency measure only, to function temporarily in times of stress. Of course, it had been conceived as a permanent banking system, but everyone knew that a short amendment to the Act would be sufficient to change its status.

Under the provisions of the Federal Reserve Act, the Secretary of the Treasury was empowered to say when the banks should begin business. Before making a decision, I talked in October with the governors and chairmen of most of the Federal Reserve Banks, and nearly all of them thought that the necessary preparations would still take considerable time. I did not want to be arbitrary, but it seemed to me that much of

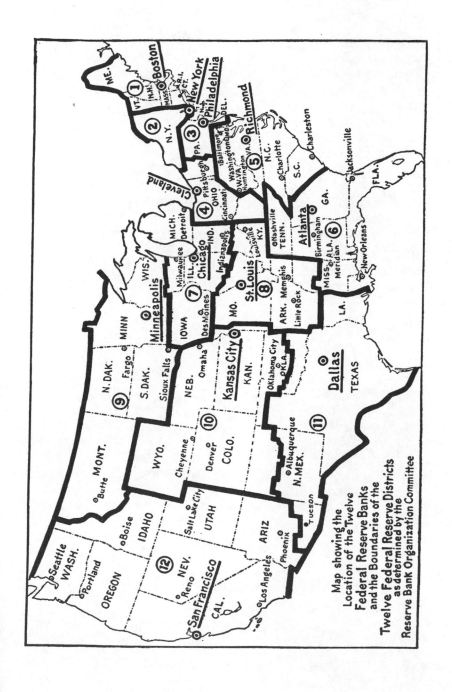

Map showing the
Location of the Twelve
Federal Reserve Banks
and the Boundaries of the
Twelve Federal Reserve Districts
as determined by the
Reserve Bank Organization Committee

the predicted delay could not be justified, as it was based wholly on the organization of inessentials. On October 25 I made an official announcement that all the Reserve Banks would open on November 16.

The representative of the Federal Reserve Bank of New York said that, as yet, the bank had no vault or safe place for keeping the large amount of gold and securities that would come into its hands.

'There is the Sub-Treasury in New York,' I suggested, 'and you can put your valuables in its vault. We'll take care of them. Or, if you are not satisfied with that arrangement, there are plenty of banks and safe-deposit companies with strong vaults. Can't you keep your money there?'

Well, there was no reason, it seemed, why the vault question should hold up the progress of affairs.

'What next?'

'Our bookkeeping system is not yet ready — the printing of forms and so on ——'

I interrupted at this point. 'Surely you can have enough printing done by November 16 to start business.'

'We can't get our office furniture by that time.'

'I wouldn't let that stand in the way,' I replied. I saw that they wanted to wait until they could start on an elaborate scale. 'Buy a few chairs and pine-top tables,' I suggested, 'hire some clerks and stenographers, paint "Federal Reserve Bank of New York" on your office door, and open up. The way to begin is to begin. When you once make a start, everything will be smoothed out through practice. We'll keep your reserves at the Sub-Treasury. You can build up your organization as the business grows.'

Much discussion. Many objections. But after I had decided on November 16, 1914, as the opening day, everybody accepted the decision and went earnestly to work. The banks opened their doors on that day, and their business ran on from the first without a hitch.

CHAPTER XIX

SHIPS AND MONEY

I

THE breaking-out of the World War in the last week of July, 1914, caused an immediate crisis in American financial circles. About nine-thirty on Friday morning, July 31, J. P. Morgan, of New York, called me on the telephone. He said that in view of the demoralized condition of the market the Governors of the New York Stock Exchange would meet at ten o'clock that morning to consider the question of closing the Exchange. He went on to say that they would be glad to have my advice as to whether or not this should be done.

I replied that I did not consider my opinion of much value on a matter of that sort and that I hesitated to offer any suggestions. Morgan assured me that they would do whatever I thought was best. I did not exactly relish the thought of assuming any part of the responsibility, but after some reflection I said, 'If you really want my judgment, it is to close the Exchange.' He said it would be done, and it was done that day.

On Sunday morning, August 2, I was at the Treasury Department when William Woodward, president of the Hanover National Bank and a director of the Federal Reserve Bank of New York, called me up. He said that the Clearing House Committee anticipated runs on the New York banks next day — Monday, August 3 — and the result might be a disastrous panic. Could I not come to New York and meet the Clearing House Committee that evening? I explained to Woodward that it was difficult for me to leave the Treasury, and asked if the committee could come to Washington. This was hardly possible, he said, as it was necessary for all members of the committee to be at their desks in New York on Monday morning. I discussed the matter with President Wilson; we concluded that it would be wise for me to go to New York.

It was a group of anxious bankers that met me in a room in the Vanderbilt Hotel at nine-thirty that evening, and I did not feel any too cheerful myself. Twenty men or more were present. I do not recall all of them, but Gates McGarrah, of the Mechanics & Metals National Bank was there; and J. P. Morgan and H. P. Davison; and William Woodward; and A. J. Hemphill, president of the Guaranty Trust Company; A. Barton Hepburn, of the Chase National Bank; Frank A. Vanderlip, president of the First National Bank; and J. W. Alexander, president of the National Bank of Commerce.

They were all unanimous as to the gravity of the situation. Sitting in the room was Edward W. Sheldon, president of the United States Trust Company, who had been a classmate of President Wilson at Princeton (class of '79), and a man in whom I knew the President had great confidence. I excused myself and left the room, sending in a message to Sheldon that I should like to have him meet me in the hall. When he came out, I asked him to tell me what he thought about it, personally.

Sheldon said that his colleagues had not exaggerated the condition of affairs; that he believed it to be fully as serious as they had represented it. When I rejoined the conference, I said that the Treasury Department would do everything in its power to relieve the strain. I asked what they thought was the most effective thing that I, as Secretary of the Treasury, could do. They replied that they would like to have emergency currency issued immediately to the limit that the law permitted.

I was entirely willing to meet the wishes of the bankers, but the Aldrich-Vreeland Act provided that emergency currency might be issued only to national banks; and only to those national banks whose circulating notes, secured by United States bonds, amounted to forty per cent of their capital stock.

When I made my announcement, Mr. Vanderlip remarked sadly that it would not be of any use to his bank. 'The National City, as you know,' he continued, 'has no banknotes in circulation.'

'And,' I said, 'I suppose you need emergency currency as much as anybody.'

'We certainly do,' Vanderlip declared. 'Probably more than anybody else. We have more country correspondents than any other New York bank.'

The fact was that the Aldrich-Vreeland Act was too narrow

in its limitations to meet the situation. I had no authority to suspend any provision of the Act, or to change it, and it seemed that the helpful thing to do was to get an amendment through Congress within the next twenty-four hours. I promised to have that done, if it were possible.

It was twelve-thirty Monday morning when the conference adjourned. The bankers were agreeably surprised and relieved when I informed them that fifty million dollars of emergency currency was already in New York, at the Sub-Treasury.

I got back to Washington that same day, and on Tuesday, August 4, Congress passed an amendment to the Aldrich-Vreeland Act under which, at the discretion of the Secretary of the Treasury, any state bank or trust company that had signified its intention of joining the Federal Reserve System might obtain emergency currency by depositing satisfactory collateral. This was a decided departure from established practice and tradition. The amendment also provided that national banks could be supplied, regardless of their note circulation, to the extent of one hundred and twenty-five per cent of their capital and surplus.

Within the next three months the Treasury issued about $370,000,000 of emergency currency to the banks throughout the country. The dormant Aldrich-Vreeland Act had been brought to life to perform one service of distinction before it finally expired. All of this emergency currency was eventually retired without the loss of a dollar.

I was as busy as several men ought to be. Not only during the roaring August of the year 1914, but from then on until I resigned from the Cabinet at the close of the war. I could not have carried on at all if it had not been for my capable and loyal assistants, such as John Skelton Williams, Byron R. Newton, W. P. Malburn, George R. Cooksey, and Brice Clagett. They relieved me of a mountain of detail, and aided materially in the executive management of important undertakings.

From the beginning of my tenure of office, my policy was to bring the Treasury Department into closer touch with the people of the country. I have no patience with the theory that the United States Treasury is a remote pyramid of money on which the Secretary sits in silent isolation.

With that idea in mind I called a meeting of business men and bankers early in August for the purpose of discussing the situation which had been caused by the war. I wanted to find out, through the medium of a general conference, what representative business men thought the Treasury might do, within its legal limitations, to be of service to commerce and finance. Men from all parts of the country came to the meeting, which was held on August 14, 1914. I invited the members of the Federal Reserve Board, Secretary of Agriculture Houston, Secretary of Commerce Redfield, Senator Owen and Representative Glass, Comptroller of the Currency Williams, and Assistant Secretaries of the Treasury Malburn and Newton to attend. This was the first publicly conducted conference of business men, I believe, that a government official had ever held in Washington.

Everything that had a bearing on the existing condition of affairs was discussed freely. Everyone said what he pleased, talked as long as he pleased and on any subject that appealed to him. The conference produced immediate and helpful results.

It was the consensus of opinion that three questions were of paramount importance, namely:

1. The restoration of the market for foreign bills of exchange.

2. Some adequate means for transporting our salable products, such as grain, cotton, and other commodities, overseas.

3. The insurance of ships and cargoes against war risks.

In the demoralization of routine international finance that came like a thunder-clap at the beginning of the war, foreign exchange got itself badly tangled up. Hardly any bills on London, or on any other money center in Europe, could be purchased, and the foreign exchange market virtually ceased to exist. The pound sterling, normally worth $4.87, sold for a while in New York at an unprecedented premium.

A feature of this problem — and a most distressing one — had to do with the condition of American tourists in Europe. When war was declared, these travelers and sight-seers found, to their dismay, that their letters of credit were temporarily of no value whatever. There was a general moratorium. Checks and drafts were not honored; cash could not be obtained on them, and many, or most, of the European hotels declined to accept anything but cash. Within a week thousands of tourists were in a serious predicament.

I thought the best thing to do was to send a warship to Europe with enough gold to supply every stranded American who had no means of procuring cash. With the President's approval I appeared before the Appropriation Committees of the Senate and House and urged that Congress provide $2,500,000 to be loaned to Americans in Europe against letters of credit or other securities.

The appropriation was granted by Congress and the cruiser Tennessee was dispatched to Europe with an initial shipment of $1,500,000 in gold. Nearly all the government's loans to stranded tourists were repaid, though some of them were lost. I am sorry to say that a few recipients of Uncle Sam's generosity who were easily able to repay simply sat tight and ignored their obligation, and in the end managed to evade payment.

2

The war was not a week old before the American nation found out, all of a sudden, that the amount of shipping under our flag was not more than a drop in the bucket compared to the magnitude of American foreign trade. It was all known before, of course, in the way of statistics; everybody who could read must have seen the figures, but one may be aware of statistics without being actively conscious of the grave potentialities behind them.

Of the forty-five millions of steam tonnage in the world at the beginning of the war, approximately one half was under the British flag. American steamships registered for the foreign trade (including all foreign vessels admitted to American registry in the first three months of the war) amounted to about one million tons, or not much more than two per cent of the world's shipping. The nations at war recalled most of their vessels; they were needed at home. The entire merchant fleet of Germany and Austria, amounting to six million tons, was blotted out immediately; by that I mean that all their ships were interned, either at home or in foreign ports. The British made some effort to carry on as before, but a large proportion of their ships was devoted, naturally, to military and naval uses.

At the conference on foreign exchange and shipping held at the Treasury on August 14, the need of a mercantile marine was one of the chief topics of discussion. The conference adopted a resolution urging Congress to do something to ameliorate the situation. What that something ought to be remained a matter of doubt, so far as the conference was concerned.

The ostensible remedy, according to the custom of our individualistic civilization, would have been to leave the problem to private effort. Shipowning and operating had become exceedingly profitable, rates were high and getting higher, and under the conventional laws of business enterprise, capital should have been attracted in large amounts to the field of ocean traffic.

That was all very well as a theory, but economic theories, as I have observed, often fail in practice. Private initiative becomes extremely timid in times of peril and uncertainty. As a result of the war, people generally were completely engrossed in problems of their own, and money was held so tightly that it was out of the question for anybody to organize a shipping concern with private capital that would be sufficiently large and sufficiently daring to create promptly an adequate mercantile marine. Shipowners were making so much money, owing to the unprecedented demand for cargo space, that they were satisfied with the existing conditions. More ships would mean lower freight rates and less profit.

The problem was too big altogether for solution in the ordinary way. I have said, in the course of this narrative, that I am opposed to the government ownership of business enterprises except in extraordinary circumstances where the intervention of the government is urgently demanded in the interest of the public welfare. The shipping question presented a perfect picture of such a case.

I conceived the idea of a shipping corporation of which the American government would own all, or a major part, of the capital stock. The underlying thought was that, while the company would be government-owned, it would be conducted as any other corporation is conducted — like the Panama steamship line, for example, which Roosevelt purchased for the nation during his term as President, and which is still being operated by the War Department.

One morning at dawn I was lying in bed, thinking about the matter, when it occurred to me that I might as well write out a tentative draft of a shipping bill which would embody the idea of a government-owned corporation. I approached the subject with reluctance, for I had enough to do already without making myself the father of a measure which was certain to run into a bitter controversy; besides, it was hardly within the province of the Treasury Department. Nevertheless, constructive action of some kind was urgently needed, and nobody else up to that time had seemed disposed to act. I went to work with a pencil and writing-pad, and the first draft was finished before breakfast. This was in August, 1914.

In the course of the day I submitted this skeleton draft to the President and discussed its main features with him. He was favorably impressed with the idea, but said that he wanted to think it over for a day or so. He remarked that the government ownership of merchant ships, no matter how desperate the need of them might be, would arouse the hostility of every reactionary in the United States, and that the bill would be opposed by all the powerfully entrenched interests. They would call it 'socialistic,' he said.

When I saw the President again, he was strongly in favor of the plan that I had submitted. He handed me back the draft of the bill and said, with a smile, 'We'll have to fight for it, won't we?'

'We certainly shall,' I replied.

'Well, then, let's fight,' he said.

We did. We fought for it, and, as I look back over the prolonged battle, I recall it as a fantastic nightmare of partisanship and politics.

Anyone who did not know the political motives behind our opponent's words would have thought that we had set out deliberately to debauch the American people, to destroy legitimate commerce, and that our shipping plan was the first step on the road to national ruin.

The bill passed the House, but the opposition in the Senate, by the use of the most extraordinary filibustering tactics, prevented it from coming to a vote at that session of Congress.

In my opinion, that filibuster cost the American people at least a billion dollars. When the bill was first introduced, ships might have been bought, or constructed, at a cost of about forty dollars a ton.

But when the measure was eventually enacted, eighteen months later, they were selling at prices that ranged from one hundred and fifty to three hundred dollars a ton.

The difficulty about shipping was further complicated by the refusal of marine insurance companies in general to undertake war risks. They were willing to insure ships and their cargoes against the ordinary hazards of the sea, such as shipwreck, collision, and foundering; but they declined to undertake insurance against floating mines, or capture, or torpedoes, or any other perils of war.

This particular trouble was solved by the creation of a War Risk Insurance Bureau, under the supervision of the Treasury Department. Congress passed the War Risk Insurance Bill on September 2, 1914, and appropriated $5,000,000 as a capital sum on which the Bureau could start operations. We began business within three or four days, even before the forms and policies of the Bureau were printed. As head of the Bureau I appointed William C. Delanoy, a well-known insurance man of New York City.

The work of the Bureau, with its insurance against every imaginable war disaster, sent the timid ships to sea. And, strange to say, it was a financial success from beginning to end, although it dealt with unknown and incalculable risks.

One of the incidental performances had to do with the camouflaging of American vessels. That came about in a curious way. At Washington there was a Naval Consulting Board on Inventions of which Thomas A. Edison was chairman. Among its most active and efficient members was W. L. Saunders, a prominent engineer and chairman of the Ingersoll-Rand Company. He came to see me one day in a state of perplexity. He said the Board wanted American shipowners to camouflage their vessels and carry some anthracite coal for use in the submarine zone, as a safety measure, but was unable to get the thing done. It seems that they had no official authority in the matter, and could not find anybody in Washington who had such authority.

'We've urged every shipowner who expects to send a vessel into the war zone to camouflage his ship and carry some smokeless coal, but they won't do it,' Saunders said.

'Why not?'

'Well, they take chances,' he replied. 'They are making money hand over fist, and they don't want to lay up their floating gold mines long enough to have them painted. We've done all we can in the way of advice. Can you suggest anything?'

It occurred to me that the indifference of the shipowners was one of the consequences of their being fully insured at low rates through the War Risk Insurance Bureau. I decided to touch their pocket-books, and I sent immediately for Delanoy, head of the Bureau. Within a few minutes we agreed to raise the insurance rates on ships that were not camouflaged and did not carry some anthracite coal, and that day an announcement of the new rates was made.

Paint was popular with the merchant marine from that time on. Within a short time virtually every American ship that sailed the war-infested seas looked like a maritime zebra. The discriminatory rate did the business.

Altogether, from first to last, the premiums on marine war risk policies amounted to more than $47,000,000, and the net profit to about $17,000,000.

3

The lack of ships had a most depressing effect on the price of cotton. About five thousand bales constitute the average cargo of a freight steamship; with seven or eight million bales awaiting export an enormous tonnage was required. Ocean freight rates rose to astounding heights, and even at the high rates, cargo space frequently could not be obtained. The wharves of every Southern port were jammed with cotton bales.

The 1913 cotton crop sold at an average price of 13½ cents a pound for middling cotton (the standard grade). By the middle of August, 1914, the price at interior points had fallen to 6 or 6½ cents. At that time the cost of growing a pound of cotton under average conditions was estimated at 9½ cents. If the new crop of about sixteen million bales was sold at the prevailing price, there would be a direct loss to the grower of $15 a bale, or about $240,000,000 on the entire crop. The Southern states, depending almost wholly on cotton for a living, were facing a gigantic disaster.

A world at war needs more cotton than a world at peace. The actual and potential demand for cotton still existed, but there was a dislocation of the bridge that normally connected demand and supply. It seemed obvious that if the new crop, then pressing against the market, could be financed and held for a time, prices would come back to a level that would keep the cotton farmer alive and out of the poorhouse; provided that something could be done in the meantime to solve the shipping problem and get the surplus crop overseas. In this connection I thought the Treasury might be helpful in promoting some kind of financial organization or plan for cotton financing.

Accordingly I called a cotton conference, which met at the Treasury Department on August 24, 1914. Tobacco was in the same distressing fix as cotton, so I invited tobacco growers and merchants as well as cotton planters, manufacturers, shippers, and bankers. The conference lasted three days, and the situation was thoroughly discussed in all its aspects. It was the consensus of opinion that the first important step was to furnish credit to cotton and tobacco planters. The primary aim was to help the farmer keep his cotton and tobacco off the glutted market for the time being.

I decided, therefore, to issue emergency currency to Southern banks for the purpose of financing cotton and tobacco stored in warehouses. The warehouse receipts were made, under proper safeguards, satisfactory banking collateral, and the banks loaned the farmers up to seventy-five per cent of their face value. I issued $68,000,000 of emergency currency to banks in the South, and in addition I deposited with them $27,000,000 of government funds.

Under this plan the cotton and tobacco planters were enabled to hold a large part of their crops for better prices. There was an immediate improvement in the situation. By the middle of September, cotton was bringing 8½ cents a pound in interior points throughout the Southern states.

There were criticisms; there always are.

All action, either affirmative or negative, in a high official position invariably stirs up criticism; and the denunciation is especially bitter if the action has any quality of originality or daring. The formula for making a pleasant impression as a Cabinet officer, or as a President, or as a Governor, is to do much talking, shake hands, slap backs, look jolly, and cultivate a knack for telling funny stories. You may not live in history by carrying out this formula, but you will live temporarily in the hearts of your contemporaries.

I expected criticism, but I wondered what there could be about such a salutary and helpful measure that anybody could criticize. Some of the New England cotton manufacturers declared that I was unwarrantably interfering with the normal law of supply and demand; that I was obstructing their right to buy cotton at the lowest possible price. One or two economists wrote and published comments to the effect that my action was economically unsound; in other words, that prices ought to be allowed to take their course, regardless of the ruin that might ensue.

I have great respect for political economy and its time-tried principles, but I think nevertheless that human welfare should take precedence of the law of supply and demand, and in cases of necessity of every other economic law. In the long run this nation gains nothing, and can gain nothing but loss and trouble, from the financial ruin of any section — North, South, East, or West — or of any class of our population.

The New York 'Times' said, in a disapproving editorial that appeared on August 24, that 'The country does not need the currency and it will be used not to *move* the crop but to *hold* it.' (The italics in the quotation are mine.)

It seems that the farmer is the one producer who is always expected to sell his product for whatever it may bring. If he holds his crop for better prices, or tries to fix the price, the consensus of reactionary opinion usually is that there is something greedy and unsocial in his attitude. Yet, at the same time, manufacturers and merchants who hold their products for higher prices and wider markets are considered good business men, full of economic foresight and sound to the core.

While these things were going on, Festus J. Wade, a public-spirited and influential citizen of St. Louis, was devising a plan of his own to help the cotton farmer carry his burden. Wade proposed to raise a fund of $100,000,000 or more, to be subscribed by banks and financial houses, which would be used in financing surplus cotton until market conditions improved.

His idea was excellent. I liked it; I did not think the Treasury ought to bear the whole load, and I welcomed coöperation. We had a meeting in New York. Albert H. Wiggin and other figures in the financial world were present. Wade's plan was approved after some important changes had been made in it. The fund was to amount to $135,000,000; and of this sum the New York banks and financiers agreed to supply $50,000,000. Fifty million dollars was allotted to banks and individuals in other large cities, and the Southern banks were expected to furnish $35,000,000.

The plan was to lend money to actual holders of cotton at six cents a pound and at a rate of interest not exceeding six per cent. Under the law the banks could not make loans for long periods, but there would be no such restrictions on the fund that we hoped to raise on Wade's plan. Loans were to be made for one year with a privilege of renewal for another six months.

We raised $97,000,000 in New York and other Northern and Eastern cities, and then subscriptions ceased. While I was sitting at my desk in the Treasury pondering over ways and means to obtain the last $3,000,000, to make the plan effective, my secretary announced Bernard M. Baruch, of New York.

I knew Baruch slightly; had met him a few times. He came in and said that he had heard about the cotton loan, and asked how much I needed to complete the fund. I replied that we were short $3,000,000.

'I will subscribe a million dollars,' he said at once and without any solicitation on my part. I suppose he must have read astonishment in my face, for he went on to say, 'If you have any doubt as to my responsibility, I will be glad to give you satisfactory New York references.' I told him that I did not

need any references; that I was satisfied with his responsibility. It was a fine thing for him to do. That was the beginning
of my friendship with Baruch.

I still needed $2,000,000, so I telephoned my public-spirited
friend Jacob H. Schiff, of Kühn, Loeb & Company, and explained the situation to him. He said at once that his firm
would subscribe the remaining two millions. In that way the
fund was completed. I may add that J. P. Morgan & Company, the Chase National Bank, and the National City Bank
were also large subscribers.

CHAPTER XX

THE STRUGGLE OVER THE SHIPPING BILL

I

In one of his interesting essays on popular government, John Stuart Mill expressed an opinion that the influence of selfish and plutocratic interests in a republic would be neutralized through the competition of such interests with one another, as well as through their differences in policy. This, he thought, would serve to protect democratic institutions and allow the popular will to take its own course.

I fear the eminent philosopher was too optimistic. The competitive strife of plutocratic interests is not sufficiently violent to destroy their prestige or their influence; they have no intention of committing mutual suicide. Their battles are like those of professional boxers who split the purse, in some fashion, between the winner and the loser.

Their various and conflicting objectives do not cancel one another, as Mill thought, for at the bottom they rest on a singleness of purpose which may be characterized, in broad and general terms, as the exploitation of the public. That is the essence of pluto-democracy, and it does not make any difference in effect who the exploiters may be — whether they are financiers or stock manipulators, or shipowners, or landgrabbers or tariff barons. The common bond between them is greed, often subtle, plausible, and insidious, but greed nevertheless. They get all they can, regardless of the public welfare and without regard to the actual value of their services or their commodities.

These reflections occur to me when I think of the adventures of the shipping bill during its long, arduous battle in Congress and before the country.

It may be accepted as a general principle, or political axiom, that whenever a beneficial measure is opposed by powerful financial interests, the real reason for the opposition is never given. The actual basis for the antagonism to the shipping bill was that it threatened the enormous profits of the shipping concerns, but the opposition could not possibly acknowledge such a reason, as it would have destroyed their standing with the public. The ostensible reason — the principal one, at any rate — was that it put the government in business, as the bill provided for government ownership and operation of the ships.

The War Risk Insurance Act had already put the United States government squarely and unequivocally in the marine insurance business. There had been no objection. Everybody was for the government handling all the war risk insurance in sight. Big business approved the idea; so did little business; shipowners; shipbuilders; exporters — everybody!

Why? Because there was a general impression that no money could be made from the business of war risk insurance. That being the case, why not let the government take the loss?

But from the day the war began, shipowning became one of the most profitable of investments. Tramp steamers not infrequently cleared their entire cost or value in a single voyage. In the course of a year an ocean-going freighter would bring in a net return — clear profit above all expenses — of three hundred to five hundred per cent on the money invested in the ship.

The shipping concerns made rates to suit themselves — not only as much as the traffic would bear, but even more than some of the traffic could possibly bear — and, as the freight offered was far in excess of shipping capacity, the vessels picked up whatever pleased their owners in the way of cargo and left all the rest lying on the wharves, often for months.

Prompt action on the part of Congress would have blown up this orgy of profiteering.

On August 19, 1914, the President called a conference at the White House to consider the proposed shipping bill. I was there, and the others present, as I recall them, were Senator Simmons, of North Carolina, who was then the chairman of the Finance Committee of the Senate; Senator Clarke, of Arkansas, chairman of the Commerce Committee; Oscar W. Underwood, of Alabama, chairman of the Ways and Means Committee of the House; and Joshua W. Alexander, of Missouri, chairman of the Merchant Marine and Fisheries Committee.

At the White House conference the proposed bill was approved, after an animated discussion, by all who were present. The next day, August 20, the matter was discussed at some length in the newspapers. Before the day was over J. P. Morgan, of New York, called on me at the Treasury. The object of Morgan's visit was to discuss shipping legislation. He was opposed to the purchase of ships or the construction of them by the government, and he said so flatly. He claimed that there was no necessity for the government taking a hand in the shipping business, but for my part I could not conceive a more urgent necessity than that which existed right then for more ships and lower rates. It was an obvious fact, so outstanding and so towering that any man could see it. He said that ocean trade was being carried on under great difficulties, and that the government's entrance into the field would be considered a menace. It is true that ships were encountering difficulties in traversing seas devoted to war. There were unusual hazards, as there always are, in wartime, but the enormous profits of the shipowners more than compensated for these risks. As for being a menace, I could not see that the government's ships would menace anything but the absurdly high rates of private shipping concerns.

2

The shipping bill was introduced in the House on August 24, 1914, by Representative Joshua W. Alexander, of Missouri. Within a week opposition of the bitterest character developed.

A swarm of lobbyists, representing the shipping concerns, descended on both houses of Congress. Some of them were known to be professionals; that is, they were paid advocates of various causes. I think that a great deal of the opposition to the shipping bill was inspired by these paid lobbyists; but that is merely my impression; I do not state it as a fact, for I cannot prove it. It is extremely difficult to trace the doings of a clever professional lobbyist, for he works almost invariably by indirection. He understands clearly the psychological value of suggestion.

Practically all the Republicans in the House and Senate, with the exception of a few Progressives — like La Follette of Wisconsin — opposed the bill, and their leaders fought it furi-

ously. We had a Democratic majority in both houses which
we counted on, but to the astonishment of the Administration
some of the Democrats announced that they intended to vote
with the Republicans on this particular question. The specter
of government ownership had scared them into a panic.

When argument failed, and the opposition had no more
ammunition in its cartridge belt, political superstition was
invoked. Timid members of our great national legislature
shivered in their seats as they heard, or were made to believe
they heard, the bloodhound of 'rank socialism' baying at the
very doors of the Capitol. Of course, I was called a 'socialist' on account of the part I took in shaping the bill and in
advocating it.

While the shipping bill was being discussed in the House, it
was pending, at the same time, in the Senate, where the opposition was led by Senators Root, of New York, and Lodge, of
Massachusetts.

Root contended that the bill would carry the government
into a business venture that was unwarranted and unnecessary.
He could not prove his assertion; in fact, he made hardly any
attempt to prove that the conditions did not urgently demand
something effective in the way of relief, and his statement can
only be taken as a declaration of political philosophy rather
than a declaration of fact.

I do not admire political philosophy when it runs into a
head-on collision with necessities. Civilization has been made,
and is kept in being today, by men and women who are moved
by a sense of immediacy, and who turn their hands to the
constructive needs of the hour, regardless of what either political philosophers or historians may say.

The pressing need of that particular time was ships —
enough ships to take American products to foreign markets at
reasonable rates. I speak advisedly when I say that neither
the President nor anyone close to him wanted the government
to be in the shipping business just for the sake of saying that
the government was in it. We were perfectly willing to turn
the entire problem over to anybody else who was properly
equipped to solve it. We would have welcomed the coöperation of any American concern which would furnish the necessary capital and provide a sufficient number of vessels with the

understanding that shippers would be treated fairly in the matter of rates and service. But there was no such coöperation in sight. Shipping interests came to the front to criticize, but not to create.

Despite all the obstacles that hindered the progress of the bill — public indifference, antagonism of shipping interests, paid lobbyists, and what not — the Democrats in the House contrived to put it through after six months' wrangling. It passed the House on February 17, 1915, by a vote of 215 to 122.

3

It did not fare so well in the Senate. The Republican opposition was encouraged by the desertion of a number of Democrats, who declared their intention of voting against the measure. These Democrats were Bankhead, of Alabama; Vardaman, of Mississippi; Hardwick, of Georgia; Clarke, of Arkansas; Hitchcock, of Nebraska; Camden, of Kentucky; and O'Gorman, of New York.

All the rest of the Democratic senators — with the exception of the seven I have just mentioned — were for the bill, and most of them worked valiantly to put it through. Senator James A. Reed, of Missouri, was one of its staunch defenders; and so was Duncan U. Fletcher, of Florida, who had charge of the bill; Williams, of Mississippi; Stone, of Missouri; Walsh, of Montana; Simmons, of North Carolina; James, of Kentucky; and Swanson, of Virginia.

The bill was supported also by some of the Progressive Republicans — La Follette, of Wisconsin; Norris, of Nebraska; and Kenyon, of Iowa.

The insurgent Democrats made a serious break in the ranks of the party that was responsible for the bill; nevertheless, Senator Stone told me, around the first of January, 1915, that the Democrats had sufficient votes anyway, notwithstanding the bolters. He said, however, that the Republican minority might use obstructive tactics and succeed in keeping the Senate from coming to a vote before the end of the session on March 4.

This is exactly what happened. Around the first of February, the Republican filibuster began, and it continued until Congress adjourned. For the information of those who may not be familiar with the term, I may explain that filibustering simply means talking a bill to death. There is no restriction on debate in the Senate; any senator is allowed, under the rules, to get up on his feet and talk on any subject until he falls dead. Some of the Republican senators almost fell dead in their passionate effort to keep the country from acquiring a merchant marine of its own. Senator Smoot spoke for eleven and a half hours without a pause, and then dropped, hoarse and exhausted, into a litter of worn-out words. Yet at that he failed to make a long-distance oratorical record, for Senator Burton, also an opponent of the bill, got up and barked vociferously against the purchase of ships for thirteen hours. Those who witnessed the feat told me that he seemed to do it without visible effort. It looked, they said, as if he had started his mouth to talking and then had gone away and left it on the job.

Senator Gallinger, discoursing on the iniquities of the bill, ran out of data in a couple of hours, but he continued to talk for five hours more. During that time he read the current news from the journals of the day, told stories of the Mexican Revolution, and quoted pages and pages of statistics on ocean transportation and ship subsidies. The stenographers of the Senate took down this farrago in short-hand, as their duty required them to do, and next day it all appeared in print in the solemn 'Congressional Record.'

On the evening of February 9, cots were placed in the Senate cloakrooms and corridors. Exhausted senators snored on them while the stream of words went on. As I reflected on the grim determination of the senators opposed to the bill, and thought of them lying down in the disorder of their improvised camp, I endeavored to put myself in their frame of mind, to grasp their motives, and to understand the inwardness of their contentions. Men who act like pickets in the presence of an enemy, and are willing to sleep in rude discomfort on the battle-field, are moved by no light impulses. Yet, with every effort to comprehend their point of view, I found that I could not do it. Their way of looking at the national emergency was so entirely different from my own that there was no meeting-place.

The Senate on that occasion was in continuous session for fifty-five hours and eleven minutes — the longest session in the history of Congress. It was a success from the Republican standpoint. Their filibustering prevented the Democrats from bringing the bill to a vote. But there were still three weeks of Congress before March 4, and the Democratic leaders thought that they might yet wrestle the issue to a show-down.

4

About five hundred thousand tons of German and Austrian vessels were interned in our ports. These ships lay idle, doing nobody any good. If they had gone to sea under the German flag, they would have been captured almost immediately by the British.

The Administration thought at one time of trying to purchase these vessels if the shipping bill became a law. This thought was never more than a nebulous idea; we never acted on it, nor did we ever enter into any negotiations in respect to the matter.

However, the idea got into the newspapers and was used by the opposition in the Senate to frighten the country into the belief that we should become involved in a war with the Allies if we acquired the interned ships. Pure nonsense. The fact is that the United States has always maintained the right to buy belligerent merchant vessels and transfer them to the American flag. It is an accepted principle of our historic international policy.

There was a rumor current about that time to the effect that somebody in the Administration was going to make a handsome rake-off, or piece of graft, from the sale of the German vessels. This yarn came into existence anonymously; it had no visible author. Nevertheless, it was effective. Senator Burton, of Ohio, for one, pretended to take it seriously. On February 2, 1915, he introduced a resolution composed of inquiries addressed to the Secretary of the Treasury. Here are the questions he asked:

1. Has the Secretary of the Treasury knowledge that any officer of the government has made overtures or addressed inquiries to the

United States was not out of danger, and that sooner or later something would happen that would force us to take a hand. It was a time of preparation; talk of preparedness was in the air. The Administration and the friends of the shipping bill came to the conclusion that our campaign for ships would be helped by combining in one objective the creation of a merchant marine and a fleet of naval auxiliary vessels; carriers of merchantable cargoes in time of peace, and carriers of men and munitions in time of war.

The speeches I made were along that line. As a matter of policy I put the idea of naval auxiliaries first, and the merchant marine second. Experience had convinced me that people as a rule are far more interested in fighting, and in preparations for fighting, than they are in any constructive commercial or industrial effort.

Representative J. W. Alexander, who had labored so valiantly in the House in behalf of the bill during the previous session, introduced it for the second time on January 30, 1916. The new bill was an improvement on the old one. It provided that the vessels that were to be acquired under it should be naval auxiliaries; it created a Shipping Board and gave the Board the power to regulate the rates of vessels engaged in interstate and foreign commerce, and to license all such vessels. The government was authorized to purchase and build ships; and to form a corporation for operating them. The bill permitted the government to own a majority interest in the corporation, and appropriated fifty million dollars to carry out the project.

Meanwhile, on January 5, 1916, Senator Walsh, who was chairman of the special committee to investigate the Administration's support of the shipping bill under the Burton resolution, filed a majority report; and a minority report was filed by Senators Sutherland and Penrose, the two Republicans on the committee. Each report agreed that the charges which the committee was formed to investigate were entirely without foundation. The definite charge 'that the Administration's support of the Ship Purchase Bill came largely from the personal interest of officials in bringing about the purchase of particular ships,' was unsupported by a shred of evidence.

Colonel Theodore Roosevelt had become entangled in the

controversy through a wholly unwarranted statement that he had made in the 'Metropolitan Magazine,' namely, that President Wilson and Secretary Bryan 'had endeavored, in the interest of certain foreign business firms, to secure for the United States the power to purchase the interned ships of one of the belligerents.'

During the last years of his life, Roosevelt was so violent in his utterances that he seemed to have lost all sense of perspective and he frequently made assertions which had no basis in reality. In this particular instance he was invited to come before the committee and give the authority for his statement. He did not appear; he had no authority to give. Instead, he wrote a long, rambling letter to the chairman of the committee which failed to throw any light on the matter in dispute.

The majority report, referring to Roosevelt's assertion, said, in part:

The writer (Roosevelt) whose eminence is naturally calculated to give weight to his utterances, finding himself without any basis even of a hearsay character for his slanderous attack upon the highest officer of his Government, simply resorted to a palpable sophistry to escape responsibility for the accusation he made.

The majority report also criticized the editor of the New York 'Times' for his reckless statement that 'there are signs that someone knows what ships are to be bought and who is to buy them for the government.' Charles R. Miller, the editor of the 'Times,' was brought before the committee. He was obliged to admit that he had no ground whatever for his assertion; that he knew nothing about the matter, although he had written as one who did know.

The minority report (written by the Republican members of the committee) said:

We find ourselves unable to agree with the strictures with reference to the statements of Ex-President Roosevelt. In reference to the resolution of inquiry it is sufficient to say that no evidence was produced which tended to establish that any options had been obtained upon any of the so-called interned ships by any person connected with the government of the United States.

The fury of the shipping interests and the financial forces allied with them was turned loose upon the new bill and the Administration.

A delegation from the New York Chamber of Commerce appeared before the Merchant Marine Committee of the House in opposition to the bill.

All the steamship companies in the United States fought the measure savagely.

The National Foreign Trade Council favored encouraging private capital rather than having a government-owned merchant marine, even temporarily.

A committee from the Boston Chamber of Commerce pointed out the dangers of the bill at a Senate hearing.

The New York Produce Exchange condemned the government ownership of ships.

Even the tugboat owners were dragged in. A delegation from the New York Tug Boat Owners' Association appeared before the Senate Committee on Commerce and declared that the bill, if passed, would injure trade. How it could possibly injure their trade was a mystery to me, and I think to everybody else. With more ships afloat they would certainly have more work in the way of towing vessels in and out of harbors.

It was quite evident that the opposition was overplaying its hand in the endeavor to make out a convincing case against the measure. There was a farcical element in their contentions. Most of those who listened to the talk of the sturdy tugboat owners got that impression. These men sat solemnly on the edges of their chairs, uncomfortable in the legislative atmosphere, and now and then they referred uneasily to papers in their hands. Apparently they had been coached as to what they were to say.

I doubt if Congress could have withstood this onslaught if the advocates of the shipping bill had not aroused the country. We began to hear from people in every state, from the average citizen, in favor of the measure. Many important newspapers, formerly indifferent or hostile, urged the prompt passage of the bill.

The battle in the House continued until May 21, 1916, when the bill was passed in spite of the determined die-in-the-last-ditch opposition of Republican leader Mann and his colleagues. Speaker Clark left the chair, took the floor, and made a vigorous speech in support of the measure. The House passed the bill by a vote of 211 to 161. Among the 211 were eight

Republicans, three Progressives, one Independent, and one Socialist. The 161 who voted negatively were all Republicans.

The contest still went on in the Senate, but in time the strength of the opposition slowly oozed away. We were practically certain that the bill would pass long before it came to a vote, and for the last month of the wrangle the efforts of the opposition were devoted to the tactics of delay. It was passed by the Senate on August 30 by a vote of 38 (all Democrats) to 21 (all Republicans), with certain amendments. The amendments were concurred in by the House; the bill went to the President and was approved by him on September 7, 1916 — only seven months before we were forced into the World War.

The two years' fight ended in the passage of the shipping bill, but the opportunity to buy merchant ships had gone. When the bill was introduced in 1914, there were substantial offerings of ocean-going vessels at forty dollars a ton. In the fall of 1916, any steamship that could manage to thrash its way across the ocean was valued at not less than one hundred and fifty dollars a ton, and from that up to three hundred dollars a ton. Few ships were offered even at these prices. The German submarines were destroying the tonnage of the Allies at such a rate that the Allied cause was facing an overwhelming catastrophe. Every ship that remained afloat was held as one holds a jewel. It was obvious to the dullest mind that if we ever intended to have any considerable amount of shipping under the American flag we would have to build it ourselves; and, moreover, we would have to go into the business of shipbuilding at a time when labor and material had both reached top prices.

6

In April, 1917, we went into the war and the American nation set out to build ships on an enormous scale. I recall that time as one recalls a fever, a delirium. Within eighteen months we spent seven times as much on shipyards and ships as the total cost of the Panama Canal. Under the pressure of a national hysteria, and the necessity for haste, money was expended in cartloads, in millions, in tens of millions, in hundreds of millions of dollars.

Appalling prices were paid for everything that had to do with a ship. Engines and other equipment were purchased at such a staggering cost that I fancied more than once that the machinery we were buying must be made of silver instead of iron and steel. The huge shipyard at Hog Island was estimated to cost $27,000,000. Its actual cost was $66,000,000. This was not a matter of graft or dishonesty; the engineers and shipbuilders did not have sufficient time to make proper estimates. Yet this $66,000,000 was a mere drop in the ocean of expenditure made inevitable by the profiteering prices of material and supplies, scarcity of labor and high pressure work. We were paying a staggering price for the filibuster of the shipping bill in 1915 and the selfish obstruction which delayed its passage until a few months before the United States had to buckle on the armor of war.

The men in the yards worked in three shifts, hammering away on unfinished ships all night under the glare of electric lights. Riveters earned almost as much as bank presidents. In the newspapers there appeared the pictures of ship mechanics, depicted as heroes of the hour.

The actual amount expended in shipbuilding was $2,645,-451,000. The twelve million tons of vessels constructed with this expenditure represented the highest cost per ton in the history of the world. I am convinced that at least one billion dollars would have been saved if the Republicans in Congress, backed by profiteering shipping concerns, had not prevented the passage of the Shipping Bill at the session of 1914–15.

Had the bill been passed at that session we would have had time to prepare the groundwork for a sane shipbuilding program. We would have begun with economy and efficiency; labor would have been properly trained; we would have been able to avoid waste; we would have entered the war largely prepared with ships to meet the demands for carrying our troops and our commerce across the submarine-infested Atlantic.

CHAPTER XXI
THE SECRET SERVICE AND DR. ALBERT

I

I AM not a Sherlock Holmes myself, nor even a living inspiration like the fictional Dr. Watson, but one of my duties as Secretary of the Treasury was to supervise the organization of detectives known officially as the United States Secret Service. When I say that I supervised their work I mean that the Secret Service was a branch of my department. I appointed its personnel, kept generally in touch with its operations, and now and then I read its fascinating confidential reports.

The United States Secret Service is frequently confused by the public with the special agents' division of the Department of Justice. They are entirely different. The United States Secret Service was organized in Lincoln's time for the purpose of running down counterfeiters, and that is still its main activity, though the scope of its operations was widened considerably during the World War. Another duty of the Service is to protect the President and his family. The next time a President of the United States comes to your town, you may observe the Secret Service men if you look for them closely, though the chances are that you will not recognize them. They look like the average man — except more so. Very likely you will not be able to distinguish them from the rest of the cheering crowd, but if you try to approach the President in an irregular way, you will quickly become acquainted with one or more of them.

An astonishing number of threatening and vituperative letters is received by every man who has a conspicuous place in public life. In the White House mail there were many every day, and not all of them were anonymous. Under the laws of the United States it is a crime to threaten the life of the President. All these letters were turned over to the Secret Service for investigation. We found that the greater part of them came from muddle-headed cranks, though now

and then the agents of the Service, or the inspectors of the
Post Office Department, would unearth a paranoiac letter-
writer — and a paranoiac running loose in any community is
more dangerous than a rattlesnake. Whenever these de-
mented people were discovered, appropriate proceedings were
begun in order that they might be confined in asylums or
looked after carefully in some other way.

It may interest psycho-analysts and others who probe into
the mysteries of human personality to learn that the most
bloodthirsty and venomous of the letters usually came from
people who were cowardly by nature and as harmless as
doves. Somewhere in the moral constitution of these letter-
writers there must have been a subconscious love of murder
and cruelty which was sublimated into written threats. Every
letter was the mental equivalent of a bullet.

Mrs. McAdoo was, for some reason, an attractive target
for letter-writing cranks and beggars. Some of their epistles —
anonymous, of course — were scurrilous beyond imagination,
and others were nothing more or less than an epistolary tangle
of murderous threats.

I went home one day and found her distressed about a
letter which she had received from an unknown woman in
Chicago. This woman wanted money. Her husband was ill,
she said, and her children were starving. She declared that
she was completely destitute. Her writing was that of a
refined person. It seemed strange to me that this woman
should feel impelled to write to some one living in Washington
for help when there were many charitable persons and institutions in Chicago. I advised Mrs. McAdoo not to send any
reply.

More letters came, all of them in the same elegant writing.
The woman's case was growing worse; she wrote that she did
not know which way to turn, and she threatened to commit
suicide if Mrs. McAdoo continued to turn a deaf ear to her
troubles. But Mrs. McAdoo was not turning a deaf ear; far
from it. The distress in my own family became acute. We
lived in an atmosphere of dense gloom, and I decided that
something would have to be done about that woman in
Chicago. But I thought we had better learn the facts about
her before sending any money.

I handed the letters to the Secret Service and told them that the matter was urgent; I wanted a report as quickly as they could get it.

Within forty-eight hours the head of the Secret Service came with some astonishing data. The woman was a professional beggar, coarse-fibered and of low degree. She had amassed considerable money at her occupation; she owned several tenement houses and had an income from rents. There were no children and no husband. She employed an amanuensis on a regular salary to write her begging letters in good English. Her mendicancy was a kind of organized industry; with filing cabinets, lists of names, and so on. The suicide letter, we learned, was Letter No. 8 in Series F.

2

The Secret Service has an ingenious system for running down counterfeiters. In essence it is a method for narrowing the field of investigation. When a new counterfeit bill or a base coin appears, the Service does not send its men wandering around looking vaguely for the trail. Everybody who has ever had anything to do with counterfeiting, as well as every suspected engraver or printer, is already on their list, and the agents of the Service are frequently led straight to the falsifier of money by the characteristics of the counterfeit itself.

There is a general impression among the public, I think, that all counterfeits are botched jobs, and that any bank teller is able to detect spurious bills instantly by the feel of the paper and the general appearance of the bill. That is not true in all cases. The records of the Treasury show that now and then a counterfeit appears that even the experts have much difficulty in distinguishing from the genuine issue.

About thirty years ago a false silver certificate, bearing the portrait of President Monroe, began to come into circulation. One of these notes was found in the cash drawer of the Philadelphia Sub-Treasury, where it attracted attention on account of the seal being slightly off color. It was sent to Washington and shown to various experts in the Treasury and to engravers in the Bureau of Printing and Engraving. They pronounced it genuine. Finally it was turned over to the Secret Service for examination, and W. H. Moran, who is now the head of the Service, proved that it was a counterfeit by discovering minor flaws in the engraving. It was considered such a dangerous imitation that the Treasury recalled the entire issue of genuine certificates from circulation.

The discovery of this note led to the unearthing of a huge counterfeiting scheme in which many persons were involved.

Despite such successful imitations as the one I have just mentioned counterfeiting on the whole is a very poor business. The actual amount of spurious money in circulation is insignificant. The counterfeiter is detected too early in his career to make much profit.

One of the most extraordinary cases in the history of the Secret Service concerned a counterfeiter who drew spurious hundred-dollar bills with a fine pen and a variety of colored inks. This happened before my time in the Treasury, and the account that I give here is made up partly from a perusal of the records and partly from conversations with the officials of the Service.

Specimens of this counterfeit came slowly into circulation in Philadelphia and near-by towns. They were almost perfect imitations — so good that practically any storekeeper would accept them without a doubt as to their genuineness, and some banks took them. Other banks turned them over and over suspiciously, and laid them aside for further examination. The paper seemed a little too thick and not as crinkly as the paper of a new bill ought to be.

Some of the doubtful bills were sent to the Treasury. Microscopic examination showed that they were not printed, but drawn by somebody with *pen and ink.*. Just consider that a moment. Think of all the fine lines, the infinite detail of curlycues and figures, the colors, the austere and rigid numbering, the portraits. All drawn with absolute perfection, except here and there the artist had taken a figure or a portrait from a bill of small denomination, and had deftly pasted it on his counterfeit. As a craftsman with the pen the creator of these counterfeits was without an equal.

The Secret Service went to work on the case, but with no success. Counterfeiters, as a rule, operate in groups. The indiscretion of one of their number often gives away the whole scheme. They get drunk and talk; they brag; they become reckless, and betray their secrets to women. Besides, counterfeiting usually requires paraphernalia — printing presses, inks, engraving tools — and the tracing of these materials is one of the reliable means of detection. But the pen-and-ink artist in question was, apparently, a lone wolf. He seemed to have no confederates, and he needed a minimum of equipment.

Eventually he was caught through an accident, after he had carried on for several years. One day a man in a Philadelphia saloon offered a hundred-dollar bill in payment for a drink, saying at the time that he was sorry he did not have anything smaller. He laid the hundred-dollar bill down on a wet spot where a glass of beer had stood. The bartender, as he picked it up, noticed that the colors on the wet side of the bill had run into a smudge. The ink was not waterproof.

The bartender reflected a moment while he pretended to look in his cash drawer. 'I haven't got a hundred dollars here,' he said. 'Wait a minute; I'll run out and get this bill changed.' The man waited; the bartender went out and brought in a policeman. When the man with the hundred-dollar bill was turned over to the Secret Service, he confessed, after some attempted evasion, that he had made the bill, and had made one of them every week for years. He had no confederates. It took him a full week to draw a bill with pen and ink, he said. When he had finished the job, he always took the bill to a store and made a purchase for a few dollars and went off with the change. He said that he had never gone to the same store twice.

One of the extraordinary features of the case was that this amazing counterfeiter was a New Jersey laborer who had never had any instruction in drawing. He was ignorant; almost illiterate. The fictional 'Jim the Penman' is predicated on this case.

3

At the beginning of the World War, the President issued a proclamation of neutrality, in which he said, among other things:

No person within the territory and jurisdiction of the United States shall take part, directly or indirectly, in the said wars, but shall remain at peace with all the said belligerents and shall maintain a strict and impartial neutrality.

It was not long before we discovered that the United States was a roving ground for every variety of propagandist and spy. Under cover, and under innocent-sounding names, formidable organizations camped on our soil and exercised their talents in pestering the American people and creating dissensions among them.

The British had an efficient and astute secret service for American operations, with headquarters in New York. The French and the Germans were also well represented. Most of the work of these foreign agencies was devoted to verbal propaganda and the dissemination of lies.

British publicity in America was characterized by an artistic unity and singleness of purpose. The main idea was to create an impression that the Germans were barbarians, and the picture was built up carefully, and by degrees, with all unessentials and contradictions eliminated. The British agents managed to make a large part of the American people believe that German soldiers had cut off the hands of Belgian children; and also that absurd and repulsive yarn about the Germans boiling the bodies of their own dead soldiers to produce fats.

All this propaganda, disguised as news and opinions, was undoubtedly a violation of American neutrality, but what could be done about it? A man may lie like Ananias, but you cannot put him in jail for that. He may say that the Allies are in the war to uphold civilization; or, if he is on the other side, he may talk himself black in the face about the marvels of German Kultur. You may not believe him in either case, yet he has a right to keep his opinion and a right to express it.

An effort was made by the Germans to purchase an important newspaper syndicate. The negotiations fell through; the owners of the syndicate finally decided not to sell. But the Germans did organize a camouflaged news bureau. However, in starting that enterprise they were not a step ahead of the Allies. The English and French governments controlled the cables. Nearly everything in the newspapers which came from Europe during the war was censored and colored in the Allied interest.

An enormous trade in munitions and food developed, but only a small part of these supplies went to Germany. The Allies controlled the seas; it was suicide for a German ship to peep out of its harbor. The American commerce with the Allies was absolutely legitimate; it was sanctioned by historical tradition and international law. We were a neutral power; our manufacturers and merchants and farmers had the right to sell anything to anybody. There is no doubt whatever that we would have sold munitions and food direct to the Germans if they had been able to take their purchases home. It was a cash-and-carry system. Yet the British blockade was far from being wholly effective. Though Germany had lost command of the sea, she did purchase large quantities of supplies in the United States and managed to get them home through neutral countries.

By the beginning of 1915, the Administration was convinced, by the most irrefutable evidence, that German agents were encouraging strikes and sabotage operations in American manufacturing plants, in order to prevent supplies from going to England and France. The German government, as we knew for a certainty, was endeavoring to influence legislation in this country.

I am not at all sure that the sabotage of a munitions plant is as malign and evil as the distortion of the public mind by editorials and false news, but you cannot do anything about the uttering of lies under the guise of news or opinions without impinging on the right of free speech. However, when propagandists conspire to destroy property or to inspire civic disorder — that is another matter, and one which furnishes a tangible basis for governmental action.

On May 14, 1915, the President — at the suggestion of Secretary of State Bryan — directed me to use the Secret Service for running-down violations of neutrality.

We kept an eye on the activities of the German embassy and we learned a lot about German behavior in regard to our neutrality laws.

Soon after the Secret Service began to observe the movements of the German representatives, we came to the conclusion that neither Bernstorff nor the embassy was the only source of illegitimate operations in this country. However, I was convinced that Bernstorff knew what was going on, even if he did not personally have the directing hand.

When the news of the sinking of the Lusitania came, Bernstorff declared that he had not known anything about it, yet notwithstanding this denial the fact remains that the German embassy printed advertisements in the New York papers a few days before the Lusitania sailed on her fatal voyage, in which the public was warned against sailing on that vessel.

The intricate German propaganda system in America appeared to radiate from Dr. Heinrich F. Albert, a Teutonic visitor to our shores, who had an office on lower Broadway in New York. Dr. Albert, who was an important personage in Germany, arrived in the United States in the early days of the war. He had no visible occupation, yet he seemed to be enormously busy. By intercepting wireless messages, sent in code from Germany to Dr. Albert through the radio station at Sayville, on Long Island, we learned that he was receiving large sums of money. This money was deposited in New York banks to his credit, and no one appeared to know what he did with it. After this country went into the war, the government got hold of Dr. Albert's account-books. They revealed the fact that he had received from Germany more than twenty-seven million dollars in all, but the records did not show how he had expended this fortune.

Dr. Albert's major activities as a German plotter came to a dramatic end on July 24, 1915, when one of our Secret Service men walked away from a New York Elevated train with the learned Doctor's brief-case under his arm.

The story of the abduction of this historic brief-case has been told in so many ways, and so erroneously, that for the sake of historical accuracy I shall give here an authentic account.

The Secret Service man who got away with the brief-case full of documentary dynamite was Frank Burke. I asked him to tell me all about it in writing, and here is his story. I give it verbatim, except for a few changes to eliminate repetitions and to clarify the narrative:

'I had intended to take the afternoon off to attend to some

personal matters,' he says. 'It was Saturday, July 24, 1915. One of our men, W. H. Houghton, had been shadowing George Sylvester Viereck for some time. Viereck, an American of strong pro-German bias, and of German descent, was the publisher of a periodical known as 'The Fatherland,' which was devoted to the advocacy of the German cause in America.

'At 2.30 P.M., just as I was getting ready to leave the office for the day, Houghton 'phoned that he had followed Viereck downtown and had seen him enter the building at 45 Broadway, which was the office building of the Hamburg-American Line.

'In spite of my desire to take the afternoon off, I told Houghton that I would join him. At three o'clock, while we were hanging about the entrance, we saw Viereck leave the building with a stranger. It was Dr. Albert, though it happened that neither of us knew who he was at that time. We followed them.

'Viereck and the other man, who was conspicuously German, went to the Rector Street station of the Elevated road and boarded a Sixth Avenue Harlem Train. They took one of the cross-seats in the center of the car. Houghton sat in the cross-seat directly opposite, while I sat just behind Viereck and his companion. The unknown man carried a large, heavily stuffed brief-case. Viereck showed him much deference and was extremely polite. From that, and also from the general manner and appearance of the stranger, I came to the conclusion that he was a man of rank and importance in German circles. I could get nothing from their conversation, because it was in German, which I do not understand.

'While passing the two in the car, I noticed the stranger had several straight oblique scars on one side of his face, which reminded me that I had been given a description of some German of importance with saber scars on his face, and after considerable thought, I remembered that six weeks before, George F. Lamb, one of the customs attorneys, had told me about Dr. Albert and described him as six feet one inch in height, fifty years old, and of about one hundred and ninety pounds in weight. Lamb had told me that Albert had saber scars on his face. He also told me he was the most important representative of the German government in the United States. I came to the conclusion that Viereck's companion was Dr. Albert.

'Having this in mind, I determined to follow him and observe his movements. When the train stopped at the Twenty-Third Street station, Viereck got off and was followed by Houghton. I remained in my seat. A young lady, who evidently boarded the train at the Twenty-Third Street station, took the seat Viereck had just vacated beside Dr. Albert and was soon interested in a book she was reading. Dr. Albert was living at the German Club located on Fifty-Ninth Street and Central Park, and to get there it was necessary for him to leave the Harlem train at Fiftieth Street and take a shuttle train that ran between Fiftieth and Fifty-Eighth Street. Dr. Albert's brief-case was resting on the seat against the wall of the car. When the train reached Fiftieth Street, the Doctor was reading and did not notice the train had stopped until it was about ready to move, when it occurred to him that he must change. He sprang from his seat and shouted at the guard to wait. As he went toward the door, the young lady sitting beside him called to him that he had left his brief-case. I am not sure that he heard her, as he had passed out of the train door and was on the platform before he started to turn back.

'When I saw that he had left his brief-case, I decided in a fraction of a second to get it. I told the girl that the brief-case belonged to me; I picked it up and started for the front door. Dr. Albert was then trying to get back in the car through the rear door. I could see, from the corner of my eye, that he was having some difficulty. A very fat woman was planted in the door; she was evidently asking something of the guard, while Dr. Albert tried to push by her.

'I suppose the young lady told the Doctor that some one had taken his brief-case when he finally got in the car, as I saw him come pouring out in a hurry. He seemed greatly disturbed. I had reached the platform by that time. There were enough passengers alighting from the train to give me a little cover. The Doctor was between me and the stairs, and I did not dare to start for the street at that moment. I went to the wall of the station, and pretended to light a cigar, striking one match after another, and blowing them out, with the brief-case against the wall, partly covered by my coat.

'After hastily glancing at the people on the platform, Dr. Albert rushed down the stairs. No train was in sight, and to remain on the platform if he returned, I knew would be disastrous, so I followed him, feeling I had more room on the ground than on the platform. When I reached the street, the Doctor was some distance out in the street where he could get a better view of pedestrians, with panic written on his face. Almost instantly he discovered me with the bag and dashed in my direction. I ran for a rapidly moving Sixth Avenue surface car going uptown. It was one of the open cars, and I jumped on the running-board near the conductor, which gave me an opportunity to tell him the man running after the car was crazy and that he had just a moment before caused a scene on the Elevated station, and if he got on the car, he would cause trouble. Certainly the wild-eyed appearance of the Doctor corroborated my statement and the conductor called to the motorman to pass the next corner without stopping so the nut could not get on. The car turned west on Fifty-Third Street.

'At Eighth Avenue and Fifty-Third Street I boarded a downtown surface car and rode as far as the car barns a few blocks down, where the car stopped for an unusual time. I got off and went in a drugstore on the corner and 'phoned Chief Flynn, who came up in his machine, and we drove to the office, where a glance at the contents of the bag, though much of it was in German, satisfied me that I had done a good Saturday's work.'

The same evening Chief Flynn (William J. Flynn, then head of the Secret Service) telegraphed me at North Haven, Maine, where my family was spending the summer, and told me that he must see me on a very important matter. I directed him to come forthwith to North Haven, and he arrived the next day, bringing the Albert brief-case with him. I spent the afternoon and evening looking over the captured documents, and the more I saw of them, the more clearly I realized their immense importance.

The question was what to do with them, what action to take. Most of the documents were of such character that they did not furnish any basis for legal action, yet they showed plainly enough that illegitimate activities were going on; that our neutrality laws were being grossly violated. I saw an opportunity to throw a reverberating scare into the whole swarm of propagandists — British and French as well as German — and I decided that this could be done most effectively through publicity.

After thoughtful consideration, I selected the New York 'World' as the medium of exposure. I went down to New York in a few days and got in touch with Frank I. Cobb, editorial manager of the 'World.' He came up to my hotel and we spent half a day in going over the contents of the brief-case. We selected some of the papers which I turned over to Cobb on one condition only — that he would not tell anyone, not even his associates on the 'World,' how they came into his possession. He promised to observe this injunction, and he did.

Our observers reported that there was consternation in the German embassy at Washington, as well as at 45 Broadway — the office of Dr. Albert. They had no idea as to who had taken the brief-case, though they suspected the British spy service. Evidently there was a lingering hope that an ordinary sneak thief had got away with the portfolio, not knowing what was in it, and that it might be recovered by offering a reward. On Monday, July 26, this pathetic little advertisement appeared in the New York 'Evening Telegram':

Lost: — On Saturday, on 3.30 Harlem Elevated train, at 50th St. station, brown leather bag, containing documents. Deliver to G. H. Hoffman, 5 East 47th St., against $20 reward.

On August 15, 1915, the 'World' began to publish the documents that were found in the brief-case. It was a startling disclosure of what was going on under the surface of events. The correspondence with Dr. Albert proved that leading officials of the German government, while outwardly professing friendship for the United States, were plotting against this country; that they were deliberately violating our neutrality. One of the most surprising facts disclosed was that no less a personage than von Bethmann-Hollweg, Chancellor of the German Empire, was participating in some of these secret undertakings.

The correspondence showed that German agents had formed elaborate schemes for the following purposes:

To control and influence public opinion by buying newspapers and establishing news services. According to the evidence of the documents, some American periodicals appeared to be receiving regular subsidies from the German government. 'The Fatherland,' edited by George Sylvester Viereck, was on the German payroll for about fifteen hundred dollars a month. Viereck denied this, but his denial was weak and not at all convincing.

To publish books, to invade the Chautauqua circuit with professional lecturers, and to finance motion pictures which would have a German bias. (I am morally convinced that the Allies were doing the same thing, but we had no documentary proof.)

To organize strikes in munition plants. The writer of one letter offered to bring about strikes in munition factories for a fee of fifty thousand dollars. Dr. Albert said later that he did not know the writer of this letter, that he was probably a crank, and that he intended to throw the letter away.

To corner the supply of liquid chlorine, used for poison gas, to keep it from reaching the Allies.

To acquire the Wright Aeroplane Company and its patents and use them in the interest of the Germans.

To organize a movement to cut off the supply of cotton from England and make it appear that the movement had originated spontaneously among the cotton-growers in the South.

To organize a movement to put an embargo on shipments of munitions. To accomplish this, the Germans hoped to influence legislation in the United States.

The correspondence also showed that while the German government was protesting against the shipment of arms to the Allies, it had, through its secret agents, purchased a large munitions plant at Bridgeport, Connecticut. The ownership of the plant was concealed under an American name. Orders for shells had been taken from the British and Russian governments, but without any intention of making deliveries.

That Captain von Papen, German military attaché, was in communication with certain labor leaders who offered to bring about strikes in American factories.

4

Twelve years after the war George Sylvester Viereck wrote:

The publication of the Albert papers was a German catastrophe. ... It was a veritable nest of intrigue, conspiracy, and propaganda that reposed placidly in Dr. Albert's brief-case. The inner workings of the propaganda machine were laid bare.... The loss of the Albert portfolio was like the loss of the Marne.

It was generally believed by the public, I think, that Dr. Albert's papers had been taken by somebody in the British service. The Doctor himself, in a published statement, laid the theft on the British. Naturally, we said nothing about our part in it, so the British fable grew. In this connection, Frank Burke, who actually did the job, adds an amusing postscript to his narrative. 'A man named Pilinas,' he writes, 'entertained myself and John Meehan one day, to our great but silent merriment, with a long account of how he himself had abstracted the Doctor's brief-case. He had formerly been in the British Secret Service. I don't know about his qualifications as a detective, but he was certainly a fine liar.'

According to another story, the brief-case was picked up by an unidentified but bright young man after Dr. Albert had left the train; that he took it home, looked into it, and realized the great news value of the contents. Thereupon he took it to the 'World' and was paid ten thousand dollars.

There was — and is yet — even another account which runs to the effect that the 'World' had been shadowing Dr. Albert for some time, and that a reporter from that newspaper captured the brief-case while Dr. Albert was having a mild after-luncheon nap on the train.

As I think of the various fables concerning this episode which have found their way into historical narratives that are supposed to be authentic, I have doubts as to the accuracy of all history — to its veracity in respect to details, at any rate.

There is a revered Chinese proverb which says: 'When two men cannot agree on the price of an onion, who can say what happened in the time of Yu?'

CHAPTER XXII
PEOPLE AND POLITICS

I

THE second change in the personnel of the Cabinet occurred in June, 1915, when William Jennings Bryan resigned as Secretary of State and the President named Robert Lansing as his successor.

Bryan was a pacifist. We were all for peace, in fact; the President and all members of the Cabinet. But Woodrow Wilson was not a milk-and-water statesman; he had no intention of looking on with a sickly smile while Germany and the Allies turned the United States into an international doormat. I knew that, and I knew also that, if we were ever forced into the war while Wilson was President, we would go in with a deadly smash and the fur would fly.

There was a great difference between his brand of pacifism and that of William Jennings Bryan. I will not say that one of Bryan's outstanding qualities was a sort of meek humility, though he sometimes gave one that impression. He was, in truth, a fighter himself — and a tough and ready fighter at that — but his battles were chiefly forensic and political.

In respect to the World War, Bryan could hardly bring himself to believe that it really existed; it was so remote from anything in his own mentality that I fancy it always seemed to him to be a kind of cosmic nightmare — this bad dream of intelligent men going out in swarms and slaughtering one another. He thought, in those early days at least, that something or other would occur, some miracle of an olive branch and the furling of flags, which would suddenly bring all the combatants to their senses.

Bryan was a firm believer in the Christian virtues; most men were good at heart, if they would only let the goodness come out and show itself. Right and truth and justice, he thought, would triumph in the end. He believed implicitly in arbitration as a solution of all quarrels. I have great faith in arbitration myself; most of the agonizing disputes that afflict human affairs could be settled, I confidently believe, by the disputants getting around a table and having a frank and cordial talk before a disinterested third party.

Yet arbitration has its limits. You cannot go into arbitration with a man who comes up and knocks you down without rhyme or reason. In such a case there is nothing to arbitrate. You may either get up, brush off your clothes, and walk away with insult and injury stirring in your heart, or you may take off your coat and pitch into your assailant.

Germany came up and knocked us down when she sank the Lusitania without warning, with a consequent loss of more than a hundred American lives; and her explanatory rhyme and reason were extremely thin and not at all satisfactory.

The German excuse was that the Lusitania carried munitions. It is true that she had some cases of small-arms cartridges in her hold, but the amount carried was insignificant — a mere nothing in comparison with the rest of her cargo — and moreover, under international law a merchant ship or passenger carrier cannot be considered a warship because a part of its cargo consists of munitions of war. As a British vessel the Lusitania was subject to capture; but if the Germans had taken her as a prize, it would have been necessary to conduct her to a German port, and the commander of the submarine that sent her to the bottom had no facilities for taking charge of prizes. Moreover, the Germans had a legitimate right, under the law of nations, to sink the Lusitania on the high seas, but not until the safety of her passengers and crew had been assured. International law does not countenance the murder of non-combatants while traveling on passenger vessels, or even when living in unfortified places on land.

The President wrote a stiff note to the Imperial German Government on the sinking of the Lusitania, and Bryan signed it as Secretary of State. Before it was dispatched, he suggested a postscript in which it was proposed that Germany meet us in arbitration over the matter, but this postscript was not sent, as the President thought it would weaken our essentially sound position. Bryan was dissatisfied, but he acquiesced and seemed disposed to make the best of it.

The German reply to the President's note was simply a polite and diplomatic evasion of the issue. The President prepared a stronger note, more direct and more emphatic. It was discussed fully at the Cabinet meeting on the first of June. I remember that Bryan had little to say at this meeting; he sat throughout the proceedings with his eyes half closed most of the time. After the meeting he told the President, as I learned later, that he could not sign the note. He repeated that arbitration was the proper remedy.

On Saturday, June 5, 1915, I had just arrived at my house for luncheon when Bryan came, unexpectedly. His face was haggard. He was visibly nervous and remarked that he had not slept well. I had never before seen him so agitated.

He began by saying that he had come to me to unburden his mind because of his personal affection for me, and because of my intimacy with the President. If the President should send the second Lusitania note, he said he thought it would surely lead to war with Germany, and that as a profound believer in peace he could not conscientiously follow the President in the proposed course. I asked him what he thought the President ought to do, and he answered that the principle of arbitration should be applied to the case. I knew that arbitration was out of the question, an impossible solution, but I said nothing.

Bryan went on to say that he thought his usefulness as Secretary of State was over, and that he proposed to resign. His purpose in coming to me was to have me take up the matter with the President and see what could be done to make his resignation cause the least possible embarrassment to the Administration.

'Colonel,' I said, 'have you said anything about this to anybody else?'

'Only to Mrs. Bryan,' he replied.

'I am glad of that, because we must keep this in the family until we can weigh it carefully,' I said. 'I think you could not make a graver mistake than to resign. I am sure that the note the President proposes to dispatch to Germany will not lead to war. But if you resign, you will create the impression that there is a difference of opinion in the Cabinet over this serious situation, and you will, I think, contribute to the very result which you say you are anxious to avoid.'

He sat in thoughtful silence for a while; then he said that he had to abide by his own feeling, his own conscience, and he felt that there was no alternative but to resign.

We went over all the ground again. In the end his decision was unshaken. I asked him to stay for luncheon, but he said that he must go home.

'Suppose I go to your house after luncheon,' I suggested, 'and talk it over with Mrs. Bryan?' She was a level-headed and sagacious woman. Her judgment was excellent, and I knew that Bryan relied on it to an unusual degree.

'All right,' he agreed. 'Come on; we'll be glad to see you.'

For a while that afternoon I saw Mrs. Bryan alone. She said that her husband had been unhappy in his position for some time on account of the President's habit of preparing important diplomatic papers himself. He had come to feel, she said, that he was not consulted as he ought to be, and that he was playing the part of a figurehead.

I replied that I knew the President had no thought of minimizing Mr. Bryan; that being responsible, as President, for our international policy, he thought he should prepare the notes to Germany himself, but that he submitted them, I knew, to Mr. Bryan and was glad to have the benefit of his counsel and assistance.

The Colonel and Mrs. Bryan looked jaded. There was an air of fatigue about each of them.

'Mrs. Bryan,' I said, 'this is Saturday. I think that you and the Colonel ought to go away somewhere for the week-end, take a rest in some quiet place, and think the matter over. When you come back on Monday, let us get together and talk about it again. Meanwhile, I will see the President and tell him of our conversation.'

She said she thought that was a good idea, and before I left their house they were getting ready to go to Senator Blair Lee's home at Silver Spring for the week-end. Mrs. Bryan records in her published diary that W. J. B. could not sleep, although the place was lovely and quiet. Instead of sleeping, he sat up for hours and read a book, published in 1829, called 'A Wreath of Appreciation of Andrew Jackson.'

That same Saturday afternoon I went to the White House and told the President of my conversation with the Bryans, omitting nothing. The President remarked that he was not

surprised at Bryan's intention to resign, as he had been growing more and more out of sympathy with the Administration
in the controversy with Germany. He said, however, that he
would like to have Bryan remain in the Cabinet, if possible.
His resignation at that critical moment might lead the German government to think that there were wide differences of
opinion in the inner circles of the Administration, and he
thought that would make our position more difficult. He
asked me to see Bryan again on Monday.

I did. I called at his home on Calumet Place as soon as he
telephoned me that he had returned. When I arrived, both
the Bryans were seated in their large, pleasant parlor. They
looked better and more refreshed.

Bryan said at once that he had not changed his mind since
Saturday. He could not go against the dictates of his conscience, he declared. I thought the situation might be helped
if I could have a private talk with Mrs. Bryan, and when I
said so her husband agreed smilingly and left the room.

When I was alone with Mrs. Bryan, I told her that I wanted
to impress upon her what I was afraid I could not impress on
the Colonel — that he was making a fatal mistake. His action
would be bitterly resented by the country; and he would be
condemned, I thought, because the American people would
believe that he had resigned for the purpose of embarrassing
the President.

Mrs. Bryan agreed with me, and said she, too, thought the
Colonel would be subjected to violent and unjust criticism,
but nevertheless, it would be better for him to resign. He
could not play a part which was not sustained by his conscience. I realized that they had conclusively made up their
minds.

As I went out, I expressed my regret to Bryan, who was in
the next room. I was genuinely sorry that he was leaving the
Cabinet, and I said so. 'You say you are convinced, Colonel,
that the dispatch of this second note about the Lusitania will
lead to war,' I continued. 'I think you are wrong. Suppose
you are mistaken, and that within the next few months that
fact is clearly demonstrated by the course of events? It will
put you in a ridiculous position; in fact, it will ruin you. I
don't want you to destroy yourself.'

Bryan looked at me steadfastly for a moment, as though he were meditating deeply on my words, then he said:

'I believe you are right; I think this will destroy me; but whether it does or not, I must do my duty according to my conscience, and if I am destroyed, it is, after all, merely the sacrifice that one must not hesitate to make to serve his God and his country.'

There was nothing else to say. I could not help admiring his high purpose, although I felt that it was misdirected.

'Colonel,' I said, 'no matter what you do, you know that my friendship and affection for you will not be diminished. I deplore your decision, but I understand how you feel about it. I will see the President and tell him what you say.'

I went immediately to the White House and related my interview to the President. He commissioned me to say to Bryan that he submitted with sincere regret to his wishes in the matter, merely because he felt that no other course was open to him. I conveyed this message in person. The next day, June 8, Bryan placed his resignation in the hands of the President.

When I told Bryan that his action would be criticized, I had no idea of the hurricane of abuse that was to howl around him. His resignation was denounced as a disloyal, traitorous act by many newspapers and public speakers. The New York 'World' declared that his resignation was 'unspeakable treachery, not only to the President, but to the nation,' and the 'World's' criticism was a fair sample of the whole body of editorial opinion. Before he went back to Nebraska, Bryan purchased, as a memento, the desk at which he had sat while Secretary of State. The New York 'Times,' commenting on his acquisition of the desk, said in its elegantly urbane manner, 'he took it away from the scenes in which Seward and Fish and Evarts and Hay thought were reverent to leave it, and carried it to Fairfield County, Nebraska, to repose among the souvenirs of his visit to Japan, and the sea-shells and snapshots, and the original drawings of cartoons in the hall, and the curious specimens of Oriental weaving in the sitting-room, and the copy of "The First Battle" on the center table.'

2

It has become the custom nowadays, among supercilious people, to depict Bryan as a clown, or a fool, or a mountebank. He was nothing of the kind. In many respects he was one of the shrewdest men I have ever known. In him, unsophistication and sagacity were strangely blended. Along with this he was truthful and square. His friendships were sincere; one could depend implicitly on his word. Yet, at the same time, he was a clever politician — the best strategist of his generation. Moreover, he was an exceptionally able man, and a fighter. He knew when to hit hard, and he never failed to do it when the occasion required hard hitting. He was certainly a formidable figure in the political arena.

With the exception of the men who have occupied the White House, Bryan — according to my judgment — had more to do with the shaping of the public policies of the last forty years than any other American citizen. He was for the income tax, for women's suffrage, for prohibition, and he was a tremendous force in putting these questions before the people.

One of his marked defects was an inability to discern clearly the real motives and purposes of men. His inclination was to have too high an opinion of anybody who professed to be his friend. It was a curious failing, for he had a personal acquaintance with more people, I should say at a guess, than any other man in the United States. A man like Bryan, who has spent his whole life in public affairs, usually grows cynical in the course of time, for such a man has every opportunity to observe the qualities of avarice, duplicity, and egotism in their most striking forms.

He kept his free silver fallacy bright and shining to the end of his life. Every now and then he would take it out and polish it up, like a man who cherishes an ancient, wartime sword. He realized that the cause of free silver was hopeless, but he considered it a righteous cause just the same. Once I attempted to discuss the free silver question with him. We did not get very far, as I soon felt that he and I were speaking different languages. On this subject, even with the best intentions in the world, we were mutually unintelligible.

He turned every public question into a moral issue. He was by nature a crusader, a reformer. Economics did not seem to have much standing-room in his mind. Whenever I began to discuss any question of economic import with him, I noticed that he usually shifted the conversation to the moral plane. He thought in terms of people bearing burdens, of the wicked in high places, of the altars of sacrifice. But anyone who pictures him as a grumpy, sour, muddled fanatic is wholly wrong. He was always amiable and cheerful, and he took his defeats with marvelous gallantry.

As I think of him there comes into my mind what somebody said of Gladstone — that to keep hating him, one had to avoid meeting him. I cannot say if this was true of Gladstone, but it was certainly true of William Jennings Bryan.

3

Bryan's place in the Cabinet was taken — after a hiatus of about two weeks — by Robert Lansing, who had served under Bryan as Counselor of the State Department; which means the department's professional expert on international law.

Before Lansing was appointed, the President asked me one day what I thought of him for the post. I said that, in my opinion, it would be a political error to put another New-Yorker in the Cabinet; we had two already — Redfield and myself — and Lansing would make three. I suggested to the President that he ought to strengthen his Cabinet by the selection of some outstanding Democrat from the Middle West.

The President reflected awhile, and then asked me if I had anyone in mind. I had not; and he remarked that he could not think of any man in the Middle West who had Lansing's excellent qualifications for the place. He let me understand that he intended to be, in effect, his own Secretary of State, and that he needed Lansing to put diplomatic notes in proper form and to act as an adviser on points of international law. I do not know whether he went into this with Lansing before he appointed him, but I presume he did.

The President, under our form of government, is directly and personally responsible for the handling of our international relations, though the routine work of the State Department is delegated, of course, to the Secretary of State and his assistants.

Whenever serious foreign complications arise, and the President happens to be a man of force and ability, the Secretary of State is bound to be, in a peculiar sense, the secretary of the President in the matter of foreign affairs. I make a point of this for the reason that Lansing undoubtedly became embittered and dissatisfied toward the end of Wilson's second term, particularly at the Versailles Peace Conference, because his advice on questions that fell within his department was sometimes disregarded by the President. His pride was hurt. It was not my affair, and I am unable to say anything conclusively about it, though I have a strong impression that he accepted his post with a distinct understanding that all negotiations with foreign powers were to be carried on by the President.

Lansing was a quiet, undemonstrative, even phlegmatic sort of man. He seemed to have no interest whatever in politics, and, although he was nominally a Democrat, his opinions about affairs in general appeared to be decidedly conservative. At the bottom he was a scholar rather than a man of action; yet I would not describe him as a philosopher, or of the philosophic type, but as a man of culture, well-read and well-informed.

At Cabinet meetings he rarely said anything unless an international question came up. Usually he sat in silence at the Cabinet table, with a pad of paper before him, and made small pencil sketches with his left hand. He seemed to draw these delineations of faces and figures almost automatically, as if he were thinking of something else while his pencil moved over the paper.

There was another change in the Cabinet when Lindley M. Garrison, Secretary of War, resigned on February 10, 1916, and was succeeded by Newton D. Baker, of Cleveland. Garrison and the Administration parted company on account of Garrison's irreconcilable antagonism toward the President's attitude on the subject of military preparedness.

Garrison had been won over completely to the idea of compulsory military service, which was then being advocated, up and down the country, and in every form of propaganda, by Theodore Roosevelt and General Leonard Wood.

The President's views as to the best method of military preparedness were radically different. He believed that the American people's deep-rooted antagonism to any form of compulsory military service was too strong to be overcome in time of peace. But, at the same time, he was open to conviction; and what he really wanted was a full and frank discussion of the entire matter in and out of Congress.

Garrison, who was strongly opinionated and dogmatic, and always impatient with opposition, wanted to force his cut-and-dried plan on Congress. When the President declined to endorse the scheme for compulsory service, or to try to dictate to the House Committee on Military Affairs, Garrison felt aggrieved and came to the conclusion that he was no longer of any use in the Cabinet. The President agreed with him in respect to the latter opinion and accepted his resignation promptly.

I have said that Lansing was a silent member of the Cabinet; that he hardly ever spoke unless his opinion was asked, or unless some question of international policy was being discussed. Garrison was precisely the opposite in temperament. He had what one might call an 'eager' mind — one that was so quick and active that he was continually anticipating what was going to be said by interjecting his own ideas. Unless you hurried up with what you had to say, he would often finish your sentences for you; and frequently they would be finished in a different way from what you intended.

There was nothing more trying to the President than to be interrupted when he was discussing a matter or making some statement to the Cabinet. Garrison was the only member of the Cabinet who did this; and, after observing him for a while, I came to the conclusion that there was something combative and controversial in his nature which he seemed unable to suppress. I know that he did not mean to be discourteous or inconsiderate, but this did not make his habit of interrupting the President any the less annoying.

Some of the members of the Cabinet gave him the nickname of 'Secretary Garrulous.' The characterization was unjust, as most humorous appellations are. He was not garrulous in the true meaning of the word; he was simply argumentative and irrepressible. What he said, in the way of interruption, was often very much to the point. Nevertheless, people who have something to say do not, as a rule, relish being interrupted while they are saying it, even by the wisest of men.

The President had long felt that Garrison was not in full sympathy with the Administration, and was relieved when he resigned. As a matter of fact, Garrison was a conservative in mental habit, and was always more or less at cross-purposes with the President's liberal policies.

After his resignation, Garrison conducted himself with admirable regard to the proprieties of the situation. He refused to take part in any criticism of the President and announced that, having retired to private life, he would do nothing to embarrass the Administration.

As I happened to be Mr. Wilson's son-in-law as well as a member of his Cabinet, there was a general impression, I think, that I was a special confidant of the President. Many people thought, during those years, that he discussed everything of importance with me, and that I had much to do with the shaping of all sorts of policies. I corrected that impression, whenever the opportunity came up, as it was entirely erroneous. In relation to the President I occupied the same position as any other Cabinet officer. He made a practice of discussing with me only such subjects as happened to fall within my sphere of action, or in which he considered my opinion of value.

For some reason, however, he made a point of consulting me about the selection of men for all kinds of positions. He did not tell me why he did this, and I never asked him, though I presume it was because I had managed the 1912 campaign and had an extensive acquaintance throughout the country; and also, perhaps, because he thought I was a good judge of people. At any rate, he asked my opinion on many appointments, from justices of the Supreme Court down to minor officials. But he did not always follow my recommendations; or, for that matter, anybody else's recommendations. He was an independent thinker and had a way of making up his own mind.

When Garrison resigned, the President discussed the selection of his successor with me, and asked me to suggest someone. I recommended Newton D. Baker. In forming his Cabinet in 1913, the President had selected him as Secretary of the Interior before the post was offered to Franklin K. Lane, but Baker was obliged to decline, as he had just been elected mayor of Cleveland by the reform element of that city, and he decided that he ought to continue in the mayor's job.

The President remarked that Baker would be an excellent man for the place, but he wanted to think it over. Several weeks went by without anything more being said on the subject. On March 6, he told me that he had decided to offer the post to Baker. At his request I telephoned to Cleveland and informed Baker that the President wanted him to become Secretary of War. He accepted, and his nomination was confirmed by the Senate the next day.

Baker used to sit at his desk at the War Department with one leg curled up under him on the cushion of his chair. On his desk there was always a fresh pansy, and he continually smoked a pipe. A small man physically, Baker looked boyish in the company of the tall and bulky generals who were usually around him.

4

The uproar over President Wilson's appointment of Louis D. Brandeis as an Associate Justice of the Supreme Court filled the air during the early months of 1916, and for a while the pro-and-con clamor over the qualities of Brandeis as a man, a citizen, a lawyer, and a judge made the news from the World War sound like a whisper.

Justice Joseph R. Lamar died in the January of that year. One day about a week after his death, the President asked me if I had any suggestion to make as to Lamar's successor; if so, he said, he would be glad to hear it.

I replied at once that I did have someone in mind. Ever since Justice Lamar's death, I had thought of Brandeis for the place, but I had said nothing, as I hesitated to make a suggestion concerning a matter of this kind unless the President asked for it. When I mentioned Brandeis, the President seemed surprised; at least, I inferred that he was from his manner and expression, but he let me know that he was immensely pleased with the idea.

'Do you think the Senate would confirm his appointment?' he asked, in a tone of doubt. I think I have already stated, in a previous chapter, that one of my unofficial duties was to keep always in touch with the Senate, and in a measure to act as the representative of the Administration in that quarter.

'Yes, he will be confirmed, I think, if you appoint him,' was my reply, 'but it will be a stiff fight.'

I knew, and he knew, that the name of Brandeis had the same effect on the great financial interests as a red flag has on a bull. They regarded him as an untamed radical, and a dangerous person; or, at any rate, that is what they said. But Brandeis was not a radical, according to the accepted definition of that term. He was, in fact, a liberal of the modern type — a keen student of affairs and a profound thinker on political, social, and economic problems. Moreover, he was one of the greatest lawyers of the time; a fact that even his bitterest opponents were ready to admit.

No doubt the President consulted others — Attorney-General Gregory among them — about appointing Brandeis, for in all such matters he proceeded with admirable caution. He told me next day that he had definitely decided to send the Brandeis nomination to the Senate, but he did not actually make the appointment until January 28. Then the storm broke.

The Washington correspondent of the New York 'Times,' sensing the fall of the political barometer and the coming of the tornado, sent that evening a long dispatch to his newspaper about the appointment. The following excerpts from the article convey its essence:

President Wilson surprised the nation today when he sent to the Senate the nomination of Louis D. Brandeis.... Mr. Brandeis' name had never been mentioned in connection with the vacant place on the Supreme Court bench, and as far as can be ascertained none of the public men who had been making suggestions to the President as to choosing Justice Lamar's successor had recommended him. He was not in any sense a candidate for the office and, in fact, he did not know of the President's desire to nominate him until a few days ago .... The selection is credited, in the best informed quarters, to Attorney-General Gregory.... Some of those who showed marked symptoms of dissatisfaction indicated that they regarded him as practically a Socialist.... That Mr. Brandeis possesses the judicial temperament is questioned.... The nomination of Mr. Brandeis was received by Senators of both parties with little less than dismay.

Within another day or two the Senate Committee on the Judiciary took up the matter and decided to make an investigation of the numerous charges against the fitness of Brandeis for the Supreme Court bench. Hearings before a committee of Congress are not governed by the rules of legal evidence. Practically anything that has even a remote bearing on the investigation can be dragged in, including hearsay evidence, newspaper articles, and even plain, ordinary gossip. Committee hearings are not public, as a rule. As soon as the nomination was announced, I got in touch with Brandeis and urged him to request the committee to hold public hearings, because I felt sure that the flimsiness of the charges against him would not stand open scrutiny.

I cannot give, in this limited space, even a meager digest of the proceedings. The opposition, according to its conventional practice, depreciated its own case by ridiculous overstatement. An effort was made to show that Brandeis was a common swindler; that he had procured the signature of an old and dying man to a deed of trust by questionable means; that he had taken fees from both sides in certain cases in which he had appeared as an attorney; that he had deserted his clients during litigation; that he was not a patriotic American; that he 'persecuted and prosecuted' the poor and pathetic United Shoe Machinery Company (the trust that controls the patents on certain shoemaking devices).

President Abbott Lawrence Lowell, of Harvard University, headed a petition of fifty-four Boston citizens — most of them lawyers — in which the Senate was asked not to confirm the nomination. But on the other hand, nine of the eleven members of the Harvard School of Law announced that they were for Brandeis. Roscoe Pound, Professor of Jurisprudence and Equity, said: 'To have one of such a stamp on the bench of our highest court at this time is a happy augury for the law.' Joseph Henry Beale, Royall Professor of Law, said that he 'did not know a man in this country better qualified in all respects for the position.'

'I have known Mr. Louis D. Brandeis forty years,' Dr. Charles W. Eliot, President Emeritus of Harvard, wrote to the committee, 'and believe that I understand his capacities and his character.... Under present circumstances I believe that the rejection by the Senate of his nomination to the Supreme Court would be a grave misfortune for the whole legal profession, the court, all American business, and the country.'

The committee eventually made a favorable report, after a four months' wrangle in which the committee itself was deadlocked; and the nomination of Brandeis was confirmed by the Senate on June 2, 1916.

He is the first Jew, and so far the only one, who has been a member of the Supreme Court of the United States.

5

A curious and wholly untruthful story that has to do with the appointment of Justice Brandeis appears in a book by the late C. W. Barron which was published in 1930 under the title 'They Told Barron.' This book is a record of Barron's conversations with people — what they told him about things in general. For the information of those who have never heard of Barron, I will say that he was for many years the proprietor and editor of the 'Wall Street Journal.'

In an entry under the date of March 1, 1916, Barron says he had a talk with somebody named Walter Newman, who told a tale of having attended a small dinner in Washington at which the others present were President Wilson, myself and Mrs. McAdoo, and Samuel Untermyer. Newman said, according to Barron:

There was at the dinner the President's daughter and her husband, Mr. McAdoo, who still owes me nine hundred dollars of real money. Samuel Untermyer was present. President Wilson said at this dinner to his son-in-law McAdoo, 'I don't know but I made a mistake in nominating Brandeis to the Supreme Bench. The opposition seems pretty strong.'

Thereupon, Untermyer rose and delivered a speech declaring what this appointment meant to the Jewish race: That he, Untermyer, and Brandeis had worked for the country and the uplift of their race and for the Democratic party and Mr. Wilson, and that he, Untermyer, had been of great assistance to Mr. McAdoo; He alluded to the progress he, Untermyer, had made and his beautiful estate up the Hudson, and declared that he stood ready, if need be, to put one million dollars into the campaign to insure Mr. Wilson's reëlection by carrying New York. He declared that the Jewish race was with Mr. Wilson in this nomination. He brought tears to the eyes of Mr. Wilson and his daughter.

Barron recorded this yarn and printed it solemnly, and without comment, in his book. Evidently he thought it would be just like President Wilson to blurt out such an astounding statement in the presence of a nondescript Walter Newman.

Here is the truth of the matter:

I never met Walter Newman in my life; I never knew he ever existed until I saw his name in Barron's book. I never owed him nine hundred dollars, or any other sum of money. President Wilson never regretted Brandeis' appointment for a moment; on the contrary, he was always proud of this particular act. Samuel Untermyer never made a speech about the Jewish race, and his beautiful estate, and a million dollars, and so on, at any dinner where I was present. I know Mr. Untermyer well. I wrote him about this Newman story and he replied that it was false and absurd; that there was no such dinner as Newman — or Barron — describes.

I have taken the trouble to notice this statement because lying gossip of this kind manages somehow to get into what purports to be authentic history, just as cockroaches manage to get into the crevices of old houses. Although my space is limited, I thought it would be worth while to pause a moment and sprinkle insect powder on this particular cockroach before passing on.

6

I shall turn here from national affairs for a moment to record some events in my own family. On May 21, 1915, our first baby, a girl, was born in our house at 1709 Massachusetts Avenue. She was christened Ellen Wilson — the name of her grandmother, the first wife of the President.

Our second child — Mary Faith — was born five years later, on April 6, 1920, in New York City. Her name is that of my mother, Mary Faith McAdoo.

The house on Massachusetts Avenue was too small for my growing family; it is astonishing how much room one small baby and its nurse can take, especially in a dwelling that is already lacking in space. In the fall of 1915 we moved to 2139 R Street, N.W., to a larger house which we managed, fortunately, to rent at the same figure — three thousand dollars a year — that we paid for the Massachusetts Avenue residence. Though this house was larger than the one we had just left, it was not entirely satisfactory.

Our physician believed in fresh air as one of the potent means of earthly salvation. At his suggestion we bought for Baby Ellen a window crib — a device consisting of a steel frame which was attached to the window-sill and into which a small ventilated metal case, or crib, could be placed. The window to the room might then be closed and the baby would be perfectly safe, suspended in the air outside the window.

For a while this crib, with the baby in it, was one of the sights of Washington, although we were not aware of it for some time. One day Mrs. McAdoo noticed a number of people standing in the street, looking up at the crib. Soon afterward a sight-seeing bus came along and stopped a moment before the house. The guide, in stentorian tones, informed his passengers that the window crib contained a granddaughter of the President. This continued, day after day, until the public curiosity, or whatever it was, had subsided.

Between the birth of my oldest child and the coming of the youngest there was a period of nearly thirty-four years. I suppose I ought to feel patriarchal when I look over my sturdy family of eight children, but I must confess that somehow the austere emotions of a patriarch have been omitted from my personality.

I am convinced that age is largely a matter of personal temperament, or mental habit. Most people become old before they should; they allow their inner life to be corroded and worn away by experience, by sad and destructive memories. When enthusiasm ceases, youth comes to an end, no matter what one's age in years may be; and thereafter life appears as a dead and fixed panorama, the spiritual equivalent of an astronomer's picture of a landscape on the moon. Many people are aged at thirty-five. We have all met them — dreary-minded young men and women who think old thoughts.

The way to keep young is to have fresh and young ideas, new thoughts, new aspirations; every day a rebirth into new life. It is not impossible to do; it is not even hard to do.

I was past the age of fifty-five when I took up flying, and since then I have flown so many thousand miles that I long ago stopped trying to keep count of the accumulated distance. I like to fly, not only because my plane takes me quickly from one place to another, but also because it lifts me above the earth. In the air I feel detached from the ordinary, humdrum details of daily existence and I acquire a sense of vista and mental perspective. Ideas that were gnarled and clotted with inessentials when I thought of them on the ground become smooth and clarified in the air.

All my eight children are living. My oldest daughter's first husband, Charles Taber Martin, died some years ago. She married again, and is now Mrs. Clayton Platt, Jr., of Philadelphia. My oldest son, Francis Huger, is a lawyer in New York City, and is married for the second time. He has children of his own, a good law practice, and an unconquerable liking for rare books and first editions.

My two other sons, William Gibbs, Jr., and Robert Hazlehurst, are both grown and married. Sally, my youngest daughter by my first wife, is married to Brice Clagett, one of the junior partners of the law firm of which I am the head. She and her husband live in Washington.

My daughter Nona, who was the social head of my household in Washington when I became Secretary of the Treasury, was married, in May, 1917, to Ferdinand de Mohrenschildt, who was second secretary of the Russian embassy at Washington. Soon after the announcement of the engagement of these young people, the Russian embassy gave a dinner in my honor. After dinner the Ambassador took me aside and told me that he was pleased to learn of the engagement. Then he said: 'Mr. Secretary, I must tell you, however, that under the law of my country a member of the Diplomatic Corps cannot marry without the express permission of His Majesty the Czar.'

I did not know whether to feel annoyed or merely to laugh it off. My acquaintance with czars is limited — in fact, non-existent — and we do things so differently in America that it was hard for me to realize that a far-distant sovereign should have anything to say about the engagement of my daughter. An idea occurred to me, and I said, as solemnly as I could:

'Mr. Ambassador, I understand, of course, the regulation to which you refer, but, you know, there is another approval which is much more important than that of the Czar?'

He looked puzzled and a little anxious. I saw that he was racking his memory for an American social equivalent of the Czar. After a moment's reflection he said: 'Ah? And whose is that?'

'The approval of the Secretary of the Treasury,' I replied. He laughed; and we both laughed. Then he remarked that the Czar's permission was merely a matter of form, and that he had already obtained it.

The marriage of Nona and de Mohrenschildt was a love match. He was a splendid young fellow, well-educated, cultured, and devoted to his work. Nona was very popular in Washington, and her wedding was one of the great social events of the time.

On account of the limited seating arrangements of Saint John's Church, where the ceremony took place, we had to confine the invitations to the President and his family; the members of the Cabinet and their families; the Diplomatic Corps; the members of the War Commissions which had been sent to America by Great Britain, France, Italy, and Belgium, and who were in Washington at the time; and to certain leading officials of the government. I had never seen so many colorful uniforms and medals together in one place before. As the father of the bride, in my ordinary cutaway coat, I was the most inconspicuous person present.

De Mohrenschildt died of double pneumonia in 1919. At that time he and his wife were living in New York and Nona was desperately ill in a hospital when her husband died. She knew nothing of his illness, and was not told of his death until several days after his funeral.

For a long time she was inconsolable and I was almost in despair about her, as her grief seriously affected her health.

Dr. Edward S. Cowles, the eminent neurologist, finally became her physician and was highly successful in his treatment. Nona remained a widow for nine years and then married Dr. Cowles. They live in New York City.

Before her second marriage, Nona insisted on going into business for herself. She told me that she must have something to occupy her mind. I consented and she opened a little shop, called Chez Ninon, for the sale of women's frocks, on Madison Avenue, in New York. This establishment is still conducted by her, and she has turned out to be an excellent business woman.

7

On December 18, 1915, Mrs. McAdoo and I attended the wedding of the President and Mrs. Norman Galt, of Washington. The President had met Mrs. Galt through his daughter Margaret and his cousin, Miss Helen Bones. They had become acquainted with her at some social affair in Washington. Mrs. Galt, a handsome, attractive woman, was a widow without children. In the summer of 1915 she visited Miss Wilson and Miss Bones at 'Harlakenden,' in New Hampshire, where the President was spending a few weeks. Their engagement was announced on October 6 of that year.

The wedding ceremony was performed by the Reverend Herbert Scott Smith, who had been a student under Mr. Wilson at Wesleyan College, and who was, at the time of the President's marriage, the rector of Saint Margaret's Episcopal Church in Washington. The Reverend James H. Taylor, pastor of the Central Presbyterian Church of Washington, which the President usually attended, assisted in the ceremony. Only a few guests were present — about forty, I believe — consisting chiefly of the families and immediate relatives of the bride and groom.

The President and his wife spent their honeymoon at the Homestead Hotel, Hot Springs, Virginia.

The new Mrs. Wilson received a warm welcome from Mr. Wilson's entire family.

CHAPTER XXIII

MAKING FRIENDS WITH SOUTH AMERICA

I

BEFORE the war the greater part of the trade of South and Central America went to Europe, notably to England and Germany. The seagoing commercial nations of Europe had built up their large South American trade by a conscious, long-continued, and uniform effort.

It was a fabric of continuity, held together not only by habit and association, but also by an efficient mechanism of banking service and ocean transportation. The British, the Germans, and the French had established steamship lines that touched every important South American port; their great banks had permanent branches in the leading cities; their commercial travelers spoke the language of the country; they took orders for goods and filled them promptly, and the goods were exactly as represented.

With the coming of the World War, this entire structure of commerce went to pieces. The South Americans were like the customers of a store that has burned down; they were looking around for a place to spend their money. The prospect of attracting a considerable part of their trade to the United States seemed promising.

But we were sadly lacking in the facilities that must accompany and be a part of all good merchandising. There was the question of payment for purchases, to mention one vexatious problem. The customs in respect to terms of credit and the financing of obligations differed in the various Latin-American countries; and, generally speaking, they were at variance in every country from the commercial habits prevailing in the United States. In many parts of South America it was impossible to buy dollar exchange. A merchant, in paying his bills to a manufacturer in the United States, usually made a remittance in the form of a draft on London; that is, in pounds sterling. At that time the English pound was an uncertain factor; consequently, payment in sterling added an additional element of uncertainty and mystery to what ought to have been an ordinary commercial transaction.

The cornerstone of the European hold on South American trade was finance. The great banking houses of England and the Continent had been ready and willing, for many years before the war, to invest money in public service enterprises, in private business undertakings, and in the bonds of the various governments throughout Latin America. On the other hand, our people knew hardly anything about South American securities. There was no market for them here. This was a heavy obstacle in the path of any program for the development of mutually profitable relations.

Another drawback was a lack of transportation facilities. The shipping bill was then in Congress (I am referring now to the winter of 1914–15) and we hoped and expected it to become a law. If it had passed at that session, we should have been in a position to establish steamship lines — controlled by the United States government — between our ports and those of South and Central America. The bill was defeated, however, at the session which expired March, 1915 — as I have stated in a previous chapter — by a Republican filibuster in the Senate.

Despite these disadvantages, I thought, nevertheless, that something effective might be done. There was good-will on both sides. The South Americans had commodities to sell, and so had we. Why not get together and create a mechanism of commerce which would function smoothly and be profitable to all?

It occurred to me that it would be a wise move to hold a Pan-American Financial Conference in Washington in the spring of 1915, to which the ministers of finance and representative business men of the Latin-American countries would be invited. At this conference they would meet our American delegates — leading business men and bankers — and discuss the various problems of reciprocal trade relations.

I submitted the idea to the President and he approved it heartily. In the closing days of the session of 1915, Congress gave the President authority to hold a Pan-American Financial Conference and appropriated fifty thousand dollars for the entertainment of the visiting delegates.

The conference was called for May 24, 1915, at Washington. An immediate and cordial acceptance of our invitation came from every country in South and Central America.

When the conference convened in the beautiful Pan-American Building in Washington, eighteen countries besides the United States were represented. Forty-three delegates came from Latin America. At the conference they met one hundred and fifty American delegates, representing the banking and commercial interests of the United States. The President delivered an address of welcome; and as Secretary of the Treasury I presided over the meetings.

The conference lasted five days, and was concluded by a banquet at the Shoreham Hotel on May 29. After that, the foreign delegates, as guests of the nation, were conducted by special train on a tour of the principal cities east of the Mississippi and north of the Ohio.

One important result of the conference was the creation of a permanent International High Commission, composed of five to seven leading citizens of each country, including the minister of finance — or, in our case, the Secretary of the Treasury. The purpose of this quasi-governmental body was to facilitate commercial treaties, uniformity of laws applying to trade, international exchange, and other measures which would tend to make trade relations smoother and more profitable to all the nations of the Western hemisphere. Congress made an annual appropriation of twenty-five thousand dollars to carry on the work of the American section. Headquarters of the Commission were established in Washington, and I became its chairman.

I regarded this organization as one of the most advanced steps that had ever been taken to secure effective coöperation between governments which desired to better their economic relations.

2

A second Pan-American Financial Conference — or, to be exact, the joint International High Commission — assembled at Buenos Aires in April, 1916. I attended as chairman of the United States section of the Commission, accompanied by its other members: Senator Duncan U. Fletcher, of Florida; Andrew J. Peters, Assistant Secretary of the Treasury; Paul M. Warburg, of the Federal Reserve Board; Samuel Untermyer, of New York; Archibald Kains, governor of the Federal Reserve Bank of San Francisco; and John H. Fahey, of Massachusetts, former president of the United States Chamber of Commerce.

The Navy Department placed the old cruiser Tennessee, with Captain Edward L. Beach in command, at the disposal of the Commission. We sailed from Hampton Roads March 8, 1916. Mrs. McAdoo went with me, and there were two other ladies in the party: Mrs. Untermyer and Mrs. Peters. There were, besides, clerks, stenographers, and interpreters. An office, complete in all details, was set up. One corner of the Tennessee looked like a branch of the Treasury Department.

On our way down an unfortunate incident occurred at the island of Trinidad. It was really a small matter, of trifling import. I am mentioning it simply to illustrate how the hatreds sown by the war, and their corresponding blind enthusiasms, had completely penetrated and distorted the minds of men.

We had to stop at Trinidad for twenty-four hours to take on coal. As the coaling of a warship, especially in the tropics, is one of the most disagreeable proceedings imaginable, the members of the Commission and their wives took quarters at the principal hotel. Our visit to the island had been extensively mentioned in the local press, and was anticipated by everybody living there, from the Governor down.

Just before our arrival ex-President Theodore Roosevelt had spent a few days on the island. He was the hero of the hour. Trinidad is, as you know, a British possession; and, in sentiment, it was more anti-German than the English themselves. Roosevelt, in his loud detestation of the 'barbarous Hun,' went straight to the hearts of the Trinidadians (or whatever they are called).

On the evening of March 11, a banquet in Roosevelt's honor was given by the Trinidad Chamber of Commerce. It was attended by the Governor and all the local dignitaries. The World War was the underlying topic of the occasion. Some of the speeches were full of satirical and harsh references to the so-called supineness of the United States. Roosevelt himself encouraged this attitude by his own speech, in which he referred to the neutrality of President Wilson (not by name, but by implication) as 'the neutrality of that arch-judge typical of all times — Pontius Pilate.'

This exhibition of bad taste would have been deplorable even if its perpetrator had been only an ordinary American in a foreign land. But Roosevelt was not an ordinary citizen; he had been President himself, and his place was one of unique distinction. That he should criticize the conduct of his own country before a provincial audience in a faraway little British island shows how far he had gone in the loss of balance and discretion.

To the inhabitants of Trinidad Roosevelt's word was gospel. They absorbed the idea that President Wilson and his Administration were nothing more than a band of irresponsible interlopers, lost to honor and dignity; that in any decent country they would have been taken by the scruff of the neck and kicked out of office. That America did not rush forthwith, and pell-mell, into the war against Germany at the beckoning finger of England was, in the public opinion of Trinidad, an unforgivable sin.

Our slim and graceful Tennessee slid smoothly into the harbor the day before Roosevelt's departure. The fort fired its nineteen unwilling guns in honor of Mr. Wilson's Secretary of the Treasury, and the cruiser replied. We landed. Trinidad is warm, exotic, and colorful, but our reception was Arctic. We made our way to the hotel, and I called promptly on the Governor, according to official etiquette. He was frigid but courteous. I sensed the ice in the atmosphere and left as soon as I could.

Under the universally accepted rules of international courtesy the Governor should have returned my visit in person. I waited at the hotel for a reasonable time and, as he did not appear, I and the members of the Commission hired some motor cars and drove around to see the places of interest on the island. I left my naval aide, Lieutenant E. C. S. Parker, at the hotel to receive the Governor if he should come. Late in the forenoon of the next day the Governor sent his aide to the hotel to return my call. Lieutenant Parker frankly informed the aide that he considered this a breach of etiquette;

that the governor himself should have come. Thereupon the Governor's aide told Lieutenant Parker that the Governor personally did not return any calls except those of admirals. Since the Secretary of the Treasury outranks every admiral the Governor's attitude was inexplicable.

We departed without official attention or official good-byes. I intended to let the matter drop, but Captain Beach and the officers of the Tennessee urged me not to ignore it. They declared that the Governor's action was not only a discourtesy to me, but to the American flag and the American nation. That was true, of course; yet it was a minor incident, so why give time and attention to it? Captain Beach and his officers were so unhappy over my decision that I reconsidered it and decided finally to make a report of the incident to the State Department.

Sir Edward Grey, British Secretary of State for Foreign Affairs, promptly apologized for the occurrence, and let us understand that the Governor was a colonial, acting *ad interim* until a new governor could be sent out from England. The new governor, on his way to take his post, came by Washington, and the British Ambassador, Sir Cecil Spring-Rice, brought him to the Treasury Department to call on me. I regretted that I had been obliged to make any complaint, but it was a matter of the flag. Personally I cared very little about it. The commotion that it caused was, I thought, wholly out of proportion to the importance of the incident.

3

Buenos Aires made me think of Paris, which it resembles in many ways. There are streets where the buildings are all of the same height, like those on the Rue de Rivoli or the Avenue Victor Hugo. Their roofs cut the sky in long straight lines. There are trees in the avenues, even in the sections devoted to business, as there are on the Parisian boulevards. The shops are bright and clear-windowed and clean. The place has an air of wealth, luxury, and vivacity.

I learned that most of the wealthy people of the Argentine live in Buenos Aires even if their financial interests are in some other part of the republic. Many of them have two houses — one on a ranch, or in some distant provincial town, and the other in Buenos Aires.

An interesting thing about the Argentineans, and Latin-Americans generally, is that, if they happen to be wealthy, they let it be known by their manner of living. If a man is worth a million dollars, he looks like a million dollars, and so does his wife, and his house. No; I am mistaken about that; I haven't done justice to the subject. I should have said that if a man is worth a million dollars, he looks like five millions, and so does his wife, and his house. They are spenders of the pure original breed. In the evening when they attend the theater — I mean the wealthy people — they go, as a rule, in magnificent automobiles that are lighted inside. Through the windows the beautifully dressed women in the cars may be seen, as if on display.

The Argentineans were extremely friendly and hospitable. They received the Commission with a roaring welcome. We were invited to so many dinners, luncheons, and receptions that, if we had accepted even a third of them, it would not have been possible to do any work. The anterooms of our apartment were crowded all day with people who had called for one thing or another, usually just to pay their respects and wish us well.

I took with me on this trip my trusted colored messenger, Richard Green, who had been in the Treasury Department for about thirty years. Richard was unusually tall — six feet three inches in height — and he was fine-looking and rather impressive in bearing. He used to sit outside my door at Buenos Aires to receive callers. It was a difficult job for him, as he felt strange and ill at ease among people whose language he did not understand. He had never been outside of the United States before.

One morning I opened the door to the hall and found him standing in a corner surrounded by a number of silk-hatted gentlemen who were talking to him volubly in Spanish and French. Richard looked as if he were surrounded by a mob about to do him harm. It turned out that the distinguished gentlemen, seeing that Richard was a negro, had mistaken him for a member of the Haitian delegation. They were paying their respects to him, as well as inviting him to some formal function. I rescued him, much to his joy.

Richard Green was one of the finest and most loyal people I have ever known. He had the soul of a gentleman — the conscientious devotion to duty, the quiet manners, the truthfulness, the honesty, the lack of assumption — all the qualities that make a man a gentleman, no matter whether he happens to be a white man or a black man. He was deeply religious and seemed to know entire chapters of the Bible by heart.

One day, while I was talking with the President, he said that he needed another colored messenger at the White House. I recommended Richard Green. I did not want to part with him, but the job at the White House would be a promotion, with a bigger salary, and I wanted to advance him. The President said, 'All right; send him over.'

I went back to the Treasury and told Richard I had some good news for him. His face brightened as he said: 'What's that, Mr. Secretary?'

I explained that the President wanted him at the White House and that, while I hated to lose him, I thought it was a promotion and I didn't want to stand in the way of his advancement. As I proceeded, the bright smile faded and his face looked as if it had been dipped in misery and allowed to set. Tears trickled down his cheeks. It was evident that he was laboring under a great emotion.

'Why, Richard,' I said, 'I thought you would be overjoyed with this news, but you act as though I had sentenced you to death. Don't you want to go?'

With quivering lips he said, 'Mr. Secretary' — hesitated a few seconds, and continued with this expressive quotation from the Bible: 'I would rather be a doorkeeper in the house of the Lord than dwell in the tents of wickedness.'

When I told the President what Richard had said, he was delighted with the humor of it and used to tell the story on himself on many occasions.

Of course, I allowed Richard to continue to be a 'doorkeeper in the house of the Lord.'

4

The Buenos Aires meeting of the International High Commission was a pronounced success. I felt, when the conference adjourned after ten days, that more had been accomplished in that time in developing a better understanding and a more practical plan of coöperation between the United States and South America than ever before.

One of the fundamentally important things agreed upon was the permanent organization of the International High Commission. Washington was selected as the headquarters for the next two years, and a Central Executive Committee was created, whose duty it was to coördinate and carry on the work of the Commission. As there were twenty sections of the High Commission, one being located in each American state, it was necessary to have a central authority to keep in touch with the various sections and direct the general work. By establishing the headquarters at Washington, a signal honor was conferred on the United States. By this action the Secretary of the Treasury of the United States became President. John Bassett Moore was elected Vice-President; and Leo S. Rowe was elected Secretary-General of the Central Executive Committee.

The Commission adopted a resolution recommending that a Pan-American Financial Conference be held every two years, so as to bring together the ministers of finance of all countries, and agreed upon the city of Washington as the place for the Financial Conference of 1917.

A comprehensive and entirely sensible plan for future progress was laid. The program covered several subjects of primary importance, such as the organization of steamship lines, the extension of banking facilities and the adoption of dollar exchange as the basis of settlement between the United States and South America, the completion of the Trans-Continental Railway from New York to Buenos Aires, enlarged radio development and increased cable facilities with reductions in cable rates. All of these were practical projects. In the end nothing, or next to nothing, came of them. The United States entered the war the next year, and for two years thereafter the whole of our national energy was given to the war and its problems. Before the necessary post-war adjustments of American industry and finance had been made, a Republican Administration under Harding came in. The interest of the new Administration in the work we had begun was so slight that the entire project was dropped. It was a pity that such a magnificent opportunity was lost.

We left Buenos Aires on a special train provided by the Argentine government and sped westward across the level pampas toward the Andes and the Chilean frontier. The pampas are prairie lands, stretching treeless and vast toward the horizon. We passed enormous herds of cattle and hundreds of prosperous-looking ranches, surrounded by wheat-fields and orchards. The climate is like that of our Middle West.

At Santiago, the capital of Chile, we were the guests of the nation for the few days of our stay. We met many of the leading men; they were unanimously in favor of closer relations with the United States, but they felt that nothing effective could be done until a large and dependable American merchant marine had been brought into existence. This, they said, was a question of the first importance.

On leaving Chile the cruiser steamed northward to Peru. The hospitable Peruvian people had planned a grand entertainment in honor of the Commission; but — alas! — that entertainment and the Commission's visit and the brass bands and the waving flags were all destined to become entangled in what may be described in its most pleasant aspect as an embarrassing dilemma. I do not know what one would call it in its gloomiest aspect; perhaps 'fiasco' is the correct word.

While we were on our way up the coast, we received a radio message from General George W. Goethals, the governor of the Panama Canal Zone, advising us that a seven days' quarantine at the Canal was in effect against ships that had touched at Callao, the seaport of Lima, the Peruvian capital. Immediately I sent a radio to Benton McMillin, the American Minister to Peru, informing him that it might not be feasible for our party to land, in view of the quarantine. He replied that 'health conditions at Lima and Callao are good. Safe to waive quarantine regulations. Peruvian authorities anxious for you to come. I join in this. The government has made arrangements to entertain your party....'

We went on in doubt, hoping for the best. Early in the morning of April 26, we arrived in the roadstead at Callao. The town is a squalid-looking place, built on low ground, close to the shore. At that time various tropical diseases were endemic there. Lima is not far from Callao — about fifteen miles, as I remember the distance — and it is situated superbly on a plateau at the base of the mountains.

In about an hour after we had dropped anchor, Captain Beach informed me that the local representative of the United States Public Health Service, who happened in this case to be a native Peruvian, had boarded the ship and reported the existence of bubonic plague at both Callao and Lima. The Captain said that under naval regulations he could not permit any officers or men to go ashore. The members of the Commission might land if they desired to do so, as he had no control over them, but he thought that such an act on their part would probably cause the ship to be quarantined at Panama.

I asked the Captain to call the medical officers of the ship into conference. Their advice was that no members of the Commission ought to go ashore; if they did there was grave danger of the bubonic plague being brought aboard the ship.

I knew that the Peruvians would not only be offended but greatly disappointed if the Commission failed to go ashore and carry out the two days' program of festivities that had already been arranged. I got the Commission together and explained the situation. My private opinion was that the danger was negligible, and I had already made up my mind to go ashore regardless of anybody else's decision. I said nothing about this, however, as I did not want to influence the others. I thought every man should decide the question for himself.

The members of the Commission, after earnest discussion, concluded to stay on board, although I do not believe any of them thought there would be any personal risk in going ashore. Their decision was in deference to the judgment of the ship's physicians. Thereupon, I said I felt that it was but my duty to go ashore, call on the President, and do what I could to mitigate the disappointment of our good friends the Peruvian officials. Mrs. McAdoo wanted to go with me, but I thought it unwise for her to do so.

While we were discussing the matter under an awning on deck, a launch, bearing the Peruvian Minister of Foreign Affairs and the rest of the Cabinet, was approaching, and in a short time a number of gentlemen with smiling faces came aboard. Our Minister, Mr. Benton McMillin, accompanied the Peruvian delegation.

As I shook hands with the delegates and thought of what I would have to tell them in a moment, I felt that I was facing one of the most awkward and distressing situations of my life. I decided, however, to let them know exactly how things stood, without any evasion. After formal greetings had been exchanged, I told them, as politely and considerately as I could, of our difficulty about the bubonic plague; the regulations of the navy; and the threatened quarantine of the cruiser at Panama.

I shall never forget the countenances of these gentlemen as I proceeded with my statement. The smiles disappeared; a deep gloom succeeded. They were thinking, no doubt, of the decorated streets of Lima, and the magnificent luncheon, and of the waiting President and assembled dignitaries. I did not blame them for looking disheartened. I was sure that they felt a decided, though unspoken, resentment against the Commission.

I tried to relieve the situation by saying that I hoped they would permit me to accompany them ashore and call on President Pardo and carry out, as far as I might within the day, such program as had been arranged. Meanwhile, there had been considerable delay while the parleying was going on and the luncheon which was being given in honor of the Commission in Lima had proceeded without the 'distinguished' guests. When I arrived, it was all over.

The President was cool and reserved when I called with our Minister, Mr. McMillin, at the palace. However, after a little conversation he relaxed and was cordial in manner. I am sure that he understood how things were and that I was doing all that I could in the circumstances.

After my visit to the President, the Minister of Finance kindly offered to be my escort for the day. He was a good-humored gentleman, full of Spanish courtesy and an ardent desire to show me every historic spot. We visited the imposing cathedral, and I saw there the mummified remains of the conqueror Pizarro, which are in a glass coffin. He was assassinated near the place, I believe, where his mummy is on exhibition. There was something strange about his appearance; he did not seem to have any neck; his head rested squarely on his shoulders. I mentioned this to my escort and he explained cheerfully that the glass coffin was too short for Pizarro's body, so they had cut off the neck and jammed his head down on his shoulders.

When I returned to the Tennessee that evening, the medical officers of the ship put me immediately into the disinfecting room, where they steamed me and did almost everything else short of boiling me alive. My clothing, in the meantime, was being fumigated. Early the next morning we sailed for Panama.

5

President Wilson's renomination in 1916 was a foregone conclusion. He was unanimously chosen by the Democratic National Convention at St. Louis in June, 1916, and Thomas R. Marshall was renominated for Vice-President.

Owing to the World War and the confusing issues that it had developed in American politics, it was extremely difficult for us to know where we stood in the matter of political strength. Party lines were shifting, and there were strong undercurrents of popular opinion which flowed aimlessly here and there.

Mr. Hughes, the Republican nominee, was, and is, a man of ability and high character, but the Republican campaign as a whole was without any real foundation. It had no constructive policy; all the constructiveness was on our side. The Republicans carried on a campaign of criticism. Professional critics are seldom elevated to positions where creative talent is the chief quality required. Moreover, the Republican volleys of criticism were directed against inessentials, or merely fired in the air, without aim or target.

Under the rules of the Democratic Party the presidential candidate has the right to select the chairman of the National Committee. It was impossible to continue McCombs in this position, so the President selected Vance McCormick, of Pennsylvania, for the post. McCormick, a progressive Democrat in the best sense of the term, was the editor and owner of the Harrisburg 'Patriot,' a daily Democratic newspaper, and had long been a leading Democrat in that hopelessly Republican state. He did a fine job in managing the campaign.

The National Committee sent me on a speech-making tour in the states of Ohio, Indiana, Illinois, and Kansas; as well as in other states. This contact with thousands of voters at that time proved to me that each side was weaker than it thought it was. I mean that the undecided and independent vote was remarkably large; a great many people evidently did not make up their minds until just before the election.

Roosevelt, in a strenuous effort to defeat Wilson, whom he hated with fierce intensity, abandoned or dissolved his own Bull Moose Party, and attempted to lead its fragments into the Republican ranks. He did not succeed entirely in doing this; a large proportion of his former adherents voted for Wilson.

As expected, we lost New York; we also lost the President's own state, New Jersey, as well as Indiana. The latter we had confidently expected to carry. But we won, much to my surprise and to the surprise of everybody on the National Committee, California, Kansas, Idaho, and Ohio, which are nearly always safely Republican in presidential elections. We also carried Nebraska, New Hampshire, New Mexico, North Dakota, Utah, Washington, and Wyoming — also usually Republican.

California furnished the outstanding sensation of the day. Normally a Republican state, it usually goes against the Democrats by a vote of about two to one, yet the Wilson electors carried it by a plurality of three thousand. The contest was so close that for several days the result was in doubt and the entire nation was in suspense.

This remarkable California victory was due, chiefly, to John B. Elliott, Collector of Customs at Los Angeles, who had charge of the campaign for Southern California, where the bulk of the Progressive vote for Wilson was cast; and to Gavin McNab, of San Francisco, who directed the campaign in the northern part of the state. James D. Phelan, the brilliant Democratic senator from California, campaigned the state and was a potent factor in the result. Francis J. Heney, at that time a progressive Republican leader in California, came out openly for Wilson and was on the Democratic electoral ticket. If California had not voted for Wilson in 1916 the whole course of history would have been altered.

It was a thrilling and tremendous victory; and it was also notable because it demonstrated that the Democratic Party could carry the country without New York and Indiana.

Democratic strategy has always puzzled me in its proverbial insistence upon nominating some man, regardless of other considerations, who is supposed to be able to carry New York in a presidential election. The Democrats rarely ever win New York in a presidential campaign; it is fatuous to chase this rainbow. New York is anchored in the Republican column in national elections for economic and financial reasons which the Democrats are unable to overcome unless there is a political revolution.

Hughes and Roosevelt based their campaign largely upon a criticism of Wilson's policies toward foreign governments. Inferentially their criticism meant that Wilson should have taken the United States into the war when the Lusitania was sunk. It was Ollie James, I think, who in one of his amazingly effective speeches on the stump devised the slogan, 'He kept us out of war.'

It was clear that the majority sentiment of the country was strongly in favor of maintaining neutrality and of avoiding, if possible, any hostile part in the great European conflict. President Wilson was tremendously earnest in his efforts to keep the United States at peace and it is an unhappy paradox that he was forced to deliver a message to the Congress within a little more than a month after his second inauguration in favor of a declaration of war against Germany.

CHAPTER XXIV
AMERICA ENTERS THE WORLD WAR

I

FOLLOWING the sinking of the Lusitania, and the ensuing controversy, the German government on September 1, 1915, assured the United States that, 'Liners will not be sunk by submarines without warning and without safety of the lives of non-combatants, provided that the liners do not try to escape or offer resistance.' That seemed to establish a definite principle, yet within six weeks thereafter the Arabic was sunk without warning and three American passengers lost their lives. The German government disavowed the act, and declared that the commander of the submarine had disobeyed orders.

Shortly afterward, the Ancona was torpedoed and seven Americans went down with her; and on November 29, 1915, the American vessel William P. Frye was sunk in violation of international law. On December 30, the British liner Persia was sunk in the Mediterranean without warning and more than three hundred of the passengers and crew lost their lives. Among them was an American consul traveling to his post. He sailed on this British ship because there was no American vessel on which he could travel.

More protests, and more lame explanations. In consequence of our demands the German government informed us on January 7, 1916, that German submarines would not sink enemy merchant vessels except in accordance with the usages of international law and 'only after passengers and crews had been accorded safety.'

Five weeks later, on February 16, 1916, the German government said to the government of the United States, through the customary diplomatic channels:

> Germany has limited her submarine warfare because of her long-standing friendship with the United States, and because by the sinking of the Lusitania which caused the death of citizens of the United States, the German retaliation affected neutrals, which was not the intention, as retaliation should be confined to enemy subjects.

This olive branch, though greatly admired and cherished, began to wilt as soon as it was received. The sinking of harmless passenger ships went right on, and we gradually came to the conclusion that the German government did not consider words and deeds as having any definite relation to each other.

On April 18, 1916, we notified the German government that, unless 'relentless and indiscriminate warfare against vessels of commerce by the use of submarines' was brought to an end, 'the government of the United States can have no choice but to sever diplomatic relations with the German Empire altogether.'

Eventually excuses and apologies were worn to shreds. The Kaiser's government, I fancy, became as tired of thinking up new ones as we were of receiving them. At any rate, on January 31, 1917, Germany came out flat-footed with the belligerent warning, effective the next day, that she would engage in unrestricted submarine warfare and that all ships, neutral or belligerent, that might be found within a zone around Great Britain, France, Italy, and in the eastern Mediterranean, would be destroyed by her submarines.

This was practically ordering the United States off the Atlantic. Our entire commerce with Europe was concentrated either within the proscribed zone or our ships destined for neutral countries had to pass through that zone. As the high seas belong to all nations in common, neither Germany nor Great Britain nor France nor any other power could limit the rights of the United States in their use and enjoyment.

In the meantime, while we had been keeping our temper and trying to avoid war, German conspiracies against the United States were being brought to light. In a preceding chapter I have said something of the doings of German secret agents in America, of their efforts to encourage strikes, to destroy munition plants, to buy press bureaus and newspapers. On January 22, 1917, the German Ambassador sent to the Berlin Foreign Office a wireless message in code which was intercepted and decoded. In it he said: 'I request authority to pay up to fifty thousand dollars in order, as on former occasions, to influence Congress through the organization you know of, which can perhaps prevent war.' As Bernstorff said in his dispatch, this was not the first time that an effort had been made to influence

Congress through secret means and the use of money. We had already learned of some of the previous attempts.

Close on the heels of these revelations came another intercepted and decoded cablegram which Zimmermann, the German Minister of Foreign Affairs, had sent to Mexico. The Mexican government was urged to make war on the United States, with the support and material assistance of Germany. In return for her coöperation, Mexico, in the event of the defeat of the United States, was to have Texas, Arizona and New Mexico returned to her. At that time the Mexicans did not love us too well, but they were possessed of common-sense. The German note eventually reached the Mexican wastebasket.

The Administration went into the war unwillingly. I make a point of this, as some of those who have written about President Wilson have not hesitated to assert that he was committed to the cause of the Allies from the beginning, and only waited for an opportune moment to take decisive action that would put the country in a situation from which it could not be extricated without war. Others have said in print that he had been completely bamboozled by British propaganda; that he had been won over to the side of the Allies by diplomacy and other subtle acts.

On the other hand, the impetuous Roosevelt and his hotheaded friends blamed President Wilson for not taking the country into the war against Germany in 1915. They said that he lacked the fighting spirit; that his attitude of neutrality was cold-blooded and supine; that he was vacillating and indecisive. Some of these critics on the pro-Ally side even went so far as to express a belief that not only the President, but the entire Administration, was distinctly pro-German.

The fact is that the President was neither pro-Ally nor pro-German; he was pro-American. The attitude of the Administration was taken without reference to the claims of the various combatants, or to the primary causes of the conflict. If the rôles of the Allies and the Germans had been reversed; if the British and French had employed their submarines to sink ships without warning and cause the loss of American lives, the Administration would have held them to stern account just as it did Germany.

The United States, led by President Wilson, went into the conflict because it was not possible to avoid war with honor. We were forced into it by the doltish stupidity and short-sightedness of the German rulers. Ludendorff declares with brazen frankness in his 'Memoirs' that Germany got the United States into the war as a part of the policy of the German General Staff. Their theory, he says, was that we could do less harm as acknowledged enemies than we did as neutrals supplying munitions to the Allies. The German General Staff had no idea that we should be able to train a fighting force in time to be effective; and the German Admiralty stated solemnly and officially that not even one American fighting unit would be permitted to reach France. 'With the help of our submarines,' Ludendorff says, 'we reckoned on a decision in our favor, at the very latest, before America with her new armies could intervene in the war.'

To have stayed out after the insults that had been slapped into our faces for more than two years would have made the word American a synonym for coward in every quarter of the world. Furthermore, such a pusillanimous policy would have failed in accomplishing its purpose. After Europe had settled its gigantic row — with Germany, in all probability, on the top of the heap — the United States would have become the universal target of contempt. Our rights would have been trampled on everywhere and the Monroe Doctrine would have gone the way of Belgium's historic 'scrap of paper.'

My impression is that the Administration would have brought the dispute with Germany to a head long before April, 1917 (probably a year earlier), if it had not been for the high-handed actions of the Allies. The President was greatly annoyed by the attitude of the British in respect to the rights of neutrals. The British government established arbitrarily a black list of American concerns, for one thing. British ships were forbidden to transport the goods of firms that had the misfortune to be on the black list, and the shipments of these blacklisted concerns lay neglected and rotting on our wharves for months. If we had had the foresight to establish a merchant marine of our own in the first year of the war (1914) by purchasing ships, and building them, the black list would have been a matter of negligible concern. But in view of the fact that there were but few American ships, the black list was a formidable impediment and vexatious sore. In most instances no explanation was given as to why a name appeared on the list, and there was no way of finding out, or of having it removed.

Another source of irritation was the practice of the Allies in declaring one thing or another contraband, apparently (in many cases) without a valid reason, to the detriment of American commerce. There was, besides, a continual succession of minor annoyances, such as the stopping and searching of ships, the censorship of the mails and cables, the detention of American citizens on the suspicion or whim of some subordinate examining officer, and the taking of American vessels and cargoes into prize courts.

Instead of being dragged into the war by the Allies, I am convinced that the reverse is true; that the actions of the Allies kept us out of it long after the patience of the Administration had been worn to the breaking point by German lawlessness.

As for me, personally, I was accused of being an ardent friend of Germany by some, and of being a fanatical pro-Ally by others. The British Ambassador, Sir Cecil Spring-Rice, wrote to Sir Edward Grey that I was hand in glove with the friends of Germany, and that Paul M. Warburg, whom he describes as a pro-German, had been my partner in business — which was not true. I had never been in business with Warburg. This was a fact that any clerk of the embassy might have checked up over the telephone.

In a letter to Sir Valentine Chirol ('The Letters and Friendships of Sir Cecil Spring-Rice,' Vol. II, p. 242), he said that Warburg 'practically controls the financial policy of the government,' and hints that everything said to the Federal Reserve Board is 'German property' — meaning clearly that if any information was given to the Federal Reserve Board it was transmitted to the German government. He goes on to say that 'if there had been a drain of gold from here' — meaning from America to Europe — 'the Treasury would have stopped gold payments and there would have been a panic.' He reported to the British Foreign Office that 'some of the millionaires would like to have court appointments in a German world empire. The Jews show a strong preference for the Emperor, and there must be some bargain.' On May 20, 1915, Sir Cecil wrote a long letter to Sir Edward Grey in which he said 'there is reason to believe that one member of the Cabinet is very closely associated with certain German political and financial interests' — and a footnote to the letter, as published, indicates that I was meant.

Sir Cecil, as anyone may see from these few brief extracts, was a prize conveyor of misinformation. As I read over his two volumes of letters, I wonder what good an ambassador does, anyway? I venture to say that any newspaper reporter of moderate experience, stationed in Washington, would have been much more serviceable than the British Ambassador in transmitting home an accurate picture of the American scene.

The custom of handling large and complicated questions through the medium of men as poorly informed as Sir Cecil — and he was not the only one in his category — made all negotiations with the warring powers extremely difficult. To obviate incessant misunderstandings, the President sent Colonel House to Europe on several occasions as his spokesman.

Even when war with Germany became inevitable, the President did not take the final step until the whole country was behind him. He did not want to lead an unwilling people into the most terrible war in the history of mankind, and much of the hesitation with which he has been so harshly accused was the result of that attitude.

The President convened Congress in special session April 2, 1917, and on the evening of the same day he appeared personally before the two houses in joint session and delivered his message. I remember the rain was pouring that evening — a soft, fragrant rain of early spring. The illuminated dome of the Capitol stood in solemn splendor against the dark, wet sky. Near the end of the President's address he said: 'We have no selfish ends to serve. We desire no conquest, no dominion. We seek no indemnities for ourselves, no material compensation for the sacrifices we shall freely make. We are but one of the champions of the rights of mankind. We shall be satisfied when those rights have been made as secure as the faith and the freedom of nations can make them.' The cheering of his audience — the members of the Senate and the House, and a crowded gallery — was so enthusiastic and prolonged that the business of the session was suspended for some time.

On April 4, the Senate passed the declaration of war by a vote of 82 to 6. Two days later, on April 6, it was passed by the House by a vote of 373 to 50.

It is the fashion nowadays to refer to the war — to America's part in it — as an unpopular movement which never had any real enthusiasm behind it, and into which the nation was pushed by political and legislative trickery.

That is not so. I feel impelled to deny any such statement for the sake of historical truth. The American nation went into the war against Germany, and went through it to the end, with a patriotic fervor that exceeded anything of the kind in our history, and I am not excepting even the Civil War. It was popular with all classes, from the top to the bottom of the nation. The war, and the energetic prosecution of it, was the one subject on which Democrats and Republicans were in complete agreement.

2

I now had to face the prodigious problem of war financing. For months I had given thought to the matter, and had endeavored to form some reasonable estimate of the amount of money that would be required. With each fresh calculation the sum had grown larger, and the figures were appalling. There were so many uncertain factors in the problem that a definite conclusion was not possible, but I realized clearly that within a few months I should be called upon to produce several billion dollars.

An outlay on such a gigantic scale could not be financed by taxation in its entirety, though I hoped to raise about half of the expenditure through taxes. We should have to sell government bonds in large quantities. In previous years, when I had more time for reading, I had studied in careful detail the history of Civil War financing. At that time I never dreamed that

I would some day be at the head of the United States Treasury; my interest in the subject was that of a student of history. Now, this reading of long ago came back in my mind. Months before the United States entered the World War, I took up again the financial history of the Lincoln Administration with the hope that it might evoke some suggestion, or starting-point, that I could use as a basis for my own procedure.

I did not get much in the way of inspiration or suggestion from a study of the Civil War, except a pretty clear idea of what not to do. The financial part of it was a hodge-podge of unrelated expedients. My predecessor, Salmon P. Chase — Lincoln's Secretary of the Treasury — tried one thing and another, and some of his measures for raising money could have originated only from a sense of desperation. He was obviously afraid of raising taxes in the early part of the war, and his bond issues — small in amount and high in interest rates — were offered quietly, almost confidentially, to banks and other financial houses under the impression, I think, that the public did not understand bonds and would not buy them. Before the war was twelve months old government bonds had become so heavy that their sale had practically ceased, except when they were offered at a large discount. Then, as the government was in dire need of money, Congress in 1862 authorized the issue of one hundred and fifty millions of 'greenbacks,' or fiat money, and made it legal tender for all debts, public and private. Eventually the amount of this paper grew to a total of four hundred and fifty million dollars.

One of the first results of the Legal Tender Act was to put a premium on gold. Consequently gold practically ceased to circulate and was traded in speculatively, like wheat or the stocks of corporations. In the middle of 1863, the 'greenback' paper dollar was worth only fifty-eight cents, and a year later it touched a low mark of thirty-five cents. This money was called 'greenbacks' because the back of the notes was printed in green.

Depreciated currency was a disastrously disturbing factor in all the fiscal operations of Chase's administration, especially in respect to the flotation of bond issues. The bonds were sold for greenbacks, yet the principal and interest of most of the issues were payable in gold. A man who possessed a thousand dollars in depreciated paper — worth, let us say, five hundred dollars — was able to buy a thousand-dollar gold bond with it, on which the six per cent interest was payable in gold, as well as the principal. People who had money made large fortunes by the manipulation of these shifting and uncertain values.

After a while Chase gave up the business of selling the war bonds as a bad job, and turned it over to Jay Cooke & Company, of Philadelphia, who became the selling agents of the government on a commission which averaged, I believe, about three-eighths of one per cent. Jay Cooke appointed sub-agents in every town and county. He organized a selling campaign which was somewhat like the modern 'drive' method that I instituted during the World War to sell Liberty bonds, though our drives in 1917 and 1918 were more diversified, more intensive, and reached the whole population more thoroughly.

Chase was evidently afraid that the public would not support him if he went directly to the people for money, so he turned the selling problem in its entirety over to private bankers, paid them commissions, and, in short, followed a policy of selling government bonds on a commercial basis.

This was a fundamental error. Any great war must necessarily be a popular movement. It is a kind of crusade; and, like all crusades, it sweeps along on a powerful stream of romanticism. Chase did not attempt to capitalize the emotion of the people, yet it was there and he might have put it to work. You may be sure that men and women who send their sons to a battle-field will not hesitate about sending their dollars after them if the need for money is properly presented.

My purpose in giving this description of Civil War financing is not to criticize Secretary Chase, or to depreciate his ability. I think he did as well as anyone could have done in the circumstances, and that most of his errors were inevitable and in the nature of things. When he came into office he found an empty Treasury, and a wholly inadequate scheme of taxation; and, moreover, the currency was in a state of indescribable confusion. The country was not prepared for large-scale financing of any kind; and this was, I am sure, the underlying reason for many of Chase's extraordinary expedients.

3

The next day after the declaration of war, I conferred with the leading members of the Ways and Means Committee of the House and of the Finance Committee of the Senate on the subject of war finance. I submitted the draft of a bill to authorize an issue of five billion dollars of bonds and two billion dollars of debt certificates — or seven billions in all.

The bill provided for loans to foreign governments to the extent of three billion dollars and it conferred upon the Secretary of the Treasury discretion to make such loans, subject to the approval of the President and to the terms and conditions of the Act. It allowed a sum not exceeding one tenth of one per cent of the amount of bonds and certificates of indebtedness for the payment of all necessary expenses and specifically prohibited the payment of any commissions on the sale of the bonds or certificates of indebtedness and the sale of any obligation at less than par; and the bonds were to be offered as a popular loan.

The bill was introduced in the House on April 11, 1917, by Representative Claude Kitchin, of North Carolina, who was at that time chairman of the Ways and Means Committee. In his remarks Kitchin said:

This bill contains the largest authorization of bond issues ever contained in any bill presented to any legislative body in the history of the world. I am happy to report that this bill has the unanimous approval and endorsement, and has the unanimous vote of the entire membership — Republican, Democratic and Progressive — of the Ways and Means Committee.

The request for such an enormous amount of money startled Congress and the country. I explained to the members of the two committees that I did not expect to offer the entire seven billions of bonds to the public immediately. The first issue would be much less than that amount — I could not say how much at that time — but I thought it would be wise to authorize the whole amount at once. I knew that it was not going to be a cheap war, and that our position in respect to financing would be more flexible if we prepared the public mind as soon as possible for a huge expenditure.

One of the outstanding features of the financial picture was the absolute necessity of lending money to the foreign governments associated with us in the war. All of them were at their wits' end for money.

My suggestion that loans be made to England, France, Italy, Russia, and other antagonists of Germany was such a radical departure from our established policy that there was, naturally, hesitation and doubt on the part of many men as to the wisdom of that course. Before I presented this idea to the Congress, I had discussed it fully with the President, and he agreed with me that it was a necessary step to take.

I confess that it was with great reluctance I reached the conclusion that these foreign loans should be made. I remember remarking to the President, at the time we considered it, that while it was an essential military measure — in fact, the only thing that we could do to save the Allies from impending disaster — nevertheless, nations are like people, and I recalled the old adage: 'To make an enemy of a friend, lend him money.'

This time-honored saying has unhappily turned out to be true. I doubt that any debtor nation of Europe is today our friend. When I read the slurs that are uttered by their public men and printed in their journals on the topic of American cupidity and dollar-chasing, I recall — with a rather unhumorous smile, I fear — their profound and eternal (and almost obsequious) gratitude when I, as Secretary of the Treasury, handed to their representatives checks for one or two hundred million dollars apiece.

In my argument, made before the Ways and Means Committee in executive session, I said that the most effective aid we could extend to Great Britain, France, Italy, and Russia was money. As we were at war with Germany, it was manifestly to our interest to see that the troops of the Allies already on the battle-front in Europe should be made twice as effective, if possible, through ample food, clothing, and necessary munitions, in order that they could not only hold the lines, but gain victories before American troops could be trained and put into action. The dollars that we sent through these loans to Europe were, in effect, substitutes for American soldiers, and the extent to which we were able to save the lives of the young men of America would be measured by the extent to which we could make operative, quickly and effectively, the credits the Allies needed to purchase supplies in the American markets.

The bill was passed by both houses of Congress on April 24, 1917, and approved by the President the next day.

CHAPTER XXV

THE FIRST LIBERTY LOAN

I

I CONCEIVED the idea of building up among the American people — among the men and women who could not go into military service — a financial front which would rest on the same inspiration and morale as the military front of the army.

Men who were left out of the war, who had to stay at home to carry on the work of the nation, would feel uneasy over their situation. I knew they would; it's human nature. They would be depressed by the thought that they were not doing their share. I felt that if all this aimless resolution and energy could be turned into the service of the Treasury it would go far toward solving the problem of war financing. A man who could not serve in the trenches in France might nevertheless serve in the financial trenches at home. He could buy Liberty bonds, and he could induce others to buy them. He could help his country by becoming a walking advertisement of the Federal Treasury, and serve effectively in the campaign to educate people as to the causes and objects of the war. That is what I mean by creating a 'financial front' which would call into its service the same qualities of discipline, self-sacrifice, and devotion that characterized those who served in the trenches.

What I have just outlined briefly was the basic idea of all the Liberty loan campaigns. That it was successful beyond all expectations is an accepted historical fact. The vital thing about it is that the entire problem was lifted above the commercial plane. I never expected to compete, in the way of terms and interest rates, with private borrowers and business enterprises. Business was good; anybody who had money could get a higher rate of interest than that carried by a Liberty bond. It would have been fatal to have attempted this enormous financing through what is commonly known as 'the money market.' We went direct to the people; and that means to everybody — to business men, workmen, farmers, bankers, millionaires, school-teachers, laborers. We capitalized the profound impulse called patriotism. It is the quality of coherence that holds a nation together; it is one of the deepest and most powerful of human motives.

That no profits or commissions should be made by anybody from the sale of war bonds followed as an inevitable corollary. The soldier in the trenches is not there for profit; he is there to fight his country's battles. So why should a man who sells his country's bonds in time of war make a profit out of them? The financial front, as I conceived it, ought to be, in every vital sense, the economic equivalent of the military front.

The problem would have been hopeless if we had not had the willing coöperation of thousands of people. No one man, nor even a thousand men, could have made more than a nibble at it in the limited time at our disposal. We put over the First Liberty Loan with a rush because so many people were willing to help. The bond and investment houses came to our aid; they put their expert salesmen in the service of the Treasury. The insurance companies gave us their solicitors; every bank received subscriptions; newspapers gave the bonds free advertising. Besides these organized selling agencies, tens of thousands of men and women volunteered. They had no experience in selling anything, but they were eager to learn and to help.

It was the business of the Treasury to organize this outpouring of energy and willingness; to organize and instruct an army of volunteer salesmen.

2

Congress had authorized a total issue of $7,000,000,000 of Treasury obligations ($5,000,000,000 of war bonds and $2,000,000,000 of certificates of indebtedness, or short-term notes), but these figures expressed simply a top limit of the issues. As Secretary of the Treasury it was my duty to decide the size of each offering to the public, and, except as to the first loan, to determine the rate of interest.

Nothing like one billion dollars of government securities — or any other kind of securities — had ever been sold to the American people before at one time or in a single effort. Yet I knew that we should have to offer more than a billion dollars

at the very start, and that the following issues would be much
larger.

The technique of administration was simple. I could sit
down at my desk and sign an order to make the first loan five
hundred million dollars or ten times that amount, and the
machinery would begin to turn. The bonds would be engraved
and entered in the Treasury books of account and offered for
sale. But suppose they did not sell? Suppose I made the issue
too large for the public to absorb? Suppose hundreds of millions of the bonds were left on our hands? The moral effect of
such a failure would be equal to a crushing military disaster.
It would not only dishearten our own people, but also the
nations across the sea whose fortunes were joined to ours; and it
would give our enemies new confidence and courage.

That was one thing to consider, yet this kind of failure could
be avoided easily by making the first loan a comparatively
small one, say five hundred millions. I knew that if a loan
of that size was offered, even at a low rate of interest, it would
be swallowed by the public instantly. But such a timid expedient would have been unwise as well as cowardly. An offer
of five hundred millions would not be enough to finance the
pressing, immediate needs of the foreign governments associated with us, to say nothing of our own requirements. Before
the ink on the bonds had dried, I should have been forced
to put out another issue, and after that another one; a war
financed in driblets.

Moreover, a small first loan would not have reached the
general public, the average man and woman. It would have
been taken in its entirety by banks, insurance companies,
wealthy corporations, and individuals. That was clearly undesirable. The war had to be brought home to the people;
they must not be permitted to get the idea that the banks
would take care of the financial end of the war, and that every
man not called up for military service might go ahead with his
office work, or his automobile repairing, or his plowing, and
forget all about it. It was not a private war; it was every man's
war; and the sooner every man realized it the better it would
be in the long run.

Then there was the question of the rate of interest. I did
not intend to sell the bonds on a strictly commercial basis.

Purchasing government securities was to be the expression of a fundamental patriotism. Nevertheless, there had to be some rate of interest. If it were too low, the result might be that even patriotic Americans of limited means would feel unable to put money in the bonds; except, perhaps, in small amounts. On the other hand, a high rate would throw the burden of a huge unnecessary expense on the people.

This rate question caused me a lot of trouble. Able and well-informed men in the banking and business world, economists of high standing and many newspapers, urged rates as high as five and five and one half per cent on the ground that lower rates were unsound from the economic standpoint and that high rates were necessary to keep the bonds at par; that it would be impossible to sell bonds to the people when they were selling below par on the exchanges.

I was not convinced by the arguments. I stabilized the rate ultimately at four and one quarter per cent, and it is a high tribute to the patriotism of the people that they oversubscribed at par every issue I offered, notwithstanding the fact that bonds already issued were selling at less than par in the open market.

Think of the enormous additional burden that the people would have been forced to carry if I had issued bonds at an increase of even one half of one per cent in the rate of interest! The four Liberty Loans I sold aggregated $16,940,000,000 in round numbers. Take your pencil and a piece of paper and figure what that extra one half of one per cent in the interest rate would have amounted to each year on $16,940,000,000. You will find that it would have increased the interest charge $84,700,000 per annum, or $1,649,000,000 in twenty years if the bonds had run that long. This will give you a vivid idea of how interest piles up.

My decision to adhere to low rates on bond issues saved an immense sum to the people of the United States. I could not reconcile myself to the idea of loading them with a huge and unnecessary burden, although I knew that it would make my task easier in selling the bonds.

3

I had formed a tentative conclusion as to the amount of the first loan. It ought to be, I thought, three billion dollars. I can hardly tell you how I arrived at the sum of three billions; the explanation would be tedious and complex, and would involve a lot of figures relating to bank deposits and national income. Yet, after all, I am sure that the deciding influence in my mind was not a mass of statistics, but what is commonly called a 'hunch' — a feeling or impression rather than a logical demonstration.

I know a good deal about the American people; when they set out to do anything with conviction and enthusiasm, they are marvelous. Three billion dollars was a tremendous amount of money, but there were one hundred million people in the United States and three billions would mean an average of only thirty dollars apiece. Besides, their subscriptions could be paid on installments. I decided tentatively on a three and one half per cent interest rate for the first loan because, for one thing, this rate was a little lower than the rates usually paid by savings banks. They were afraid that large withdrawals of their deposits would be made if the rate was higher, just at a time when the great shrinkage of their investments would make it difficult for them to stand the strain.

To clarify my own mind on these debatable topics, and to get as much advice and information as the situation demanded, I called into consultation leading bankers, specialists in bond-selling, the partners of investment houses, the members of the Federal Reserve Board and the Federal Advisory Council, members of Congress, and representatives of various industries. I gave, besides, a hearing to anyone of responsibility who had anything to say on the subject.

To my surprise and disappointment, virtually all of those whom I consulted disagreed with me, both as to the amount of the loan and the rate of interest. They pointed out the fact that the American people as a whole knew nothing about bonds; that the total number of investors in that class of securities was only three hundred and fifty thousand or thereabouts. I replied that we had to educate the people. It was true that they knew little or nothing about government bonds, but we would tell them. Doubt was expressed as to whether that could be done in a short time. The general impression among my banker advisers was that our chief reliance — on the first loan, at any rate — would have to be financial institutions and the regular bond-buyers.

Every financier whom I consulted or who volunteered an opinion thought that an issue of three billions was more than the country would absorb. White, Weld & Company said, 'We believe that the United States could today float a loan of between one billion and two billion dollars of four per cent bonds, having a life of, say, twenty to twenty-five years.' Guy Emerson, then vice-president of the National Bank of Commerce, of New York, wrote, 'There is a general feeling that the first issue ought not to be in excess of one billion dollars.'

J. P. Morgan, from whom I had asked suggestions, wrote me a long memorandum on the subject under date of April 27, 1917. His paper is too lengthy for reproduction here, but I give some pertinent extracts:

From my enquiries it is clear that the general opinion here is that not more than one billion dollars of these bonds should be issued at one time.

Contrary to my own views, he thought that not more than about twenty per cent of the total expenditure for the war should be covered by taxation.

It is exceedingly important [Morgan wrote] that investors of all size should not be discouraged, as they easily may be, by a scale of taxation which is felt by them to bear unjustly upon the investing class of the country....

I would suggest also that the amount of money which can be, not appropriated but actually spent for the purposes of the United States in the war during that year, should be ascertained with some approach to accuracy. And that a proportion not exceeding twenty per cent of this amount should be considered as the sum to be obtained by taxation.

Among all the men of wide financial experience, Paul M. Warburg was the only one who thought that the issue could be above two billions. 'If you ask me, as an old-time banker,' wrote Mr. Warburg, 'fixing the plan to suit myself, I should say that two billion five hundred millions would be as much as I would like to handle at the first bite.... If it is two billions for the Allies and five hundred millions for ourselves as a starter, I think the banking community would go at it with a will and with confidence that they would make it a full success.'

4

By the side of these problems ran the related and collateral question of taxation. When I first went into the subject, I concluded that about half the cost of the war ought to come from taxes. On further consideration I decided taxation on such a scale would be excessive, and perhaps destructive to some extent of the capitalized energy which keeps the wheels turning. If you take the whole of a man's surplus income through taxes, you cannot expect him to buy bonds, nor can you expect industry to expand and prosper.

I realized that a policy of raising even one third of the expenditures of the government during the war would lay a heavy burden on the people; yet, at the same time, it was the better choice of two evils. The emission of great quantities of government bonds and short-time obligations would necessarily create a tremendous inflation, and this in turn would lead to large increases in the prices of commodities of all kinds. The only possible way to restrain inflation, to some extent at least, was by the imposition of heavy taxation and by preaching constantly to the people the necessity for saving their money and investing it in government bonds and of refraining from extravagance and waste in every form.

On May 14, 1917, I announced that the first loan would be two billion dollars, and the rate of interest three and one half per cent. Subscriptions would be received up to and including June 15, 1917. The bonds were to have a life of thirty years, with a proviso that the Treasury might, at its option, redeem any or all of them after fifteen years. They were exempt from all taxation except estate and inheritance taxes. It was further provided that purchasers of this issue would be permitted to convert their holdings into bonds of any subsequent issue which might bear a higher rate of interest.

I thought the loan should have a distinctive name, something that would carry more fire and meaning than 'government 3½ per cents.' I decided to call it a 'Liberty Loan,' and on April 28, 1917, I gave out this statement to the press:

The great bond issue which will soon be offered to the public will be known as Liberty Loan of 1917. The money to be raised by this loan is for the purpose of waging war against autocracy. It is to supply the sinews of battle in the interest of free government. It is peculiarly appropriate that as the negotiation of this loan will constitute the first great step of the United States in the prosecution of the war, it should be issued in the name of freedom.

The selling campaign was memorable — and, in many ways, astounding. Our unpaid helpers, men and women, went to work with a patriotic fervor that still thrills me with admiration when I think of it. They reached, I believe, every home in the United States and every adult person. There were volunteer committees in every city and sizable town in the country. Women's clubs turned themselves into selling agencies. Factories and workshops stopped their plants and assembled their workmen so they might listen to Liberty Loan speeches and subscribe for bonds. The newspapers and the billboard people contributed space. When you rode in a street car you faced an advertisement of the bonds, given gratis by Barron G. Collier, of New York, who controlled the street-car advertising agencies.

Anybody who had the cash to make a small down payment could buy a bond, and pay the rest in a series of installments extending over months. The people bought Liberty bonds with enthusiasm and on a scale that had no parallel in our national history. Within thirty days the subscriptions to the First Liberty Loan ran up to a larger amount than the total of all the bond sales of the federal government during the four years of the Civil War.

Yet, in the midst of all this patriotic fervor, there were jarring notes. There were some pro-Germans, of course, who looked with disfavor on the whole proceeding; and a few vociferous theorists who refused to have anything to do with the Liberty Loan on the ground that it was unnecessary; they said that the war should be financed by an unlimited issue of paper money.

Among those who threw cold water on the campaign was
Senator Warren Gamaliel Harding, of Ohio. This was the
Harding who, after the war, became President of the United
States, through a curious turn of Fate.

While the First Liberty Loan campaign was going on, I put
in four weeks on a speaking tour, going around the country,
making sometimes three or four speeches a day in behalf
of the loan. It was one of the hardest four weeks I ever spent.
I traveled every night in a sleeping-car, made speeches all
day, and my voice was worn to a frazzle toward the end.

I left New Orleans one night and arrived at Birmingham the
next morning. A number of reporters met me at the station
and asked what I thought of Harding's speech. This was
Saturday, June 9, 1917. I replied that I had not heard of it.
They showed me a morning paper which contained a colloquy
in the Senate between Harding on one side, and Senators J.
Hamilton Lewis and James A. Reed on the other. It appeared
that Harding had made a Memorial Day address at Columbus,
Ohio, in which he said that the campaign for the Liberty Loan
was 'hysterical and unseemly.' Lewis and Reed attacked
him because of this. Lewis said, among other things:

The Senator from Ohio knew that what he said would injure the
effort for the Liberty Loan. It must have been deliberate. He gave
vent to a sentiment that was calculated to put heart into those
whose sympathy might be against the prosecution of the war against
Germany.

Harding rose and said that he had no hesitancy in repeating
the remarks he had made in the Memorial Day speech.

I have believed the Liberty Loan campaign hysterical and unseemly [he said]. I have not wished to hinder it. I only wished that I
might make the conditions which would have made this seemingly
hysterical campaign unnecessary, and I am hesitant to say on the
floor of the Senate why it is so.

Mr. President, in normal times I am a partisan. In times like this
I am hesitant to express my partisan impressions. If I were of a mind
to do so, I could stand on this floor today with criticisms well founded
and substantiated by facts which would prove a sensation to the
hundred million of Americans who are on the anxious seat today.
And since the question has been raised and some specification seems
necessary, I say to you that America with ability to buy seventeen
billion dollars of bonds on any day, is reluctant to buy because of
lack of confidence in the present Administration.

He continued:

I have not meant to be ugly in my reference to hysteria. There is very eminent authority for the use of that word over a little unseemly excitement.

At this point Harding was interrupted by J. Hamilton Lewis. Continuing, a moment later, he said:

If I could have recourse to the record of a recent secret session of the Senate, I would be able to produce the remarks of certain gentlemen who divulged facts concerning our part in this war that would startle the American people. I would like to refer to their statements that there were things that ought to be investigated. But I cannot talk of it here, for it was in secret session that it happened.

Senator Reed interrupted here to challenge Harding's assertion that 'any charge of misconduct of the war' had been made in the executive session either by himself or any other senator. Thereupon, Harding insisted that observations had been made which indicated a disgust on the part of some senators over America's unpreparedness. Reed replied that nothing was stated in the executive session about unpreparedness that the American people had not already known.

I have no doubt that Harding's remarks were ingeniously contrived to obstruct the Liberty Loan by conveying to the American people an idea that there was some hidden and mysterious iniquity connected with the conduct of the war. He was obviously playing politics and had for the time being overlooked the fact that all parties had tacitly agreed to let partisanship drop. His attitude was exceptional among public men. Throughout the war Republicans as well as Democrats worked for the success of the Liberty Loans.

5

I have always wondered, and am still wondering, why the Republicans nominated and elected Harding in 1920. He was, as everyone knows, soft and pliable and easily managed. Apparently, if one may judge from his record as President, he was ready and willing to turn over the major functions of the government to 'privilege' and to give his sonorous approval to its policies. That was, of course, a desirable thing from the standpoint of the vested interests; but, even so, it seems that a Republican with more stamina and a more distinguished record, who would not have brought discredit on the Administration, might have been selected.

The anonymous author of 'The Mirrors of Washington' says of Harding:

As a legislator he left no mark on legislation. If he had retired from Congress at the end of his term, his name would have existed only in the old Congressional directories, like that of a thousand others. As a public speaker he had nothing to say that anybody could remember. He had passed through a great war and left no mark on it. . . .

He neither compelled attention by what he said nor by his personality. Why, then, without fireworks, without distinction of any sort, without catching the public eye, or especially deserving to catch it, was Warren Harding elected President of the United States?

One plausible reason why he was nominated was that given by Senator Brandegee at Chicago, where he had a great deal to do with the nomination. 'There ain't any first-raters this year. This ain't any 1880 or any 1904. We haven't any John Shermans or Theodore Roosevelts. We've got a lot of second-raters, and Warren Harding is the best of the second-raters.'

The author, who was one of the best-informed of the Washington newspaper correspondents, though he prefers to keep his anonymity, goes on to say that Harding was elected because the American people were tired of 'the high thinking and rather plain spiritual living of Woodrow Wilson.' They desired a man in the White House who would cause the country no more moral overstrain than would be caused by any man one might meet, by chance, in the smoking compartment of a Pullman car.

Harding was a likable person. His manner was pleasant and ingratiating; and he was a 'good fellow' in the ordinary locker-room, poker-game sense of that term; far too much of a 'good fellow,' in fact, to be entrusted with great authority. The possessor of an adjustable conscience, which could be altered to fit every changing circumstance, Harding went through life with good cheer and gusto, believing thoroughly that a man can get along very well if he can only fool some of the people some of the time.

He was a speechmaker; he spoke on every convenient occasion in a big, bow-wow style of oratory. He would use rolling words which had no application to the topic in hand, and his speeches left the impression of an army of pompous phrases moving over the landscape in search of an idea. Sometimes these meandering words would actually capture a straggling thought and bear it triumphantly, a prisoner in their midst, until it died of servitude and overwork.

6

It was a matter of great importance to secure the coöperation of the bankers, both in respect to the selling of Liberty bonds and the Treasury plan of taxation. I hoped to raise sufficient money through taxes to cover at least one third of the total cost of the war. I realized, of course, that bankers and millionaires, like everybody else, would pay whatever taxes Congress saw fit to impose; and I knew also that they would take their quota of Liberty bonds — but there is a great difference, in effect, between doing a thing grudgingly and doing it eagerly and willingly. A grudging act, done with grouchy discontent, exudes a social poison which permeates the community. In the end all dissatisfaction is destructive. I wanted the bankers, and all wealthy people and rich corporations, not only to buy their full share of Liberty bonds, but to buy them gladly. And I wanted to get them in a frame of mind that would lead them to pay their income taxes, which would be necessarily high, with cheerfulness.

For that reason I made it a point to discuss my fiscal program in the frankest spirit with the financiers. Their response was stimulating. It was not long before I felt that bankers and financiers, as well as the rest of the country, were solidly behind the Treasury.

On May 5, 1917, a luncheon was tendered to me at the Bankers' Club in New York at which Benjamin Strong, Governor of the Federal Reserve Bank, presided. Among those present were: George F. Baker, of the First National Bank; Frank A. Vanderlip, of the National City Bank; A. H. Wiggin, of the Chase National Bank; William Woodward, of the Hanover National Bank; J. P. Morgan; and Jacob H. Schiff.

When I rose to speak, I talked without any mental reservations and laid all my cards on the table. I expressed the conviction that the soundness of the economic and financial situation, as well as the effective prosecution of the war, could be had in no other way than by raising at least one third, and possibly one half, of the cost of the war by taxation; that necessarily the great bulk of this burden would fall on individual and corporate incomes. I said that war, as they all knew, was serious business, and that, when the government would have to conscript the lives of men, it could not be expected to be less stern in conscripting the means by which those men might be enabled to fight with the maximum of benefit to the country.

That these statements were platitudes is a fact of which I was well aware; but on certain occasions platitudes are not to be despised. There are times when they are far more efficacious than any variety of brilliant and original thought. My experience has proved to me that when one is discussing far-reaching issues that touch the lives of millions of people — and on which immediate action is imperative — it is always best to shape one's utterances in well-worn and familiar forms, into images which are easily recognizable and which are a function of the common experience of mankind.

At that time, and until he died recently (in 1931) at the age of ninety, George F. Baker was the foremost and most authoritative of American bankers. He sat by my side at the luncheon, and when my speech was concluded Governor Strong called on him. Mr. Baker was a reticent man, of an unemotional type. Ordinarily his words, encrusted with caution, came slowly. I was surprised when, in a fervent and emotional talk, he declared that he approved all I had said about taxation and about the general policy I had in view for financing the war; that so far as he was concerned, the government could take half of his income and more, if needed, for war purposes. His speech was stimulating and had, I think, more effect in reconciling the influential group at the luncheon to heavy taxes than anything that was said by anybody else.

To finance the government temporarily, in view of its large daily expenditures, the Treasury issued certificates of indebtedness, or short-term notes, which were sold to bankers and to the public. The authorizing act (that of April 24, 1917) limited the maturities of these certificates to one year as a maximum. Most of them ran much less than a year — a great many for only one month.

Through the use of these certificates we were able to anticipate the cash returns from Liberty bond sales. They served
also to keep our finances in order until the rather ponderous
and slow-moving taxation program got into operation. As
the Treasury certificates were sold chiefly to banks, we made
thousands of them depositaries of Treasury funds, and upon
selling them certificates of indebtedness we kept the money
on deposit in the purchasing bank until it was needed. In
this manner we avoided a sudden shifting of funds and a consequent dislocation of the country's financial system.

As money came into the Treasury from the sale of Liberty
bonds, or from the receipt of taxes, we paid off the certificates
of indebtedness and canceled them; but, while this was going
on, new certificates were being issued. There was a constant
inflow and outgo of funds.

When the subscription books were closed, on June 15, 1917,
the First Liberty Loan had been oversubscribed by more
than one billion dollars. Subscriptions amounted to $3,035,-
226,850, or fifty per cent more than the amount offered.
The number of purchasers was in excess of four million, and
ninety-nine per cent of them subscribed in amounts ranging
from fifty dollars to ten thousand dollars.

7

In all probability the war would have been won by Germany if America had not been forced into it on the side of the
Allies. That is my considered opinion, formed at the time,
and it has been strengthened by reading and research since the
close of the war.

We did not enter the conflict a moment too soon. The
Allies were in dire straits in the spring and summer of 1917,
from a military as well as from an economic standpoint. In
confidential communications their representatives made no
effort to minimize their gloom over the deadly seriousness of
the situation.

The Germans had beaten Russia to a standstill, and in
1917, German troops that had been employed in the East
were appearing in masses on the western front. Many military experts considered the position of the enemy in France

impregnable; others believed that the line might be broken, but only at a huge cost in men. The Germans had had two years or more to dig themselves in, and they had done it thoroughly. Besides, they possessed the enormous advantage that modern methods of warfare give to the defenders of highly fortified positions. French officers told me that it would cost a million men, at the least, to dislodge the enemy from the Hindenburg Line, if it could be done at all. France was almost bled white; she had no million men to lose; nor had the British.

The problem of the submarine was still unsolved, and the sinking of Allied ships went on at a staggering rate. In the early months of 1917, German submarines were destroying about three hundred thousand tons of shipping a week, on an average. In one month the submarines sank nearly as much shipping as the entire tonnage of steam vessels under the American flag at the outbreak of the war.

Across the sea came the dismay of the British — a dismay that carried a deepening note of disaster. There was a fear, and a well-grounded one, that England might be starved into abject surrender before we should be ready to do anything effective. On April 27, 1917, Ambassador Walter H. Page reported confidentially to the President that the food in the British Isles was not more than enough to feed the civil population for six weeks or two months.

The special British War Mission reached America on April 22. Arthur James Balfour, who came as the head of it, was accompanied by Lord Cunliffe, Governor of the Bank of England, and others. Balfour called on me shortly after his arrival. I found in him a delightful gentleman with an unmistakable air of breeding and culture. If I had not known his antecedents, I should never have taken him for a man of affairs. The mark of the university was all over him; he made me think of quiet English lawns and historic buildings of gray stone, of dons and prebendaries, of scholarly and grave professors.

He emphasized the imperative need of immediate financial assistance and said that he wanted to get a clear idea of what to expect. I told him that I felt great responsibility in the matter; that I ought not to act on impulse and turn over vast sums of money to the Allies without knowing to what use they were to be applied. Furthermore, I said that I should like to get the opinion of their best military minds as to the probable duration of the war. If, in their opinion, it would last five years longer, I should have to arrange a scheme of financing quite different from the one I should adopt if the war was to last only one year longer. Our loans, I remarked to him, must be distinctly related to military necessities, and, therefore, I should be grateful if he would submit a memorandum showing in general the uses to which these loans would be applied.

Mr. Balfour assured me that the information would be supplied. He remarked, in the course of this first conversation, that all the Allied powers, including Great Britain, had exhausted their credit in the United States. The financial situation was, he declared, more alarming than any other phase of the war; that it prefigured even a greater catastrophe than the submarine peril.

In various memoranda the British — and after them the French, Italian, Russian, and other Allies — laid before me the vast and tangled skein of their debts and fiscal expedients. Much of the data was secret and confidential; it had never been divulged, so I was told, even to the legislative assemblies of their countries. This information revealed a complex of urgent necessities. I realized that the war could not be continued successfully unless we supplied the Allies with enormous sums of money.

I was willing to do everything that it was possible for me to do, under the authority given to me by Congress, but I could not, of course, make the United States Treasury an open cash drawer from which the Allied powers might help themselves. What I tried to get from the nations that borrowed from us was: (1) a clear, definite statement of what they intended to do with the funds advanced by the Treasury; (2) a statement of the relation of our loans to their own financial efforts.

On July 10, 1917, I sent a communication through the State Department to Bonar Law, the British Chancellor of the Exchequer, for the purpose of establishing a clear understanding of our position, and of what I thought should be done by both sides to keep it clear. In the course of this cabled letter I said:

The United States reserves to itself at all times complete independence of decision and freedom of action with respect to financial matters. The Secretary of the Treasury does not undertake to define America's policy except as to financial matters. The financial policy will be dictated by a consistent desire to coöperate to the fullest extent possible with the several powers making war in common against Germany, but America's coöperation does not mean that America will assume the entire burden of financing the war.

I learned with regret later on — months later, in fact — that this frank statement had hurt the feelings of the British officials. They objected particularly to the implications of my phrase: 'America's coöperation does not mean that America will assume the entire burden of financing the war.' So they said, anyway, to Ambassador Page, unofficially, in the course of a conversation. It is needless to say that I did not mean to give offense, though I desired to have it clearly understood that we did not care to tie our hands financially, and that our purpose was to give assistance wherever, in our judgment, it would be most effective in furthering the common aim to win the war.

Congress passed the Loan Act on April 24, and the first loan was made to the British the next day. I decided to let them have two hundred million dollars at once to cover their immediate needs. Lord Cunliffe received the check officially on behalf of the British government.

In the course of time I came to know Cunliffe well, and I was much pleased with his way of doing things. He was calm, unperturbed, clear-headed, and thoroughly at home in everything pertaining to finance. I like men who know their business. Lord Cunliffe knew his.

He was much impressed by my promptness in advancing two hundred million dollars to his government without red tape or circumlocution. He looked at the pen with which I had signed the check and remarked that it had made history, or something of the kind.

'Would you like to have it as a souvenir?' I asked, and he replied that he would. I told him that I would be glad to give it to him, but would send it to the Bureau of Printing and Engraving first to have a record of the event engraved on the penholder.

Not long afterward I made a loan of one hundred million dollars to France. Ambassador Jusserand called to get the check. While I was signing it, I remembered that my gift of a pen to Lord Cunliffe had been mentioned in the newspapers, and it occurred to me that Jusserand might feel slighted unless I offered him a pen, too. After I had signed the French check, I asked him if he would like to have the pen. To my surprise he declined to accept it. 'No, thank you,' he said, 'I don't care to have it.' I was at a loss to know what to say. He seemed piqued, for some reason that I could not divine.

A short time afterward I learned that he was resentful because I did not give him a check for two hundred millions, the same amount that I had advanced to Great Britain. In subsequent conversations with representatives of France and Italy, they said to me, in effect, that they thought they ought to receive the same amount in loans that I extended to Great Britain, on the theory that their nations were first-class powers, too, and that all should be treated alike.

I informed them that the allocation of credits was determined solely by my conviction, after the most careful studies I could make, as to where those credits could be employed with the greatest advantage for the prosecution of the war. If I thought the entire three billion dollars I was authorized to lend to foreign governments could be used by Italy alone, or France alone, or Great Britain alone, with the greatest effect in bringing the war to a swift and victorious conclusion, I should lend it all to that power.

My reason for giving the larger check to the British at the outset was not alone because their war needs clearly indicated it, but because Great Britain had already borne an undue share of the financial burden of the war. She had, in fact, advanced, up to that time, out of her own treasury five or six hundred million pounds to France and a less amount to Italy and Belgium.

With a few exceptions all the members of the War Missions — British, French, Italian, and the rest — were war-weary, jangled, nervous, and some of them were on the ragged edge of hysteria. Is it any wonder they were, considering the fact that they and their compatriots had been in the thick of the fight for nearly three years?

As time went on, most of the details of the British loans were worked out with Sir Richard Crawford. He was unusually well informed in such matters. Often when he came to my office to discuss the war and the needs of his country, and especially during some of the gloomiest periods, his emotions got the better of him and tears streamed down his face. I felt the deepest sympathy for him because I knew what he and his countrymen had endured. 'You must forgive me — overstrain,' he used to say, with a smile, when I noticed his emotional state.

In September, 1917, Lord Reading, Chief Justice of England, arrived in Washington. He was a special envoy of the British War Cabinet to deal with financial questions that might arise between the United States and the British government during the war.

Reading was peculiarly fitted for this mission. Like Lord Cunliffe, who had returned, meanwhile, to England, he was thoroughly informed about financial matters. He had a keen and penetrating mind. He saw the problem in the large, and it was a great relief to me to have a man of his fine ability, common-sense, and good judgment with whom to discuss the complicated questions that were constantly arising. Reading was a handsome man, with a charming personality. Our relations were soon established on a plane of complete candor and confidence. Subsequently he succeeded Spring-Rice as ambassador at Washington.

The latter part of April, 1917, the French War Mission, headed by former Premier René Viviani, arrived in Washington. Marshal Joffre, the hero of the Marne, accompanied him. Viviani was an eloquent orator; the French, I believe, considered him the greatest orator in France. When he addressed Congress, he made a profound impression.

About the middle of May, André Tardieu came to Washington as French High Commissioner. He spoke no English and my early interviews with him were through an interpreter. I soon discovered that he was a highly intelligent, level-headed, unexcitable man, with a comprehensive knowledge of financial, as well as of military, affairs. He began to study the English language shortly after his arrival. I was amazed by his quickness in learning. In a remarkably short time we dropped the interpreter and carried on our negotiations in English.

Before long I discovered that it was utterly impossible for me to conduct negotiations in person with these diplomats. It took too much time. They were, as a rule, loquacious and accustomed to leisurely conversation and to a scheme of personal duties which, I honestly believe, carried the tacit implication that they were supposed to do only one thing a day. On the other hand, with a thousand things to do every day, I had to be "snappy." That is all right with Americans. They understand, and when they have said their say, in brief phrases, they get up and leave, or I could make them go by courteously indicating my lack of time.

But one cannot terminate an interview with an ambassador or a minister; that would be a breach of etiquette. On occasions I had to listen for a long time to things that had no relation to the immediate problems in hand when important people were champing at the bit in my outer room and sometimes raging because of my seeming lack of consideration. Assistant Secretary Crosby was, therefore, put in charge of foreign loans until he was sent to Europe. Then I appointed Albert Rathbone, of New York, a lawyer of high standing and ability, as Assistant Secretary and entrusted him with the direction of this important division of the department.

8

When we entered the war all my boys volunteered promptly. They joined the navy under the impression, which was prevalent at the time, that the navy was the arm of the service that would get to the other side first.

My oldest son (Francis Huger) began as a provisional ensign and was sent to the officers' training camp in Annapolis July 17. He made an excellent record and was detailed first to the command of a submarine chaser at Norfolk. During the latter part of the war he was made a lieutenant and assigned to one of the destroyers of the squadron operating in the submarine zone with headquarters at Queenstown, Ireland.

William G., Jr., was a senior at Princeton when war was declared. He served in the naval flying corps and saw duty as an aviator in France.

Robert H., my youngest boy, was not of military age when the war began. He was in St. Paul's school in New Hampshire, and I wanted him to complete the spring term, but he was so dissatisfied that I had to give in and let him enlist. He became an ordinary seaman, and after serving as a 'gob' for six months he was permitted to join the flying corps. When the Armistice was signed he was just completing his training as a naval aviator at Pensacola, Florida.

While Robert was a 'gob' he was ordered one day to report to a petty officer on shore at Norfolk. When he presented his orders, the petty officer, who was something of a roughneck, said, gruffly: 'McAdoo! McAdoo! Any kin to the Secretary of the Treasury?'

'Yes,' replied Robert, 'he is my father.'

'Aw, come off, young feller. Don't gimme any guff. If your father was Secretary of the Treasury, you'd be an admiral!'

CHAPTER XXVI
PROVIDING THE SINEWS OF WAR

I

THERE was a distinct lack of coördination among the Allies when we went into the war; by that I mean not only a lack of coördinated effort, but also a lack of coördinated ideas. In purchasing supplies in the United States, they were bidding against each other, and prices were lifted to fabulous heights by their competition. That was one of the primary causes of the general inflation which was seriously disturbing the economic condition of the country. It seemed to me that they should be required to buy in our markets through a purchasing commission, created by authority of our government, which might also coördinate the purchases of the Allies with the purchases of the United States. This commission should have authority to determine the reasonable needs of the allied governments and to give them the benefit of the same prices our government would pay in the open markets. Authority existed already in the government to establish reasonable prices for materials and supplies required for war purposes.

Early in May I proposed the establishment of an Inter-Ally Purchasing Commission which would act as a buying agency for all the Allies in the United States. At the same time I suggested, as a corollary to the purchasing commission in America, an Inter-Ally Council in Europe which would decide on the European destination of supplies purchased in the United States, and submit recommendations to me as to the amount of credit which we should, from time to time, grant to each country making war in common against the Central Powers. The Treasury, I thought, should be represented on this Council.

With the President's approval, I discussed these ideas with the representatives of the Allied Powers at Washington and submitted to them a tentative draft of an agreement. They accepted it with the diplomatic phrase 'agreed to in principle,' together with suggestions as to certain modifications which they thought should be made in my plan.

After that the matter dragged along in the usual leisurely diplomatic way. Though the need for a purchasing commission in the United States became more insistent every day, I could get no action.

The British government appointed Lord Northcliffe to succeed Mr. Balfour (who had returned to England) as head of the British War Mission in the United States. Northcliffe arrived in Washington about June 15, and shortly afterward conferred with me about British credits and the financial problems arising out of the war. In the course of our conversation I discussed with him the proposed Inter-Ally Council in Europe, and told him frankly that I felt somewhat impatient with what appeared to me to be procrastination on the part of the allied governments in dealing with a matter of such outstanding importance.

I have met few men who had such a quick comprehension as Northcliffe. It was never necessary to explain anything to him twice. He reminded me more of the higher type of American business executive than any foreigner I have ever known. He was dynamic, his phrases were vivid, his ideas crisp and clear, and he had a way of getting down at once to the vital thought in any question under discussion.

But Northcliffe was not a financier, nor did he pretend to be one. He preferred to leave matters involving financial technique to Lord Cunliffe and Sir Richard Crawford. His strong point was in determining how to do things — the shortest and surest road to accomplishment. He had a fine political and publicity sense; he always thought of the effect of actions on public opinion.

I told him that I objected strongly to financing the war on an unnecessarily inflated basis. Under the Liberty Loan Act the Secretary of the Treasury was empowered, in making advances to foreign governments, 'to enter into such arrangements as may be necessary or desirable for establishing such credits and for purchasing such obligations of foreign governments,' and I said to Northcliffe that I considered the establishment of the proposed commissions to be among the 'arrangements' I was authorized to enter into by virtue of the Act.

He agreed with my suggestions and said that he would do everything in his power to help carry them out. I knew he would; I was impressed by his candor and good-will. But I knew, too, how ponderous and slow-moving all governmental machinery is, so I thought it wise to add something suggestive of an ultimatum in order to speed things up. I informed him that I should feel compelled to withhold credits from the Allies after August 15 unless, by that time, an agreement had been reached for the establishment of a purchasing commission.

Nevertheless, action was delayed. Neither I nor Northcliffe knew why. In the meantime I discussed the matter with André Tardieu, the French High Commissioner. He said he was in favor of the plan and that he would recommend it to his government.

Finally, in August, the idea was approved by the principal Allied Powers, and became an actuality. The Purchasing Commission, with headquarters in Washington, was composed of Bernard M. Baruch, Robert S. Lovett, and Robert S. Brookings.

There was some trouble over the appointment of Baruch as the head of the Purchasing Commission. I had urged the President to make him chairman of that body because I considered him well qualified for the post on account of his character and demonstrated business ability.

The President said that Lovett did not want to serve under Baruch and that Secretary of War Baker also objected to his appointment. Why? 'Because,' the President replied, 'they say Baruch is "a Wall Street speculator."' Baker's objection was the more important of the two, since the Purchasing Commission should have his confidence if it was to handle purchases for the War Department, as well as for the Allies.

I never had the least doubt as to Baruch's capacity and fitness for the job. He was a man of vision and ability; he had a thorough knowledge of business and of American industrial production. Moreover, his personality was pleasing and he was just the man for a place where one has to meet and deal with a large variety of people.

After a few days' consideration the President took my view of it and Baruch was appointed. His services as chairman of the Commission were highly satisfactory. Subsequently the

President made Baruch chairman of the important War Industries Board, which did a work of tremendous importance in the industrial field in the United States and in coöperation with the Allies during the war.

Shortly after the Purchasing Commission was appointed, we reached an agreement with the Allies for the creation of an Inter-Ally Council, with headquarters in London. As the American representative I sent Oscar T. Crosby, who was one of the Assistant Secretaries of the Treasury. Crosby, who was a graduate of West Point, and an accomplished, well-informed man, had the requisite technical knowledge to enable him to relate military operations to finance. He spoke French fluently. When the Inter-Ally Council was organized in Paris, he was made its president.

The loans to foreign governments began to pile up at a tremendous rate. By the middle of July, 1917, the Treasury had let the British government have $686,000,000; and, besides, had advanced $427,000,000 to other associated powers — a total of $1,113,000,000. I thought that was a great deal of money for the Allies to have drawn in three months. Later on I was to learn that it was only a drop in the bucket compared to what they needed and what we had to lend them during the course of the war.

2

I had to enlarge my immediate Treasury staff to meet the demands of the war. Congress authorized two additional Assistant Secretaries, making five in all, as well as an Assistant to the Secretary of the Treasury. I promoted George R. Cooksey, my private secretary, to the post of Assistant to the Secretary. He was succeeded by Brice Clagett, correspondent of the Associated Press in Washington. Clagett was a man of unusual ability, tact, and intelligence. His wide experience with public men and affairs as correspondent of the Associated Press had given him exactly the training he needed to perform the difficult duties of private secretary during that strenuous period.

In reorganizing my staff of Assistant Secretaries, I took Byron R. Newton away from Washington and sent him to

New York as Collector of Customs, which was a post of greatly increased importance during the war. My war staff of Assistant Secretaries consisted of James H. Moyle, of Utah; Thomas B. Love, of Texas; Leo S. Rowe, of Pennsylvania; Russel C. Leffingwell, of New York; and Albert Rathbone, of New York.

In making these appointments I was not moved by partisan considerations. Moyle, Love, and Rathbone were Democrats, while Leffingwell and Rowe were Republicans. Leffingwell, a lawyer of fine ability and high character, was particularly well informed on questions of finance. He became my assistant in fiscal matters, and while his point of view and mine were frequently at variance, nevertheless these differences were brought out in argument and enabled me to reach decisions with greater confidence and satisfaction to myself than if he had agreed with me about everything. Whenever I made a final decision Leffingwell acquiesced and carried it out with loyalty and energy.

I put Thomas B. Love in charge of the Division of War Risk Insurance and Internal Revenue. It was a tremendously important job, and one that only a big man could fill satisfactorily. Love made a splendid record. He had been Banking and Insurance Commissioner of his own state of Texas, and had a thorough knowledge of financial and insurance matters. When I appointed him he was practicing law; he sacrificed his lucrative practice to take this unremunerative post.

Rathbone took over the Division of Foreign Loans. Rowe had the Division of Customs, and supervised, also, the Treasury Department's relations with Latin America. He had long been known as a specialist in South American affairs. Moyle was put in charge of public buildings and miscellaneous bureaus. Daniel C. Roper, of South Carolina, was made Commissioner of Internal Revenue, and John Burke, of North Dakota, was appointed Treasurer of the United States. They were all good men, of constructive talent and genuine ability. I was fortunate in having them around me.

The problem of organizing the Treasury for the vast work the Liberty loans would entail had to be dealt with immediately. It was necessary to create a publicity bureau to acquaint the country, not alone with the purposes of the war, but with the necessity for financing it through subscriptions, large and small, from all the people. This was immensely important. I appointed Robert W. Woolley Director of Publicity for the First Liberty Loan. Woolley was, at that time, Director of the Mint, but he gave up that job, took hold of the publicity bureau, and managed it ably. After the close of the First Liberty Loan drive, Oscar A. Price succeeded Woolley as Director of Publicity. Price was subsequently my private secretary and one of my assistants when I became Director-General of Railroads.

The speakers' bureau was put in charge of Charles F. Horner, of Kansas City, who had large experience as a director of Chautauqua lectures. He took hold with a perfect understanding of what was required, and his work was so good that I do not see how it could have been excelled. You remember, no doubt, the four-minute Liberty loan speakers who appeared between the acts at the theaters, and the street-corner lecturers who would pop up from nowhere, mount a soap-box and tell the passing crowd about Liberty bonds. They were all under Horner's direction.

Louis B. Franklin was president of the Investment Bankers' Association of America. He volunteered and came to the Treasury. He gave up a valuable business and fine connections in New York and devoted himself with great energy and ability to the Liberty loan work.

About the same time I brought another Franklin (George S. — not related to Louis) into the department. He came as legal adviser to the Liberty Loan Division. When I resigned as Secretary of the Treasury and resumed the practice of law in New York, he went into partnership with me as one of the members of the firm of McAdoo, Cotton & Franklin. The Cotton in this firm, by the way, was Joseph P. Cotton, who became Under-Secretary of State in the Hoover Administration and died in the spring of 1931.

My experience in large affairs had convinced me that the selection of the right men as executives and assistants is a matter of incalculable importance. You may have wonderful ideas and constructive plans in your head; you may be a giant locomotive in the way of energy; you may have the best intentions in the world and you may know exactly what you

want to do; nevertheless, if you are put at the head of a great
and far-flung undertaking, you will buzz around like a bee in a
box unless you have the capacity to pick the right men.

The chief trouble in selecting men for important posts is
that they are frequently picked out, not for the work they have
to do, but for some other reason. Very few people, including
those in high places, are able successfully to separate reason
from prejudice. One is unconsciously swayed by personal likes
or dislikes. You may turn down a man because he spits on
the floor and wears striped shirts. You don't like spitting on
the floor, let us say, and you don't like striped shirts. But that
is not your conscious reason for erasing him from the slate; it
is your unconscious one. You just don't like him, so you let
him go, yet he might be the very man you need; or he might
not be. The point is that you have let an extraneous and
superficial circumstance make a decision.

Another difficulty in man-choosing lies in the subtle error,
hard to evade, of selecting a man solely because he has a
good understanding. Many a man who understands exactly
what you are trying to do, and who is so intelligent that he
sees all the angles of your problem at the first explanation,
turns out hopelessly inefficient when you put him to carrying
out your plans. Every man is a combination of qualities, good
and bad, and sometimes the mixture is peculiar. Understanding and intelligence are excellent traits, and undoubtedly desirable, but they must be accompanied by energy and administrative capacity.

In selecting men for executive positions, I have always attached much importance to the capacity for 'finishing the
job' — to use a phrase which expresses precisely what I want
to say. If a man cannot finish what he starts out to do, there
is no use starting; and I must say, speaking from personal
observation, that the lack of finishers in the world is appalling.
Many men, for some reason, lose courage, or enthusiasm, or
interest, before the job is done. Others go at their work so
carefully, and with such perfection of detail, that they become
hazy and profound, and finally evolve into mere dawdlers
from whom nothing in the shape of definite results can be
expected.

I had good men in the Treasury. Men who went at things

with intelligence and vigor, and who had the knack of finishing whatever they began. They were poorly paid, but I could do nothing about it. All able men in the government service are underpaid. There were men under me, working for five thousand dollars a year, who could have earned eight or ten times that amount in business.

One of my plans was to put the women to work selling Liberty bonds. Strangely enough, there was great opposition to this idea. Some of the objectors thought the women would be a hindrance instead of a help; that they knew nothing about finance and could not sell bonds, while others thought that it was beneath the dignity of women to go around selling anything. The women were eager for patriotic service, and I knew that they could be quickly welded into a powerful force, through their clubs and their enthusiasm, to arouse the spirit of the people and to tell them the real reasons for the war. Still, the objections continued, particularly the one about the work being undignified, though I never heard of any of the objectors saying it was beneath a woman's dignity to work in an office, or to stand behind a department store counter.

Anyway, the women went ahead and organized a National Women's Liberty Loan Committee under the auspices of the Treasury Department. The committee was composed of Mrs. W. G. McAdoo, of Washington, D.C.; Mrs. Antoinette Funk, of Pennsylvania; Mrs. Kellogg Fairbank and Mrs. George Bass, of Illinois; Mrs. Guilford Dudley, of Tennessee; Mrs. George T. Guernsey, of Kansas; Mrs. Frank A. Vanderlip, of New York; and Mrs. Francis L. Higginson, of Massachusetts. Miss Mary Synon, of Chicago, was appointed secretary.

A sub-committee of the National Committee called on me and said that it was the unanimous desire of all members (except, of course, Mrs. McAdoo) that Mrs. McAdoo be made chairman, and asked if I had any objection to it. I replied that I thought it would be getting too much 'McAdoo' into the campaign, since I must necessarily direct the whole Liberty Loan movement. Mrs. McAdoo was already at the head of the largest Red Cross Auxiliary in Washington, composed of 4400 women employees of the Treasury Department and was burdened with heavy responsibilities. I was reluctant to add to her many cares and duties, but on the Committee's insistence I finally consented to her selection as chairman and executive in charge.

Mrs. Antoinette Funk, who was a practicing lawyer in Chicago, was elected vice-chairman. She gave up her practice, came to Washington, and devoted her whole time to the work. Combined with decided executive ability and abounding energy, she had a delightful personality which made her work doubly effective in the Liberty Loan campaigns.

Miss Mary Synon was another of the able women who served on the National Liberty Loan Committee. A magazine writer of wide reputation, she abandoned her private affairs and for two years devoted herself to the Liberty Loan work with fine patriotism and devotion. She is the author of a biography of me, which appeared under the title 'McAdoo' in 1924.

The National Women's Liberty Loan Committee did immensely valuable work. During the Second Liberty Loan sixty thousand women enlisted as bond salesmen. They sold one billion dollars of bonds. When the Fourth Liberty Loan came along one year later, between seven and eight hundred thousand women served and got two billion dollars in subscriptions.

When I entered the Cabinet in 1913, the Treasury was a somnolent and gloomy institution, characterized by a remote and cold austerity. It had an air of standing apart from everything else in the United States — an air of abstraction, of carefully counting dollars and putting them away in secret places.

By 1917 all that was changed. The ancient secretaries would have had difficulty in recognizing the department, with its manifold activities. We were dealing with everybody in America. The humblest citizen was on our books and was our valued customer. The historic stone building was a place of energy, vitality, and movement.

3

Long before the summer of 1917 was over, we began to lay our plans for a second Liberty loan. I was disturbed by the tax-exempt features of the first loan, the income from which, as you will recall, was exempt from all taxation except inheritance and estate taxes. I was impressed by the obvious fact that large numbers of people of wealth could put most, or all, of their fortunes in Liberty bonds of the first issue and escape taxation altogether. Such investors would receive only three and one half per cent; not a large return, I admit, but even at that it was larger than they would receive from a five per cent investment that was subject to the normal income tax and super tax. That was one point to be considered, and another was the unhealthy effect on the social economy of a large and wealthy class of tax-free persons.

I recommended to the Ways and Means Committee of the House that the bonds of the second issue be made exempt from all taxes *except* estate and inheritance taxes, and graduated additional income taxes (commonly known as surtaxes), and excess profits and war-profits taxes. This recommendation was adopted by the Committee.

As the bonds were deprived of most of their attractive tax-exempt features, it was necessary to compensate, in a measure, for their loss by raising the interest rate a peg higher. I accordingly made it four per cent.

It was provided that, if any issue of bonds at a higher rate should be put out before the termination of the war, the bonds of the second loan might be exchanged for them.

The Second Liberty Loan campaign was begun October 1, 1917. The issue was three billion dollars, the rate four per cent; and the Treasury announced that it would accept one half of any oversubscription.

The lists closed on October 27, so we had one day less than four weeks for the campaign. We were much better organized for intensive effort than we had been in the days of the first loan.

The offering was a phenomenal success. Total subscriptions amounted to $4,617,532,300 — approximately fifty-four per cent oversubscribed. More than nine million subscriptions were received, against four million for the first loan.

The aggregate amount of the bonds allotted under the agreement to accept half the oversubscription was $3,808,-766,150.

The Third Liberty Loan was floated in the spring of 1918. At that time the existing issues — the bonds of the first and second Liberty loans — were selling slightly below par; in other words, the public seemed to have bought bonds already to the point of saturation. That was the reason which some of my advisers gave for their decline. I did not think the reason was a convincing one. We had sold, up to that time, less than six billions of Liberty bonds, and according to the best estimates of the nation's wealth and net income, the country should have been able to absorb twice six billions in twelve months.

However, a fact is a fact, whatever the fundamental cause may be; and in this case, the fact that the bonds were selling below par was undeniable. I decided, in the interest of stabilizing the price, to make the third loan more attractive from a purely financial standpoint, so I put the interest rate up to four and one quarter per cent. The conversion privilege (that is, the right of the holder to convert the bonds into future issues bearing a higher rate) was omitted from the third loan. The bonds were non-convertible.

The offering was three billion dollars, and the Treasury reserved the right to allot additional bonds up to the full amount of any oversubscription. The campaign started April 6, 1918 — the first anniversary of America's entrance into the war — and the lists closed May 4. Like the first two loans, the third was largely oversubscribed. The aggregate amount of subscriptions allotted was $4,176,516,850. The number of subscriptions ran up to the gigantic total of 18,376,815. Many people subscribed to bonds in two or three places, so while it would have been erroneous to assume that the actual number of subscribers was above eighteen million, I thought we were safe in estimating them at about fifteen million. When the returns came in, I began to feel, for the first time, that we were really getting to the heart of the great mass of the American people.

The Fourth Liberty Loan was offered to the public on September 28, 1918. The amount was six billion dollars and

the interest rate was four and one quarter per cent. To make
the loan more attractive to a certain class of investors, it was
provided that interest on thirty thousand dollars of these
bonds held by one person would be exempt from surtaxes until
two years after the close of the war.

The subscription list closed on October 19 — about three
weeks before the Armistice. Nearly 23,000,000 subscriptions
were received, and the total sum was $6,989,047,000. It was
the largest flotation of bonds ever made in a single effort anywhere or at any time.

The next issue — and the final one — was called the Victory
Liberty Loan. It was sold to the public in 1919 under the
direction of Carter Glass, who succeeded me as Secretary of
the Treasury upon my resignation in December, 1918. The
object of the Victory Liberty Loan was to raise money to fund
the floating debt, which was rapidly accumulating as the result of expenditures in the months succeeding the close of the
war. This Victory Loan was in the form of United States
notes running for comparatively short periods — three or four
years — and convertible, at the option of the holder, into
bonds having a longer life.

The loan was offered to the public on April 21, and subscriptions were limited to a total of four and one half billion
dollars. It was oversubscribed, but not to the extent of the
previous loans, as the war was over and much of its enthusiasm had waned.

The total amount raised by the Treasury on the five loans,
over a period of two years — from May, 1917, to May, 1919 —
was $21,439,394,500. Of this total, $16,940,000,000 came from
the four Liberty Loan campaigns that were carried out under
my direction.

4

It is hard to say, with accuracy, what would have happened
if the war had continued another year. The total expenditures
of the government for the fiscal year ended June 30, 1918,
amounted to $13,791,907,895, including the sum of $4,739,-
434,000 which was advanced in the form of loans to foreign governments; and toward the close of the fiscal year the
monthly outgo was increasing rapidly. I saw that plans would

have to be made for raising not less than $24,000,000,000 in the fiscal year beginning July 1, 1918, and ending June 30, 1919.

On May 23, 1918, I wrote a letter to the President in which I described the financial situation in bald terms, devoid of poetry and romance. I said, in part:

We cannot wisely contemplate nearly doubling our cash disbursements in the fiscal year 1919 without providing additional revenue. We cannot afford to rely on four billion dollars only from taxation, because we shall then have to depend on raising twenty billion dollars by loans. This would be a surrender to the policy of high interest rates and inflation, with all the evil consequences which would flow inevitably therefrom, and which would, I firmly believe, bring ultimate destruction upon the country. We cannot afford to base our future financing upon the quicksands of inflation or unhealthy credit expansion....

On the basis of the present revenue laws we should have to raise in the fiscal year 1919 twenty billion dollars by the sale of Liberty bonds, or by loans of one sort or another. Personally, I do not believe that it can be done. I believe that if we are to preserve the soundness and stability of our financial structure, we must raise not less than one third of our expenditures by taxation....

I went on to summarize the main features of the tax legislation which I proposed:

(1) Such legislation should be calculated to provide in cash during the fiscal year ending June 30, 1919, not less than one third of the cash expenditures to be made during that year. According to my estimates, eight billion dollars should be raised in taxes payable in cash into the Treasury during that year.

(2) A real war profits tax at a high rate should be levied upon all war profits. This tax should be superimposed upon the existing excess profits tax in such a way that the taxpayer would pay whichever tax were the greater, and the existing excess profits tax should be amended in certain important particulars so as to remove inequalities.

(3) There should be an important increase in the amount of normal income tax upon unearned incomes. Under existing law earned incomes above certain exceptions are taxed four per cent as an income tax and eight per cent under the name of an excess profits tax, making a total of twelve per cent, while unearned incomes, derived from securities, etc., are taxed only four per cent. The eight per cent tax should be recognized as an income tax and the rate of twelve per cent retained in respect to earned incomes, while a higher rate than twelve per cent should be imposed on unearned incomes.

(4) A heavy tax should be imposed upon all luxuries.

The fear of some of the party leaders that this program for taxation, if adopted, would cause the Democrats to lose control of Congress was well founded. The November election took place while the revenue bill was still in Congress. The unpopularity of the bill, with its proposal to increase taxes generally and to bear heavily on large corporate and individual incomes, was undoubtedly the most potent factor in the defeat of the Democrats. We lost enough seats in Congress to give the Republicans a working majority.

Yet, in the same situation today, I should make the same recommendations. I would have been false to my responsibilities, and to the trust that had been imposed on me, if I had permitted a thought of political defeat or victory to influence my decision in a matter of such grave consequence, or had jockeyed about this tax measure, or had endeavored to please the country by presenting a more attractive and less adequate scheme. It was no time for politics; we had to do the right thing, even at the risk of Democratic overthrow.

Within a week after the November election the war came to an end. The financial pressure was relieved. I sent a new recommendation to Congress for much lighter taxes, reducing previous proposals by two billion dollars!

Here we have the irony of fate. If the Armistice had occurred a month earlier, I am confident that the Democrats would have won the election and that the history of the next two years would have been vastly different.

As I have already said, the fiscal plan I formulated at the beginning of the war was based on the idea that one third of the total expenditures of the government should be covered by taxation; and the remaining two thirds by loans.

The actual results ran very close to the calculation. In the two war years — July 1, 1917, to June 30, 1919 — the total expenditures of the Treasury were approximately $24,-300,000,000. This sum does not include advances made to foreign governments; they were not expenditures, but loans.

The receipts from taxes (including customs and miscellaneous) for the same two-year period were $8,800,000,000 — or a little more than one third of the total expenditures.

CHAPTER XXVII
THE MONEY EUROPE OWES US

I

AMERICA's power, thrown into the scale at the critical moment, won the war for the Allies. It was won with our men and our money. This is not a boast; it is not a reflection on the gallant armies of the Allies. It is a mere statement of fact. I know that it has been, and is, disputed, but it is nevertheless true. No one who was in the inner circle of the Wilson Administration, or close to the Administration, doubts it. When the desperate plight of the Allies was revealed to us, after the United States entered the war, we had a distinct impression that it might be too late to save the Allied cause.

On July 20, 1917, Ambassador Page urged me by cable to increase the financial assistance to the British government. I thought I had been pretty liberal up to that time. We had been in the war hardly three months, but I had already loaned to the British nearly seven hundred million dollars. At the close of his message Page said: 'Greater fear and depression has been caused by the financial situation than has heretofore been felt from any cause since the start of the war.'

About the same time, in July, 1917, Bonar Law, the British Chancellor of the Exchequer, cabled me an urgent message of many pages — thousands of words and masses of figures. It was a carefully prepared memorandum which gave the status and outlook of the British Treasury in detail, as well as briefer analyses of the financial condition of the other Allied Powers. Bonar Law said in the course of this statement:

In short, resources of the United Kingdom which are available for payments in the United States are exhausted. Unless the government of the United States can meet fully our expenses in America, including exchange, the entire financial fabric of the alliance will collapse. This conclusion will be a matter of days, not months.

The question is one requiring the taking of a large view. If matters continue on the same basis as they have during the past few weeks, it will not be possible to avoid a financial disaster of the first magnitude.

With these omens written on the sky, I tackled the job of furnishing as much assistance as I could. The Treasury had to lend the Allies the money to pay for almost everything they bought in this country after we entered the war. They did not have the money and leaned on us absolutely. By establishing the Purchasing Commission and the Inter-Ally Council, which I referred to in the last chapter, we managed to keep the prices of supplies within fairly reasonable wartime limits; and we endeavored, with a good deal of success, to prevent extravagant and wasteful buying.

The whole amount advanced to foreign governments was $9,466,000,000, of which $2,170,000,000 was lent after the Armistice. These post-Armistice loans were not made under my direction, but by my successor. I mention them in order to complete the picture. Some of them were represented by credits entered on the books of the Treasury before the Armistice was signed. On the faith of these credits the Allies had made contracts for supplies in the United States which had to be liquidated. Further advances were necessitated to clean up the situation.

Although small payments on this stupendous debt have been made by some of the debtor nations since the war, it has not diminished, but has actually increased, owing to the accumulation of unpaid interest, as well as to adjustments and miscellaneous items of one kind or another. On November 30, 1930, foreign governments owed the United States $11,279,-990,878. The items in the total run in an ascending scale from Hungary ($1,920,315), Latvia ($5,775,000), Lithuania ($6,235,207), up to Italy ($2,017,000,000), France ($3,865,-000,000), and Great Britain ($4,426,000,000).

Since it fell to my lot to initiate the policy of foreign loans, as the Act of Congress gave authority to 'the Secretary of the Treasury, with the approval of the President,' to make them, I know, perhaps better than anybody else, the origin of these loans and the circumstances under which they were negotiated.

During the last few years I have heard, at times, arguments to the effect that the money we advanced to friendly governments during the war were not loans at all, except in form; that they were, in reality, gifts or contributions; and that they were made by us, and accepted by the borrowers, without any expectation of repayment. These arguments or assertions have no basis in fact or in anything but the imagination of those who make them.

I do not hesitate to say that it would have been impossible to secure from the Congress of the United States authority to make gifts to the Allies of the stupendous amount of money represented by these loans. Every borrowing government understood that it was receiving loans, not gifts, and that it was expected to repay them. Moreover, every one of them gave to the United States its written obligation in this form:

The government of [name of foreign government] for value received, promises to pay to the United States of America, or assigns, the sum of [number of dollars in words] on demand, with interest from date hereof, etc.

The obligation further provides that the principal and interest thereon shall be paid in gold coin of the United States without deduction for any taxes, present or future, that may be imposed by such foreign government. I took demand obligations in order that they might be refunded after the war into definite maturities.

In lending money to a foreign nation, you lend it, of course, upon the faith and honor of the people of that nation. There is no doubt whatever in my mind that every one of our debtors acted in good faith.

Their ability to pay is another matter, which I shall discuss further on. The point I am establishing here is the historical one that our financial assistance was given in the form of loans; that there was a definite agreement to pay both principal and interest in gold; and that there was no implication in the loan agreements or otherwise that the loans were not to be repaid or that repayment depended in any degree on German reparations, or on the willingness or ability of Germany to pay such reparations to the nations indebted to us.

When I went to the people of the United States, on a long speaking tour in the First Liberty Loan campaign, I had to explain with meticulous care to every audience I addressed that all advances to foreign powers were loans which would, from time to time, be repaid to the United States, just as the United States itself would, from time to time, repay the money it was borrowing from its citizens to enable it to make loans to these foreign powers. It was on this specific point that our people wanted to be informed and assured. I do not over-state the fact when I say that, if the American people had not been convinced of the good faith and honor of the borrowing governments, the United States would never have been able to sell its bonds to its own people for the purpose of making these foreign loans.

In contrast to the gratitude for our financial assistance which the Allies then expressed, there is now a disposition throughout Europe to call America an international Shylock and money-grabber, and to take it for granted that the com-posite American mind is incapable of perceiving anything that rises above the level of the dollar mark. It is well, in, consider-ing these baseless aspersions, to remember that the United States is the only nation which was arrayed against Germany that did not seek or receive indemnities and colonies when the war was over. We expected nothing in the way of reparations and we got nothing. The only debt that Germany owes us today is a comparatively small amount to cover the actual expense of our army of occupation on the Rhine.

2

What I have said, in the last few pages, sets forth the legal basis on which the loans were made. Technically, and actually, it is a perfect case of creditor and debtor.

But is it wise to consider it persistently from that point of view? To look at the problem through the calculating eyes of an ordinary, conventional money-lender serves only to keep it entangled in a web of threadbare and feeble sophis-tries which lead us nowhere. You cannot collect a debt, no matter how sacred it is, from a debtor who lacks the means of payment. Nor is it wise to impoverish whole nations in or-der to balance the books.

These thoughts have occurred in the past few years to

many thinking people in America, and some of them have proposed that we cancel the entire foreign debt as a solution of the question. I must say that I do not agree with them, primarily because cancellation would be an abandonment of the whole problem as insoluble. I do not consider it insoluble, and I do not think that cancellation should be discussed seriously until every other resource is an acknowledged failure.

Instead of wiping out the foreign loans, at an expense of eleven billion dollars which would have to be paid by our own people, I think we and our debtors ought to exhaust every rational and honorable means to liquidate these debts with a minimum of strain on the European economic structure.

In my judgment cancellation is an academic question. The great body of public opinion in the United States is opposed to it. I doubt that our people will ever consent to any plan which includes an outright cancellation of these loans. They are keenly aware of the fact that Great Britain, France, Germany, and the rest of them did not ask our advice before they began the war. If they had consulted us, we would have advised them not to fight. But they did not want advice; on the contrary, all of them rejected our offers of mediation, not only at the beginning of the war, but later on — even as late as 1916. The war grew out of purely European conditions, and was provoked largely by military tension. It was not our war at first. We were forced into it finally against our will through Germany's systematic policy of trampling on our international rights. Moreover, we entered the war as an independent power. We never joined the Allies; we coöperated with them, but our military coöperation was simply for the sake of convenience and efficiency. Their aims were different from ours. They wanted territory and indemnities, while our object was to protect our rights against the militaristic empire of Germany.

A cancellation of the foreign debts cannot be made without the consent of the people of the United States, as the American people collectively are the creditors in this case. The debtors cannot *cancel;* they can only *repudiate.* But no honorable nation would do that. It would be ruinous; such a course would destroy the national credit; and the repudiator would be unable to command capital for economic needs and enterprise or to meet a desperate emergency in time of war.

Aside from these considerations, and waiving, for the sake of discussion, questions of honor and economics, would it be wise for the United States to cancel eleven billion dollars of obligations, when our generosity might encourage these same powers to engage, at some future time, in another colossal war, with the subconscious idea in the back of their minds that they might force us into the conflict again and lay upon us a large part of the cost in blood and treasure? This may be considered a remote conjecture, but it is not as far-fetched as it may seem. Who would have thought, in the summer of 1914, when the nations of Europe began a war that was wholly European in origin and purpose, that we would be dragged into it; that before we got out of it we would have to spend about twenty-seven billion dollars, besides many more billions in indirect costs; that nearly three hundred thousand of our young men would be killed or wounded; and that twelve years after it was over the nations of Europe would still owe us more than eleven billion dollars? In 1914 such a prediction would have been looked upon as having no more validity than the phantoms of a nightmare, but it came true just the same. One way of stopping war is to make it too costly for anybody to afford.

3

Unusual and extraordinary problems require unusual and extraordinary solutions. Such problems can be solved only by insight and imagination, backed by courage.

When we look at the foreign debt problem closely, we cannot fail to observe that the chief difficulty in liquidating these obligations lies in the form of payment and the mechanism of transferring wealth from debtor to creditor.

As the matter stands today, the loans are in the form of obligations of one government to another. For instance, the government of Great Britain owes the government of the United States a certain sum of money, payable in semi-annual installments covering interest and amortization. France and Italy, and other governments, owe the United States, in

like manner. It is stipulated that these semi-annual installments must be paid in gold. Since the United States already
possesses almost as much gold as all other nations combined,
and since, in the course of foreign trade, balances must be
settled in gold, and since the production of new gold is insufficient to meet the world demand, the burden of gold set-
tlements is becoming more and more difficult and oppressive
for the debtor governments.

France has the only remaining large stock of gold outside
the United States, but France cannot part with any considerable proportion of it without depreciating further the value
of the paper franc. French currency is now fairly stabilized;
to dislocate its equilibrium again would still further disturb
the economic condition of the world.

The most obvious method of repayment is for the debtor
nations to send us gold or commodities. If you owe a debt,
you must pay it either in money — and the kind of money
the creditor will accept — or you must turn over to him something that he is willing to take instead of money. Lacking
gold, the debtor nations might export their manufactured
goods to the United States, sell them here, and create a fund
or balance that could be used in paying their debts to us.

But that would not do. Our tariff is too high to permit the
importation of such a huge amount of foreign commodities.
That is one reason. Another is that a flood of foreign goods
coming into the United States would seriously disturb American industry by raising up cheap competition, on a large
scale, against our own manufacturers.

Since payment in gold or in commodities involves, apparently, insuperable obstacles in the present condition of the
world, the question naturally arises: Is there any way in
which these vast governmental debts can be liquidated or
transformed into other obligations which will ease or relieve
the situation and accomplish their ultimate extinguishment
with honor to the nations involved?

I think there is. We might consider the proposal made by
Lord Rothermere in 1919. He said:

We are enormously indebted to the United States, but we also
possess assets of extreme value which the United States Government might be willing to acquire in liquidation, wholly or in part, of
our American liability.

I suggest that we should endeavor to dispose of the Bermudas, the Bahamas, and some of the West Indian islands—but not Jamaica, Barbados or Trinidad — to the United States. We might even offer to cede British Guiana and British Honduras.... It would be a blow to our pride, but when a man is near bankruptcy he sells some of his assets. Landowners and others in Great Britain are doing this. The nation is no exception; it must cut its cloth to suit its circumstances.

I thought there was virtue in the Rothermere suggestion, and, in the early part of 1920, I expressed approval of the idea that the United States liquidate a part of the British and French debt by taking over their West Indian possessions even if we had to take them at a price far in excess of their value, not only because it would benefit these debtors financially, but it would bring under our flag islands which could be used with great effect against us as military and naval bases if we should ever be at war with either or both of these powers.

Great Britain owed us, as of June 30, 1930, the total sum of $4,426,000,000; France owed us on the same date $3,865,000,-000. If they would transfer to us their West Indian possessions, together with British and French Guiana, we could afford to accept them in liquidation of a large part, perhaps as much as half, of their indebtedness. This is far more than the intrinsic value of the islands, and, to the extent that it is, we would be cancelling a large part of the debt. But I am sure that public opinion in the United States would approve this generous treatment, especially if it was provided that a just part of the excess value at which we took the islands and other territorial possessions should be applied by Great Britain and France to a reduction of their claims against Germany. Under the Young plan there is an agreement that in case of a reduction of the Allied payments on the debt to the United States, two thirds of such reduction is to be allocated to Germany and one third to her creditor nations. I do not know how this arrangement would work out in the event that payment by our debtors was made in territory instead of in gold, but the Young plan might be amended to fit these conditions. The manner of liquidation that I have suggested here would, if carried out, have the effect of reducing the war debts all around with great benefit to the general economic situation.

I am unable to judge the value of the commerce of these

islands, but I imagine that it is not great. I can conceive of no reason, other than sentiment, why either Great Britain or France should want to hold on to them unless they regard them as useful for military operations in case of war with us. If that is their reason for holding them, then the reason is all the stronger why we should want them transferred to us. Such a transfer would allay the irritation which the American people naturally feel because Great Britain and France maintain, or can maintain, military bases on these islands which are close to our shores and which would put the United States at a considerable disadvantage if hostile conditions should ever arise. Moreover, these islands are a part of the Western Hemisphere and come properly within the sphere of our influence.

In any transfer of sovereignty the rights of the people in the various islands and the commercial interests of Great Britain and France should be protected for a term of years by conditions in the treaty. This could be done by making Great Britain and France 'favored' nations as to tariff and other commercial arrangements in respect to their former colonies for the next fifteen or twenty years.

The plan just outlined would, if carried out, relieve Great Britain and France of a large proportion — perhaps as much as one half — of the annual payments they are now required to make in gold to the United States.

What about the remainder of their indebtedness?

For that the United States could afford to accept in settlement stocks and bonds in railways, steamships, telephone and telegraph companies, in manufacturing concerns and other enterprises in their respective countries or colonies, or in foreign countries, and also real estate in some of their large cities.

It is feasible to do this, not only in the case of Great Britain and France, but also in dealing with other debtor nations.

The question may be asked: How are these governments going to acquire the assets in question? The answer is: By giving their own bonds to their own citizens in exchange therefor.

During the World War Great Britain did exactly that. While I was Secretary of the Treasury we lent Great Britain more than four hundred million dollars to take up a like amount of her obligations to American banks. These obligations were secured by collateral representing British investments in various countries of the world. Great Britain had obtained them by giving her subjects British bonds in exchange. Their estimated value was between five hundred and six hundred million dollars. When we took up these British obligations the Treasury obtained this collateral as security.

By the same method, Great Britain, France, Italy, and our other foreign debtors could obtain and transfer to us a sufficient amount of securities to liquidate their obligations. There are, of course, difficulties in the way, but they should not be insurmountable. Where all parties have the will to clear up matters of this sort, a way can be found.

If a settlement of this character could be effected, the United States would then have an interest in British, French, and Italian industries. The debts would cease to be debts and would become investments. To handle them a United States holding corporation might be organized, with our government as the sole stockholder. The various governments would then be indebted to their own nationals; and that is a different thing from owing foreign debts. The interest on the debts would remain at home instead of being sent abroad.

Here an objection arises. The investments turned over to us would presumably earn interest or dividends and, under ordinary conditions, these would have to be sent to the United States, so the transfer of gold (or commodities in lieu of gold) would still continue. This could be obviated by an agreement on the part of the United States that all such dividends or earnings, or a major part of them, should be invested in the countries of our debtors for a long term, say ten or twenty years. We might receive no cash returns from these investments for that period, but their value should be constantly increasing.

Meanwhile, as favorable opportunities were presented, the United States corporation might sell its assets, or its own stock, from time to time, to the nationals of the countries in which its investments were located as well as to our own citizens. Eventually the American interest in the corporation would be liquidated. We should have our money, with interest or earnings, whatever they might be, and the entire operation would have been carried out with a minimum of disturbance to the world's finances.

I am aware of numerous objections that can be offered to this plan. It is not an ideal solution — an *ideal* solution is not possible — but it seems to me that it would be a far better arrangement than to insist on payment in gold or in commodities which might seriously depress our own industries. And whatever its defects may be, the plan is, I think, better than cancellation or repudiation or tacit agreement to allow the debts to go permanently into default. Any of these courses would mean simply an abandonment of the entire problem, without any further honorable attempt to solve it. I advance the idea with the hope that it may provoke healthful discussion.

The Allies borrowed from the United States government during the war period and the post-war period (up to November 1, 1920) $9,466,283,000 but they spent in the United states during that period $11,867,943,000; or about two billion dollars more than they borrowed. The figures covering expenditures are given on the authority of Harvey E. Fisk, who was employed by the Bankers' Trust Company, of New York, to make a thorough study of the subject; I assume that they are correct. I do not know how much profit was made by munition-makers and others, but, from a fair though generalized knowledge of what went on during the war in the way of profiteering, I should say, as a guess, that it must have been at least twenty-five per cent, or about $2,700,000,000.

But these profits did not reach all the American people. They went into the bank accounts of a comparatively small proportion of our citizens. A few thousand people made fortunes running into millions. For some of the remainder there were higher wages; for the greater number there was little benefit. For nearly everybody the higher cost of living increased the difficulty of making both ends meet.

The profits of the profiteers are safe. The makers of munitions and the dealers in war supplies have all been paid. We made loans to the Allies to square these accounts, and we raised the money by selling Liberty bonds to our citizens.

The profiteers, with their profits tucked away, will not be hurt if the war debts are cancelled or cannot be collected.

On the other hand, the Liberty bonds which furnished the money to the Allies are still outstanding. They constitute a charge against the whole people. They will have to be paid, and they will be paid, both principal and interest, regardless of what happens to the foreign loans, because the United States is and always has been jealous of its honor. Cancel these foreign debts, and the result will be that Mr. Everyman and his wife and his children, in proportion to their means, will have to pay the colossal sum that the war profiteers have already put in their pockets.

There must be no profits or profiteers in the next war — if it comes! Nobody should be allowed to make a dollar out of munitions or war supplies.

CHAPTER XXVIII
IDEAS THAT BECAME REALITIES

I

It is a curious fact that the hard and perilous trade of soldiering is, in all countries, one of the poorest paid of human occupations. The fighting man has always been expected to take the greater part of his reward in glory. That worked out well enough when armies were small and filled with harum-scarum adventurers, devoid of home ties, who went to war for the sake of excitement. Soldiers were like firemen; they were expected to keep out of sight until they were needed, and then they appeared, all of a sudden, as the heroes of the hour.

In the course of time this simple military formula became obsolete. War today means the mobilization of entire nations; men are drafted by the million. The rank and file of modern armies, in time of war, is composed of men who come from the heart of the nation's economic life. They have careers of their own, and they leave their paying jobs, their farms and their workshops, to fight their country's battles. A large proportion of them have dependents, wives and children, or aged parents, who lose their means of support when the bread-winner of the family is called.

To the President and to the entire Administration, the financial and economic condition of the soldier and of the soldier's family were matters of grave concern. Long before the World War I had had some personal experiences of my own that had brought the question vividly to my mind.

In 1898 I was eager to go into the Spanish-American War, to take part in the military campaign in Cuba. At that time I was not well established in New York and was having a hard struggle to get along. After a good deal of thought I regretfully came to the conclusion that I could not afford to leave my law practice and my family — as it would have meant disaster for the practice and poverty for the family — so I had to give up the idea of a military career.

However, there was much to be done in New York in the way of assisting the dependent families of soldiers. Most of them were left without any provision for their support. As I recall it, a private at that period was paid either fifteen or sixteen dollars a month when in active service. If the entire amount had been turned over to his dependents, it would not have gone far toward their maintenance.

An organization was formed for the purpose of giving aid to the wives and children, and other dependent relatives, of the men at the front. It was under the direction of Major John Byrne, who had served in the Union army during the Civil War and was well known in New York as a philanthropic helper of the needy and forlorn. I became associated with him in that work.

I could fill pages with stories of the destitution that we encountered among the soldiers' families. Many of them were penniless and starving.

It took some time to arouse the people of New York City, but when they learned the true condition of affairs they responded generously, yet the assistance they gave was haphazard and uncertain. It depended too much on the whims of individuals and the well-meaning efforts of sketchy, loose-jointed organizations. It was all done in a pervading atmosphere of charity. When I think of it now, I smell second-hand clothes and see mental pictures of baskets of food being carried to the doors of tenement houses by liveried footmen. Homes were invaded by prim investigating committees; application blanks were handed out; shabby women and children waited uneasily in the chilly corridors of public buildings.

It happened, incidentally, that our campaign for the relief of soldiers and sailors turned Captain Richmond Pearson Hobson, a shy naval hero, into an orator.

Everybody was talking about him at the time. He had thrilled the country by a spectacular and daring attempt to block the mouth of Santiago Harbor. Under cover of darkness Hobson and a crew of courageous volunteers took a heavily loaded steamer into the entrance of the harbor with the idea of sinking it in such a way that it would close the channel. The attempt failed; the tide was so strong that it swept the sinking ship to one side and left the channel free. If this exploit had succeeded, the Spanish fleet inside the harbor would have been bottled up without a possibility of escape.

Hobson was the hero of the hour. While everybody was talking of his adventure Hobson himself, just released from a Spanish prison, arrived in New York. It occurred to me that if we could get him to speak at a meeting in the Metropolitan Opera House his appearance would be tremendously helpful in raising money for the dependent families of soldiers and sailors. I went to see him and explained the situation.

'Why, I never made a speech in my life,' he said, and looked at me with unconcealed dismay.

'Oh, it's not difficult,' I assured him. 'Just get up and talk. Be natural.'

He shook his head. 'No, I can't do it,' he said in a faltering tone. 'I wish I could.' I saw that he was appalled by the thought of facing a large audience; a case of premature stage fright. He said something about the Metropolitan Opera House being so big, and so many people, and so on.

'Yes, but everybody knows you're a hero,' I said, and continued, jokingly, 'Do you mean to tell me that you are squeamish about facing five thousand of your friends, though you were not afraid to take a ship over torpedoes and mines, and sink it at midnight right under the enemy's guns?'

'That was different,' he replied.

It took a long time for me to persuade him to appear at all, or to say anything, but finally he agreed to sit on the stage and make a few remarks when he was called upon. 'Just a few sentences,' he said. 'That is all I can promise.'

What occurred that evening was an illustration of the fact that every man has hidden and unsuspected capacities. Hobson came, and was introduced in a stirring speech by my law partner, William McAdoo. There was thunderous applause; he stood quietly facing the audience while it continued. Then he began to speak in a hesitating manner. But as he went on he gained confidence; his voice gathered volume and resonance. He had a wonderful command of words. His speech was amazingly eloquent in its simplicity, directness, and dramatic power. Hobson turned out to be a natural orator with an instinctive capacity for emotional expression.

I do not believe he ever had stage fright again. Since that time he has been a member of Congress, has made speeches in all parts of the country, and has a fine reputation as a lecturer.

2

When it became virtually certain that the United States
would go into the World War, I thought the time was ripe for
the establishment of a plan which would put the men in the
military and naval service on a better economic footing. The
basis of the family's support, it seemed to me, should be an
allotment of a fixed proportion of the soldier's pay. As this
would not be enough, it would have to be supplemented by a
definite contribution from the government; and the government's share should depend on the circumstances — such as
the number of children in the family. The main idea was to
work out a plan which would take the problem out of the field
of charity.

A fresh consideration of the pension system was inevitable.
The existing scheme of soldiers' pensions was as unscientific as
the distribution of prizes from a Christmas tree. It had come
into being right after the Civil War, and it had grown year by
year. In 1917, there were 673,000 names on the pension rolls.
This army of pensioners included thousands of men who had
never seen a battle; and thousands whose entire service consisted of a month or two spent in a training camp, a period of
frolic and boyish escapades; for this they were on the pension
list for life. But it included, also, many thousands of gallant
veterans who had gone through four years of the Civil War,
and had been in its most memorable conflicts. In short, the
existing pension scheme was mechanical, inequitable, and unjust. Some men received too much, and others too little. Nothing could be done about the pensions that had already been
granted, for the good faith of the government was behind them;
but I thought we might make a fresh start on a better plan.

Parallel to the plan of compensation there should be, I
thought, a system of optional — not compulsory — life insurance at low rates, to be paid for by the men.

On June 23, 1917, I wrote a letter to the President in which
I said that I had in mind

a plan which I am going to discuss with you for the enlargement of
our present War Risk Insurance Bureau so as to permit insurance
on the lives of officers and men of the army and navy. This is a big
problem, but not too big for us to tackle. I shall not, at the moment,

discuss the merits of the proposition. That can, I think, be deferred until we can take the step I now propose, namely, that you permit me to call a conference of the leading life insurance companies to meet me at the Treasury department in Washington at an early date for a full discussion of the question of insurance upon the lives of the officers and men of the army and navy. If, as a result of that conference, a satisfactory plan is not devised for such insurance, then we can consider seriously enlarging the present War Risk Insurance Bureau to perform the service.

The President was deeply interested. A day or two after he received my letter, we had a talk on the subject, and he approved my idea of calling the life insurance people into consultation. Accordingly, I issued an invitation to sixty-five of the leading companies to attend a conference at the Treasury Department to be held on July 2.

In the meantime I learned that the Council of National Defence was also considering the matter. The President suggested that I get in touch with the Council so that we might agree on a single plan. The question was in the hands of the Committee on Labor of the Advisory Commission of the Council. Samuel Gompers, at that time president of the American Federation of Labor, was chairman of the committee, and Judge Julian W. Mack was closely associated with him. They gave me their whole-hearted coöperation. I asked them to attend the conference of July 2, and I sent invitations also to the Secretaries of War, Navy, Commerce and Labor.

The representatives of the insurance companies were not enthusiastic over the idea of the government going into the business of insuring the men in service, yet it was not a new departure, except as to magnitude, for we had already begun to insure the lives of the officers and seamen of American merchant vessels through the War Risk Insurance Bureau of the Treasury. Their opposition was based chiefly on the fear that the government would set up a permanent insurance bureau, which would eventually be extended to insure civilians as well as soldiers; and that it would compete actively with the life insurance companies.

There was no ground for this apprehension. The insurance that we planned was to cover soldiers and sailors only, and most of its functions — particularly that of writing new insurance — would end with the war. We intended to write

'term' insurance only; policies which had a life of only one
year, and which had to be renewed annually. The rates on
this form of policy are low. Our actuaries figured that the
peace-time rate on men between twenty-one and thirty-one
would be only eight dollars annually for a thousand-dollar
policy.

We proposed to insert a provision in the policy, however,
which would permit any insured man to convert his policy
after the war, into long term insurance.

I was convinced that government insurance, touching the
lives and welfare of millions of men, would be a great educational demonstration of the value of life insurance. I told the
insurance executives that our plan, instead of injuring their
business, would popularize the insurance idea; that it was the
most effective form of advertising that could be conceived.
They gazed at me gloomily; I could see that they did not
share my views; they feared that we were out to draw business
away from the life insurance companies; that what we proposed was the specter of government ownership in a new form.

I asked them for alternative proposals, and expected to hear
that the insurance companies were ready to take the whole
thing off our hands. To my surprise they said that the companies were not eager for the business; it was too risky, and
the total amount was too large.

I have said that the peace-time rate on term insurance averaged — for healthy young men between the ages of twenty-
one and thirty-one — eight dollars a thousand. That was the
rate for men in civil life, but these men were going to war. The
losses would probably run into large figures; and the premium
which was intended to cover the extra hazard would naturally
have to be much higher than eight dollars a thousand. Right
there I thought the resources of the government ought to come
in. As the nation had taken the men from their peace-time
occupations and put them into an extra hazardous service, it
was only fair and right for the government to assume the difference between peace rates and war rates. Gompers and Judge
Mack, as well as all the other representatives of the government, were in entire agreement with me in this conclusion.

That was the underlying basis of the insurance plan. In
working out the details as to rates, methods of payment, and

general set-up of the insurance mechanism, we had the assistance of Captain S. H. Wolfe, of the War Department; Major Henry Leonard, of the Navy; Assistant Secretary Sweet, of the Department of Commerce; and Miss Julia Lathrop, of the Department of Labor. Captain Wolfe had been an insurance actuary before he went into military service; his technical knowledge and advice were of great value. In addition we employed a number of insurance actuaries and administrative experts as special advisers.

The Military and Naval Insurance Bill was drafted by Judge Mack. In scope it was not limited strictly to the insurance feature; it covered, in fact, the entire subject of the soldier's economic relation to the government. After much discussion in Congress, the bill was passed by a unanimous vote of both houses October 6, 1917, and the act went into effect immediately.

The government paid the enlisted man — the private soldier — $33 a month in foreign service, which was the largest pay ever given to the rank and file of an army in all military history.

We insured the officers and men at the basic rate of $8 a thousand. The minimum amount of insurance that a man was allowed to take was $1000. From that the policies ran upward, in multiples of $500, to $10,000, which was the maximum amount on a single risk. The largest policy was within the means of any man in the service; the rate was low enough to permit even a private at $33 a month to take that amount. A policy for ten thousand dollars cost $6.60 a month; but the insurance was not compulsory; no man was obliged to insure himself. The policies covered total disability as well as death; that is, total and permanent disability was considered equivalent to death by the terms of the policy.

Every enlisted man who had a wife or child was obliged, under the law, to allot one half of his monthly pay for their support. The government contributed an equal amount, together with an additional monthly allowance for each child.

A wife with two children received $16.50 from the soldier husband and $34 from the government, or a total of $50.50 per month. For each additional child the government allowed $5 more per month, so that a wife with four children received $60.50 per month. All this was a new departure in the economic history of warfare. Charity was eliminated; the support of the fighting man's dependents was put within the frame of urgent necessities.

After deducting $6.60 as a monthly premium on a $10,000 policy, and his allotment of $16.50, from his pay of $33, a married man would still have left $9.90 per month as spending money. Clothes, food, and medical service were furnished to him, of course, by the government. Nine dollars and ninety cents a month was a generous amount of spending money for a soldier in France during the war. It was, in fact, several times more than the entire pay of a French soldier in the ranks.

Another section of the Act set forth the compensation which the government was to pay in case of death or disability resulting from personal injury or disease. This compensation was entirely independent of the insurance feature. It did not make any difference whether a man was insured or not; in case of injury or death, the government would pay his compensation just the same. If he carried insurance, however, the payment to his family in case of death or total disability would be increased by the amount of the insurance.

I shall not give the details of these provisions. They were comprehensive and generous; in fact, no nation had ever made such a dispensation for its fighting men. In addition to all the benefits I have described, the Act provided for hospital treatment and care of the partially and totally disabled, and also for the training, education, and rehabilitation of those who were so badly injured that they had to be taught new methods which would enable them to do something useful and, at the same time, escape the tedium of lives of inaction and idleness. The War Risk Insurance Act was, I think, one of the greatest humanitarian measures ever enacted by any government.

3

I appointed William C. Delanoy of New York, Director of the War Risk Insurance Bureau. It became, all of a sudden, one of the best patronized institutions in America. Within three weeks nineteen thousand applications for policies had been received, and the aggregate amount of insurance applied for was $161,500,000. From that time on, the volume expanded daily. There were days when more than *fifteen thousand* applications came in, and as I looked over the situation, I realized that we were in danger of being swamped by the pressure of such an overwhelming amount of routine work.

We set out to reorganize the Bureau, and to increase its personnel. It was a difficult job, one of the hardest and most perplexing that I have ever encountered. I can compare it only to the refitting of an ocean liner, the installation of new engines, and the drilling of a fresh crew, while the ship is in mid-ocean and is head-on to a hurricane.

One of our urgent troubles was lack of room. We did not have a square foot of floor space in the Treasury for the Bureau, nor did I know where any available space could be found. It was not possible to wait and hold up the operations of the Bureau while new buildings were being erected. In this emergency I thought of the National Museum, of its wide, generous floors, of its huge rooms filled with exhibits. I shall never forget the dismay of the Board of Regents when the suggestion was made that the War Risk Insurance Bureau might move into their building.

'It is impossible!' they declared. 'It simply can't be done.'

They said that if we took the building they would not know what to do with the exhibits; there was no place to put them. I suggested that they be moved to one side, but the Regents shook their heads sadly, and said that it would be a ticklish job to move the great articulated skeletons of the ichthyosauri and the huge mammals. The skeletons might be injured; might possibly fall to pieces. I realized that they were probably right about that, but I insisted that our soldiers and their families were of even greater importance than the skeletons of prehistoric lizards.

I had a talk with the President, who was the *ex-officio* head of the Board, or so-called 'Establishment' which conducts the Smithsonian Institution and the National Museum. He told the Regents that the emergency was imperative, and he hoped they would permit the Bureau to use the Museum. When they understood the extreme necessity, they assented pleasantly enough. The huge skeletons, the showcases of rare stones, the weapons and implements of primitive life, were all carried over to one side, or picked up and packed closely in a few rooms. The Bureau moved into the Museum. For a few weeks we had all the space that was needed; then the building began to fill up with card files and typewriters and we had to look elsewhere for more room. In a few months the Bureau had grown so rapidly that it occupied sixteen buildings, large and small, in various parts of Washington. Early in 1918, we began the erection of the eleven-story fireproof Arlington Building which is now occupied by the War Risk Insurance Bureau. It was not completed until 1919.

General Pershing was one of the first to take out a ten-thousand-dollar policy. 'The army in France,' he said in a cablegram to me, 'is pleased at the announcement that the Soldiers' and Sailors' Insurance Bill is now a law. By this act our government has given its soldiers a privilege which no other country has ever granted. The very low rate and other advantages of this insurance are so manifest that it is hoped that every man in the army who needs insurance for those dependent upon him will avail himself of this generous offer. I have made application for insurance myself.'

One of the most vexatious of difficulties encountered in the work of the Bureau came from many men in the service bearing the same name. There were thousands of John Smiths, William Browns, and Thomas Joneses among our four million policy-holders, and every ordinary name had many hundred duplicates. There were three miles of card files, with thirty million cards, filed under different headings according to the information they contained. They were arranged alphabetically, and according to geographical location. Now imagine what happened when the wife of John Smith, of Chicago, or of William Brown, of New York, wrote to ask about her husband's allotment or his life insurance. The immediate question was, what John Smith or William Brown was meant. That entailed correspondence — letters to and fro between Smith's or Brown's wife and the Bureau. It was a tedious job. Some of the men spelled their own names differently at different times. Others enlisted under initials which were unknown to their families; at home they were known only by nicknames. The War Department finally decided to give each man a number; but, unfortunately, this was not done until February 28, 1918, when there were two million men on the rolls. The numbering brought order out of chaos. By starting with any soldier's number, the Bureau was able to establish his identity.

Before the war was over, nearly nine tenths of the officers and men in the service carried government insurance. Up to October 31, 1918, the Bureau had received 4,090,031 applications; at that time the total number of men under arms was 4,727,928. The average policy was $8744.

The amount of insurance carried by the Bureau on October 31, 1918, was in excess of $35,000,000,000, against less than $30,000,000,000 of life insurance carried by all the insurance companies in the United States.

Did the operations of the War Risk Insurance Bureau injure the life insurance companies? That is a pertinent question, but I shall not go into an argument over it. The figures tell the story; they furnish a complete answer.

In 1908, the total life insurance in force in the United States — including all forms of policies — was $14,518,962,000. In ten years (to the close of 1918) this total had increased to $29,797,068,000. In other words, the amount of life insurance in force was doubled in the decade before the insurance of soldiers and sailors was taken up by the government.

Now let us go ten years further — to 1928. At the close of that year the total amount of life insurance in force in the United States was $95,206,314,000, or more than three times the total of 1918, and almost seven times the total in force in 1908. The War Risk Insurance Bureau was established in 1917, but did not get into full operation until 1918. The next decade — from 1918 to 1928 — witnessed an unparalleled growth in the volume of life insurance. Every company in the country broke all previous records in the writing of new business. Government advertising of the value of life insurance and the four million policies taken by the men in the service proved the greatest boost the life insurance companies had ever had in their history.

4

Another constructive development of the year 1917 was the beginning of the Federal Land Banks. The germinating idea at the root of the farm loan plan was identical with that which inspired the establishment of the Federal Reserve System.

The banks in the Federal Reserve System are permitted to discount notes based on agricultural transactions, as well as obligations having to do with the sale or purchase of livestock, provided such notes mature in six months or less. The farmer is thus given the benefit of six months' credit instead of the three months' maturities which are permitted for commercial paper.

Although this was helpful to the farmer, it did not touch the heart of his problem. A loan to the average farmer is a synonym for mortgage. He is accustomed to borrowing money on land, and to extending his acreage and developing his property through the use of money obtained through mortgages. But the rates of interest on farm mortgage loans were so exorbitant, and the money-lenders so grasping, that hundreds of farming communities lived in a state of perpetual fear and poverty.

The ordinary farm mortgage ran, usually, about three or five years, and at its expiration the farmer was frequently unable to get a renewal. He had to pay the principal of the debt or lose his land. Statistics show that he generally lost his land. The maturity of the mortgage came too soon, as a rule, and the interest rates were too high. Tens of thousands of farmers paid as much as twelve per cent for the use of money, though in some of the more favored agricultural regions — in Iowa, New York, and Ohio, for example — the rates were much lower.

What was urgently needed was a mortgage system similar to that in Germany or France, where the farmer is able to borrow on mortgage for a term running from twenty to thirty-five years at a low rate of interest. He pays the interest annually and a small part of the principal. At the end of the term — say, thirty years — the mortgage is liquidated without having been a serious, overwhelming burden at any time.

The time seemed propitious in the spring of 1916 for the consideration of a farm mortgage system. In coöperation with Senator Henry F. Hollis, of New Hampshire, I worked over the general structure, as well as the details, of a rural credits bill.

Hollis was a member of the Senate Committee on Banking and Currency and chairman of the sub-committee in charge of the Rural Credits Bill. I found him able, energetic, and enthusiastic, and a true friend of the farmer. He was considered a radical by the reactionaries in the Senate, but that means nothing. They called anybody with liberal ideas a radical. Hollis was an advanced liberal, and not a visionary.

While the Senate was considering the bill brought in by Senator Hollis, the House was discussing a similar measure which had been prepared by Representative Carter Glass and the House Committee on Banking and Currency. The differences between the two plans were smoothed out in a joint conference and the compromise bill passed both houses in July, 1916. The banks, organized under the Federal Farm Loan Act, were opened for business in the spring of 1917.

5

Twelve Federal Land Banks were established. Each bank was required to have an initial capital of $750,000, divided into shares of five dollars par value, but the amount of the stock fluctuates according to the volume of outstanding loans, or mortgages.

The Act provided for a Federal Farm Loan Bureau in the department of the Treasury. This Bureau is administered by a Federal Farm Loan Board, consisting of the Secretary of the Treasury as chairman *ex-officio*, and four members appointed by the President. One member of the Board, designated as the Farm Loan Commissioner, is the active executive head of the system.

Upon my recommendation the President nominated for these positions Herbert Quick, of West Virginia; George W. Norris, of Pennsylvania; W. S. A. Smith, of Iowa; and Charles E. Lobdell, of Kansas. These appointments were promptly confirmed by the Senate. George W. Norris was made Farm Loan Commissioner, a position analogous to that of Governor of the Federal Reserve Board.

In founding the banks the government acted in the capacity of midwife and nurse. By that I mean that the Treasury set up the plan and mechanism, started it to going, and advanced

practically all the capital at the beginning. Through the
operation of an ingenious device, which I shall describe, the
ownership of all the banks was gradually transferred to the
borrowers, so the entire stock-ownership in the Land Banks is
now in the hands of the people to whom its funds are loaned.
The system is supervised, not only in a general way, but in
thorough detail, by the Federal Farm Loan Board at Washington.

One of the first and most important questions the Board
had to decide was: Shall the rate of interest on farm mortgages (which the Board had the right to fix) be uniform
throughout the United States, or should the Board, recognizing the fact that money commanded a higher rate in some
sections of the country than in others, establish different
rates of interest in different sections of the country?

There was a difference of opinion in the Board, but all
members finally agreed to the establishment of the uniform
rate.

It was expected, when the banks were organized, that the
initial capital of $750,000 for each bank, or $9,000,000 in
all, would be taken by the public, but when the stock was
offered, the total public subscription was little more than
$100,000. The Act provided that the Treasury should take
all the unsubscribed stock at par; consequently the government purchased $8,880,315 of Land Bank stock and became
the principal stockholder in each of the twelve banks.

The local representatives of the Land Banks are known as
National Farm Loan Associations. Any ten farmers in a
community can get together and organize a local association
— provided that the aggregate amount they desire to borrow
on first mortgages is not less than $20,000.

Applications for loans are sent to the Land Bank of the
district through the local associations, but loans are not made
until an expert farm appraiser of the Land Bank looks over
the land and reports on its value, as well as into the reputation
and capacity of the applicants.

The Land Banks make loans only on first mortgages, and
for an amount not larger than sixty per cent of the value of
the land. The loans run for long periods; for ten, twenty,
thirty, or even forty, years. Interest is paid semi-annually,

each payment including a small amount toward the amortization of the principal.

For example: Suppose a farmer borrows $5,000 for thirty-three years at six per cent. He will have to pay the interest — $300 a year — in semi-annual payments of $150 each; also one per cent of the principal — or $25 — each half year. Every six months he pays $175, and in thirty-three years he has paid not only the interest, but the principal of the debt.

When loans are made, ten per cent of the amount is deducted for investment — five per cent in the stock of the Federal Land Bank of the district and five per cent in the local association to which the borrower belongs. The borrowers become, in that way, stockholders of the banks and the dividends which their stock earns are paid to them.

A National Farm Loan Association that borrows, let us say, $40,000 on behalf of its members receives $38,000 in cash and $2,000 in land bank stock. The capitalization of the bank is increased accordingly. It was provided in the Act that when the stock held by the local associations in any Land Bank equaled the initial capital of the bank — that is, $750,000 — the bank thereafter would devote one fourth of any addi tional increase in its capital stock to retiring the initial capital. That is the method by which the government gradually withdrew its original investment.

The Land Banks are owned now wholly by farmers (through their local associations), and every stockholder is a borrower. When a loan is completely liquidated, the stock that it represents is retired.

The Land Banks get the money to lend on mortgages from the sale of Federal Land Bank bonds. These bonds are obligations of the entire Federal Land Bank System, but not of the United States government. If any bank in the system should fail, the other eleven would have to redeem its bonds.

The Act also provided for the organization, with private capital, of Joint Stock Land Banks to be conducted under the direction of the Federal Farm Loan Board.

The Federal Farm Loan Act says that bonds issued by Federal Land Banks 'shall be deemed and held to be instrumentalities of the government of the United States, and as such they and the income derived therefrom shall be exempt from federal, state, municipal, and local taxation.'

While the bill was in Congress this tax-exempt provision was bitterly opposed by those interested in the lending of money on farm mortgages. After it became a law, the opposition continued, and the Farm Mortgage Bankers' Association, representing banks and bankers in the farm mortgage business, instigated a suit to test the constitutionality of the Act.

The first case that I argued in court after I returned to the bar in 1919 was this suit. I appeared for the United States as a special assistant Attorney-General; and I also represented the Joint Stock Land Banks. The constitutionality of the Act was upheld by the United States District Court of Kansas City. The Supreme Court of the United States, to which the case was appealed, sustained the decision of the lower court; thus all question of the constitutionality and validity of the Act was finally laid to rest.

The Federal Land Banks have grown enormously in volume of business and net assets since their establishment. On June 30, 1929, the amount of mortgage loans outstanding was $1,204,000,000; and the total of Land Bank bonds on the same date was $1,177,000,000. The capital stock of the twelve banks had increased to more than $65,000,000, and the reserves and undivided profits were over $17,000,000. The government's original investment in the stock of the Land Banks has been repaid in full.

Not only have these banks done a huge volume of business, but, over and beyond that, their influence in the field of agricultural credits has been highly beneficial. The activities of grasping money-lenders in the mortgage business have been reduced to a minimum. Any farmer who has good security in land need not pay a higher rate of interest on a first mortgage today than that established by these banks.

6

In 1917 and 1918, the greater part of the new funds of the American people — that is, the net income of the nation —

went into Liberty Loans and other money-raising expedients connected directly with the carrying-on of the war. Much of the fresh capital which, in ordinary times, would have been applied to the expansion of industry was absorbed by the needs of the government.

Before the war had continued six months the effects of the diversion of capital into government financing began to be felt. In many cases industries essential to the prosecution of the war could not sell their bonds or other securities, or procure funds needed for capital expenditures. This condition bore heavily on lumber and coal-mining concerns, on public utilities and other useful enterprises, and on some of the manufacturers engaged in producing war supplies. Under the incentive to greater production, many industries had expanded enormously, and they needed more capital than they could command in the securities market.

In some parts of the country the savings banks were hit rather hard by our Liberty Loan campaigns. The Second Liberty Loan bonds carried interest at four per cent, and the third and fourth loans, four and one quarter per cent. These rates were higher than those paid by the savings banks in certain sections, and as a result much money was drawn from savings and invested in Liberty bonds. Some savings banks were facing the necessity of selling a part of their assets — bonds, stocks, mortgages, and real estate — at whatever they would bring.

To meet this emergency, Congress, on my recommendation, which was approved by the committees of both houses in charge of financial affairs, created the War Finance Corporation, with a capital of $500,000,000. All the stock in the corporation was owned by the United States. The Act was approved April 5, 1918, and the corporation began business on May 20.

The War Finance Corporation was managed by a board of five directors, of which I was chairman, *ex-officio*. The other members, appointed by the President with the approval of the Senate, were W. P. G. Harding, of the Federal Reserve Board; Clifford M. Leonard, of Illinois; Eugene Meyer, Jr., of New York; and Angus W. McLean, of North Carolina.

The corporation made loans to 'essential' industries, either through banks or direct (in some cases). The purpose of the Act would have been distorted if the corporation had gone into the business of lending money indiscriminately, so an inflexible rule was made that only 'exceptional cases' of financial necessity would be considered. The applicant had to prove, first, that the assistance requested was essential to a war industry; and, second, that it could not be financed in the ordinary way.

To assist the cattle industry of the Southwest, the War Finance Corporation established agencies at Kansas City and Dallas. More than three and a half million dollars was advanced to the growers of livestock.

Another rule of the corporation was to charge whatever rate of interest was current in the industry to which the loan was made, and the rate varied from five to eight per cent. The ruling was necessary to prevent diversion of loans from the banks. In short, the War Finance Corporation did not compete with existing financial institutions, but was conducted so as to be an auxiliary to them.

One of the functions of the corporation was to protect as far as possible the market for Liberty bonds. To do this, it had authority to buy bonds and resell them. Up to November 30, 1918, the corporation had purchased $378,000,000 of bonds and had sold $272,000,000, at a gross profit of $2,851,000.

Though the loans made by the corporation were of great assistance, the corporation's 'moral' influence in the field of finance was even more beneficial. For example, the canning industry experienced immense difficulty in securing needed funds, but as soon as the War Finance Corporation came to the aid of the industry by advancing the comparatively small sum of $200,000, confidence was restored and the banks thereafter took care of the situation.

The Capital Issues Committee, which was also created by the War Finance Corporation Act, coöperated with the program of war financing by passing on all proposed new issues of securities for the purpose of deciding whether or not they were essential. The Committee consisted of C. S. Hamlin, John Skelton Williams, and F. A. Delano, all of whom were members of the Federal Reserve Board; and H. C. Flower, Frederick H. Goff, John S. Drum, and James B. Brown.

The effectiveness of the Capital Issues Committee was impaired, to some extent, by the fact that Congress failed to confer authority on the Committee to forbid issues which were not approved. They could only give an opinion, and let it go at that. Fortunately, their rulings were observed voluntarily and as a patriotic duty by most of the concerns that proposed to float new issues of stocks or bonds, though there were some rather vicious exceptions.

7

People ask me now and then how I could find time to get through the work that was piled on me during the period of the war; how I managed to be, all at the same time, Secretary of the Treasury, chief sales manager of the Liberty Loans, and administrator of the huge soldiers' and sailors' insurance plan; chairman of the Federal Reserve Board, financial negotiator with the Allied Powers, chairman of the Federal Farm Loan Board, chairman of the War Finance Corporation and Director-General of two hundred and fifty thousand miles of railroads.

I will tell you how it was done.

In the first place, it was through simplification. You may recall what I said about that in connection with the Hudson Tunnels. I said that the secret of doing a big job is to reduce it to its simplest elements. Most men who fail in positions of great responsibility allow themselves to be smothered by inessentials. They worry over details, and lie awake at night thinking of something that cannot make any difference in the final result one way or the other.

There is a key to every problem. I always endeavor to find the key, and then I shape everything else around it. The key is the core of the subject; it is the one element which means the difference between success or failure. The key to the flotation of the Liberty Loans was the creation of a financial front, or fighting line, which would be analogous to the military front. The problem was to take the question right to the heart of the nation, to make the men and women who bought bonds, or got others to buy them, feel that they were doing a service to their country which could not be measured by commercial standards. I applied the whole energy of the Treasury Department to that one point.

In the second place, there is the delegation of authority and responsibility. Its success depends largely on picking the right men. When I selected a man for an important post, I always made up my mind that I would trust him absolutely until he proved unworthy. Nevertheless, I continued to keep my eye on him. Every man has his own individual way of doing things, and you must allow for that. Two men may have the same goal in view, and, though they travel different roads to reach it, each of them may get there. There were thousands of men and women, of all types and temperament, under my direction. Frequently I came across people who were doing what they had to do in a different way from the course I should have pursued in their place, but I made it a rule to say nothing about it — to make no comment unless I saw that they were headed in the wrong direction. A small-minded, carping executive who goes about rasping and fault-finding over trifles inevitably destroys efficiency. Subordinates who have ideas in their heads shut up like clams; they lose initiative and vigor; and, if such a policy is continued, many of them become fawning, boot-licking toadies and hypocrites.

It is much better, in the long run, to risk the making of mistakes than to encourage inefficiency by giving your subordinates a daily scare. All men and women have a deep streak of loyalty in their nature. The business of an executive is to find it and develop it. *Esprit de corps* is a magnificent asset.

The way to get loyalty and service is to pick men with great care. Have all your doubts and misgivings before, and not after, you give them responsible posts. If you cannot erase your doubts, then it is unwise to take that particular man. But once the man is selected, tell him what you want clearly and frankly. Keep nothing in reserve; let him have your whole mind. Then give him enough rope to do the job.

My experience with men and affairs convinced me, long ago, that a keen and vivid interest in one's work is half the battle. A man who is not interested in what he is doing is bound to make a failure, no matter how simple the job. It may be nothing more than nailing covers on packing-boxes. If the man who does the nailing is not interested in hammers and nails and packing-boxes, and takes no pride in having everything secure and tight, he will make a mess of his work.

Loss of interest is the worst thing that can happen to a man in relation to his employment. The virus of a discontented employee, who has lost interest and does not care about anything but pay-day, has a way of spreading and growing, like typhoid germs in water. In a short time a lackadaisical employee becomes the center of an area of infection. The only thing to do is to get rid of him, and as soon as possible.

But neither interest, nor loyalty, nor energy takes the place of brains. Nothing can supersede ordinary common-sense; it is a fundamental quality. I have always tried to avoid fools, and I think I have succeeded fairly well in doing it. A fool can cause more mix-ups in two hours than a dozen men can disentangle in a month.

I was able to hold half a dozen important positions at the same time, and to administer all of them, because I had able men as my subordinates. They were loyal; they were interested in their work; they understood and trusted me, and I understood and trusted them. I had a way of simplifying the problems that came before us, and they had clear ideas of what was to be done.

I used to work fifteen or sixteen hours a day, for weeks on end, but I was seldom fatigued. The work was constructive, and I have a deeper love for constructive ideas and accomplishments than I have for any sort of game. I went to my desk every morning with the eagerness of a boy going to a ball game; I liked to feel that I was a part of the nation's life; that I was doing something fundamentally helpful.

CHAPTER XXIX
THE PLIGHT OF THE RAILROADS

I

IN ALL important respects the United States is a single economic and social organism. A citizen of Maryland who goes to California finds himself, when he gets there, further from home than an Englishman would be in Syria. But a Londoner in Damascus would always be a stranger, while a man from Baltimore would feel at home in Los Angeles or San Francisco. The people he met would look and act as do those in the East; they would wear the same pattern of clothes, speak the same language, eat the same kind of food, and listen to the same brands of phonograph and radio. He would find in the stores all the customary material equipment of daily life. Without the least trouble he could procure his favorite toothpaste and razor blades, shirts and collars. In the street he would see the twin brother of the automobile that he had left in the garage at home. At a counter in the hotel lobby he could buy his habitual cigar, not a bit different from those sold in Baltimore. He would find nothing strange about the hotel, either. The clerk behind the desk, the news-stand with its array of well-known magazines, the attendant bell-boys, the furniture from Grand Rapids, the plate glass and the gilt lettering would all seem familiar to this stranger from a distant state.

This homogeneity is one of the most striking aspects of American life. There is nowhere else in the world an area of like extent and population in which the essential texture of material existence has so little variety. Such a pronounced standardization may not be attractive from an æsthetic point of view; we would undoubtedly be more picturesque if we had a wider range of clothes, houses, and furniture. But, however that may be, there is no denying the fact that the economic results are beneficial. Standardization leads to the mass production of essential commodities, to the development of a high order of technical skill, and to the lowering of prices.

The railroads are among the chief factors in bringing this

about. They bind the vast, far-flung regions together; they give easy access to every part of the national domain. Their economic influence is enormous — incalculable in its potential force. With their help commerce spreads; local concerns grow into national enterprises; and the products of a town, sold everywhere in the United States, may become better known than the town itself.

At the same time our system of transportation has the effect of segregating industries and activities. Various sections of the country have turned to a specialization which would be impossible without the railroads. Pittsburgh is a specialist in iron and steel; Minneapolis produces flour; Danbury makes hats. Florida and California grow oranges; the Northwest grows wheat; the South grows cotton. Connecticut makes clocks and tools; the North Carolina towns specialize in cigarettes and other tobacco products, while Detroit is a huge automobile factory. The food you eat, the clothes you wear, and the furniture in your house constitute an assemblage of articles that originated in at least a hundred different places.

The parts of the United States are as dependent on one another as the heart is on the lungs or the hand on the eye. Rivers of merchandise move in all directions, flowing steadily, like blood in the human arteries. The railroads are the vital force which keep these economic life currents in circulation. If they should stand still for twenty-four hours, that day would mark the first stop toward national economic disintegration. If they should stop for a month, the result would be chaos.

Around the close of 1917 the service of many of the railroads, especially those in the North and East, was actually on the verge of collapse. A breakdown was averted by the federal government's action in assuming control of all the railroads as a war measure.

I was appointed Director-General of Railroads with an authority that was as nearly absolute as any power can be in America, and I served in that capacity until the end of 1918, when I resigned from the government.

The saving of the railroads from disaster, their operation under government control, and their rehabilitation, form one of the most dramatic and instructive chapters of war history.

2

During the years 1914 and 1915 the American railroads had a comparatively easy time. There was a pronounced slump in traffic following the outbreak of the World War and the consequent disturbance to the channels of world trade. On June 1, 1914 — two months before all Europe went forth to battle — the number of idle cars in the United States was around 240,000. Traffic fell off in volume, so that ten months later (April 1, 1915) the number of idle cars had risen to 327,000. At that time one freight car in eight was unemployed. This condition was soon to change.

The enormous orders for supplies which were given to American concerns by the Allies began to strain the capacity of the railroads in 1916. Traffic increased enormously. From a total of 277 billions of ton-miles in 1915, it leaped upward dizzily to 366 billions in 1916 — an increase of thirty-two per cent — and the railroads were not prepared, either in equipment or personnel, to handle it efficiently. A ton-mile, I may say for the information of those not familiar with the term, is the unit of measurement of railroad freight traffic. It means one ton hauled one mile. A passenger-mile, in like manner, means one passenger carried one mile.

Cars were no longer idle; the figures began to show on the other side of the statement. On March 1, 1916, there was a shortage of 19,000 cars; and by November 1, the car famine had grown to formidable proportions. On that date the shortage amounted to 115,000 cars. This means, to put it another way, that goods which would fill 115,000 freight cars were ready for shipment, but could not be shipped because the cars were not to be had. You may visualize these figures by imagining a freight train, made up solidly, and reaching clear across Central Europe — from Paris to Warsaw, across France, Belgium, Germany, and Poland.

The car shortage represented only one feature of the railroads' inadequacy. They were, unfortunately, lacking in other ways. For years they had been under-maintained in the matter of equipment, tracks, and yard facilities. There was not enough trackage in the terminal yards of many of the roads, especially in the ports on the Atlantic seaboard, with the result that the terminals became almost hopelessly confused and crowded. Miles of loaded cars stood for days and weeks, waiting for room at the wharves or alongside the unloading sheds. The car-shortage problem was aggravated accordingly.

It was an established custom of the roads to keep empty cars at the points where they had been unloaded until freight for a return trip had been accumulated. This was done to save expense, as it costs almost as much to haul an empty car as it does to haul one with a paying load. Since exports — consisting of war material and food — were much greater than imports in 1916 and 1917, the rule which kept empty cars at the point of unloading gradually led to an enormous accumulation of empties on the Atlantic seaboard. They had brought commodities destined for Europe, but the return loadings fell far short of the capacity of the empty cars. Yet, at the same time, there was an unparalleled deficiency of available cars throughout the country. One hundred and forty-five thousand cars had accumulated at Eastern terminals in February, 1917. A month later (March 31, 1917) the net car shortage was reported at 144,797. There is an obvious connection between these figures. If the congestion at the Eastern terminals had been broken up there would have been no car shortage at all.

I have referred to the under-maintenance of the roads before we entered the war, and I shall give some data on the subject further on. It is sufficient to say here that an unusually large percentage of the rolling stock was in bad repair. In some instances locomotives which should have been retired long ago to the old-age service of yard and switching duty were still in daily use on main lines. Cars which should have been in the shop were patched up hurriedly in some fashion and sent forth to lurch along as well as they could. The number of defective cars in service kept constantly increasing.

Furthermore, the actual number of cars in existence and in use had diminished through the scrapping of worn-out equipment. In 1914 the American railroads owned 2,349,734 freight cars; in 1916, instead of owning more, they owned twenty thousand less. There were at that time 2,329,475 cars in possession of the roads.

Much of the roundhouse and shop equipment was out of date. Roundhouses which had been built twenty or thirty years before to shelter the small locomotives of that time were still being used. In numerous instances the larger locomotives could not be handled or repaired in the roundhouses. They were left out-of-doors, and the overhauling was sometimes done in freezing weather. Steam pipes, injectors, air pumps, and even cylinders froze and burst during the winter.

It must be understood that these observations are necessarily general in character. Some of the roads were in better condition than others, but they were exceptions. What I have said applies to the whole American network of roads, considered as a single transportation system. It was like a chain with many weak links in it.

Just before the United States went into the war — on March 22, 1917 — Samuel Rea, president of the Pennsylvania Railroad, testifying before the Interstate Commerce Commission, said, 'the condition of the railroads today presents a menace to the country, not alone to the owners of the properties, but as affecting directly the international situation.'

He said further, at another hearing:

The evidence of the last two years has proven, I think, that many of the railroads — and I know it is true of the Pennsylvania system — are far behind in improvements, extensions, and additions to facilities should be provided years in advance of their need....

At the present time we are urgently in need of terminal facilities in New York harbor, which will cost about twenty million dollars. The terminal facilities in Philadelphia, Pittsburgh, Baltimore, and on the system west of Pittsburgh, and many other points, are inadequate....

3

In 1916 a dispute over the hours of labor between the railroad managers and their employees brought on a crisis that threatened a general strike and a consequent nation-wide tie-up of the railroads. The men, through their labor unions, insisted on an eight-hour day. The President gave a number of hearings to representatives of each side, but neither the railroads nor the unions would budge an inch from their respective positions.

Finally, to avert the national disaster which would have come from a cessation of railroad work, the President recommended to Congress the enactment of a measure now known as the Adamson Eight-Hour Law. It was passed by Congress August 29, 1916, and signed by the President a few days later.

Under the Adamson Law an eight-hour day was made obligatory on all the railroads, with provisions for payment for overtime when such overtime was necessary. The railroads contended that the act was unconstitutional and carried their opposition to it into the courts. After the case had been there for several months without a decision, the railroad labor organizations gave notice of their intention to call a strike unless the eight-hour day was established at once without waiting for a judicial ruling on its constitutionality. The railroads yielded to these demands early in the morning of March 19, 1917. Some few hours later, during the same day, the Supreme Court upheld the constitutionality of the Adamson Law.

I have given the precise chronology of the Adamson Bill and the events following its passage for the reason that, after I retired as Director-General of Railroads, a persistent effort was made to create the impression that I was responsible for the eight-hour day on the railroads.

Though it had my entire approval, which was merely the approval of a citizen looking on, I had nothing to do with the enactment of the Adamson Bill. It had been in operation for nine months before I became Director-General.

The difficulties in respect to railroad labor were greatly increased by the drafting of men for the army. A competent train man, or shop employee, or even a good track-layer, cannot be made in a week or a month. All railroad workers become efficient through experience and training. The indiscriminate drafting of men needed in the technical service of the roads, such as locomotive engineers and machinists from the shops, bore heavily on the efficiency of the transportation system. After I was appointed Director-General, I had some investigation made, and found that many of our skilled workers, drafted for military duty, were employed in training camps as cooks, or bootblacks, or in other menial occupations which could have been done just as well by any untrained youth. In endeavoring to have the drafting of technical employees of the roads stopped, or reduced to a minimum, I pointed out that a locomotive engineer, considering the current conditions of railroad transportation, certainly contributed as much by his railroad service to the winning of the war as any soldier in the trenches in France. My arguments were not very successful, though after I had made numerous protests, a little more discrimination was used by the draft boards.

4

Upon our entrance into the war the leading railroad executives of the country met (on April 11, 1917) in Washington at the request of the Council of National Defense to consider the transportation problem in its relation to the national emergency. They selected a committee of five executives, known as the Railroads' War Board. This committee sought, through voluntary action, to operate the railroads as a national unit. The railroads pledged themselves to 'coördinate their operations in a continental railway system, merging during such period [meaning the duration of the war] all their merely individual and competitive activities in the effort to produce a maximum of national transportation efficiency.' This action of the railroads was approved and encouraged by the Administration.

The Board accomplished a good deal toward an immediate improvement of the situation. Embargoes were placed on the congested areas, and Europe-bound traffic was diverted to less active ports. The Board organized a Commission on Car Service which led to the pooling of all freight-car equipment. Unnecessary passenger-train service was abolished for the purpose of saving coal. Shippers were required to utilize all available car tonnage to its full capacity instead of sending off cars with a partial load. As a result the average carload was increased nearly ten per cent. This meant, of course, that one car in ten was released for additional service.

On May 1, 1917, there was a shortage of 148,000 cars. Through the energetic action of the Railroads' War Board this was reduced to a shortage of 34,000 cars in August. Between May and October 157,000 cars were requisitioned from roads where the traffic was not abnormally heavy and turned over to the roads which had more urgent need of them.

The pressure on the roads was so great that long delays in the delivery of shipments of all kinds became ordinary and usual. To facilitate the movement of commodities essential to carrying on the war, a system of priorities, or preferential shipments, was established; and the War and Navy Departments, as well as the Shipping Board, were given authority to issue priority orders. The system was utterly lacking in coördination. Thousands of government agents throughout the country were given bundles of 'preference' tags. A tag placed on a car meant that it had the right of way, and that it was to be sent to its destination ahead of all untagged freight. The tags were used indiscriminately, and were often handed out to shippers as personal favors.

Some of the well-meant efforts to move government freight through the use of priorities were devoid of all common-sense. Consider, for instance, the forwarding of construction material to Hog Island, the site of the proposed government shipyard. Thousands of cars containing lumber, structural steel, and other building material were rushed by priority orders toward Hog Island weeks before there was a railway track on the site, or any facilities whatever for unloading. These cars stood in long lines in the Philadelphia terminals, and for miles back in the country. Instead of relieving the congestion, they added to it.

In August, 1917, Congress looked over the chaotic confusion of the priority scheme and attempted to put an end to its abuses by the passage of a priorities statute; which created the office of Director of Priority in Transportation. Judge Robert S. Lovett, of the Union Pacific Railroad, was appointed Director of Priority by the President.

The new arrangement was not much better than the one it superseded. Lovett came to the conclusion, apparently, that he did not have authority to cancel priority orders already issued, but he did not increase the difficulty by issuing any new priorities himself, except in four or five cases of extreme urgency.

Toward the close of 1917, the Pennsylvania Railroad reported that eighty-five per cent of all the freight traffic on its Pittsburgh division was moving under priority orders. This large proportion made the entire scheme ineffective and ridiculous. When practically everything carries a priority tag, preference loses its virtue. In short, the priority system was an acknowledged failure.

Yet, despite the existence of complications and incredible difficulties on every hand, much of the work of the Railroads' War Board was sound and helpful. But the Board did not and could not solve the vast underlying problem. Its achievements were, at the best, no more than palliatives or salves laid over a deep-seated wound. The impact of the continually increasing volume of traffic was too much for the vital strength of the roads. Their burden was so close to the limit of endurance that they were always on the very edge of a general breakdown in service. Such fortuitous occurrences as bad weather, storms, and ordinary accidents had prolonged and disastrous reverberations. The railroads were like a man who is carrying a load on his back that is too heavy for him. If he stumbles, he has great difficulty in getting on his feet again.

Before the Railroads' War Board had been in existence three months, all observers of perception and judgment realized that the chief difficulties of the situation were unchanged. There was only a temporary and superficial improvement, which was good as far as it went. In the first place, there was no unity of control, notwithstanding the resolution of the railroad executives to turn all the roads into a 'continental railway system' for the duration of the war. The Railroads' War Board, though created by the carriers themselves, had no actual authority. It was merely an advisory body and the carrying-out of its rulings depended wholly on the good-will of the constituent members.

Sharfman, an authority on railroad economics, says in 'The American Railroad Problem' (page 94):

The Railroads' War Board showed a marked reluctance to translate into concrete action the general professions of the resolution of April 11, 1917. The merely individual and competitive activities of the roads were accorded undue consideration. Radical changes in administration were postponed as long as possible. There was a concerted determination to discourage the assumption of authority by the government in the administration of the roads; but this determination seemed to be unaccompanied by a willingness to take such measures as would render governmental action unnecessary.

The reluctance of the executives of the roads to establish a unified or 'continental' railway system of operation in actuality instead of in theory arose from the fact that these executives were still responsible to the stockholders of their companies for earnings and dividends. The unified system, as contemplated by the Railroads' War Board, went only halfway. The Board proposed to pool operations, but not to pool earnings. Under such a plan traffic would be diverted from some roads and given to others, yet each road had to stand on its own feet financially. It was not practicable to abolish competitive tactics or to establish a unified system on such a basis.

Moreover, the unification of the railroads, even temporarily, was impossible under the law while the Anti-Trust Act and the regulations of the Interstate Commerce Commission remained in force. Under the Anti-Trust Act of 1890 they were forbidden to merge competing lines or to make rate agreements among themselves. Congress had failed to suspend these restrictions, and whatever was accomplished in the way of unified service was done with hesitation and timidity.

The financial condition of the roads was another obstacle to improvement. Fresh capital was needed — not in trickles and driblets, but by the hundreds of millions — for new and more efficient equipment, for more locomotives and more cars. Everything was wearing out, and the money for replacement could not be found. The credit of the railroads had been impaired for several years before the war, and they had experienced much difficulty in selling their securities. With the government taking every available dollar in Liberty loans, this difficulty was enhanced to the point of impossibility.

The Railroads' War Board declared, in a formal statement, that much of the confusion, delays, and inefficiency of the service was the result of a lack of equipment. The roads needed two thousand additional locomotives and one hundred and fifty thousand new freight cars. 'This,' the Board said, 'is not more than the railroads require every year, and at present prices represents a cost of approximately five hundred million dollars.'

In the matter of income and expense the railroads were caught between two jaws of a vise — between the Interstate Commerce Commission on one side and the demands of labor on the other. Wages were desperately low, far below the scale in other industries, and the railroad worker was urgently in need of better pay.

I have no doubt that the railroad companies would have raised wages, or would have been forced to raise them, if they could have increased their own revenue in proportion. But the Interstate Commerce Commission had repeatedly refused to permit an advance in rates. As late as June, 1917, the Commission denied the applications of the carriers for even a moderate advance in rates, except on coal, coke, and iron ore, and a few classifications in the Eastern territory. In the meantime the purchasing power of the railroad dollar was dwindling. Everything from coal to cross-ties had to be paid for at inflated prices.

As to labor, there were employees of the roads in 1917 whose wages were actually as low as ten cents an hour; and approximately half of the total number of those employed received seventy-five dollars a month or less. On the other hand, unskilled laborers were getting as much as five dollars a day in war industries. Nobody in the land who wanted a job was out of work. Any railroad hand with a bit of gumption could leave the railroad any day and be at work next morning somewhere else at larger pay. The labor turnover became enormous. As experienced men and skilled workers left for better wages in other industries, inexperienced men took their places.

The Railroads' War Board reported to the Senate Committee on Interstate Commerce December 22, 1917, in response to a questionnaire, that 'the railroads are finding it increasingly difficult to keep their equipment, and particularly their locomotives, in proper repair and efficient condition on account of the shortage of skilled labor.'

As a result of these various corrosive solvents, the American railroads were disintegrating as an industrial and commercial entity around the close of 1917. Their disintegration was so rapid that it was no longer a state of being, but an active movement which could be seen advancing day by day.

F. D. Underwood, president of the Erie Railroad, described concisely the condition of affairs in his statement before the Interstate Commerce Commission in November, 1917, when he said: 'It needs no gift of prophecy to foretell the financial end for railroads in the northerly and easterly sections of the United States except their net earnings are increased. There is a short word that indicates it — Smash!'

In discussing the operation of his own road Underwood said:

The Erie Railroad broke down this last winter; it failed to do its duty by the public.... It fell down because it went into the winter with power depleted to eighty per cent of its normal operation, with cars in about a like proportion, and it had no money to employ help to transform its deficient equipment into its normal condition, for the reason that its costs had mounted up beyond any precedent and beyond its ability to foresee.

A crisis was reached in November, 1917, and it became evident to all who were familiar with the situation that something radical would have to be done, and done soon, or there would be a general collapse of railroad service.

On the Eastern lines the loaded cars, standing on the tracks, numbered 180,000 above normal. The car shortage was increasing daily; on November 1, it amounted to 158,000 cars. New England was threatened with a coal famine. The harbors on the Eastern seaboard were crowded with ships that could not depart on their voyages on account of a lack of coal; on the other hand, the coal could not be brought to the ports because of the congestion on the railroads. Things were moving in a vicious circle.

The Interstate Commerce Commission made a special report to Congress on December 1, 1917, in reference to the existing conditions of transportation. The Commission called attention to the fact that the unification which had been hoped for under the supervision of the Railroads' War Board had not been accomplished, and declared that 'Unification in the operation of our railroads during the period of conflict

is indispensable to their fullest utilization for the national
defense and welfare.'

Federal control of the railroads was, in fact, inevitable.
There was no other way to handle the existing situation.
Neither the President nor anybody else in the Administration
wanted to take them over. It was done as an imperative
war measure. In this connection it is worth while to mention
the fact that the United States was the last of the nations engaged in the war to adopt this course. In England, where the
railroads are owned by private corporations as they are in the
United States, all the lines were put under control of the government on the day Great Britain declared war on Germany.
In France, too, where some of the roads are owned by the
state, the privately owned lines were placed under government
direction immediately. The railroads in Germany and Italy
were already owned and operated by the governments of those
countries.

5

In the fall of 1917 the President was more disturbed over
the condition of the railroads than he was over any other
problem of the Administration. He knew that I had a considerable knowledge of railroad transportation and he discussed the difficulties of the railroads with me on numerous
occasions. I advised him to take control of the railroads as a
war necessity. His own judgment, he said, ran in the same
direction, but he wanted to give the Railroads' War Board
every chance to show what it could accomplish before the
government interfered.

In the course of these conversations he remarked that what
disturbed him most was to find a competent man to run the
railroads if the government took them over. The selection
of the right man, he said, was a matter of grave concern. 'It
must be someone,' he went on to say, 'in whom I have implicit confidence, for in the end I am responsible. I must
select a man of experience and vision, and, above all, I want
a man of hard, practical common-sense.'

I suggested the names of several men — railroad executives
and others — who, I thought, were of the right caliber for

such a large undertaking. We talked of them, and of others whom he mentioned. Finally he said, rather suddenly:

'Mac, I wonder if you would do it.'

Before I had time to speak, he continued: 'I know you are already overburdened with the Treasury and I hesitate to suggest that you assume further responsibilities. But you have a wonderful capacity for organization, for getting the right men about you, and for doing things. That is why I would like to have you direct the railroads. I don't want to urge it; I am merely asking if you think you could undertake it?'

After a little reflection, I replied that I thought I could do the job. 'The railroad problem,' I told the President, 'involves more than the question of transportation. It is a matter of finance as well as of operation. The great shrinkage in railroad securities is a serious menace to banks, fiduciary institutions, and investors throughout the country. It is of vital importance that the financial situation shall be protected in every direction in order that the government may be able to sell the tremendous issues of war bonds which we must continue to offer, from time to time, to the public.

'I am inclined to think that it would be less of a burden for me to have direction of the railroads, and thus be able to control the financial problems involved, than to have the railroads under the direction of someone with whom it might be impossible for me to coöperate.'

'Exactly,' the President agreed. 'I had that in mind.'

'If you decide to take over the railroads and put me in charge,' I continued, 'I can at least organize the situation and get things started. If I find then that the load is too much for me to carry, we can turn the job over to someone else.'

I learned, not then but some months later, that I had been recommended for the place by a considerable number of the President's friends. Among them was Commissioner C. C. McChord, of the Interstate Commerce Commission. In a letter to the President on December 7, 1917, Commissioner McChord said:

The right man must have had administrative experience in the field of transportation and in finance. The first for obvious reasons, the latter because the question of finance is a very vital matter and is so closely interwoven with the other factors in the present situation. In fact the need of money for capital expenditures is of as much importance as the question of revenues for operating expenses, taxes and income, which is presented in the rate cases.

I suggest Secretary McAdoo as having both of these qualifications, and I believe he could see the thing through. The objection that he is already carrying a very heavy burden of responsibility at once presents itself, but he would have the assistance of Comptroller Williams, who has had large experience in railroad administration. He would also have the assistance of one or more expert advisers who can be furnished by the Commission together with its working force of inspectors.

On December 26, 1917, the President took possession of the railroads by proclamation, on behalf of the United States, under the authority given him in a provision of the Army Appropriation Act.

Federal control was an emergency war measure, and nothing else. I emphasize this point for the reason that some prejudiced or ill-informed commentators on these events have endeavored to show that federal control concealed a sinister and unrevealed design. It has been said that federal possession was intended as the first step toward government ownership of all the railways. There never was a word of truth in such assertions. The Administration assumed control of the roads with great and genuine reluctance. It was never intended by me, or by President Wilson, or by anyone else in the Administration, to use temporary control as a stepping-stone to government ownership.

In addressing Congress, January 4, 1918, the President said, in reference to the railroads:

It had become unmistakably plain that only under government administration can the entire equipment of the several systems of transportation be fully and unreservedly thrown into a common service without injurious discrimination against particular properties. Only under government administration can an absolutely unrestricted and unembarrassed common use be made of all tracks, terminals, terminal facilities and equipment of every kind. Only under that authority can new terminals be constructed and developed without regard to the requirements or limitations of particular roads.

The control was made effective at twelve o'clock, noon, December 26. In the same proclamation the President appointed me Director-General of Railroads.

As Director-General I was instructed, by the President, to operate the roads either through the executive heads and officers of the companies, or to supersede them with officials of the Railroad Administration, according to my own judgment. Although the proclamation stated that the carriers were to remain 'subject to all existing statutes and orders of the Interstate Commerce Commission,' it declared further that the Director-General 'shall have paramount authority and be obeyed as such.' In substance this definition of my authority gave me the power to change the existing rates, to raise or lower wages, and to use all facilities of the roads, regardless of ownership, in the best interest of the public.

The executive heads of the railroads did not oppose the assumption of federal control, when it finally came about, by argument or otherwise. On the contrary, their attitude was distinctly one of relief. They had been long entangled in a complicated dilemma of inadequate financing, under-maintenance, and insufficient equipment. They were, speaking frankly, at their wits' end.

The illuminating letter, which I give below, from Thomas DeWitt Cuyler, states clearly the views of the railroad executives at that time. Mr. Cuyler was one of the most influential directors of the Pennsylvania Railroad as well as the president of the National Association of Owners of Railway Securities. This letter — dated December 31, 1917, says:

My dear Mr. McAdoo: May I venture to express to you, and through you, to the President, my admiration and approval of the manner in which the President has acted in taking over the railroads for national operation. The method was of course a most difficult one to decide upon and it seems to me that no wiser plan could have been devised either in the interests of the people of the country at large or the owners of the property. A most difficult situation has been met with consummate ability. The right man in the right place has been selected to carry out the plan and I am sure that you will have the coöperation of every official and director of the properties taken over.

As chairman of the Road Committee of the Pennsylvania Railroad for many years and a director and on the Executive Committee of both the Atchison, Topeka & Santa Fé and the New York, New

Haven & Hartford, I have been filled naturally with anxiety as to just how the situation would be met. The railroad officials and directors have done their best under the existing laws to carry out the operation of the roads in a manner that would be best conducive to the interests of all concerned. That they have been unable to do so, I think you will agree with me, is largely due to the laws under which they were compelled to operate, rather than from want of ability or desire upon their part.

May I add that I wish you every success in the trying responsibilities you have assumed, and if I can be of any assistance in any way you have but to call upon me.

With warmest sentiments of regard, I am very faithfully,

(Signed)   Thomas DeWitt Cuyler

CHAPTER XXX

DIRECTOR–GENERAL OF RAILROADS

I

THE most pressing duty of the Railroad Administration was to utilize the railroads to help win the war. They had been taken under federal control as a war measure; therefore the Railroad Administration could justify its existence only on that ground, no matter what else it might accomplish. The first and most imperative problem was to relieve the congestion of traffic on the Atlantic seaboard; to get trains moving regularly and quickly to and from the ports; to keep a steady stream of men and supplies flowing to Europe.

But war or no war, the American nation had to live, and industry — with its absolute dependence on the railroads — had to go on. While we were getting the route to Europe open, it was essential, at the same time, to give service to the public. This implied not only an efficient use of existing railway equipment, but also the expansion and improvement of the entire mechanism of the railroads.

These two objectives, winning the war and public service, stood like lighthouses on my horizon; yet there were other essentials of almost equal importance. The railroads were business enterprises and it was fundamentally necessary to keep them, as nearly as possible, on a profit-making basis. I realized the extreme difficulty of doing this when the primary motive of the whole proceeding was to give service, regardless of cost. Nevertheless, I was certain that it could be done in time, but not until the roads had been rehabilitated and their facilities expanded to handle traffic efficiently. The thing that lay under my hand and control was not a continental railway system in any true sense of the term. It was a run-down, confused, chaotic mess; an entire industry that was sliding rapidly downhill. It was anæmic, undernourished, and subject to alarming attacks of heart failure.

I knew that there was an instant need of restoratives, or the patient's condition would grow even worse. Rates and wages would have to be raised; sound economies would have to be enforced; waste in money and effort would have to be eliminated; and a stronger sense of loyalty and willingness in the vast army of railroad workers would have to be cultivated.

This program fell naturally into a series of common-sense formulas. It was simple enough when stated on paper, in the limits of a few paragraphs, but its practical execution was a different matter.

All problems in which human factors are involved increase in difficulty in proportion to Numbers and Distance. It is easier, for instance, to deal with one man than it is to deal with ten; and it is easier to reach an agreement with a man while he is sitting before you than it would be if he were a thousand miles away. As head of the Railroad Administration I was in control of 240,000 miles of railroad lines, owned by hundreds of competitive corporations; and their employees — who had become employees of the Administration for the time being — numbered nearly two million. To inspire this entire mechanism of men and machines with a single purpose and a single policy was obviously one of the major difficulties of the situation — a task that was doubly hard because there was scarcely a man among them who was satisfied with his wages or salary or working conditions.

The magnitude of the railroad business was, in itself, a stupendous phenomenon. Close at hand, its bulk and shadow were overpowering. It was like standing at the foot of Niagara Falls, where the sky overhead is a chaos of roaring water. One loses a sense of perspective. I realized that I should have to put a gap of mental distance between myself and the entire problem; and that I should be hopelessly lost in a jungle of detail and expedients and makeshifts unless I could reduce the railroad panorama to its simple outlines.

As a first step toward simplification I set up, in my own mind, a conception of the transportation industry as a single commercial unit, in very much the same way as the proprietor of some local enterprise — say, a department store — looks at his own business, at its sales and expenses.

The business of the railroads consists of the selling of service to the public. The railroad companies own a machine for carrying goods and people, and their income is derived from the hire of the machine. They receive money from the public; and, on the other hand, they pay out money for labor, supplies, new equipment, taxes, and so on. The remainder is their profit.

Now, it is perfectly obvious that if one's livelihood comes from a machine of any kind, the machine must be kept in good order; otherwise it will be impossible to deliver satisfactory service; and it is equally obvious that the wages paid to the hands who operate the machine must be fair, and equivalent to the wages paid in other industries for the same class of work. If not, these wage-earners will eventually abandon the machine and earn their living in some other way.

But the owners of the machine cannot keep it in good repair, nor can they pay satisfactory wages to their employees, unless the public is charged enough for the service to cover these two objectives.

I applied this simple reasoning to the railroad situation, and above the fog of detail and controversy appeared these outstanding peaks of cardinal necessities: Rates, Wages, Equipment. 'If we can get these three things fixed right,' I said to myself, 'we shall solve at least ninety per cent of the problems confronting the railroads.'

The results of railroad operation for the calendar year 1917 had not been compiled when I was appointed Director-General, but I obtained from the Interstate Commerce Commission an accurate forecast of the figures applicable to Class I railroads.

For statistical and other purposes the American railroads are divided into three classes. Class I includes all roads that earn $1,000,000 or more per annum; Class II, all roads that earn less than $1,000,000 but more than $100,000; and Class III, those that earn less than $100,000 a year. All the large and important roads are in Class I, and the condition of Class I carriers — their income and expenses — indicates the state of the industry as a whole. The Class I roads represent 98 per cent of the total revenue of all American railroads.

I was at the head of a business concern, as appeared from the Class I figures, that had a gross income (or operating revenue), in 1917, of a little more than four billion dollars. I give here the various items of income.

Revenue:

Freight	$2,833,000,000
Passenger	827,000,000
Mail	58,000,000
Express	107,000,000
Miscellaneous	189,000,000
Total operating revenue (Class I roads) for 1917	$4,014,000,000

Now let us turn to the items of expense for the year 1917:

Expense:

Labor	$1,739,000,000
Fuel (for locomotives)	394,000,000
Material and supplies	489,000,000
Loss and damage to goods and injuries to persons	78,000,000
Depreciation and retirement (such as the scrapping of obsolete equipment)	115,000,000
Hire of equipment	36,000,000
Insurance	14,000,000
Uncollectible revenues	700,000
Taxes	214,000,000
Total operating expense (Class I roads) for 1917	$3,079,700,000

If we deduct the total expense from the gross income we have:

Income	$4,014,000,000
Expense	3,079,700,000
Remainder	$934,300,000

This remainder — $934,300,000 — represents the net return on the investment of the railroad companies — their profit. The property investment in Class I railroads at that time, as estimated by the Interstate Commerce Commission, was $17,762,152,000. The roads earned, therefore, in 1917 a net profit on capital invested of 5.26 per cent.

We learn from these figures that about seventy per cent of the revenue of the railroads came from hauling freight and about twenty percent from passengers. The railroads are primarily freight carriers.

I noted that forty-three cents of every dollar received by the railroads was paid out to labor, which was by far the largest item of expense. Ten cents of every dollar went for fuel, and a fraction more than twelve cents for 'material and supplies' — which means rails, cross-ties, replacements, and the thousand and one things that a railroad needs. Add up these major items — Labor, Fuel, Material, and Supplies — and the total is sixty-five cents.

There were, then, four factors of primary importance. In the field of income, the chief factor was revenue from hauling freight. In the category of expense, labor was of first importance, then fuel and then material and supplies. It would not be true, or sensible, to say that the remaining factors on either side of the equation were negligible. They were important, too, but not decisive. I came to the conclusion that, in considering the railroads as a business enterprise, the greater part of my attention should be concentrated on the four items that I have mentioned.

The figures that I have given here are for the year 1917, but that year was abnormal — a fact that had to be kept continually in mind and for which due allowance had to be made, or every conclusion in respect to the situation would contain destructive fallacies.

These abnormal conditions were reflected in several ways. For instance, consider earnings. In the year 1917 the railroads had the biggest business in their history — the gross earnings of Class I roads being $4,014,000,000. They had carried all the traffic they could handle, to the limit of their equipment. I reached the conclusion, therefore, that the revenue for 1917 was approximately the highest possible with the existing equipment and the existing rates. There was just one way to increase revenue; and that was to raise rates and to augment the carrying capacity of the roads by increasing efficiency and providing more and better equipment.

The rate structure of American railroads is exceedingly intricate. It is unscientific in an economic sense, the result of a long evolution in which concessions and allowances and arbitrary arrangements of one kind or another were dominant factors. Several different and conflicting principles were employed at the beginning in laying down the rate forms. The original causes for these arbitrary distinctions have disappeared, but in the meantime the essential rate structure has become incorporated into the nation's economic fabric, so that it would be difficult or impossible, at this late day, to change the underlying basis of the existing rates. All that can be done without a radical reorganization of the rate structure is to raise rates or lower them. I knew that the rates, as they were in 1917, were altogether out of line with other prices, and I contemplated raising them, but before going further in the matter I wanted to have before me some definite comparisons.

You cannot compare the freight rates of one period with those of another and reach any satisfactory state of enlightenment unless the changes have been pronounced, for the reason that so much depends on the volume of the various commodities that comprise the traffic, and also on the length of haul. The proper standard of comparison is the revenue per ton-mile.

I found that the revenue per ton-mile on all American railroads in 1913 — which was a normal year — was 71.9 cents. In 1917 it was slightly lower; the revenue per ton-mile for that year was 71.5 cents. In short, rates — as measured by their income-effect — had not increased at all since 1913. It is true that the earnings of the roads from freight were much larger in 1917 than in 1913 — about thirty per cent larger — but that was because the roads had carried more freight in 1917. They were not paid any more for a piece of work; their income was larger because the volume of traffic was greater. But in doing more work they used up their equipment more quickly.

Having established these comparisons, I went further and, with the aid of the statisticians, ascertained the relation of rates at these two periods — 1913 and 1917 — to commodity prices. It was a matter of common knowledge that the price of almost every kind of commodity, including labor, had soared upward since the beginning of the war. I was well aware of that fact, but I wanted to have it reduced to precise figures.

For that purpose we assumed that the index number of commodity prices (wholesale) and freight rates each stood at par in 1913; that is, each could be expressed by 100. The railroad dollar and the commodity dollar were at that time equal to one another. In 1917, freight rates, as shown by their results in revenue per ton-mile, remained on the same level as in 1913, while the index number of commodity prices had risen to 176. To equalize freight rates with commodity prices, I should have had to raise rates 76 per cent.

Such an unprecedented and sudden raise was out of the question, for two reasons. One was that the country could not stand for it; to certain industries it would have been disastrous.

The second was that a gigantic raise in rates would have added materially to the inflation that we were trying strenuously to avoid.

This decrease in the purchasing power of the dollar had its effect in other ways that bore directly on the welfare of the railroads. For instance, in 1913 the railroads (Class I) expended $433,000,000 in 'material and supplies' — that is, in ordinary maintenance; in 1917 their expenditure under the same heading amounted to $489,000,000, or $53,000,000 more than in 1913. But the figures were deceptive. The expenditures in 1917 were made with dollars that had decreased about forty per cent in purchasing power, so the material and supplies purchased in 1917 might have been purchased by an outlay of about $300,000,000 in 1913. Instead of having made a larger expenditure in 1917, the amount expended was much smaller than in 1913, as measured by the actual volume of material and supplies. These figures were reflected in the state of under-maintenance of the railroads. I realized that the expenditures for maintenance would have to be greatly increased if the roads were to be kept in working order.

There was a long vista of perplexing problems before me. I have mentioned a few of them; it would take pages to enumerate them all. From all parts of the country the complaints of shippers and merchants on account of undelivered freight and bad service poured in on the new Railroad Administration. As I listened to this steady roar of dissatisfaction, I realized that we had inherited a problem of gigantic proportions.

And above all loomed the question of wages, the most insistent and pressing of the thousand and one problems that demanded my attention. Men were on the verge of striking; were ready to lay down their tools and quit, despite the call of patriotism and their own sense of loyalty. They were getting ready to strike because they had long and vainly sought relief from the railroad managers and the conditions of their existence were unendurable. When it was announced that the government would take control of the roads, they remained at work, hoping that something beneficial would be speedily done for them.

3

The first thing I did after the President's proclamation had named me Director-General was to ask A. H. Smith, president of the New York Central Railroad, to come to Washington. Smith and I had been friends for some years, and I knew that he was thoroughly familiar with every phase of the railroad business. He had begun as a track hand and had filled many important positions on his way up to the presidency of the New York Central Lines. I had confidence in his judgment.

He came to Washington immediately, and in the course of a long discussion we considered plans for relieving the tremendous railroad congestion, particularly the blockade of traffic on the Pennsylvania and the Baltimore & Ohio Railroads. These two systems penetrated the largest coal and industrial districts in the United States. They were locked up as tight almost as a bank safe, and it was imperative that something be done quickly if a grave disaster was to be averted. I asked Smith if he would act as my assistant, *pro tempore*, until an organization could be effected. He consented.

'What,' I said, 'is the most exigent problem, other than the congestion of traffic, that confronts the railroads?'

'Labor,' he replied. 'Wages. That is certainly the first thing.'

'I am going to do something about wages,' I said. 'How far do you think we should go in that direction?'

'You'll have to go a long way,' Smith declared, 'to bring wages up to a normal level. Railroad labor is grossly underpaid. We're losing our skilled men daily; they are going into war industries where the pay is much higher. And the draft is taking them, too, regardless of the disastrous effect on the operation of the roads.'

'What do you think I can do about it; I mean immediately — right now?'

'You can raise wages,' Smith said. 'You have the power to do it.'

I did not like the idea of dealing casually and offhand with such a complicated question. 'It seems to me,' I said, 'that before taking definite action I ought to have a thorough investigation made of the whole subject of wages and working

McADOO AS MAN OF ALL WORK
Cartoon by Ding depicting Mr. McAdoo's varied activities in 1918

conditions. That would necessarily require some time, but when I got the facts, I would be able to act intelligently.'

'That's a good idea, but' — he said after a moment's reflection—'the men will not stand for the delay. Do you know that strikes are impending on the most important roads at this moment? The men haven't enough to live on; they can't exist.' He was impressively earnest in his manner.

'Well,' I said, 'suppose I announce that I will appoint a commission to investigate wages and working conditions and require it to report promptly and that whatever increases I make will be retroactive to January 1. That is, when the raises are made every man will receive back pay from January 1 on the increased schedule. How would that do?'

Smith said he thought it would be an ideal arrangement — that it would satisfy the men.

On January 18, 1918, I appointed a Railroad Wage Commission consisting of Franklin K. Lane, Secretary of the Interior; Charles C. McChord, of the Interstate Commerce Commission; J. Harry Covington, Chief Justice of the Supreme Court of the District of Columbia; and William R. Willcox, former Public Service Commissioner of New York. The Commission was instructed to investigate the subject of railroad wages in relation to wages in other industries and in relation to the cost of living, and to submit recommendations.

The report of the Commission, made on April 18, 1918, was the basis of my action in raising the wages of railroad employees. I shall discuss this report further on.

My immediate staff, or 'cabinet,' was composed of railroad executives of distinction and ability. Each member of the staff was put in charge, under my direction, of a clearly defined division of administrative work.

I appointed Carl R. Gray, who is now president of the Union Pacific, Director of the Division of Transportation. From the Atchison, Topeka and Santa Fe Railroad I took Edward Chambers, vice-president in charge of traffic on that system, and made him Director of the Division of Traffic. Chambers was recognized as one of the ablest traffic men in the United States. John Skelton Williams was appointed

Director of the Division of Finance and Purchases. William S. Carter, who, at the time of his appointment, was president of the Brotherhood of Locomotive Firemen and Enginemen, came into the Railroad Administration as Director of the Division of Labor. He was a man of fine intelligence and loyalty. To our deliberations he brought the point of view of labor in a calm and striking way that was extremely helpful.

As Director of the Division of Public Service and Accounting I appointed Charles A. Prouty, who was at that time a member of the Interstate Commerce Commission. John Barton Payne was made General Counsel of the Railroad Administration. He was a distinguished member of the Chicago bar and had been counsel for some of the leading railroad companies of the West.

Theodore H. Price, of New York, the highly talented editor and proprietor of 'Commerce and Finance,' served as Actuary — a title which was not very exact in definition of his duties. Much of his work had to do with public relations, and he rendered immensely valuable service in that connection. Besides myself and John Skelton Williams, he was the only man in the Railroad Administration who received no compensation for his services. I did not believe in the principle of the government employing men for nothing or for nominal pay, and I insisted that Price should receive the salary that I thought the position justified, but he resolutely declined and said that I would have to dispense with his services altogether unless he was permitted to serve the country without charge. He was so valuable to me in the work I had to do that I made an exception of his case.

To the position of Assistant Director-General I appointed Walker D. Hines, of New York. At the time of his appointment he was chairman of the board of the Atchison, Topeka and Santa Fe. Hines was, and is, a man of unusual ability. His mind is one of perfect clarity and logical precision in everything that relates to railroad economics. When I resigned at the end of 1918, he succeeded me as Director-General.

Oscar A. Price was my Private Secretary and was subsequently made assistant to the Director-General.

For some time after the beginning of federal control I met

with the railroad cabinet every day. The members of this so-called 'cabinet' had no vote at its meetings; the responsibility was mine and, necessarily, I had to make the decisions, but the experience and practical wisdom which these advisers brought to our discussions were immensely helpful.

The question of salaries was a ticklish subject, as the custom of small pay for government work is a long-established American tradition. What would Congress say if I paid these men salaries approximating as much as they had received as executive officials of the railroad companies, in view of the fact that the highest salary paid by the United States government — with the exception of the President's — was twelve thousand dollars a year? The members of my railroad cabinet had all left positions in which their salaries ranged from fifty thousand to one hundred thousand dollars. I am sure that they would have cheerfully accepted the ordinary government pay; in fact, most of them would have served for nothing — or for a nominal dollar a year — if I had asked them. But the dollar-a-year principle of government work (even during the war) was, in my opinion, thoroughly unsound. For one thing, it kept poor men of ability out of the service; and, for another thing, it wrapped the entire subject in a romantic atmosphere of unreality and make-believe. Furthermore, there were even graver defects in the system which I shall not discuss here.

The Railroad Administration, as I saw clearly, was no place for romanticists, nor for half-hearted service given with the air of conferring a favor. It was highly desirable, I thought, for everybody in the Railroad Administration to realize that it was a business institution carried on in a business-like spirit. These considerations led me to the decision that I would pay reasonably large salaries to men in important posts, though in no instance as much as they had been paid in private employment. If any discussion over the matter arose in Congress, I stood ready to give the reasons for my action, and take whatever blame there was.

I fixed the salaries of members of the 'cabinet,' or executive staff of the Administration, at twenty-five thousand dollars a year, and of the Regional Directors, who had charge of the various districts, at forty thousand or fifty thousand dollars a year, depending on the size of the territory under their supervision. I did not receive any salary myself as Director-General. My own pay continued at twelve thousand dollars a year, as Secretary of the Treasury.

The expected criticism did not develop. Congress and the country were apparently satisfied with these salary arrangements.

At the outset of federal control I retained the various railroad corporations as the agents of the Director-General for the operation of their respective properties. Federal control was to be temporary and it was incumbent upon me to preserve the integrity of the various railroad properties and organizations while I had charge of them. This was scrupulously done, notwithstanding the false statements which were repeatedly made at the time, for political effect, that the railroads were so 'scrambled' under my administration that it would be impossible to restore them to their original status upon the termination of federal control. Each property was returned in its full integrity to private ownership when government control ended and without the slightest difficulty or complication.

The country was divided into three regions, or districts, and a Regional Director — who represented the Railroad Administration — was appointed as supervisor of each region. The railroad companies operated, not in their corporate capacity, but as agents of the Railroad Administration under the general supervision of the Regional Director.

This arrangement, as it turned out, was not satisfactory. There were exasperating complications, confusions of authority, and things generally moving at cross-purposes. The system lacked directness and simplicity. The basic policies were determined at Washington and orders were directed to the various corporations to put them into effect. Frequently these orders were misinterpreted from passing through so many different minds, and this caused great dissatisfaction and annoyance. This was particularly true with respect to labor. The workingman didn't know who was the boss; he wanted the government to be his boss, but he couldn't tell whether it was or not.

Most railroad men were undoubtedly loyal to the government, but instances were brought to my attention where they were not and where they were doing as much as they could to thwart the policies of the Railroad Administration. This resulted in a kind of sabotage, carried on by some high in authority, for the purpose of discrediting government operation of the roads. There were, besides, a few natural malcontents who were instinctively opposed to any power higher than their own. Julius Kruttschnitt, chairman of the Southern Pacific Railroad, was a man of this type. I have a feeling that he consciously and deliberately set out to cause all the trouble he could, with the purpose of bringing discredit on the Railroad Administration. On the other hand, William Sproule, president, and other high officials of the Southern Pacific, gave me fine support.

The monthly earnings of the roads began to show a distressing downward droop. For the first five months of 1917, while the companies were operating the properties, the net operating income was $346,439,522.

Keep those figures in mind and compare them with the first five months of 1918. The companies, during the latter period, were still operating the railroads — but under government control, and as agents of the Railroad Administration. The wages paid to employees and the rates for service were practically the same in both periods. (To be perfectly accurate, I should say that both rates and wages were a little higher in the first five months in 1918 — the raise in one offsetting the raise in the other.) During both periods the roads had all the traffic they could carry.

But for the first five months of 1918 the earnings of the carriers dropped to $215,278,241. The same management, the same relative wages and rates, and full-capacity business in both cases; yet the earnings fell off $131,000,000 in the 1918 period, despite all the aid and assistance given by the government. I came to the conclusion that the sooner I took the railroads completely out of the companies' hands, the better it would be all around. Therefore, I decided to dismiss the corporations as the agents of the Director-General and to appoint federal managers, selecting in each instance a responsible officer of the corporation for that purpose, and to have these federal managers report direct to the Regional Directors.

In carrying out this revised plan, which went into effect about June 1, 1918, I divided the country into seven 'regions' instead of three, and appointed a Regional Director for each region.

The Regional Directors were:

Eastern Region: A. H. Smith, formerly president of the New York Central. Headquarters at New York.

Allegheny Region: C. H. Markham, formerly president of the Illinois Central. Headquarters at Philadelphia.

Pocahontas Region: N. D. Maher, formerly president of the Norfolk and Western. Headquarters at Roanoke, Virginia.

Southern Region: B. L. Winchell, formerly Director of Traffic of the Union Pacific System. Headquarters at Atlanta, Georgia.

Northwestern Region: R. H. Aishton, formerly president of the Chicago and Northwestern. Headquarters at Chicago.

Central Western Region: Hale Holden, formerly president of the Chicago, Burlington and Quincy. Headquarters at Chicago. Until his appointment as Regional Director, Mr. Holden had been a member of the Railroad Administration's central staff.

Southwestern Region: B. F. Bush, formerly president of the Missouri Pacific. Headquarters at St. Louis, Missouri.

Referring to these appointments Sharfman says ('The American Railroad Problem,' page 108):

The easy transition from private operation to federal control was due, in no small measure, to the great personal capacity of the first Director-General, and to his willingness to choose able subordinates, as manifested throughout his incumbency of the chief executive post in the Railroad Administration.

The Regional Directors represented the best railroad talent in the United States.

The appointment of A. H. Smith, of the New York Central, as Regional Director of the Eastern Region, was deeply resented by the Pennsylvania Railroad. There was an intense rivalry between these two great systems, but I had to appoint somebody, and Smith was selected by me on account of his recognized ability and experience.

I knew how deep the rivalry of the Pennsylvania and the New York Central was, but I had no idea that any official of the Pennsylvania would be offended by Smith's appointment. In view of the fact that the country was at war, I thought such jealousies would be buried for the time being. Anyway, it would not have made any difference to me or to the Railroad Administration. There had to be a Regional Director — and Smith was my choice.

Not long since, in talking with a friend of mine, he said that one of the Pennsylvania officials complained bitterly to him only recently of my action in putting Smith, of the New York Central, 'over their property during the war.' Smith had diverted their traffic, this Pennsylvania official said, and had disorganized their business.

'The business of the Pennsylvania was already disorganized — in fact, demoralized — when Smith became Regional Director,' I said. 'We took the railroads over during the war for the purpose of doing exactly what Smith did, diverting traffic and reorganizing their disorganized business.'

'For diverting their traffic?' my friend asked.

'For operating them as a unified system to meet the national crisis. It was necessary to move the traffic without regard to the business of any one company or system, and, moreover, why should the government have paid the railroads as rental an average of the best three years of earnings in their history unless it could use all their facilities in common to help win the war?'

'Some of the Pennsylvania Railroad people think their road was discriminated against.'

'They're mistaken,' I said. 'There was no discrimination against any railroad. We moved the traffic by the shortest or most available routes, and consequently some of the Pennsylvania's traffic went to other roads; but, on the other hand, some traffic that had been carried by other roads went to the Pennsylvania. If that is what they mean by disorganization, then they were disorganized.'

I learned, soon after I took control of the railroads, that the Pennsylvania was in a worse condition than any other railroad in the United States. The congestion on the Pennsylvania lines, combined with an inadequate and run-down equipment and general inefficiency in operation, had just about brought freight traffic on that railroad to a standstill. Samuel Rea, its president, had said to the Interstate Commerce Commission, on March 22, 1917, that 'the Pennsylvania system... was far behind in improvements, extensions and additions to facilities' — a statement that we learned was unfortunately too true. Under Smith's direction, and with the coöperation of the other railroads under federal control, the wheels on the Pennsylvania began to turn again.

The Railroad Administration spent far more money on the Pennsylvania in the matter of new equipment, additions, and improvements than on any other railroad system in the country. During the period of federal control the total amount expended on all railroads for additions and betterments — not including new cars and locomotives — was $774,184,000. Of this amount $160,382,000, or more than one fifth of the whole, was expended on the Pennsylvania.

At the conclusion of federal control the government's bill against the Pennsylvania Railroad for expenditures, covering the items stated above, together with charges for *overmaintenance* and other things, was $187,117,000. The railroad contested the government's claim for full reimbursement. It presented a long array of counter-claims and offered to pay $53,814,000, or less than one third of the government's expenditures. In the end the Pennsylvania did pay the government $90,000,000 as a settlement in full. This was done after I resigned as Director-General. I had nothing to do with it, and am quoting the figures from the official records.

Considering these facts, I must say that it is difficult for me to see how and where the Pennsylvania Railroad was injured by the Railroad Administration. If the business of the road was 'disorganized,' I venture to assert that it was the most profitable disorganization in the history of railroading. Instead of being gloomy about it, the officials of the road ought to be pleased; the advent of the Railroad Administration was the happiest occurrence of the Pennsylvania's corporate life.

The principle of sending all freight by the shortest route was vigorously applied by the Railroad Administration. We found that goods were often carried hundreds of miles out of the way, by roundabout courses, in order to keep the business for a single railroad. This was a common practice, carried on every day and almost everywhere. In one instance that came to my attention it had been the custom to haul coal cars one hundred and seventy miles to a destination which was only thirteen miles from the point where the shipment originated. That miracle of inefficiency served its purpose of getting the revenue for one road even if that road did haul the coal at a loss. We stopped all that.

There was a large aggregate saving of labor, coal, and the wear and tear of equipment — as well as a saving in time — by the re-routing of traffic. In the Central Western region alone the Railroad Administration saved 12,065,849 car-miles by short routes. This saving was equivalent to the distance traveled by one hundred freight trains, each consisting of fifty cars, moving 2413 miles.

3

The relation of the government to the railroads was similar to that of a tenant who rents a furnished house. The occupant agrees to take care of the house and its furniture, to pay a stipulated rental, and to return the property to its owner in as good condition as it was when he took possession.

The amount of rental, or compensation, for the use of the roads and their equipment was a matter of argument, which was settled on March 21, 1918, by an Act of Congress known as 'The Federal Control Act.' It was provided that each carrier should be guaranteed a compensation equal to its average annual railway operating income for the three years ending June 30, 1917. These three years — called 'the test period' — furnished an excellent basis for an average, as in the matter of earnings 1915 was a poor year, 1916 was a better one, and 1917 was the best year that the railroads had ever had in their history.

The average net operating income for the three-year test period was approximately $906,000,000, including the income of railroads of all classes. This amount was guaranteed to the carriers; it was to be paid to the companies annually during the term of federal control, regardless of whether the government lost money or made a profit from railroad operation. The companies were treated generously under this arrangement. After paying interest on their funded debt, they would have enough left to pay eight and a half per cent annually on their capital stock. By virtue of the guarantee, every share of railroad stock became as good as an eight and a half per cent government bond. It was also provided in the Federal Control Act that the property was to be kept in working order and returned to the railroad companies not later than twenty-one months after the end of the war in as good repair and with as good equipment as when taken over.

Under another section of the act a Revolving Fund of $500,-000,000 was appropriated as a working capital for the Railroad Administration. This fund was used in providing new equipment for the railroads and in meeting the maturing obligations of the companies in cases where their own funds were not sufficient.

It should be kept in mind that during the term of federal control the railroad companies were entirely outside the sphere of railroad operation. They existed only as corporate entities, as actual owners of the roads. The Railroad Administration paid them the annual guarantee, or compensation, and out of this the companies took care of their own bonded indebtedness. When they were not able to do so, the Railroad Administration lent them money for that purpose. Permanent improvements, such as new equipment, new buildings and extensions of lines — anything that would be ordinarily classed as a capital expenditure — was charged against the railroad companies. Ordinary maintenance was charged against current earnings and assumed by the Railroad Administration.

I ordered, from the builders, 1930 new locomotives and 100,000 new freight cars, at a total cost of $380,000,000. This ate a large hole in the Revolving Fund, but the new equipment was charged to the railroad companies. Some of them paid for it, eventually, in cash; others gave their notes in payment. Some of the companies contested payment on the ground that they did not need the equipment; that it was unnecessary. As a matter of fact, the necessity for it was not only obvious but overwhelming. My impression is that all of the companies paid the government for this rolling stock in the end, though some paid with much grumbling.

CHAPTER XXXI

RAISING WAGES ON THE RAILROADS

I

Upon assuming control of the roads, the Railroad Administration began immediately to expedite traffic. Every possible means that fell within the limits of efficiency was used to keep the trains moving and to avoid congestion.

A 'permit' system was established to control the movements of essential commodities. No freight was accepted without a permit, and before the requisite permission was granted the shipper had to give a satisfactory reason for moving his goods. A careful watch was kept on the handling of the permits, as the system might easily have become the source of discrimination. It worked well, however, and was a potent factor in relieving the stress of traffic. The chief purpose was to serve essential industries promptly. In cases where delay was inevitable, the weight of it was put as much as possible on inessentials.

A Car Service Section was created to control the permit system, the movement of cars generally, and their allocation to various railroad lines. Empty cars were not kept waiting on the Atlantic seaboard for return loads, but were sent back at once. More than 850,000 empties were moved, in the year 1918, from congested districts to the points of origin of essential traffic. The hauling of these empty cars added considerably to the expense of the Railroad Administration, but it was in the line of service and, in fact, an absolute necessity.

We found that there was a large expenditure of useless effort in the cross-hauling of coal; that is, the shipping of coal from one producing region into territory that could be supplied more economically from another coal region. For instance, coal from Eastern mines was hauled a thousand miles and sold in places that were within a hundred miles of Western mines in full production — and Western coal was sold and consumed to a considerable extent in the East. These conditions had grown up through the competition of coal producers.

The Railroad Administration declined to do long and unnecessary hauling of coal. As a consequence of this coal-zoning system the saving in car service was large.

To avoid the shipping of goods in less than carload lots, we devised a system of so-called 'sailing days.' Package freight was held at certain points until specified days of departure, so as to provide full carloads. The beneficial results of these measures began to appear in a few weeks. The average carload in April, 1918, was 29.4 tons against 25.7 tons in April, 1917.

The transportation of troops was, of course, a primary duty of the Railroad Administration, and it took precedence over all other passenger traffic. From the date of my appointment as Director-General to the time of the Armistice — a little more than ten months — the railroads under federal control carried 6,496,000 men, or an average of 625,000 a month. We operated more than nine thousand special troop trains.

For the purpose of expediting overseas shipments, I appointed, by agreement with the Secretary of War and the Secretary of the Navy, an Exports Control Committee. This committee was put in charge of exports of every kind. Instead of sending goods to Europe through only a few ports — such as New York, Boston, and Philadelphia — traffic was diverted to other harbors on the Atlantic and Gulf. The work of the committee was extremely helpful in solving the problem of congestion and senseless overcrowding of yards and terminals.

As a measure of economy, as well as of convenience, I had the ticket-offices of the various roads consolidated in the cities where such offices were maintained apart from the terminal stations. One staff of clerks sold tickets for all the roads, and only one rental was paid for the offices.

Terminal stations were unified and were used by all lines irrespective of ownership. There was also a joint use of repair shops and railroad yards. When a locomotive broke down it was sent to the nearest shop, even if that shop belonged to another road.

Competition in all its aspects was eliminated. Advertising is one form of competition, so the advertising of features and special services — and, in fact, advertising of all kinds — was stopped. In competing with each other the roads were operating many unnecessary passenger trains. I abolished many of them. Altogether one sixth of the total passenger-train miles was eliminated.

These various economies amounted to a considerable saving. Walker D. Hines says, in his 'War History of American Railroads,' that $110,000,000 of annual expense was obviated, as follows:

Elimination of passenger-train service.	$60,000,000
Unification of terminals and consolidation of ticket-offices.	35,000,000
Saving in advertising.	5,000,000
Miscellaneous.	10,000,000

The number of dining-cars was reduced, but just as many people were fed. That was accomplished by abolishing the *à la carte* service and furnishing only *table d'hôte* meals. Of course, this was a war measure, its purpose being to reduce waste of food and to increase the usefulness of each dining-car, of which there was a great scarcity, in order that our troops, as well as the public, might have the benefit of these facilities. It was not a popular measure to interfere with people's appetites, and there was much grumbling about it, but it had to be done.

2

In 1917, after the United States went into the war, Herbert Hoover was appointed Food Administrator. He had just returned from his task of distributing food to the people of Belgium. One of his duties was to direct the sending of food supplies abroad — not only for the Allied armies, but to feed the civilian population.

Hoover promised deliveries of 1,100,000 tons of foodstuffs a month, but owing to the breakdown of railroad service under the Railroads' War Board the actual deliveries ran far behind this program. There was a shortage in December, 1917, when I became Director-General, of about 500,000 tons; and in January this was increased by another shortage of 400,000 tons. The food situation in the Allied countries of Europe became extremely critical. The United States government was informed confidentially by the prime ministers of Great

Britain, France, and Italy that unless the program of food deliveries was maintained the Allies would not be able to continue the war. The rations of the French army had been reduced once, and those of the Italian army twice. In England there was only a two weeks' supply of food of all kinds. That shows how near starvation the English were, and by what a close margin the war was won.

This information was kept from the public for fear of its effect on the morale of the nations opposed to Germany and her associates. It was conveyed to me, however, though its substance was old news. I understood the situation even before I became Director-General, and for the month of January the energy of the Railroad Administration was concentrated on keeping the lines from the West to the Atlantic seaboard clear, in order to facilitate shipments of food. In a few weeks things were in better shape.

About the time conditions began to improve, through the work of the Railroad Administration, Hoover gave an astonishing interview to the New York 'Times,' which was published February 22, 1918.

His statement appeared in the 'Times' under this heading:

SIXTY DAY CRISIS IN FOOD FACES US
ASSERTS HOOVER

Rail Congestion Has Brought a Serious
Situation for America and Her Allies

Cereals and Livestock Are Tied Up
and Serious Losses Are Threatened
He States

At Odds With McAdoo

Some Relief Measures Refused
It Is Said

Wilson Likely To Take Drastic Action

Hoover declared, in this interview, that the shortage was extremely serious. 'It is true,' he said, 'that since December 1st we have fallen far behind our agreed food program with the Allies.' This was a fact that everybody in authority already

realized. Its publication could have no possible effect on the
situation except to give encouragement to our enemies. He
declared further, with faint praise for the Railroad Administration:

This deficiency is due solely to the railway congestion since that
date. The Railway Directorate since coming into control on January 1st has made an effort to find a remedy, but during the month
of January the weather was insuperable, and although progress
has been made since February 5th the situation is the accumulation
of three months' delays.

Then he goes on to present some statistics, such as 'one
hundred and thirty thousand carloads of potatoes' which
were ready for transportation on November 1, and since that
time only twenty-eight thousand carloads have been moved.
He said, further, that 'There is a great deal of livestock which
has been ready for the market for some time, but is still held
in the farmers' hands through inability to secure transportation.'

He said, a little further on in his statement, that the failure
to transport foodstuffs in the requisite quantities to the seaboard 'has not been due so much to the actual inability of the
railways' giving priority to foodstuffs for Allied shipping as it
has been to bringing products from the farms to the terminal
markets where it can be aggregated, prepared and purchased
by the Allies.'

Notwithstanding the revelation of the true state of affairs,
as given in the last paragraph, the net import of his interview
was that the railroads and the Railroad Administration were
hopelessly swamped, and that not only were the Allies in the
utmost peril for lack of food, but that a desperate domestic
food shortage was on the near horizon and would soon be
among us.

At that time the Railroad Administration had the matter
well in hand, and the problem was being solved rapidly, day
by day. Hoover must have known of this, as he had every
opportunity to be well informed. One of the best traffic men
in the country had been detailed by me to give his whole time
to the Food Administration, and he was a member of Hoover's
office force.

The country was greatly alarmed by the dire prophecies

of the Food Administrator. No doubt his statement was promptly communicated to Germany through the secret news service of our enemies, and that it gave comfort to their waning hopes. One of the interesting features of the case was that Hoover had made no complaint to me personally, or to the Railroad Administration.

Immediately after reading the 'Times,' I wrote Hoover the following:

You are, as I understand it, the sole purchaser in this country of food supplies for the allied governments. You must, therefore, know the location of the food supplies which you from time to time purchase and the ports in this country to which you desire such supplies shipped.

If you will notify me from time to time of the location of the specific supplies and the port or ports in the United States to which you wish to have such supplies transported, I will guarantee the necessary transportation subject alone to interruptions from blizzards and floods.

His reply to this letter was not particularly informative. Here it is; date, February 23, 1918:

My dear Mr. McAdoo: I am grateful for your note of the 22nd, and I wish to express the great relief of myself and my colleagues at your assurance that not only will the allied foodstuffs be promptly moved, but that there will be no delays in our domestic distribution causing any danger of suffering, which necessarily implies the collection of our food materials from the country to our terminals, mills, and packing houses before either the domestic or allied supplies can be aggregated for transportation to points of consumption or export.

I am certain that this assurance from you will greatly quiet the growing apprehension in the country of the last few weeks. Faithfully yours.

(Signed)   Herbert Hoover

You will observe that Hoover's letter did not answer any question that I had asked. What I wanted to know was the location of the food supplies. His colorless letter contributed nothing to the problem in hand.

I replied that he had not answered my questions and I, therefore, repeated them. If he would give me the information called for, I said, 'the transportation will be provided.' Hoover did not answer this letter, but his legal adviser, Mr. Glasgow, of Philadelphia, called me on the telephone and asked for an interview for Hoover and himself.

They came to my office. Glasgow did all the talking. Hoover sat with downcast eyes, like a diffident schoolboy. Beyond the greeting as he came in, and his good-bye when he left, I do not recall that he had anything to say. Glasgow told me, on Hoover's behalf, that the Food Administration wanted to coöperate with me in every possible way; that Mr. Hoover regretted his statement that had appeared in the 'Times'; that the publication was a mistake and he hoped it would not interfere with our cordial relations.

I said that I had been giving the Food Administration a preference all along in transportation and that I would continue to do all I could to help, but that I thought Mr. Hoover should make his complaints to me and not to the public through the newspapers. Mr. Glasgow said, while Mr. Hoover made a minute examination of the floor, that Mr. Hoover would do that in the future. Mr. Glasgow finished his say, Mr. Hoover completed his inspection of the floor, and they took their departure.

The work of clearing up the overseas food shortage was continued by the Railroad Administration with unabated vigor. By March 15 the vessel capacity of the Allies had been satisfied and there was available at North Atlantic ports an excess on wheels of 6318 carloads of foodstuffs exclusive of grain on cars and in elevators.

The traffic on American railroads reached, in 1918, an unprecedented total of 403 billion ton-miles; it was the heaviest traffic year in the history of railroading up to that time. The ton-mileage was thirty-three per cent greater than for any year previous to the war.

The operating efficiency of the Railroad Administration is proved by the fact that there was a steady improvement in results throughout the entire year.

We broke up the congestion on the railroads. We reduced the car shortage from 148,000 in November, 1917, to an actual surplus of cars by October, 1918.

The threatened coal famine of 1917 was definitely averted. We increased the number of coal cars from the mines and delivered coal wherever it was needed, and in sufficient quantity, anywhere in the country.

Sharfman remarks ('The American Railroad Problem,' page 139) that the record of federal control was 'a decidedly creditable one.' He says, further, 'The conclusion seems warranted that the Railroad Administration succeeded in moving all essential traffic with reasonable efficiency and expedition, and that the restrictions upon general transportation were reduced to a minimum, in view of the imperative character of the war demands.'

3

The Railroad Wage Commission that I appointed on January 18, 1918, made its report on the following April 30 in the form of a remarkably thorough and informative study of wages and economic conditions.

The Commission found that the increase in living expenses of industrial workers generally, including railroad employees, had been about forty per cent in the two years between December, 1915, and December, 1917. As an indication of the extensive basis of fact from which their conclusion was drawn, the Commission stated that the figures showing the relative prices of food, clothing, and rentals were gathered in forty-two cities. The United States Department of Labor, coöperating with the Wage Commission, obtained the budgets of more than eleven thousand workingmen's families. They were checked up and compared by statistics from independent sources.

The cost of living had advanced approximately forty per cent — which meant that a dollar was required to buy, in 1918, the amount of food, clothing, and other necessities of living that could have been bought by the expenditure of seventy-one cents in 1915.

The Commission said:

It has been a somewhat popular impression that railroad employees were among the most highly paid workers. But figures gathered from the railroads disposed of this belief. Fifty-one per cent of all employees during December, 1917, received $75.00 per month or less. And eighty per cent received $100.00 per month or less.... Between the grades receiving $150.00 to $200.00 per month there is included less than three per cent of all the employees (excluding officials), and these aggregate less than sixty thousand men out of a grand total of two million.

Another section of the report gave, for purposes of comparison, the railroad wage scale in 1915 in columns parallel to the wage scale at the end of 1917, when the Railroad Administration took control. The railroads themselves, before the government came in, had raised wages in 1916 and again in 1917. These raises were generally small in amount and quite unequal in their distribution over the whole body of employees. They had been made without system, and were, as a rule, the result of pressure from the labor unions.

The Commission decided to take the year 1915 — that is, the wage scale of that year — as a basis for the contemplated advances. The amount of the raise for each type of wage-earner was indicated by a percentage of the 1915 wage scale. The lowest paid workers received the highest percentage of raise, the theory being that those who received the smallest wages were more affected by the increased cost of living than those near the top of the scale. This theory, in my judgment, was sound.

All employees whose pay was under $46 a month received a flat increase of $20 a month. From there on, up to wages or salaries of $250 a month, the increases were in gradually diminishing percentages. Those who had been paid from $46.01 to $50 a month in 1915 got a raise of 43 per cent. In other words, a man whose wages in 1915 were $50 a month received a raise of $21.50.

As I have said, the percentages of increase diminished in the upper reaches of the scale. Employees who received $150 a month got an increase of 16.17 per cent; those at $200 a month got an increase of 8.375 per cent; and those at $250 got no increase. Here are some of the actual increases in dollars:

	1915	1918
Crossing flagmen, per month	$ 39.50	$ 59.50
Section men, per month	37.68	57.68
Freight conductors, per month	131.59	158.95
Passenger train engineers per month	178.46	198.90
Electricians, per month	78.44	111.39
Yardmasters, per month	131.09	158.95
Passenger train brakemen, per month	85.23	119.85
Engine-house men, per month	56.58	80.37
Firemen on freight trains, per month	94.10	127.50
Section foremen, per month	64.30	91.65
General foremen, per month	127.77	155.55

In General Order No. 27, issued May 25, 1918, I directed that the new wage scale be put into effect immediately. It was retroactive to January 1, 1918. All employees who had been with the roads before the adoption of the new scale received back pay.

'When women are employed,' I announced in Article V of this General Order, 'their working conditions must be healthful and fitted to their needs. The laws enacted for the government of their employment must be observed, and their pay, when they do the same class of work as men, shall be the same as that of men.'

In Article VI, I abolished the immemorial discrimination in the matter of wages against colored firemen, trainmen, and switchmen and put them on the same wage basis as white men employed in the same capacities.

The weight of the wage increases was reflected, necessarily, in an increase in operating expenses, as shown by the comparative figures given here:

Cost of labor in 1918............................$2,614,000,000
Cost of labor in 1917............................ 1,739,000,000

Increase in 1918 over 1917......................$ 875,000,000

4

I have never done anything in my life that gave me so much satisfaction as raising the pay of the railroad employees. To have been the means of providing a decent living wage for two million men and women makes me feel happier than to have been President of the United States.

Yet there is nothing I ever did, in my entire public career, that brought down so much criticism on my head. Not then; not when it happened. At that time everybody was for it. I do not recall even one objection to the raising of wages when it occurred. Every railroad executive with whom I discussed the matter thought the subject should receive my immediate and most urgent attention.

After the war, however, there was a different tone. Some commentators declared that I had spoiled the whole body of railroad employees by giving them more pay all around. Other invidious critics said and wrote that I had a political purpose in mind; in other words, I had shrewdly schemed to raise wages so the railroad men would help elect me President of the United States. Professor Charles Seymour, in his 'Woodrow Wilson and the World War,' says that I made 'concessions to labor' and implies that my so-called concessions put labor on a high horse, with a consequent result of general demoralization.

For the benefit of Professor Seymour and of others like him, I say here that when I became Director-General the subject of raising wages had passed completely out of the sphere of argument, and had become a long-standing national disgrace. It was not a matter of concessions. The real question was whether the roads could be operated at all on starvation wages. I solved it by giving the men and women of the railroads at least enough to live on.

CHAPTER XXXII
I LEAVE THE PUBLIC SERVICE

I

To MEET the higher cost of operation which was brought about as a result of the general raise in railroad wages, it was necessary to raise freight rates and passenger fares. As I have already pointed out in a preceding chapter, the price of transportation was far under the level of commodity prices in 1918. I realized that a seventy-six per cent raise in rates — which would have brought the price of freight transportation up to the general level of commodity prices — would be unwise, as it would have caused an almost catastrophic disturbance to commerce and industry; and would have given new impetus, besides, to the wave of inflation which was advancing the price of necessities.

After many conferences with my railroad cabinet, I decided to make an advance in rates which would be just sufficient, as nearly as we could calculate, to cover the increased cost of operation on account of the advance in wages. For several months I had the rate experts of the Railroad Administration working on the new schedules. I approved their recommendations and the raise in rates was announced in General Order No. 28, issued May 25, 1918, simultaneously with the announcement of the raise in wages.

The increase in freight rates amounted to about twenty-eight per cent; at the same time passenger fares were raised eighteen per cent, approximately, and an extra charge was made for Pullman fares.

The raise in rates went into effect on June 25, 1918. Any attempt to have made this increase in rates retroactive, parallel with the retroactive increase in wages, would have been impossible though I would have made the increase retroactive if there had been any practical method of doing it.

The Railroad Administration paid the higher wages, therefore, for the full year 1918, while the higher rates were received for only a little more than half a year. The result is shown in these comparative figures for 1917 and 1918:

	1917	1918	Per cent of increase
Revenue from freight and passenger transportation....................	$3,660,000	$4,487,000	22.3
Cost of labor......................	1,739,000	2,614,000	51.4

Actual increase in revenue.................$827,000,000
Actual increase in cost of labor............. 875,000,000

Walker D. Hines, who succeeded me as Director-General, has calculated that if the higher rates had been effective from January 1, 1918, the additional net operating income of the Railroad Administration for the year would have been approximately $412,000,000. These figures, which were made with great care and from abundant sources of information, may be accepted as authoritative.

2

The railroads were the largest consumers of coal in the United States; they bought about one third of the total quantity produced. The requirements of the roads were regular; month after month a railroad would take a certain percentage of the output of any mining company with which it had a contract. The mine operators were enabled, therefore, to calculate for a long time ahead and adjust their production and labor supply accordingly. In view of these facts the mining companies had been willing to accept contracts from the railroads at prices considerably below those paid by the public. It was a fair arrangement all around; the regular demand from the railroads stabilized coal production, and consequently the mine-owners made concessions in price to the railroads.

In the spring of 1918, H. A. Garfield, who was then head of the Fuel Administration, abolished the special price contracts and announced that the Railroad Administration would have to pay, in the future, the same price for coal that was paid by the public. The reasons for this decision, as given by Garfield, did not seem to me to be logical or sound at the time, nor has their obscurity been illumined by the passage of years.

There was considerable controversy over the matter, but in the end the Railroad Administration had to pay the same price as everybody else. While the dispute over the price of coal was in progress, I sent — in my capacity as Secretary of the Treasury — to the Internal Revenue Bureau for the tax returns of the coal companies for the year 1917. It had been asserted that the mine-owners could hardly make both ends meet, owing to the exactions of labor, war conditions, and so on, and I thought I would check it up. There were returns from more than a thousand companies. Not having time to look over them all, I picked out twenty-four at random, with the idea that a chance selection of that number would be fairly representative.

The business of coal mining had been so profitable in 1917 that a perusal of the bare figures of the income tax returns gave me the feeling that I used to have when, as a youth, I pored over the diamond-strewn and fantastic adventures of the 'Arabian Nights.'

The earnings for the year of the twenty-four companies, expressed in percentages (to their capital stock) are given here.

No. 1: 516	No. 9: 399	No. 17: 76
No. 2: 271	No. 10: 8	No. 18: 0.3
No. 3: 121	No. 11: 289	No. 19: 10
No. 4: 11	No. 12: 252	No. 20: 28
No. 5: 1223	No. 13: 83	No. 21: 7
No. 6: 91	No. 14: 158	No. 22: 561
No. 7: 4.6	No. 15: 1106	No. 23: 308
No. 8: 146	No. 16: 55	No. 24: 35

There you have as fine a specimen of war profiteering as I have ever seen. Of the twenty-four companies, two had profits of more than a thousand per cent in one year. Every dollar invested brought in more than ten dollars in dividends. Ten companies earned between one hundred and six hundred per cent, and four between fifty and one hundred per cent. Only eight of them made less than fifty per cent. The Railroad Administration and the public, in paying exorbitant prices for coal, furnished the wherewithal for these swollen profits.

Coal cost the American railroads $106,000,000 more in 1918

than it had cost in 1917. Of this amount about $60,000,000 was due to the ruling of the Fuel Administration which set aside the coal contracts between the mining companies and the railroads.

The railroads, under federal control, earned nearly $700,-000,000 net in 1918. As the guaranteed compensation to the companies had been fixed at $906,000,000 per annum, the net income of the roads for the year fell short by $216,000,000 of meeting the rental charge. Several causes contributed to the production of the deficit. The most important one lay in the fact that, while it had been necessary to pay the higher scale of wages for the whole year, the higher rates were in force far less than seven months. If it had been practicable to make the increased rates retroactive — to have collected them back to January 1, 1918 — the Railroad Administration would have earned a surplus of not less than $196,000,000 after paying all charges, including compensation to the companies.

Another cause was the increased price of coal; and still another was the large amount that had to be spent on maintenance. In 1918 the Railroad Administration expended $638,000,000 on 'material and supplies' — that is, on ordinary maintenance — against an expenditure for the same purpose in 1917 of $489,000,000.

The underlying factor of operation for the period, the one that determined the direction and impetus of the Railroad Administration, was to help win the war. Our first duty was to keep the trains moving, regardless of cost or profits. That was done.

If a profit could be made, so much the better; but, if not, then the deficit had to be faced as a part of the cost of the war.

2

During this strenuous year I made every possible effort to dissociate myself from political movements or to have anything to do with public affairs outside of my multifarious duties. It was an excellent resolution, but one that was not always easy to carry out. The nation was passing through an era of progress and change, and some of the reforms then at their crucial turning-point had been advocated by me so long and so fervently that I could hardly disregard their call on my time.

In September, 1918, the question of woman's suffrage — after years of struggle — reached the United States Senate. The Nineteenth Amendment to the Constitution was pending, and, as you know, a two-thirds affirmative vote of each house is necessary in order that a constitutional amendment may be submitted to the states. The resolution concerning the amendment had passed the House of Representatives, but a preliminary canvass of the Senate indicated that it would have hard going in that chamber, and might be defeated.

I got in touch with the leading Democratic senators, and learned from them that the resolution had a majority, but not the necessary two-thirds. After a week's hard work we took a fresh count and found that we lacked only two votes. There we stuck. A miss is as good as a mile, as the old saying goes, and a deficit of two Senators could frustrate the entire woman's suffrage campaign.

On Saturday evening, September 28, 1918, Mrs. Antoinette Funk, of Illinois, and Mrs. Gilford Dudley, of Tennessee, called to see me at my house, as a committee of the National Woman's Suffrage Association, for the purpose of conferring about the critical situation. In the course of the conversation I asked them what they wanted me to do and they said they wanted me to have another talk with certain senators, and they produced a list. I looked it over and — alas! — I had to tell them that nothing could be done with those particular men. I had already talked myself hoarse in pleading with them. Mrs. Funk and Mrs. Dudley left in a state of discouragement.

Early next morning (Sunday) it occurred to me that something might be gained if the President could be induced to go before the Senate the next day, October 1, and deliver a special message on the subject. If it was to be done at all, it had to be done on October 1, because the Senate was to vote the following day. What I had in mind was a most unusual procedure for the President. There was no precedent for the Chief Executive's addressing either house of the Congress in person in behalf of any pending measure. The President's messages always related to legislation in general or to the state of the union, but never to a specific bill which either house had under consideration.

I knew that the President did not like to discuss, or consider, any public question on Sunday. This was an immutable rule with him which he never violated except in case of emergency. Nevertheless, I felt that this matter was of sufficient importance to justify me in bringing it to his attention, so I called on him at the White House at ten o'clock Sunday morning.

I told him what I had in mind. I said that, while I was afraid that nothing he could say would change two of the negative votes into the affirmative, I felt that since no President of the United States had ever spoken in favor of woman's suffrage, and that since we were fighting a war for democracy, it seemed to me that we could not consistently persist in refusing to admit women to the benefits of democracy on an equality with men. I went on to say that I believed that, even if his message failed to produce the desired result at that session of the Congress, it would undoubtedly exercise such a profound impression on public opinion that enough senators favorable to the amendment would be elected in November, 1918 (about a month away), to make sure of the passage of the Woman's Suffrage resolution at the next session.

The President listened patiently, as he always did, until the case had been presented to him. He said, at once, that there was no precedent for such a course on his part and that he thought the Senate might resent it. The situation in respect to the pending resolution was thoroughly familiar to him; all the work I had done was with his approval and, in fact, at his request, so he knew that it was a question of bringing just two senators over to our side. He thought it would be hardly possible to get them to change their minds — nothing whatever could change them, he thought — but he promised to consider my suggestion and let me know his decision.

About five o'clock that Sunday afternoon, Mrs. Wilson called me on the telephone and said that the President was writing the message. I conveyed this information, in confidence, to Mrs. Funk and Mrs. Dudley, with an injunction

that they should tell only Mrs. Catt and Dr. Anna Howard
Shaw. It would be most unfortunate, I explained to them,
if the news of the President's intention to address the Senate
should happen to come out prematurely.

The next day, October 1, the President addressed the
Senate. His coming was entirely unexpected. It was clear
that his appearance was bitterly resented by all those opposed
to the amendment and that even those who favored it were
influenced by senatorial tradition and the feeling that the Chief
Executive should not plead for any particular measure which
the Senate had under consideration. An air of hostility, a frigid
atmosphere, always heightened ·President Wilson's powers.
It did on this occasion. He spoke only fifteen minutes. His
speech was powerful and impressive and carried a fighting
edge. Although it had no effect on the Senate's vote, it made
a profound impression on the country. I have no doubt whatever that it was the determining factor in the election of
enough senators favorable to the cause to pass the resolution
during the next session of the Congress. As a result, the
resolution submitting to the states the Nineteenth Amendment, which provides that no citizen of the United States
shall be denied the right to vote on account of sex, was
adopted by Congress on June 4, 1919. Within a little more
than a year it was ratified by three fourths of the states.

3

When the Armistice that ended the World War was signed,
November 11, 1918, I felt a great relief, not only because the
war was over, but also because I saw the end of my own public
service approaching.

I had promised the President that I would remain as a member of his Cabinet until the close of the war. It is true that I
enjoyed the work, but my duties were so onerous and required
such long hours and such close attention that I had almost
reached a state of exhaustion.

There was another reason which became more pressing
every day. I was spending more than I earned, several times
more, and my financial means were dwindling. The cost of
living in Washington had gone up to fabulous heights; the
monthly deficit made a tremendous hole in my assets.

Three days after the Armistice, on November 14, I sent my resignation to the President:

Dear Mr. President: Now that an armistice has been signed and peace is assured, I feel at liberty to apprise you of my desire to return, as soon as possible, to private life....

For almost five years, I have worked incessantly under the pressure of great responsibilities. Their exactions have drawn heavily on my strength. The inadequate compensation allowed by law to Cabinet Officers (as you know I receive no compensation as Director-General of Railroads) and the very burdensome cost of living in Washington have so depleted my personal resources that I am obliged to reckon with the facts of the situation....

I cannot secure the required rest nor the opportunity to look after my long-neglected private affairs unless I am relieved of my present responsibilities.

I am anxious to have my retirement effected with the least possible inconvenience to yourself and to the public service but it would, I think, be wise to accept now my resignation as Secretary of the Treasury, to become effective upon the appointment and qualification of my successor so that he may have the opportunity and advantage of participating promptly in the formulation of the policies that should govern the future work of the Treasury. I would suggest that my resignation as Director-General of Railroads become effective January 1, 1919, or upon the appointment of my successor.

I hope you will understand, my dear Mr. President, that I would permit nothing but the most imperious demands to force my withdrawal from public life. Always I shall cherish as the greatest honor of my career the opportunity you have so generously given me to serve the country under your leadership in these epochal times.

I knew the President would understand fully why I felt compelled to retire from the public service, as I had previously discussed the matter with him. On November 24, 1918, he sent me this gracious reply, in accepting my resignation:

My dear Mr. Secretary: I was not unprepared for your letter of the fourteenth, because you had more than once, of course, discussed with me the circumstances which have long made it a serious personal sacrifice for you to remain in office. I knew that only your high and exacting sense of duty had kept you here until the immediate tasks of the war should be over. But I am none the less distressed. I shall not allow our intimate personal relation to deprive me of the pleasure of saying that in my judgment the country has never had an abler, a more resourceful and yet prudent, a more uniformly efficient Secretary of the Treasury; and I say this remembering all the able, devoted, and distinguished men who preceded you. I have kept your letter a number of days in order to suggest, if I could, some other solution of your difficulty than the one you have now felt obliged to resort to. But I have not been able to think of any. I cannot ask you to make further sacrifices, serious as the loss of the Government will be in your retirement. I accept your resignation, therefore, to take effect upon the appointment of a successor, because in justice to you I must.

I also, for the same reasons, accept your resignation as Director-General of Railroads, to take effect, as you suggest, on the first of January next or when your successor is appointed. The whole country admires, I am sure, as I do, the skill and executive capacity with which you have handled the great and complex problem of the unified administration of the railways under the stress of war uses, and will regret, as I do, to see you leave that post just as the crest of its difficulty is passed.

For the distinguished, disinterested, and altogether admirable service you have rendered the country in both posts, and especially for the way in which you have guided the Treasury through all the perplexities and problems of transitional financial conditions and of the financing of a war which has been without precedent alike in kind and in scope I thank you with a sense of gratitude that comes from the very bottom of my heart. Gratefully and affectionately yours.

(Signed) Woodrow Wilson

My resignation was a surprise to the nation, so far as I could judge from the newspapers, as well as from the thousands of letters that poured into my office.

Practically all the journalistic comment was eulogistic. I was given credit not only for what I did, but also for achievements which properly belonged to my subordinates and associates. The New York 'Times,' which on various occasions had been a severe critic of mine, generously said (in part) on November 23, 1918:

That for personal reasons or for any reason Mr. McAdoo should feel constrained to resign the Secretaryship of the Treasury is an occasion for regret as general as it is sincere....

Mr. McAdoo takes his place among our great Secretaries of the Treasury.... His counsel and his influence were valuable in the organization of the Federal Reserve System, which ranks with our man power and our industries among the forces that enabled us to bear our part in the war. That tower of strength he put to use with courage, foresight and wisdom, and with results in the raising of billions upon billions in Liberty loans that will ever be an occasion for pride and confidence. His management of the loan campaigns was admirable, and his personal part in them was inspiring.

To these herculean tasks of wartime there was added the direction of all the railway systems of the country, and again his great abilities, his sagacity in the choice of assistants, and his marvelous industry and untiring devotion to duty were manifested....

We hope they [the American people] will feel some sense of shame withal that the niggardliness of our democracy toward its servants has again compelled a public officer of the first order of worth and capacity to resign an ill-paid office at a critical time to repair his private fortune, no small part of which has been spent to pay his living expenses while in office.

I was profoundly touched by the letters I received, when the news of my resignation was announced, from the men who had been closely associated with me in the service of the nation. It is fine and comforting to have the esteem and confidence of your fellow-men, especially of those who have worked by your side. The letter I quote here, from B. L. Winchell, Regional Director of the Southern Region of the Railroad Administration, is typical. Mr. Winchell wrote, on December 16, 1918:

It has been a privilege to be associated with you for ten months, and I hope I shall always profit thereby.

We have all learned much from you, and I am only sorry that I did not meet you thirty years ago. I admit that I might not have been able to duplicate all of your methods, but the mere effort to do so would have been good for me.

My resignation loosened a flood of verse. Here is a sample. This was composed by Arthur Guiterman. Perhaps the author meant to throw an ironic and satirical javelin into my cosmos, or maybe he intended his poem as a tribute. It is so clever and amusing that I reproduce it here, with the author's permission.

> The Who, preëminently Who,
> Is William Gibbs, the McAdoo.
> (Whom I should like to hail but daren't,
> As Royal Prince and Heir Apparent.)
> A man of high intrinsic Worth,
> The Greatest Son-in-Law on Earth —
> With all the burdens thence accruing,
> He's always up and McAdooing.
> From Sun to Star and Star to Sun,
> His work is never McAdone.

He regulates our Circumstances,
Our Buildings, Industries, Finances,
And Railways, while the wires buzz
To tell us what he McAdoes.
He gave us (Heaven bless the Giver)
The tubes beneath the Hudson River.
I don't believe he ever hid
A single thing he McAdid!
His name appears on Scrip and Tissue,
On bonds of each succeeding issue,
On coupons bright and posters rare,
And every Pullman Bill of Fare.

POSTSCRIPT

But while with sympathetic croodlings
I sing his varied McAdoodlings
And write these eulogistic lines,
That thankless McAdoo resigns.

The employees of the railroads read that I was resigning because I could not afford to live on my pay, and many of them wrote to me that they would contribute a portion of their wages to keep me at the head of the Railroad Administration. Within a short time this impulse, without my knowledge, had assumed the proportions of a national movement. The idea was that every railroad employee, man or woman, would contribute one dollar a year to give me a salary. On November 25, three railroad workers at St. Louis — J. H. Kirkland, H. J. Garrigan, and O. E. Sumner — wired me that St. Louis had filled its quota; that $24,000 a year had been pledged by the wage-earners of the roads centering in that city.

As there were two million or more railroad employees, if each had contributed one dollar, I would have had a salary of $2,000,000. Of course, I could not permit this, so I declined with warm thanks for the generous impulse of the fine men and women who had worked so devotedly under me.

I resigned without having secured a job and without having decided what I would do. The imperative need was rest to restore my health and I did not want to assume responsibilities of any kind that would disturb me. But I began to receive numerous offers of important positions, all of which I declined. One, however, I was anxious to accept, and would have accepted if I had been equal to it. That was the receivership of the Brooklyn Rapid Transit Company. James N. Wallace, president of the Central Trust Company of New York, was not only one of the ablest, but he was one of the most independent, of the New York bankers. A warm friendship had sprung up between us. He had served with ability and unselfishness as a member of the Finance Committee of the Railroad Administration. Wallace called on me in Washington, December 18, and told me that the Brooklyn Company would have to go into the hands of a receiver, January 1, 1919; that he and Nicholas Brady and his brother James, who were also friends of mine and were largely interested in the Brooklyn Company, were anxious for me to take hold of this great property and reorganize it. On the next day after Wallace's call I received the following letter from Nicholas Brady, who was then in New York:

Mr. Wallace has told me in detail of his personal talk with you, as a result of which I hope that you will see your way clear to undertake the job.

While I would not presume to advise you, the opportunity to me seems great — the rehabilitation of a great public service, and a great property freed for a time from unreasonable exactions by the local authorities as well as immediately improved in credit.

Whether it is our fault or not, we are at this moment so absolutely bereft of public confidence that any new man would be welcomed by the public, and if that man were W. G. McAdoo the battle would be more than half won at the start. You would, of course, be free to make your own selections as to counsel or any other position. As you know, we would like to have you take the job, but I would not urge it if I were not certain that you would make a success of it, with corresponding credit to your reputation as well as financially. As we have very little time to make our arrangements, I hope to hear favorably from you very soon.

Whatever your decision may be, I want to thank you for your uniform kindness and consideration, in which Jim joins me.

With best personal regards, I am yours very truly

N. F. Brady

This would have been congenial work because I was thoroughly familiar with the local transit situation in New York, having had large experience with it while I was building and operating the Hudson Tunnels, but I had to pass it up because, after all, health is certainly the most valuable asset in human life.

The President asked me to suggest my successor as Secretary of the Treasury because he said I knew, better than anyone else, the problems with which the Treasury had to deal, and he was anxious, therefore, to have the benefit of my judgment in making an appointment of such great importance.

I told him that there were two men whom I thought qualified and available. One was Bernard M. Baruch, who had shown great administrative ability in directing the War Industries Board, and whose knowledge of finance was extensive and sound. The other was Representative Carter Glass, who was unusually well informed about the Federal Reserve System and whose high standing and political influence would make him a valuable member of the Cabinet.

The President knew each of these men well and had a high opinion of them. He authorized me to sound them out. I spoke first to Baruch, saying that the President had him under consideration and that I should like to know if he would care to take the office if the President should decide to appoint him. Baruch said that the honor was far beyond his merits and that he was most grateful to the President and to me for being thought worthy of such a great office. He thought, however, that he had better finish the work he was doing as head of the War Industries Board, and therefore he would prefer not to be considered for the post.

When I saw Carter Glass, he expressed doubts as to his own qualifications. He said that all of his experience had been in the legislative branch and that he doubted his capacities as an administrator. I told him that he ought not to hesitate on that account because the Treasury was highly organized; it had an admirable staff of assistant secretaries and I was sure that he would find no difficulty in carrying on the work.

I reported the result of my interviews to the President and he appointed Carter Glass. On December 16, 1918, I turned my office over to him. Walker D. Hines, who had been Assistant Director-General of Railroads, succeeded me on January 11, 1919. I had urged the President to make this appointment because I knew Hines was a man of unusual ability and well qualified for the task.

After a three months' holiday with Mrs. McAdoo in Santa Barbara, California, I went to New York and engaged in the practice of law at the head of the firm of McAdoo, Cotton & Franklin.

4

Federal control of the railroads continued, for fourteen months after my resignation, under Walker D. Hines as Director-General. The roads were returned to their owners on March 1, 1920. I had nothing to do, of course, with the Railroad Administration during these last fourteen months, but I shall give a short résumé of its operations to complete the picture.

After the Armistice there was a sharp and unprecedented falling-off in railroad traffic. War orders had come to an end; manufacturing industries of all kinds were adjusting themselves to a peace basis; and, besides, a policy of financial deflation was making itself felt in all sections of the country. By March there was a surplus of approximately five hundred thousand cars. This was the largest total of idle cars in the history of American railroading. In only two months of the year 1919 — January and October — did the railroads carry a larger traffic than in the corresponding months of 1918.

These conditions had a seriously adverse effect on the earnings of the Railroad Administration, an effect which was heightened by the great steel strike of September and the coal strike of November. The operating expenses of the roads were increased unavoidably in various ways; in a higher payroll, for one thing. The cost of labor was $230,000,000 higher in 1919 than it had been for the preceding year. Another huge item of expense was that of material and supplies. For this item — or for maintenance, to put it another way — it was necessary to spend $801,000,000, against an outlay for the same purpose in 1918 of $638,000,000.

To meet these increased and absolutely necessary expenditures the only resource of the Director-General would have been to make another raise in rates. I have shown, in a previous chapter, that the rate increase in 1918 was known, at the time, to be inadequate because it did not bring freight rates up to the general level of commodity prices, or anywhere near it. Director-General Hines decided, however, not to put the burden of higher traffic rates on the country in 1919. Business was undergoing a drastic deflation. There was imminent danger of a prolonged period of depression and unemployment. A raise in rates would have added materially to the troubles of industry and commerce. The course he adopted was to keep rates down and let the government assume the deficit.

The railroads earned $455,000,000 net in 1919, or about one half the rentals guaranteed to the owner corporations by the government. For the whole period of federal control — the twenty-six months from January 1, 1918, to March 1, 1920 — the net operating income of the Railroad Administration fell short of the guaranteed rental for that period by approximately $714,000,000. Of this deficit $216,000,000 was incurred in the year 1918, while I was Director-General. The remainder — $498,000,000, or thereabouts — was incurred in the next fourteen months.

Federal control was an emergency war measure, and the war, so far as the economic status of the railroads was concerned, did not end with the Armistice. The period of readjustment continued for more than a year, and it was inevitably a period of loss and liquidation.

The Railroad Administration's deficit seems large, but compared with other war costs it is a bagatelle. Here is one item of comparison, for instance. In the Meuse–Argonne offensive, under the direction of General Pershing in the fall of 1918, a continuous battle was kept up for forty-five days on a front of only nineteen miles. The cost of this barrage in shells and munitions, including transportation, has been conservatively estimated at $762,000,000. In short, the American artillery fired away, in a period of less than seven weeks, on a narrow military front, shot and shell that was greater in cost than the deficit incurred by all the American railroads in twenty-six months. It was a part of the price we paid for victory and there has never been any reason, except selfish and partisan ones, to whine about it and to distort and misrepresent it.

And, it must not be forgotten, this deficit was not a deficit in the true sense of the term. It did not express an actual loss in operation. The railroads always made money under federal control. Their operation showed a handsome profit, but they did not earn the full amount the government had agreed to pay their owners as rental for the property.

5

At the end of federal control the railroad companies began to file their claims against the government for damage to their property. It was a frenzied assault on the United States Treasury.

The most extravagant claims were made on account of alleged under-maintenance, depreciation, breakage, wear and tear, loss and damage to equipment, defective track-laying, defective machinery, loss of tools, and hundreds of other items. Anyone who heard the testimony in support of these claims could not help wondering how the railroads could be operated at all, in view of the general smash-up which the government was charged with having inflicted on them.

But most of the claims were exaggerated beyond all reason, and were nothing more than barefaced attempts to get huge sums of money out of the Treasury on a pretext that started out by being plausible and ended by being ridiculous.

As an illustration I give here a few examples of the railroad companies' demands, taken at random from a long list:

The International and Great Northern Railway wanted $5,316,000, but this dwindled ·to $100,000 when the claims were examined.

The Erie Railroad's claims aggregated $10,494,000, but in the final settlement the shoe appeared on the other foot. Instead of the government paying the Erie anything, that railroad had to pay the government $3,250,000 for additions and betterments made while the road was under federal control.

The Central Railroad of New Jersey put in a claim for $22,546,000, which was settled for $4,500,000 — or twenty-five per cent of what it tried to get.

The Atlanta, Birmingham and Atlantic wanted $590,000. Its claim dwindled, in the light of analysis, to the insignificant sum of one dollar.

The Wabash Railway demanded $13,694,000; the claim was settled by the government paying the road $1,500,000.

The Hocking Valley Railway Company considered itself injured to the extent of $563,000. The government experts did not agree with this conclusion, and the matter was closed by the railroad paying into the National Treasury $700,000!

The Pullman Company made a claim for $24,424,000 which contained, among other items, a charge of $571,000 for sheets lost or destroyed, $417,000 for towels, $256,000 for pillow slips, and $114,000 for porters' coats. The company's property was undoubtedly damaged on account of the heavy service to which its cars were subjected in transporting troops; but, after all, $256,000 will buy an enormous number of pillow slips. The claim of over $24,000,000 was settled for less than one third of the total; the government paid the Pullman Company $7,250,000.

The total amount of the railroads' claims for under-maintenance of way and structures and under-maintenance of equipment was $677,510,607. In the process of investigation, which took the time of a corps of experts four years or more, these claims were finally settled for $222,696,015. In other words, two thirds of their claims were lopped off. Many observers, of sound judgment and extensive information, still think that, even with two thirds of their claims disallowed, the railroads, in settlement, received the juiciest plum in their history.

In the vast post-war controversy which arose on account of the return of the railroads to their private owners and the necessary legislation to carry it into effect, as well as on account of the huge claims of the carriers for damages to their property while under federal control, it seemed to be important to the campaign of the railroads that I should be held up to the public as the villain of the piece, as an arch-devil who had 'ruined the railroads.' This was iterated and reiterated, ad nauseam, from one end of the country to the other. Professional publicity agents were employed to carry on this propaganda, and during the whole of it nothing whatever was said about the fact that my successor, Walker D. Hines, had had any part in the operation of the railroads, although he succeeded me as Director-General and acted as such for a term two months longer than mine. I was charged with responsibility for all that he did, as well as for all that I did. These attacks upon me were a great surprise. Throughout my term as Director-General I had retained in the service the ablest railroad men in the country; I had given them my confidence and had relied upon them, largely, for the operation of the properties. I had given them ample and wide authority. If the railroads were ruined during the twelve months that I was Director-General, then I am afraid that the able railroad men who assisted me were equally guilty. But the railroads were not ruined; they were saved, and the fine body of railroad men who served with me and under me rendered great service to the country in the difficult transportation crisis engendered by the war.

The real motives behind these attacks were twofold — one, to excite public sympathy for the railroads so that they could get the most favorable legislation for their return to their owners, and the other was political. Men and women all over the country were talking of me as a possible nominee of the Democratic Party for President. The opposition naturally wanted to keep out of the race any Democrat who had a record for constructive achievement, and the best way to do that, they thought, was through a campaign of disparagement.

The plain fact is that the Railroad Administration was a godsend to the railroads and their owners. Federal control, instead of ruining the roads, put them on their feet, made them more efficient, and returned them to the companies with better credit and in better shape than they had ever been during their existence.

The railroads were restored to their owners under the Transportation Act on March 1, 1920. While this act was on its passage through the Congress and after it became a law, I attacked it in numerous public speeches as providing no real solution of the railroad problem. For once, at least, I had the gift of accurate prophecy! The railroad crisis is again upon us and in a more serious form than ever before. The solution of this problem will require more brains than have yet been exhibited in dealing with it.

6

With the arduous and busy years of my government service behind me, I felt like a man who has returned home after a long voyage on which he has seen many strange and interesting sights. My judgment had been broadened by experience, and I had grown, I hope, in vision and understanding.

CHAPTER XXXIII
WOODROW WILSON

I

I HAVE never seen, among the millions of words that have been printed about Woodrow Wilson, any description or analysis of his personality that presented a rounded portrait of the man I knew.

He was many-sided. His knowledge of things, his collection of ideas, his impressions of people, were astonishing in depth and variety. This many-sidedness was, I think, one of his most striking characteristics, but it is a trait that has been confusing to historians and biographers. He seemed different to different people because he was different. Men who saw only one side of Woodrow Wilson thought they had seen all there was to see, that they knew the whole man. He has been the subject of innumerable incomplete delineations which depicted a single aspect of his intellectual profile while all the rest remained in shadow. One had to be acquainted with him a long time, to observe him closely in many diverse circumstances, to see him in many moods, to understand even passably well the trend and genius of his character.

Woodrow Wilson was a great man in the true sense. He possessed vision and creative power, the two primary qualities of a great mind. He looked over the heads of other men, above the confusion of contemporary events, to distant horizons. There was no trace of intellectual squalor in his life; none of his ideas came from the slums and back alleys of thought; he had an innate capacity for lifting all his mental processes to a lofty plane.

Greatness is a mystery. It flows from a mysterious source, and it passes through the world carrying in its heart springs and motives of action which are often incomprehensible to the common run of mankind. To say that greatness is always misunderstood is well within the truth; and it is equally true that myths and fictions always cluster around it.

In one sense I knew President Wilson well; I was in contact

with him almost every day for six years. I served under him in an important official capacity and I had the rare privilege of seeing him in the more intimate relation as a member of his family. I knew his mental habits; I saw clearly the general pattern of his thought and life. But in another sense I hardly knew him at all. There were wide and fertile ranges of his spirit that were closed to me; and, I think, to everyone else except the first Mrs. Wilson. As far as I am aware, she was the only human being who knew him perfectly.

I do not mean to imply that he was secretive, evasive, or non-communicative. His ideas ran ahead of his epoch; he had gleams of prescience, flashes of foresight, which did not fit into the grooves of speech or into the pattern of current vernacular thought. He kept them to himself, buried deep in consciousness, but anyone who was close to him saw their reflections now and then, as one sees the reflection of a distant fire on a dark sky. I believe that it was this wealth of unuttered ideas that gave such pungent illumination to his speech.

There was none of the windiness of the ordinary speechmaker in his make-up. When he said anything to the public, it meant something; it had meat and substance in it. Only a few Presidents have had his capacity for expressing dynamic truths in a few words; just now I can think of only four others — Washington, Jefferson, Jackson, and Lincoln — who possessed it. I was always impressed by the remarkable manner in which he could make himself understood by the average man. He had a gift for striking at the heart of a problem, for holding up to the general view the essential part of any complicated situation.

We have here the intellectual aristocrat who speaks from the high tower of intelligence; whose words are vivid with the essence of the world's culture, whose ideas are neat and clear and precise.

Clarity was one of his outstanding traits. When I recall the events of my long association with him, I cannot remember an instance where he was at a loss for the right word to express his thought. In conversation there were no fuzzy expressions, no jumbled, incomplete phrases. He never used slang, which he considered an indication of slovenly mental habits. His mind was so luminous and orderly that when he wrote anything — a letter or a state paper — he seldom made any serious changes in the first draft.

Language, in the service of politicians, often becomes an outstanding vice. But Woodrow Wilson always subordinated talk to action. The purpose of discussion was to bring men together to unify their ideas, to give them a common aim. When that was done, discussion had reached its objective and had to give way to achievement. 'There are times,' he said, 'when words seem empty and only action seems great.' He had a way of actually carrying out plans which, in the hands of other people, would have ended in mere gestures. Yet the American public's impression of him has been so distorted by misrepresentation that — I venture to say — nine out of ten of our people think of Woodrow Wilson as a talker rather than as a great creative force.

One has only to point to the distinctive and far-reaching achievements of the Wilson Administration — achievements that surpass in number and importance those of all preceding administrations for the past fifty years — to correct this misleading notion.

Greatness is always creative. Productivity is one of the cardinal distinctions between a great mind and a small one. In Woodrow Wilson there was a deeper impulse for accomplishment than I have ever seen in any other man. Ideas that led nowhere — mere speculative thoughts — never made an impression on him. He called them blank cartridges. He detested the routine work of administration, the signing of papers, the reading of stale reports. He was happy only when he was engaged in work that was definitely constructive.

But he was not an impetuous leader. He never rushed into action; he considered everything that could be said on every side of the question before making up his mind. When he finally made a decision, the argument was closed; once the vessel was under steam and headed for the other shore, there was never any thought in the captain's mind of turning back.

He was grateful for information and advice, to which he was always receptive, but he reached his conclusions in his own way, after thorough consideration of every aspect of the matter; and it did not make any difference if everybody else thought him wrong. His enemies have delighted in describing him as obstinate. Nothing is further from the truth. He was tenacious of purpose and nothing could deflect him from his objective once he made up his mind, after the most careful deliberation, as to the proper course of action. These are the essential characteristics of a great leader. Unless one has the conviction that his cause is right and is determined to achieve it, he cannot succeed.

Throughout human history the great leaders who have written their names high on the roll of fame are those who have been inflexible of purpose in the pursuit of great objectives. Washington was not turned from his purpose by the miseries of Valley Forge, nor by faint-hearted compromise measures. Frederick the Great, beset on all sides by powerful enemies, never lost his determination or his confidence in ultimate victory. There was a strain of this dauntless quality in Woodrow Wilson.

He did not hesitate to differ from the leaders of his own party when he thought they were wrong, and he decided against them in such instances. He was not unwilling to compromise on inessentials, but he would not compromise principles or morality. I remember when the so-called 'mild' reservations were proposed to the League of Nations Covenant to the Versailles Treaty. Some of the Democratic leaders were eager for him to accept them. I discussed the matter with him. He said that he would not be averse to the ratification of the treaty with the so-called 'mild' reservations, but that the opponents of the treaty had not advanced them in good faith and the moment there was any indication on his part of a willingness to accept them, partisan opponents would immediately propose other and more objectionable reservations which it would be impossible to consider. They were, he said, determined to prevent ratification of the treaty at whatever cost; therefore, it was impossible for him to discuss compromise.

Subsequent events proved clearly the correctness of his judgment. Lodge and the opponents of the treaty were determined to defeat it, regardless of consequences. They saw a partisan advantage in that course. During my discussion with him he said, 'Mac, I am willing to compromise on anything but the Ten Commandments'; by which he meant there could be no compromise where the moral law or high principle was involved.

His inflexible purpose saved the Federal Reserve banks. The influences against a regional bank system — and in favor of a huge central bank — were immensely powerful. These influences pervaded the entire country and raised opposition to the Administration's plan in the most unlikely places. The President decided that a regional bank system was essential to the welfare of the country. He reached this conclusion after a long and careful examination of every fact and factor that entered into the question and he could not be swerved from it. Time has vindicated his judgment. The successful establishment of the Federal Reserve System could never have been achieved if he had been a weak and irresolute leader, who was not sure of his position and who was not ready to battle for it. This is not obstinacy; this is statesmanship.

In many of the controversial measures enacted during the Wilson Administration, he relied upon me largely to reconcile the conflicting views of the members of our own party in the Senate. Many times compromises and adjustments were made, but they did not involve surrender of essentials. As a matter of fact, he was one of the most reasonable of men in the discussion of any question or problem that came before him, but he had an instinctive distaste for makeshift devices or political expedients. Like Andrew Jackson, he was a good hater, and when he saw that a man was capable of duplicity, and was playing the part of a hypocrite or a demagogue, he crossed him off, so to speak, and the crossing-off was final. His list of antipathies was small, but their roots ran deep. To illustrate, I quote here the final paragraph of a public letter which he wrote, April 18, 1922, about Senator James A. Reed, of Missouri:

To those who have closely observed Mr. Reed's career in Washington, he has shown himself incapable of sustained allegiance to any person or any cause. He has repeatedly forfeited any claim to my confidence that he may ever have been supposed to have and I shall never willingly consent to any further association with him.

2

The popular idea that he was a relentless thinking machine with the intellectual and moral austerity of a mid-Victorian schoolmaster is a misconception that is about as wrong as anything can possibly be. He was simply not that kind of man at all, but of a different, and opposite, type.

Yet, as I bring the events of the Administration period into my memory, I can see and understand how this myth originated. He was easily bored, and was always terribly bored by egoists who praised themselves; by self-seeking people who came with an ulterior motive thinly disguised under a transparent veil of liberalism; and by men who started by telling him what he already knew. In such cases — and there were many of them — he had a way of retiring within himself and dropping the light and witty play of speech that he liked to employ in other circumstances. For the time being he became pure logic, clothed in garments of patience and courtesy. There was no 'rise' to him, no sparkle of humor or fancy. His callers would go away with the conviction that they had met a modern impersonation of Jonathan Edwards.

They would have been astonished, I am sure, if they had heard and seen him mimic their attitudes and manner of speech after they had departed. Sometimes in the family circle at the White House he would spend part of an evening giving imitations of various people. He had a most vivid sense of picture, and he could depict a scene — even one of many years back — with startling realism. On these occasions he would act the parts of the various people in his story, taking up one character after another. He had such perfect control over his facial muscles that he could change his expression instantly — and completely. His imitation of a dull-witted, sluggish, haw-haw Englishman would have made a reputation on the stage. Another one of his rôles was that of a drunken man, with thick-tongued speech and wobbly bearing. He could imitate me, too, and when he did he looked and acted more like McAdoo than I did; that is, he had an actor's feeling for salient characteristics. I asked him once how he had acquired the ability to make these astonishing changes in facial expression, and he told me that it had come from long practice. He had cultivated it as a hobby to amuse himself.

Imagine the delight of the newspapers if they had discovered that the occupant of the White House had such an extraordinary power of mimicry. But they never knew anything about it.

President Wilson had an intense dislike of newspaper stories about himself and his family. I remember one day when someone showed him a long article on the subject of his daughters. It was full of conjectures — really nothing more than idle gossip — about the probability of the President's daughters marrying this man or that. The President always kept his temper under control, but he came pretty near losing it on that occasion. His face flushed; he laid the paper down with a gesture of annoyance. The next time he met the Washington correspondents in a body, he told them emphatically that he considered the article out of taste and offensive, and that he did not want anything of the kind printed in the future.

When he was in the mood for it he would sometimes — in the course of an evening — start to discuss an idea, or a conventional notion, or an argument of one kind or another — and play with it for an hour. It was a kind of mental gymnastics which I find difficult to describe. You have seen magicians, I suppose, produce gold pieces and Easter eggs from astonishing receptacles. Well, it was something like that, if you substitute ideas and conclusions for material objects. Sometimes he would show, in a playful manner, that the most startling contradictions were folded up in commonly accepted notions or courses of conduct.

He loved children, and he could make himself delightful to them by inventing games. I used to watch some of these spontaneous games with astonishment at his readiness of invention. He could make a game out of anything — a lead pencil, a toy dog, or a set of alphabet blocks — and they were the kind of games that hold children spell-bound. It was a form of extemporizing. When he was asked by the children whom he had amused to play the same game on some subsequent occasion, he could seldom remember what it was, but he would invent another one on the spot with instant readiness.

One of his little-known traits was a persistent, lifelong shyness. He did not like to meet people. I have never known why this was so. Without the encouragement of the first Mrs. Wilson, I doubt if he ever would have entered public life at all. It was she who encouraged him to take part in political affairs, and to a great extent her influence shaped his career.

He possessed an extraordinary quality of self-control, so that he could make himself do whatever was to be done without revealing his own feelings. Although his personality was sensitive, vibrant and high-strung, he was able to make his countenance a perfect mask. Most people who heard him speak, or saw him in public, thought he was enjoying himself. As a rule he wasn't.

The inevitable attributes of political life — the hand-shaking and the turmoil and the wordy reiteration of old arguments — annoyed him, but he concealed his annoyance under the cloak of patience. 'Almost every man who comes here,' he said to me at the White House one day, 'starts out by telling me that the question he comes to discuss is important, and that it ought to be considered seriously. I know that I am considering serious problems. That happens to be my job; no one has to tell me that.'

Sometimes, at conferences where the subject of discussion had been worn to shreds by much talk, he would sit listening to the flow of meaningless and shallow words, an image of official courtesy, with a remote and faraway look in his eyes. His attitude, as I recall it, makes me think of the definition of a good listener by Abe Martin, the barbed-wire philosopher. 'A good listener,' said Abe, 'is usually a fellow who is thinking of something else.'

He was one of the most accomplished public speakers of his time, yet he was not an orator in the emotional, declamatory sense of the word. He never harangued, he never paced the platform like a caged tiger, or gesticulated wildly. His diction was perfect and his power of definition amazingly clear. His voice was mellow and especially pleasing.

I have heard him speak to audiences of from ten thousand to fifteen thousand people in auditoriums where the acoustics were atrociously bad, but he reached these vast audiences without apparent effort. I once asked him the secret of his

PRESIDENT WILSON AND ELLEN WILSON McADOO
1915

power to project his voice without raising it particularly, so as to make himself understood by crowds of such magnitude.

He told me that he had studied and practiced elocution assiduously for a long time, and that he considered it a definite art, like painting or sculpture. I mentioned the names of some excellent speakers who seemed to me to be natural orators. He said that he thought some men had a natural gift for oratory, but even they would be greatly benefited by a course of training in elocution. In addressing a large audience, where there might be difficulty in making himself heard, his method, he said, was to select some person about the center of the audience and begin as if he were speaking directly to that person. He would begin in a normal and rather low tone, without any effort to raise his voice to a high pitch, and he could tell by the facial expressions of the particular person or group that he was addressing if he was not clearly understood. Then, as he went along in his speech, his voice would rise naturally and without effort.

3

I have never known anyone who had a more sincere and more ardent love for humanity than Woodrow Wilson. His mind translated all events, all ideas, all problems into human terms. His mental background was a panorama of people rather than a panorama of things. For him the world consisted of human beings, of men and women. England, Germany, the Treasury, ships, railroads, dollars, books, ideas — these were all mere abstractions. There was only one reality behind them all, and that reality consisted of people. Take the human race out of the world and you have no world left, no matter what remains of buildings and battleships. The most splendid civilization is of no value unless people are reasonably contented; unless there are equal opportunities for all men, unless every man has a legitimate field for his talents and his energy.

These ideas, as I have expressed them, are not in his words, but they give the texture of his thought. Again and again, in his discussion of the problems of the Administration, he would come back to these conceptions. In his first inaugural address he said:

We see that in many things life is very great. It is incomparably great in its material aspects, in its body of wealth, in the diversity and sweep of its energy, in the industries which have been built up by the genius of individual men and the limitless enterprise of groups of men....

But the evil has come with the good, and much fine gold has been corroded. With riches have come inexcusable waste.... We have been proud of our industrial achievements, but we have not hitherto stopped thoughtfully enough to count the human cost, the cost of lives snuffed out, of energies overtaxed and broken, of the fearful physical and spiritual cost to the men and women and children upon whom the dead weight and burden of it all has fallen pitilessly the years through. The groans and agony of it all had not yet reached our ears, the solemn, moving undertone of our life, coming up out of the mines and factories and out of every home where the struggle had its intimate and familiar seat.... The great government we loved has too often been made use of for private and selfish purposes, and those who used it had forgotten the people.

Any man who has these convictions is bound to be a Democrat at heart, no matter what his political party happens to be called. He believed, with Lincoln, that genius and greatness grow upward from the soil. They are sturdy plants with their roots in the earth rather than in the air. The intangible ideas on which civilization rests — the sense of mutual forbearance, the honesty of purpose, the love of justice, the desire to be independent, the ambition to strive and achieve —all these, he thought, had to exist in the great mass of humanity to give validity to democratic institutions. He said, 'I believe in the ordinary man. If I did not believe in the ordinary man, I would move out of a democracy and, if I found an endurable monarchy, I would live in it.'

In the spiritual aspects of his personality Woodrow Wilson reminds me of Robert E. Lee, though these two leaders were miles apart in mental outlook. General Lee believed in God; so did President Wilson. Both of them relied on the wisdom of God. They both believed that God is an ever-present force — active, and not passive — in the affairs of men. I know that in this age of doubt a belief in God seems antiquated to many people. Science has classified Him as either the doormat of the universe or as a remote, intangible Something which exercises its energies in forces as impersonal as gravity and as meaningless as the gyrations of a humming-bird. I am not arguing the question; I am only setting down Woodrow Wilson's belief as one may record an historical fact.

When ideas and plans on which he had set his heart went wrong, or were overthrown, he accepted the verdict as the will of Providence. The failure of the United States to enter the League of Nations was a great blow to him, but he said, 'I am not so sure that the delay is not for the best. The people should be unmistakably back of the government's action. After all, Providence knows more about these things than any of us. Anyone is a fool who questions Its ways.'

Now and then I told the President some story or other; stories that were supposed to be funny. One day I told him one about a circus aeronaut and a negro cornfield hand. In the 1880's almost every circus that visited the little Southern towns made a big feature of a balloon ascension. These balloons would go up and drift over the neighboring countryside for a while and come down in some field a few miles from the starting-point. The thrilling part of the entertainment was usually provided by a trapeze performer, who would go up in the balloon swinging to a bar. While he was in the air he would go through various stunts — holding on by his toes, or by his teeth.

Well, on the occasion that I am telling about, the balloon came down in a cornfield in which an old negro man was at work. He had never heard of a balloon, or of the circus, or of hardly anything else. Picture his astonishment when the great saggy brown globe settled on the ground, and a young man in blue tights, with gold stars and spangles, leaped out and walked toward him.

The old negro was transfixed. Bowing low, he said humbly: 'Howdy do, Marse Jesus; how's your pa?'

At this point laughter is supposed to burst forth. The President did not laugh; he did not even smile. He looked at me silently for a moment, and then said:

'Mac, that story is sacrilegious.'

I had never thought of it in that light, but it was the last of that kind I ever told him.

Duty was a paramount motive in President Wilson's life. I am again reminded of General Lee and his saying that 'Duty is the sublimest word in the English language.' The President had no use for any man who did not perform his duty to the best of his ability, and this rule was without exceptions. I think that the coldness — or a large part of it — which he sometimes displayed toward men had its origin in this deep underlying trait. He did not want to get in a position where he would be moved, in his attitude on public measures, by a personal liking for the men behind them.

There was a popular impression that I had great influence with him, and that I could do anything I pleased and 'get away with it,' as the saying goes. It was entirely erroneous. The only influence I had with the President came from his knowledge that I tried to do my duty in my own sphere. If I had neglected my work, or had attempted to influence him in any way that was harmful to the public service, he would have asked for my resignation as quickly as he would have asked for the resignation of anybody else.

He told me one day that the consciousness of representing all the American people, and not a single political party, was always in the back of his mind. He said he thought that he should endeavor, in his administrative capacity, to obtain the best results without adhering rigidly to party affiliations. In this statement he showed the generosity of his nature as well as his strong sense of duty to the whole people. It was an excellent idea in theory, and it should have been equally excellent in practice, but it did not always turn out to be so. For instance, when, in the beginning of the Administration, we consulted Republican senators about federal appointments in their states, we sometimes found that the men they approved were obviously poor material. It was not a Republican administration, and from a narrow political point of view there was no special reason why a Republican politician should try to make it a successful one.

During the World War — that is, after the United States entered it — politics was 'adjourned,' to use the President's phrase, and he appointed many Republicans to high administrative positions. It was a wise course, and with some exceptions it worked out splendidly. Incidentally, it gave some of the Republican leaders of today their start in political life. Herbert Hoover was one. Hoover was a practically unknown man who had spent most of his adult life abroad. He was as completely out of touch with American affairs, or with the American people, as one might expect of a man who had lived years in China, years in Australia, and years in England. His chief distinction had been acquired in distributing free food to the Belgian people in 1915 and 1916 — a celebrity easily won, I fancy, as I judge from long observation that the job of giving away things requires very little wear and tear on one's ability.

After this accomplishment Hoover was appointed Federal Food Administrator by the President, and that started him on his road to the White House.

President Wilson's temperament did not readily adapt itself to political strategy. He had an incurable distaste for professional politicians; he did not understand their ways and did not want to learn. With his abiding faith in the people, in their ultimate soundness, his instinctive preference was to build his administration on principles and achievements rather than on political chess play.

'I am sometimes very much interested,' he said on one occasion, 'when I see gentlemen supposing that popularity is the way to success in America. The way to success in this great country, with its fair judgments, is to show that you are not afraid of anybody except God and His final verdict. If I did not believe that, I would not believe that people can govern themselves. If I did not believe that the moral judgment would be the last judgment, the final judgment, in the minds of men as well as at the tribunal of God, I could not believe in popular government.'

This attitude was incomprehensible to the average political leader, and in the course of time the President acquired a reputation among the politicians as an impracticable idealist. The term is a misnomer; he was an idealist, but there was nothing impractical in his motives or in his objectives. His idealism differed from the immediate expediency of the hour in that it was founded on a wider vision, a longer foresight, and a deeper understanding of social problems. 'The most expedient thing to do today,' he said, 'is frequently not the best thing to do in the long run.' As I write this paragraph there comes to my mind a saying of James Gordon Bennett, the elder, who founded the 'New York Herald.' Popularity was his aim, and he made the 'Herald' the most popular newspaper of the time. 'I make it a rule,' he declared, 'never to be more than a day ahead of the people, and never an hour behind.' Woodrow Wilson was never behind the people or the politicians, but he was years ahead of them. Like Jefferson and Lincoln, he will be understood better by posterity than he was by his contemporaries.

I know there is a widespread impression, which has been carefully nourished by his political adversaries, that he was ungrateful to his friends and political supporters; or, as one writer puts it — and this man never knew him, by the way — 'as soon as Mr. Wilson got to the top he threw down the ladder on which he had climbed.'

The accusation is unjust and malicious, and is without any basis in fact. It is true that some of his political and personal friendships ended in coldness and misunderstanding, but it was through no fault of his own. In every instance there was an element of selfishness in these supporters. The President was disillusioned when he found that they demanded something of him which would conflict with his sense of duty and responsibility to the whole people. He never wanted anybody's support primarily for himself, but for the principles he advocated.

He had a whole-hearted detestation of war profiteers. The thought that anybody would, and could, make money out of destruction and death filled him with horror. Yet the profiteer was all over the land, and nothing effective could be done about it, as profiteering and legitimate business were so thoroughly scrambled together that it was not feasible to kill one without doing serious injury to the other.

4

President Wilson's distinguished literary style was acquired through years of attention and laborious practice. He had studied — had read and re-read — the classical English authors so thoroughly that he could repeat long passages of their prose from memory.

He said there are no synonyms, that every word has a precise meaning of its own, or a shade of meaning that distin-

guishes it from every other word. In writing he endeavored
to find the exact words to express his thought.

Excess verbiage, he declared, had the effect of weakening
the projectile force of a statement. It was much better to express an idea in twenty words instead of in forty; then, if it
could be cut to ten, even still better. An excess of words
around an idea was like too much water in one's coffee; the
coffee was still there, but it did not taste the same.

One day, while reading something that I had written, he
stopped, looked at me and said: 'Mac, why do you write *under*
the circumstances?'

'Why, Mr. President,' I answered, 'I've heard that expression all my life. People say "under the circumstances."
It's common usage. Isn't it correct?'

He took up a pencil and, smiling meanwhile, drew a circle
on a piece of paper. '*Circum* and *circumference*, you see. It
means something round; an enclosure,' he explained. 'The
word *circumstance* comes from *circum*, which indicates an
enclosure, and *sto*, to stand. It means "standing around."
You can be *in* a circumstance, but not *under* it. The correct
expression is "in the circumstances."' I give this anecdote
merely to show his careful attention to modes of speech and
writing.

When the new post-office alongside the Union Station was
being erected in Washington, the Treasury Department
(which has charge of all public buildings) requested Dr.
Charles W. Eliot, of Harvard, to write two inscriptions, to be
cut in stone panels on the façade of the building.

I did not know that the inscriptions had been written by
Dr. Eliot. The Supervising Architect brought them to me and
asked for my approval. They struck me as exceptionally fine,
but it seemed to me that they needed some slight changes.
While I was trying to improve the wording, according to my
own ideas, it occurred to me, that as a great master of English
was in the White House, I would send them over to the
President with the request that he either approve them or
change them.

The inscriptions came back with some alterations made by
the President.

Dr. Eliot had written:	President Wilson changed it to:
Carrier of News and Knowledge	Carrier of News and Knowledge
Instrument of Trade and Commerce	Instrument of Trade and Industry
Promoter of Mutual Acquaintance	Promoter of Mutual Acquaintance
Among Men and Nations and Hence	Of Peace and of Good Will Among
Of Peace and Good Will	Men and Nations

Dr. Eliot wrote:	The President altered it to:
Carrier of Love and Sympathy	Messenger of Sympathy and Love
Messenger of Friendship	Servant of Parted Friends
Consoler of the Lonely	Consoler of the Lonely
Bond of the Scattered Family	Bond of the Scattered Family
Enlarger of the Common Life	Enlarger of the Common Life

After the inscriptions (with the President's corrections) had been engraved on the panels, some newspaper reporters came to learn why I had made changes in Dr. Eliot's words. They said the learned Doctor was annoyed. I was surprised to learn that he was the author. I sent for the Supervising Architect. 'Why, yes, Mr. Secretary,' he said, 'we paid Dr. Eliot an honorarium to write those inscriptions.'

'Why didn't you tell me?' I asked.

'I thought you knew,' was his reply. 'And when they came back changed, I thought that was what you wanted, so we put them on the building.'

When I told the President, he said that if he had known that Dr. Eliot had written them, he would not have made any changes. He was sorry that Dr. Eliot was annoyed, but it was too late to do anything about it. He smiled; and I smiled; and we let it go at that.

Anyway, the Washington post-office building has the distinction of bearing inscriptions which are the joint product of two great modern masters of English.

His letters to his friends were luminous with grace and charm. Even while he was prostrated by the long, lingering illness from which he never recovered, he would write me notes, like this one of June 11, 1922:

Dear Mac: Thank you for your letter of June 2nd. We are always hungry for news of you all and hope you will find it possible to repeat your kindness frequently and keep us posted as to what is happening to you. It is particularly delightful to realize how comfortable and happy you all evidently are because — say what you will — you and Nell are not at home in the West and a certain period of adjustment is inevitable. Fortunately that period promises to lack the trying features which usually attend such adjustments. Both of you are very adaptable and with children such changes do not count....

Things are going about as usual with us. I suppose and believe that I am getting better but not in a way that would startle you with its rapidity or at all excite you with a sense of haste. Patience has never been my long suit but it now contains evidently all the winning cards, and I must do the best I can to simulate it at least. The real burden, of course, both of the waiting and the planning, falls on dear Edith [the present Mrs. Wilson] and that is of course for me an element of great distress. She carries everything off so wonderfully that you never could tell by watching her that there was any strain, but that alas does not alter the fact.

Edith joins me in loving messages to you all. I wish that Nell and you and the children could realize how often and with what solicitous love I think of you and hope for frequent reunions not too long delayed. After all, the continent is not too wide or too broad to be bridged by our thoughts and affections, and there is no danger that our section of the bridge will fall into disrepair. Our thoughts are constantly sending you loving messages and we shall make you aware of it as often as possible. If I ever get strong again I am sure that I can find many means of making our intercourse more conscious and vital.

I congratulate you, my dear fellow, on the promising beginnings of your law practice. Affectionately yours.

(Signed)   Woodrow Wilson

I dissolved my New York partnership and in March, 1922, I moved to Los Angeles and opened a law office. Hence the reference to the West and to 'the promising beginnings' of my law practice in the President's letter.

Although the breadth of the continent was between us, we had the happiness during his last years to have 'frequent reunions.' On one occasion Mrs. McAdoo and I carried Ellen and Mary Faith with us. The President's delight in seeing his grandchildren and having them around him will always remain vividly in my memory.

POSTSCRIPT

I

WHEN I began to write these memoirs, my intention was to carry them on through the 1920 and 1924 campaigns, and to tell the dramatic story of the 1924 National Democratic Convention. I found, however, that any adequate description of these events would increase the length of the book so greatly that it would have to be published in two volumes. This would not be desirable for many reasons.

Accordingly, I have ended the record with my resignation from the government service in January, 1919. At some future time, if I ever have the leisure and the inclination, I may write of the part I played in each of these historical campaigns. If done at all, it will have to be done on a broad canvas; a picture vivid with fire and drama.

2

As I look back over the long road of experience, I realize that the constructive impulse has been the chief motivation of my life. I like movement and change; I like to make things better, to reshape old forces and worn-out ideals into new and dynamic forms.

Like all human beings whose lives are projective in character, I have had defeats as well as successes. But I have always thought, and still think, that even a defeat is better than standing still. What is life worth if one spends it like an oyster fastened securely to a rock? In my opinion a sense of effort is the finest thing in life. Nothing else gives me so much joy as the solution of a difficult problem. Even if I find it insoluble, there is a deep inspiration in having attempted to solve it.

Defeat, when it has come my way, has never left me sour or disappointed; and I can say with sincerity that through good luck or bad, fair weather or foul, success or failure, cynicism has not conquered me nor has my faith in humanity been impaired. My life has covered a wide range and it has been full of interesting and unexpected adventure. I have no quarrel with Fate, no matter in what moods I have found her, and no matter what her decrees have been. I have had a glorious time!

THE END

INDEX